WARRIORS
WAY

Books by

Robert S. de Ropp

If I Forget Thee

Drugs and the Mind

Man Against Aging

The Master Game

Sex Energy

The New Prometheans

Church of the Earth

Eco-Tech

Warrior's Way

WARRIOR'S WAY

The Challenging Life Games

ROBERT S. de ROPP

A Merloyd Lawrence Book

DELACORTE PRESS / SEYMOUR LAWRENCE

A MERLOYD LAWRENCE BOOK
Published by
Delacorte Press/Seymour Lawrence
1 Dag Hammarskjold Plaza
New York, N.Y. 10017

Grateful acknowledgment is made for permission
to quote from the following copyrighted material.

From WITNESS by J. G. Bennett: Published by Omen Press, Tucson, Arizona, 1974. Used by permission of Elizabeth Bennett.

From MAN, THE UNKNOWN by Alexis Carrel: Copyright 1935, 1939 by Harper & Row, Publishers, Inc.: renewed 1967 by Anne De La Motte Carrel. Reprinted by permission of Harper & Row, Publishers, Inc.

From REFLECTIONS ON LIFE by Alex Carrel: Copyright © 1952 by Alexis Carrel. By permission of Hawthorne Books, Inc. All rights reserved. Copyright Librairie Plon 1950, 1978 and used by permission.

From FLIGHT AND LIFE by Charles Lindbergh: Used by permission of the Estate of Charles Lindbergh.

Manufactured in the United States of America
First Delacorte printing

Designed by Oksana Kushnir

LIBRARY OF CONGRESS CATALOGING IN PUBLICATION DATA
De Ropp, Robert S.
    Warrior's way.
    "A Merloyd Lawrence book."
    Includes index.
    1. De Ropp, Robert S.   2. United States—Biography.
I. Title.
CT275.D366A38   973.91'092'4 [B]   78-26917
ISBN 0-440-09438-0
ISBN 0-440-59385-9 (pbk.)

God said: Do thou grant his earnest request.
Enlarge his faculties. Give him freewill.
Freewill is the very salt of piety,
Without it heaven itself were a matter of compulsion.
Put a sword in his hand and take away his impotence.
Let us see if he turns out a warrior or a robber.

(Rumi *Mathnawi*)

The basic difference between an ordinary man and a warrior is that a warrior takes everything as a challenge while an ordinary man takes everything either as a blessing or a curse.

(Don Juan in *Tales of Power*, Carlos Castaneda)

CONTENTS

1 Warriors and Slaves   1
2 The Spire Aspiring   7
3 And One Clear Call for Me   13
4 Rats in the Ruins   19
5 Education of a Peasant   26
6 Dust   33
7 A Season in Hell   39
8 Gentle Warriors   44
9 The Banquet of Knowledge   56
10 Politics in Fog   62
11 The Smerdiakovs Will Triumph   68
12 The Shock of Recognition   79
13 Ouspensky Fourth Dimension   92
14 Harvest and Suffering   107
15 Lion into Rabbit   116
16 An Evening with the Baron   122
17 If Fault of Planets . . .   129
18 The Sinking Ship   134
19 Keep Careful Notes   141
20 Mad Song   149
21 To the New World   157
22 Morbio Inferiore   166
23 Prayer of the Heart   179
24 Hungers in Conflict   190
25 Fair-Weather Sailor   197
26 King in Exile   204

27 Take Fate by the Throat   218
28 Drugs and the Mind   231
29 Sly Man and Superman   237
30 In Dubious Battle   255
31 I Have Been Here Before   271
32 The Great Psychedelic Freakway   279
33 Reluctant Guru   292
34 Warriors in the Tree House   303
35 Sarmoun and Psychotron   314
36 Seeker After Truth   336
37 The Trickster's Way   354
38 Leaving the Lab   364
39 The Watercourse Way   376
40 On the Beach   385

I

WARRIORS
AND SLAVES

Today is my birthday.

The face that looks back at me from the mirror is the face of a man of sixty-five. My hair is grey and my hairline is receding, my skin is wrinkled and the lenses of my eyes are hardening. My arteries are hardening too. It is part of the program. The body is programmed to last for only a certain time. It will hold together, if treated properly, for about a hundred years. I have treated it properly. As a result it remains healthy. I never have a day's illness and seem immune to practically everything. But I cannot alter the program. No matter what I do my body will age, weaken, and finally disintegrate. The organizer that formed it in the first place and now holds together the atoms of which it is made will lose its power. The elements of my body will scatter like the beads of a necklace when the string breaks.

I have made the voyage of life aboard a ship of fools with a motley crew, each member of which thought itself important. I have been a mystic and a scientist, an author, a house builder, a boat builder, a gardener, a fisherman, a father of four children, a Whole-earther getting his food from the soil he cultivated. These various characters made up the crew of my vessel, and their often conflicting aims determined the course the vessel took. They argued, fought, stole from each other. Each tried for a time to become master of the ship. But now there is harmony aboard, and the various fools have made peace with each other. Their aims do not conflict, because none of them considers himself important. It's the effect of aging.

One thing I learned fairly early in the course of the voyage. It is our privilege as human beings to live either as Warriors or slaves. A Warrior is the master of his fate. No matter what fate throws at him, fame or infamy, health or sickness, poverty or riches, he uses the situation for his own inner development. He takes his motto from Nietzsche: *That which does not destroy me strengthens me.*

The slave, on the other hand, is completely at the mercy of external events. If fortune smiles on him, he struts and boasts and attributes her favors to his own power and wisdom—which, as often as not, had nothing to do with it. If fortune frowns, he whines and weeps and grovels, putting the blame for his sufferings on everything and everybody except himself.

I learned that all life games can be played either in the spirit of the Warrior or in the spirit of the slave. My life games were determined by the predelictions of the various members of my ship of fools. The author dreamed of writing books. The scientist dreamed of performing experiments. The mystic dreamed of penetrating new worlds of the mind and of consciousness. The Whole-earther dreamed of a little farm on which he would be self-sufficient. The fisherman dreamed of the ocean with its white surf and floating seaweeds and of the good fish dinners it provided when conditions were right.

So each of the crew members had his own game.

I realized, again rather early, that I was far more slave than Warrior, and that if I ever wished to master my own fate, I would have to train myself to stop behaving slavishly.

In the course of my voyage I met several other Warriors who, by the example of their own lives, encouraged me to try to live in a manner worthy of a free man. To become a free man is no easy matter.

I have set down here a log of my personal voyage. I do

not consider that voyage particularly inspiring, but I happen to know more about it than I do about anyone else's. I have included brief accounts of the voyages of others who managed to live in a manner worthy of a Warrior, though they did not necessarily think of themselves in these terms. There are conscious and unconscious Warriors, those who know what they are fighting for and those who just fight.

The genetic endowment that was dealt me by fate was not bad as genetic endowments go. I resulted from the union of a Teutonic knight and an English lady. My father, the Teutonic knight, was a descendant of that band of German adventurers who cajoled and bullied their way along the coast of the Baltic and carved for themselves large estates in Lithuania, Latvia, and Estonia. They were all barons, and called themselves *von* this and *von* that and lorded it over the hordes of peasants. My father, who chose to live in England, dropped the *von* and called himself simply de Ropp. His gene pool had been further enriched by his Cossack mother, Lydia Gurjef (a name that, with a somewhat different spelling, was to become very familiar to me later), a wild spirit who came from the Crimea. My mother, a proper English lady, belonged to the Fisher tribe, which had its quota of distinguished members—a historian, an admiral, a banker—good solid members of the bourgeoisie, whose influence tended to stabilize the more volatile elements I inherited from my father.

As for the society into which I was born, it appeared at the time of my birth to be prosperous and safe. I entered the world in 1913, the last year of the great Age of Optimism. Most judges of human affairs assumed that, with the help of science, conditions of life would get steadily better and better. The great powers of Europe had carved up the rest of the planet. Kings, Kaisers, and Czars strutted and postured. Their representatives ruled millions of "natives" in various far-flung empires, of which the British was far-flungest. It stretched from Africa to China and was colored pink on the map. The structure looked stable enough, but before I was two years old the Age of Optimism ended. The whole towering system collapsed in a mess of mud and blood as the great powers of Europe used all the resources of their famous science for the sole purpose of tearing each other to pieces.

The sound of that crash reverberated through my young life and caused me, at a very early age, to feel alienated from the world I had entered. I remember being bundled into a blanket by my obviously terrified mother and hastily carried down from our upstairs flat to one in the basement. We lived in London, in Chelsea, near the river. The Germans were making their ultimate contribution to civilization by sending over zeppelins to bomb the inhabitants of London. All the inhabitants—men, women, children, cats, and canaries.

Of course this bombing of open cities became routine later on, and no one thought it unusual when whole cities were reduced to rubble; but in those days remnants of civilized attitudes survived, and the bombing of London was considered barbaric behavior.

My mother did not want me to know about the bombs. It was close to Christmas, so she told me a story. She said all the bangs and crashes we were hearing were due to Father Christmas. The jovial old boy was driving over the rooftops in his sled and dropping a package or two in the process.

> When what to my wandering eyes should appear
>   (CRASH!)
> But a miniature sled with eight tiny reindeer
>   (BANG! CRASH!)
> On Donner and Blitzen!

Donner and Blitzen with a vengeance! *Gott strafe England!*
And noting that the Father Christmas ploy had done little to reassure me (for I could sense her fear, as children can), she began in a quavering voice to sing a carol:

> Bringing tidings of comfort and joy
> Comfort and joy!
>   (CRASH! BOOM!)
> Glad tidings of comfort and joy.

And only a few days later my suspicion that, carols and Santa Claus notwithstanding, something frightful was happening, was fully confirmed. My father, who spoke four languages fluently and was therefore in the British Intelligence Service, came home on leave with a package wrapped in dirty newspaper. Opening this he revealed fragments of a zeppelin that had been shot down over London. Included in the wreckage was a torn, scorched piece of uniform from one of the crew members. And I could not avoid a sense of astonishment over the satisfaction in my father's voice as he told us that the crew of the zeppelin was roasted alive in a flaming mass of gas; that zeppelins were death traps, sitting ducks for antiaircraft guns; and that their use proved again that the Germans were fundamentally a very stupid people. In fact I was so distressed by the thought of that roasted crew member that I shed tears—not realizing, in my innocence, that he was one of "the enemy" and so deserved all he got.

Some days later my tears flowed again, this time so copiously and for so long a time that my father and mother were worried. This time the cause of my grief was a music-hall song sung by the nursemaid then looking after me. I can remember only a fragment, but that fragment is significant.

> When you're all dressed up and nowhere to go
> Life is weary, weary and slow,
> And tumpty-tum, tum, tum, and something, tumpty, tum,
> When you're all dressed up and nowhere to go.

This produced in my childish mind a sense of such total desolation that—although all concerned tried to reassure me, telling me it was just a song and a silly one at that—I could not be consoled but wept and wept. For I knew, without being able to formulate my ideas, that I had joined the wrong species, on the wrong planet in the wrong solar system, that we were all of us dressed up with nowhere to go, that our proudest gestures were rooted in futility, like those huge, idiotic zeppelins sent over to kill and terrorize and to provide a fiery death for themselves and their crews.

2

THE
SPIRE
ASPIRING

The Great Plague of the twentieth century killed almost as many people as World War I and completely changed my line of fate. The influenza pandemic of the winter of 1918–1919 destroyed 20 million men, women, and children.

It killed my mother, who had just given birth to my sister.

It nearly killed me.

I was hustled out of plague-ridden London to my grandmother's house in the country, where I quietly began to die. A step, another step, and yet another. Further and further into the Unknown Region. I was barely seven years old, but quite willing to go. I could scarcely breathe. In the night Death came near me, hovering among the shadows cast by the night-light.

You want me, Death? Ready when you are.

But Death passed me by.

My lungs healed. My health was slowly restored. I was motherless. My whole line of fate had been changed by a minute virus one hundred millimicrons across.

One result of my motherless state was that I was placed in a boarding school at a very early age. Another was that I never had a home, was shuffled from relative to relative for the holidays. I stayed at my aunt's house in Leicestershire. She was married to a purple-faced colonel who kept a stable of hunters and rode to hounds. I stayed at my grandmother's house near the village of Pottern. I stayed in my great aunt's house in the town of Salisbury.

My holidays in Salisbury helped to shape my personal myth, the intricate web of symbols and ideas that formed the substrate of my inner world. This myth crystallized around two enormous memorials and a fish. The enormous memorials were Stonehenge, which stood on Salisbury Plain not far from the town, and the Gothic cathedral that towered above the river Avon. This river ran at the bottom of the garden, and in the river was the fish, a huge trout of great age and wisdom that no one could catch, the third component of my myth.

Sweet Avon, flow softly . . .

The river was an enchanted place. It emerged from the shadow of an old stone bridge; it was shaded with great trees. Rippling water weeds, like the tresses of Undine, waved in the current. My great aunt, an imaginative old lady with no children of her own, was very fond of fairy tales. She would tell me about Undine, the water spirit, who haunted streams and whose voice could be heard in the babblings of the river. There were all kinds of fairies in the garden, fairies in the hollyhocks and scarlet poppies, fairies in the delphiniums, the gladioli, the foxgloves, the peonies, the fragile forget-me-nots and love-in-the-mist. The place swarmed with spirits of one sort or another.

As for the fish, it was a symbol of power and of mystery. Again and again I tried to catch it, on worms, on maggots, on lumps of bread, on flies. It mocked my efforts. It had eluded anglers far more skilled than I. Now and then I caught sight of its shadowy form, swift and powerful, pursuing something or other. My great aunt said it was a magical fish. No one could catch it. If they did they would never be able to lift it from the water. The fish was the companion of Undine, the water sprite. Perhaps, if caught, it would change into Undine herself.

The magic fish, the river, the garden with its flower-fairies—all these, like the threads in a tapestry, formed part of a design. They formed part of the Magician, that shadowy archetype who, with the Scientist, danced a duet through my life.

Stonehenge added other components to the Magician. Stonehenge, whose megaliths lay like fallen giants on the empty plain, was not much visited then. It was possible on Salisbury Plain to feel all sorts of presences, for the whole plain was dotted with remnants of lost cultures, from the great mound of Old Sarum, to the traces of Saxon fortifications and Roman roads that had been built in the age of the Antonines. The presence that haunted Stonehenge was huge and terrifying. Not during the day. By day larks sang above the plain and fragile harebells bloomed, and the huge memorial had a calm benign aspect. But in the evening, when elongating shadows picked out the old monuments, the megaliths became very threatening. Like the great fish they were symbols of power and of mystery.

The cathedral made a different impression. It did not threaten. It sang. Seen from the water meadows across the river Avon, floating against the sky above its own reflection, the great building had an ethereal lightness, as if it were about to leave the earth. The impression of lightness, of soaring, was due, of course, to the tremendous spire—that spire which distinguishes Salisbury from all other Gothic cathedrals, that gives it its grace, its balance, its quality of transcendence.

I learned a lot about the cathedral. My father, anxious that I should not forget all the knowledge painfully forced into my brain at the very expensive preparatory school I attended, insisted that I visit a tutor during the long summer holidays. So I would dawdle along the banks of the river Avon and arrive at the home of my tutor. I forget his name. He was a white-haired scholar, probably a reverend. Salisbury swarmed with parsons.

The worthy old gentleman had two passions, the cathedral and Greek poetry. He was supposed to teach me Latin but kept lapsing into Greek. I would sit in a kind of daze as he rolled off sonorous passages from Homer or Aeschylus. I could not understand a word of it but knew that it was great poetry. Listening to the old scholar I realized the meaning of the word enchantment—for the melodious Greek had a truly spellbinding quality. It was hypnotic.

His love of the cathedral formed the real bond between us. Shyly, with a conspiratorial air, as if he were about to initiate me into a mystery, he led me to a shed behind his house. There, on a large table, were spread out thousands of fragments of colored glass. The old scholar contemplated the glass long and sadly.

"A labor of love," he said, "a labor of love. And, I fear, useless. Quite useless. And yet I continue. Ten years of work to repair a crime committed by a fool in a few minutes."

Later he told me the nature of the crime he was trying to repair. Apparently, at the end of the eighteenth century the bishop and dean of the cathedral appointed a certain James Wyatt to the position of cathedral architect.

"The wicked wanton Wyatt," said my old tutor, shaking his white locks, a look of wonder on his gentle face. How could God in his wisdom create such monsters?

Anyway, this Wyatt, in addition to destroying the great campanile and leaving the cathedral voiceless, tore out of the windows vast amounts of stained glass, much of which was thrown into the city ditch, then in the process of being filled. It was this glass that my tutor had rescued, digging it up piece by piece. It lay on the table like a huge jigsaw puzzle that he was trying to assemble into some meaningful design. The task was hopeless, as my tutor sadly admitted, for the glass had been broken and much was missing. Yet he struggled to fit it together.

"If we could only recreate one window—what a triumph!"

The second secret my tutor revealed was more disturbing. One afternoon we took a walk to the cathedral and he led me inside. Around us the soaring Gothic arches of the nave and choir sprang effortlessly up to the vaulted roof. My tutor led me to a slender column near the choir.

"Put your head against it," he said, "and look up at the roof."

I did so. Suddenly the frightening truth dawned on me. The column was bent! It was slowly being crushed under the enormous weight of the spire. That spire, so airy and delicate seen from a distance, contained a terrifying weight of stone.

"Can't they take the columns out and straighten them?"

My tutor shook his head sadly. Gothic cathedrals could not be taken apart like cars and have spare parts inserted.

"I will tell you a secret," he said. "The people who built the cathedral never meant it to have a spire. The foundations aren't strong enough. One of these days the spire will fall in through the roof."

I left the building hastily. My tutor tried to reassure me, saying that the spire had stood for six centuries and would probably last another six.

"It is a miracle," he said. "It should have fallen in long ago but it has stood for six hundred years. How can one account for it? It is protected by the hand of God."

Dear old man! Did he really think that God had such a special interest in the building? Both he and "wicked wanton Wyatt" have niches in my special collection of archetypes. Wyatt is the archetype of all destructive lunatics who, for one reason or another, ruin the treasures of the past. My tutor is the archetype of those patient souls who—lovingly, patiently, but often ineffectually—strive to repair the damage wrought by the wicked Wyatts.

But far more important for me is the symbolism of the cathedral. Built on the soggy chalk of the Avon valley, subject to flooding, surmounted by a tower and spire it was never designed to support, how does it manage to stay up? Were its designers, especially those who added the great spire, geniuses or madmen? For me that cathedral, rising out of its spacious lawns, the tip of the spire more than four hundred feet above the ground, is by far the most beautiful building in the world, more beautiful than Chartres or Notre Dame, the Blue Mosque or the much overrated Taj Mahal. My knowledge of its structural weakness only adds to the awe that it arouses.

For the cathedral is Man, the Adam Kadmon.

Only man, of all the living things on earth, carries about with him that aspiring spirit, reaching toward heaven.

But that soaring spirit is supported by a structure that never was designed to carry such a load. Man, the naked ape, with his feet in the mud, can scarcely bear the burden that has been placed upon him. It crushes him, as the great spire crushes and distorts the slender pillars that were never designed for such a burden. The spire is a menace to the cathedral as well as its crowning beauty. The aspiring spirit is a menace to man as well as the sense and purpose of his existence. Whenever I think of the cathedral, I remember the words of Nietzsche's Zarathustra:

> Man is a rope stretched between the animal and the Superman—a rope over an abyss.
> A dangerous crossing, a dangerous wayfaring, a dangerous looking-back, a dangerous trembling and halting.
>
> (*Thus Spake Zarathustra*)

Will there come a time when the spiritual descendants of the wicked Wyatt will dismantle the spire stone by stone because it is too dangerous and might fall in and squash a few tourists? Such an act would certainly make the cathedral much safer, with a little stub where the soaring spire had been. And the cautious bureaucrats who might order the spire dismantled would have a good excuse for their action. The cathedral was not designed for a spire in the first place.

I think this is entirely possible. The great spire represents the Warrior spirit in man, his willingness to take risks, face dangers, master his fate. But the spirit of our age is opposed to the Warrior's attitude. We want to be safe and snug and coddled and cared for.

"The spire was all very fine and beautiful, but the cathedral will be a great deal safer without it."

3

AND
ONE CLEAR
CALL FOR ME

"I don't think that would be suitable," said the music master. "No, I don't think that would be at all suitable."

"In that case I won't choose a hymn."

Defiant of authority. The music master, shaggy and opinionated, took offense, as such types will. Why did he take offense? It was the privilege of all boys who were leaving Cheam School to choose a hymn at one or another of the last services to be held before they left. I was leaving, prematurely, torn out of the place by my father, who was broke. The Great Depression was starting. The school was very expensive. I had to go.

So I chose my hymn—not really a hymn at all. "Crossing the Bar" by Alfred Lord Tennyson, which for some reason had been incorporated into *Hymns Ancient and Modern*, the hymnal we used at that school. I liked it. It summarized my feeling of not belonging, of needing to go, to set out on a greater voyage, to cross the bar and enter a larger ocean.

> Sunset and evening star
> And one clear call for me
> And may there be no moaning of the bar,
> When I put out to sea.
>
> But such a tide as moving seems asleep,
> Too full for sound and foam,
> When that which drew from out the boundless deep
> Turns again home.

Home! Where is home? I am a stranger in a strange land. I must set out on a voyage, a Journey to the East. I do not belong here. These thoughts were barely formulated in my young mind. I was conscious only of an overwhelming nostalgia, a longing for something else, for somewhere else. But of course to the music master, poor literal-minded clod, the crossing of the bar referred to death, and it was not nice for a twelve-year-old boy to be thinking about death. Not suitable at all.

But I got my hymn. Our worthy headmaster, a "reverend" as most of them were in those days, was somewhat more perceptive than his underlings. He may even have been a genuinely religious man. In any case he realized that this oversensitive, bewildered twelve-year-old who was being torn prematurely out of school had chosen that particular hymn not on account of the working of the Freudian death wish but because he felt vague yearnings for a further journey. Just to be sure that this was understood, he chose the theme "Crossing the Bar" for his Sunday evening sermon, explaining that the bar, in nautical language, was the dividing line between the quiet harbor and the stormy ocean. In facing life, the worthy man assured us, we would have to cross many bars, to proceed from many snug harbors into howling storms.

The headmaster paused and glanced at the school war memorial. It consisted of panel after panel of oak, carved by the school carpenter with the names of the dead. We lived surrounded by ghosts of slaughtered men.

Our headmaster's generation had crossed the bar with a vengeance, leaving the snug harbor of civilized life for the filth, the boredom, the danger, the horror of the trenches. He had seen his friends shot to pieces. He had felt his faith in God shaken. He had survived. He still believed that they had fought in a good cause and that the dead were heroes. He liked to draw our attention to the central panel, on which was carved in large letters the following verse:

SONS OF THIS PLACE, LET THIS OF YOU BE SAID,
THAT YOU WHO LIVE ARE WORTHY OF YOUR DEAD.

Yes, in those days (it was the year 1925) the myth of
heroism still flourished and was duly instilled into the
minds of the young. The bitter comments on the war written by some of the war poets had not been read and certainly not been marked, learned, or inwardly digested by
our spiritual instructors.

Despite the wreckage left by the "Great War" in the form
of shattered bodies, ruined minds, oceans of tears, and he-
tacombs of dead, we were still told that it was sweet and
decorous to die for one's country. And believed it. And
were perfectly ready to join the ranks of the dead heroes,
who always in our young imaginations died with arms outstretched, with smiles on their faces, smiles brought on by
the thought that they were dying decorously and sweetly.

So I sat listening to that last sermon surrounded by the
ghosts of slaughtered men, thinking that I too might one
day die decorously and sweetly. Behind me lay my
disrupted childhood, in which the only unifying theme was
the school, with its regular sleepings and wakings, its regular games and lessons, its regular prayers.

Lessons. Looking back at the wasted years my gorge
rises. Even there, at that early age, the Scientist in me was
hankering for nourishment. *If he ask for bread will you give
him a stone?* Stones were all that Cheam School offered in
those days. A "classical" education. Latin, Greek. The mildewed remnants of a ruined world. As far as Cheam School
was concerned, science did not exist. Newton might never
have lived, or Lavoisier, or Faraday, or Pasteur, Lister,
Planck, or Einstein. So nothing remains in my head from all
those years that could have been so rich in new impressions
but a few fragments of Ovid and odds and ends of English
history. A farce of an education. And yet it was considered
a good school, suitable for the training of officers and gentlemen.

Ah, yes. The empire still existed in the twenties, a bit frayed at the edges but more or less whole. And to maintain this monstrous structure—on which, its admirers insisted, the sun never set—a steady supply of guardians was required. These guardians needed to develop the qualities of watchdogs, and know when to bark and when to bite. They were expected to maintain stiff upper lips, to serve without complaint in various remote spots, often extremely unhealthy, and to bear something vaguely defined by Rudyard Kipling as the White Man's Burden.

This task called for an educational system calculated to produce a neat blend of intelligence and stupidity. The stupidity consisted chiefly of a smug conviction that because one was British and had a pinkish-white skin one was in some way superior to others who were not British and had skins ranging from black to yellow. The white *bwanas* who ruled large chunks of Africa and the *Pukka Sahibs* who ruled India were expected to behave in a manner befitting a superior race. They did not mix with the natives, they did not sleep with native women, they dressed for dinner even when alone in darkest Africa, they stood to attention and drank a toast on the King's (or Queen's) birthday.

It was to create such types, I suppose, that preparatory schools and the so-called public schools (which were anything but public) existed. It was an atrocious system that only the British, who love dogs but dislike children, could have invented. At a tender age the unfortunate boy was torn from his home, dressed in a uniform like a little convict, sent to a massive establishment reminiscent of a prison, subjected to insults and beatings from pompous pedagogues, dragged through interminable games of cricket in summer, soccer in winter, and taught absolutely nothing that could be of any conceivable use in a complex, highly technical world dominated by science.

Meanwhile, in the chapel twice daily, the weird assumptions of the Judeo-Christian guilt cult were force-fed into our young minds. Turning to face the altar, we declared that we believed that a certain Jewish carpenter had defied the laws of biology by getting himself conceived of the Holy Ghost and born of a virgin, that he was the only Son of God the Father Almighty, and that after being crucified dead and buried he somehow contrived to rise three days later and ascend into heaven in defiance of the laws of physics.

I was young and naive. It never occurred to me to question these assertions. It was good to believe in God. I believed passionately. God was a presence, a divine father, far better than my earthly father, whom I hardly ever saw. One could ask God for anything, for help, for advice, for consolation, for protection. God could guide one through life, and at death one returned to his kingdom. It was a comforting idea. It explained my sense of not belonging. I had come from another place and to it I would return. Jesus had died and risen again. Death was not the end.

An extraordinary thing happened to me at the time of my confirmation. The kindly old bishop who placed his hands on our heads preached a sermon on a text from the Gospel of St. John.

I am the true vine and my father is the husbandman. He that abideth in me and I in him the same bringeth forth much fruit.

I was swept by sudden overwhelming emotion. I could not understand my own thoughts. Something else was thinking through me, something with extraordinary power and extraordinary vision. I have never forgotten that moment. It convinced me that lurking in my brain, scarcely ever used, lay a magnificent supermind capable, if I could only contact it, of revealing all the mysteries of creation. That mind showed me in a flash of insight that the myths we piously pronounce in the form of the Athanasian creed had nothing to do with the real teachings of Jesus. Jesus symbolized the god in man. His crucifixion and resurrection symbolized the struggle between Warrior and slave. Only slaves or foreigners were crucified. Insofar as we are slaves, we are crucified daily, subjected to pain, degradation, and inner death. But the god in us, our Warrior spirit, can rise above this degradation, can unite with something greater than itself and bring forth fruit on a different level of being.

Naturally I could not formulate all this. How could a twelve-year-old boy understand a vision that contained in itself the entire mystery of Christ's teaching, of the Great Work of the alchemists, of the sacred knowledge of the hierophants? What I thought at the time was that there existed in me a temple, as lofty and beautiful as the great cathedral at Salisbury, but completely spiritual, a temple not built with hands. Within that temple were contained the answers to all the mysteries of life. Only in that temple could one worship truly. But the way to the temple was hidden and difficult to find, guarded by monsters, hedged about with dangers. And the thought occurred to my young mind that all my life would be wasted unless, somehow or other, I could rediscover the inner temple that I had briefly entered on the occasion of my confirmation.

4

RATS
IN THE RUINS

The family von der Ropp, so my records inform me, took its name from a river in old Livland called Ropp or Raupa. The name was first recorded in 1221 attached to a certain Theodoricus. From that point on Ropps of various kinds kept cropping up in that corner of northern Europe called Livland or Lettland. In 1292 Johann von der Ropp was a vassal to the Archbishop of Riga. In 1303 Dietrich von der Ropp was a Cistercian monk. In the generalized slaughter that accompanied the Thirty Years' War all Ropps but one were killed. From the single survivor all the present Ropps are descended.

So on my father's side I came from a breed of Baltic barons, of whom it has been said that they are Germans with Russian souls. Others have been unkind enough to suggest that we combine in our gene pool the worst characteristics of both Slav and Teuton. I am quite sure this is true in my own case. My personal heredity, that "salad of racial genes" as Nabokov would say, was further complicated by the fact that my paternal grandmother was a Cossack from the Crimea. To the influence of that Cossack grandmother I attribute some of the weirder manifestations of my psyche.

Anyway—Wilhelm Edmund Karl Reinhold Alexander Baron von der Ropp (whew!) was my paternal grandfather. He owned in Lithuania, then part of Russia, an estate called Daudzegir. My father, the youngest son, inherited a share of the estate. He never visited the place. He was one of those Russian-souled Germans who became fascinated with the English. He imitated the English in everything, including sleeping with the windows open even when the outside temperature was below zero. He was what Turgenev called an Anglophile.

My Anglophile father settled in England, became naturalized, married an Englishwoman, fought in the British army in World War I. But he was still partial to his title and enjoyed being addressed as Baron.

In 1925 my father was broke. He had tried to make his fortune in Kenya (then Kenya Colony and part of the British Empire) and had succeeded only in losing what little money he had. He had retired temporarily to the family estate in Lithuania because he had absolutely no place else to go.

The great house at Daudzegir, so I have been told, was once the pride of the neighborhood. It was enormous. Huge rooms on the main floor provided place for as many as fifty guests. There were large conservatories in which exotic plants were carefully nursed through the Lithuanian winter. There were lofty bedrooms but no bathrooms. The toilets used large iron tubes to conduct the waste into a cistern, which was periodically emptied by a group of drunken peasants. (The job called for a special issue of vodka, which was generally consumed on the spot.)

Underlying all this splendor, in a semisubterranean termitary, were rooms that resembled prison cells in which the swarms of servants that accompanied the aristocracy found shelter. The serfs were liberated very late in Lithuania. In those prisonlike rooms serfs had been housed. A girl was supposed to have been buried under the foundations or walled up in the massive masonry. Her ghost was said to haunt the building.

Any splendor Daudzegir may have possessed had faded by the time my father took refuge there in 1925. The whole area had been a battlefield in World War I. Shell fire had scarred the walls and damaged the roof. Marauding troops—German, Russian, Red Army—had sheltered in the house and left their marks. The mildewed, faded wallpaper was scrawled with obscenities in several languages. The great ceramic wood stoves, ornamented with human figures, were partly smashed and all the figures decapitated. Not a stick of the once splendid furniture was left in the place. And there were rats, huge rats, that lived in every nook and cranny.

To this monumental wreck I found myself transported, a timid boy of twelve straight from the ordered life of my English prep school. It was my father's plan, aided and abetted by his second wife, to house me in this ruin until he could ship me off to Australia, a convenient dumping ground for unwanted offspring.

He was not a good father.

He and his wife managed to scrape up some money from somewhere and departed soon after my arrival for Berlin, where they lived in style in an apartment on the Kurfürstendam.

For two years I was left in the family ruin, my sole companions a family of Latvians who farmed the land. They were old family retainers. The father had been the gardener and the mother the cook. They spoke four languages: German, Russian, Latvian, and Lithuanian. They could read, write, and do simple arithmetic, and considered themselves a class apart—far above the Lithuanians, whom they despised as mere peasants.

After two years in the ruins among the rats and the Latvians I was well on the way to becoming a peasant myself. My expensive education drained out of my head. I went barefoot in summer, wore peasant moccasins made from a single slab of leather in winter. I learned the meaning of poverty, the meaning of starvation.

Yes, starvation. I did not starve myself. The old family retainers saw to it that I was fed, though I doubt that my father sent them any money. But I was living among peasants whose tiny plots of land barely sufficed to keep them alive. They grew little patches of rye, wheat, and potatoes; they made a barrel of sauerkraut and another of dill pickles. Their scrawny hens laid a few eggs, and there might be just enough pasture for a cow. But a really bad year left them with barely enough food in store to survive the winter. Their thin, gaunt faces spoke of hunger.

My stay in that rat-ridden ruin was in part a time of discovery, in part a time of terror. The terror reached its height during the winter months. It gets incredibly cold in the winter in Lithuania, and the winter nights are very long. My father, with that snobbery typical of the Germano-Russian aristocracy, refused to let me live below stairs with the peasants, where I might have kept warm and felt reasonably safe. Instead I was forced to inhabit one of those large lofty upstairs bedrooms. It was bitterly cold, and the cracked plaster of the ceiling seemed likely at any time to fall on my head. All round me were empty rooms in an even worse state of repair than the one I occupied.

On the deathly still winter nights, when the cold outside crept around like a wolf in the snow, those empty rooms became haunted with ghostly presences. Sitting at my rough table by the light of one candle, trying to read one of the few books my father had left me, I shivered with a combination of cold and terror. The sounds I heard or imagined I heard in the empty rooms made my flesh creep. Sometimes I heard footsteps, sometimes voices, now and then a faint scream or the sounds of sobbing.

Indeed there had been enough violence and bloodshed in and around the house—what with the war, the revolution and the starvation that went with it—to supply the place with a whole army of phantoms. So I would sit trying to read as the ghosts racketed around in the empty rooms, then, without undressing, dive in terror into the mattress of straw that was my bed and pull a blanket over my head to keep out the ghostly noise.

I added to my own terrors by placing a skull on a pole on the decaying veranda that stood outside my bedroom. The skull had been fished up by the peasants out of one of the ponds in which the flax was retted. It had a gaping hole in the side of the cranium, the skull of a victim of war, German or Russian, who could tell. The peasants had thrown it into a culvert, from which I had recovered it and stuck it on the pole outside my window. This action was a manifestation of the more shamanistic aspect of my Magician archetype. The shaman within me regarded that skull as a power object.

At night the skull took on a life of its own and started peering through the window, sometimes festooned with partly decayed flesh. This added greatly to my nocturnal terrors, yet I could not bring myself to bury the wretched object. My shaman-magus was very attached to that skull.

The Magician, for me, represents skillful means or magical power (the Juggler of the tarot cards). Shamans, sorcerers, magicians all use this power, which they draw from certain power objects in nature. During the time I spent in the family ruin, the Magician archetype began to emerge and to dominate much of my behavior. I knew nothing at that time about archetypes or sorcerers, but I knew about power objects, especially power plants. It was intuitive knowledge derived from the collective unconscious. My expensive English prep school had ignored the whole subject of biology. We had not even been encouraged to collect wild flowers. Yet here I was passionately addicted to gathering roots, berries, and fungi. From these, in an old enamel bowl picked up somewhere, I would concoct mysterious stews that I felt sure had magical properties.

Fortunately a residue of caution prevented me from partaking of these elixirs. Had I done so I might well have poisoned myself, for the ingredients I favored—the scarlet fly agaric, the berries of the spindle bush and nightshade— are all quite toxic. It seems to me now that my Magician knew they were toxic in spite of my lack of botanical training. He chose them for his brews because they were poisonous.

But the Magician was more than a brewer of magical potions. He understood the voices of spirits, especially the spirits of woodland and water. There were extensive woods near the house, remnants of the great forests that had once covered the area. During the summer months, when the short nights were a mere interval of twilight between one day and the next, these woods swarmed with spirits. To commune with these spirits my Magician would lead me to the woods and have me wandering around all night listening and looking. The spirit voices of the summer woods were very different from the terrifying ghosts that haunted the winter house. The woodland spirits spoke of the mysteries of nature, symbolized by the ignis fatuus, the pale fire that glowed among the marshes. They spoke of the holy life force that inhabited certain trees.

In Slav and Teuton alike this mystical response to forests lies deep in the soul. Trees were sacred to both races, as they were also to the Celtic Druids. For myself I can testify that the racial memory exists. I am, in part at least, a man of the woods. Trees speak to me.

So, in those days in Lithuania, as a lonely abandoned boy in a strange land, I sought from the trees the "forest murmurs," influences that could reassure me, nourish my spirit. I sought them also in the streams that ran through the meadows at the edge of our estate. Here, among yellow kingcups and water lilies, the water spirit Rusalka sang her song, inviting young men to join her in her underwater realm. I bathed naked in the stream; I listened to Rusalka; I gathered crayfish, sticking my fingers into the holes in which they hid, drawing them out by their pincers, eating them cooked with dill.

My Magician also had a taste for graveyards. There was one of which it was especially fond near the river Tatolla. The shrine by the entrance had been used for target practice by the Bolsheviks during their brief occupancy of Lithuania. The Christ figure was scarred with machine-gun bullets. Inside over the graves were large wooden crosses. The wooden figures on the crosses had mostly decayed, so that the bodies hung down by the feet while the two arms dangled from the crosspiece. A ruined chapel with garishly painted figures of various saints stood amid the crosses.

The ruined shrine had some sort of message, some magic, like the megaliths of Stonehenge. It had to do with death and the world beyond death, the dark realm, the labyrinth with its monster, the mystery of the unconscious. My Magician knew about these things, but he could not formulate in words just what he knew. He was an archetype, and he carried the wisdom of that archetype.

Only years later, when I began to study the works of Carl Gustav Jung, did I realize how much an archetype can know.

5

EDUCATION OF A PEASANT

"If you come with me I'll show you the fish traps."

Siegfried towered above me, a regular giant. He was twenty-four years old, the eldest son of the Latvians who took care of me. They were passionately pro-German and anti-Russian. A daughter was called Brunnhilde.

Siegfried and Brunnhilde in the same family!

I had been in Lithuania only a few weeks and my German was rudimentary. But I realized he was saying something about fish, so I trotted off with him. All my life I have been fascinated by fish. Still am.

It was the time of the spring thaw. The meadows were flooded. Water was pouring along the drainage ditches. The country swarmed with frogs. Never in all my life have I seen frogs in such profusion. They hopped and crawled everywhere. One could not avoid stepping on them. Among them, like dignified gentlemen in formal attire, the storks—newly arrived from Egypt—strutted on their long legs. They stuffed their stomachs with frogs and flew off to their nests. Throwing back their heads they brought them forward again with the curious clapping sound that gives them their German name (*Klapperstorch*). They regurgitated the frogs into the open beaks of their young.

We splashed across the flooded meadow. Across a drainage ditch a temporary dam of willows had been placed. In the center was the fish trap. Siegfried heaved it out of the water, revealing a fine pike. I did not know at the time that

I was looking at a fish trap whose design had not changed since the Neolithic Age. It was cunningly woven of willow stems, one cone within another. The fish could enter but not exit.

From that point on Siegfried became my teacher. The Latin verbs, fragments of Ovid, odds and ends of history, and other residue of an expensive and useless education drained out of my brain. Instead I learned how men survive. I learned where my food came from. I learned of the great cycles and the great laws.

The laws were absolute, inescapable. Break them and you perish. All peasants know this. They know it instinctively, as animals know, as the storks know when they must migrate, as squirrels know when they must gather their winter store.

In a land with a savagely cold winter and a short growing season no time could be wasted. As soon as the land had drained and become workable the ploughs were in action. I learned how to harness a horse to the plough. I learned the feel of the damp earth flowing over the mold board, how to keep a straight furrow by pressing on one or other of the handles.

In June when the grass was lush in the water meadows I learned how to swing a scythe with the mowers. In those June days when the nights were short the peasants were inexhaustible. Truly they were extraordinary! All day, in the full summer heat, they would swing their scythes, working in unison across the acres of grass, which was still scarred here and there by shellholes and the mounds of old trenches. They would come homeward singing, the men in front with their scythes, the kerchiefed women behind them carrying wooden rakes.

Did they then collapse in exhaustion? Not a bit of it. They stuffed themselves with curds and rye patties cooked in oil, drank kvass or homemade beer, produced guitars, mandolins, balalaikas—and danced! Danced like maniacs, leaping and turning, no prissy ballroom stuff but real Russian-type folk dance. All that after ten hours' mowing in the summer heat!

And the songs! Never have I heard such singing. The Lithuanians are a very ancient people, and their language is akin to Sanskrit. They have these songs, *daino* they call them, which must also be very ancient. Though the Lithuanian dances are very lively, the songs are melancholy. The peasants would sing when going to their work and when returning from it, sing in perfect harmony, the women taking one part, the men another. Over the broad meadows these sad harmonies could be heard, expressions of the soul of a people whose lot had always been hard, ground between two giants, Slavs and Teutons, in an impoverished land with poor soil and a savage climate.

After the hay was brought in, the rye and wheat were harvested. Again I learned from my mentor the ancient art. It is one thing to drive a reaper or a combined harvester. It is quite another to confront twenty acres of rye with nothing but a scythe or sickle. Then you really earn your bread in the sweat of your brow. A scythe, to be effective in cutting wheat, must be equipped with a cradle. This enables the harvester to keep the stems neatly together for binding into sheaves. The cradle added considerably to the weight of the scythe. It was heavy labor indeed. But the inexhaustible peasants swung their way through acre after acre, pausing now and then for a drink of kvass, or to sharpen their scythe blades.

The women followed the men, binding the sheaves with straw. There was a special trick to this that I still remember, a way of twisting and dividing the stalks, knotting them together and tucking in the ends. It was truly backbreaking toil, but the women were as tough as their men and worked on without pause, laying the sheaves together in stooks as they went until the field was covered with tentlike structures.

Last of the major crops was flax. The stalks, with their spherical brown seed pods, were pulled up, roots and all.

The pods were removed by the men, who passed bundles of stalks through a rippling comb. Then the stalks were tied together, dumped in a pond, and weighted down with rocks. Sometime later they were fished out and laid on the banks to dry, and the whole land stank. This was the retting process, designed to liberate the fibers from the pith and bark. Later, during the winter, the bundles were taken to a village nearby, where—in a special building maintained at a high temperature by a roaring wood stove—the stems were crushed by a heavy wooden roller pulled in a circle by a blindfolded horse.

To all these was added a host of other tasks. Mangolds had to be harvested for the cattle. Cabbages had to be converted into sauerkraut, cucumbers into dill pickles; great loaves of rye bread had to be baked in brick ovens; cows had to be milked and milk turned into cheese. The peasants grew their own tobacco, which they cured themselves. It contributed a special element to their peasanty smell, which was quite distinctive, musky, like the smell of an animal. The idea of odorless man is an artifact of modern culture. Normal man smells, and so does normal woman.

The peasants knew nothing of baths. Their tiny log cabins had two compartments. In one half lived the peasant and his family, in the other lived the cow, the horse, and a pig or two and some chickens. They did not even have an outhouse but shat outside winter and summer. Twice a year in the spring and fall they took a steam bath. For this they used the village smokehouse, which for the rest of the year was used for smoking ham. They would make a pile of stones, light a fire under it, pour water over the stones, and sit in the scalding steam scouring the dirt and dead skin from their bodies with bundles of birch twigs. From these biannual orgies of cleanliness they emerged with a strong aroma of smoked ham.

In winter, when the huge snowdrifts often rose to the eaves of their cabins, they virtually hibernated. They ventured out occasionally to load their sledge with combed flax, and drove ten miles to the market town, where the Jews stood in line along the road to bargain with the peasants. Combed flax was their only cash crop.

Once he had money in his pocket, a terrible struggle began in the soul of the peasant. His angel told him to take it home to his wife. His devil told him to spend it on vodka. As often as not he listened to his devil. It seemed impossible for the peasant ever to observe moderation in his consumption of alcohol. He drank himself into a stupor, was loaded onto his sledge by his companions. He did not need to drive. His horse knew its way home.

Now and then the animal became entangled with a snow drift, the sledge turned over, the peasant fell out. He was dug out later frozen stiff. It was a good way to go.

At Easter, when the snow began melting, the peasant would take his horse to the blacksmith to have its winter shoes changed for summer ones. He would also polish his own boots. He would bring into his house birch branches, which opened their buds in the warmth. At church, to celebrate the rising of Christ, he would painfully change from his peasant moccasins into his boots, which were worn only in church, often handed on from father to son. At midnight a carved and caparisoned doll was hoisted aloft by the priest, while the whole congregation burst out in a shout of triumph.

Christ is risen! Christ is risen!

I remember the rapture on those peasant faces, the triumphant cry bursting from the very soul. The joyful cry went back far beyond Christianity, back to the pagan festivals that celebrated the return of the sun, giver of light and of life. Christ is risen! Life will be renewed. We have emerged from the tomb of winter. Under the melting snow the earth is reawakening.

Ah yes, there were lessons to be learned among the peasants. Far from the phony world of my English prep school, from the Ovid and history, French verbs and football and cricket, I learned the realities of life—the essence values.

How well I understood why Tolstoy, tormented in soul, found refuge finally among the peasants. Their weaknesses were obvious. They got beastly drunk, they were often brutal, they were ignorant and superstitious. But by God they were genuine! There was nothing phony about them. They faced cold, hunger, poverty with patience and good humor. They never complained of their hard lot. When conditions became too impossible, they simply died.

Their lot was hard not only because the climate was harsh and the soil poor, but because they were placed, geographically, between two giants. Again and again the clash between Slav and Teuton had sent invading armies pouring across the Lithuanian plain. In World War I the villages had been overrun by Cossacks, plundered by Junkers, collectively raped by the Bolsheviks, and impartially ravaged by diseases, chiefly typhus. It was really a miracle that anyone survived.

The aftermath of the war was also ruinous. Thinking that the Russian ruble might lose its value, our old family retainers changed part of their savings into German marks. Then the mark became every bit as worthless as the Czarist ruble. I well remember the old peasant woman who took care of me opening a drawer with a woebegone expression, as if revealing a guilty secret. In it lay piles of rubles and marks, the savings of a lifetime. They were nothing but bits of paper, completely worthless, but she clung to them still, cherishing some vague hope that they might regain their value.

The sight of those piles of paper impressed me deeply— and effectively undermined, at that early age, any ideas I might have formed about the value of money.

So fate rained blow after blow on the heads of those patient peasants, but they responded like true Warriors, overcoming enormous difficulties to rebuild their homes and bring their ravaged land back into production. And what instinctive wisdom they had, what reverence for the great cycle of existence! I remember walking beside Siegfried when his plough turned up some bones. They were obviously human, some victim of the war. He picked up the bones.

"Poor fellow, I'd give him a Christian burial if I knew his beliefs. But I might put him in the wrong cemetery, and he wouldn't rest easy. Ah, well, clay is brother to us all, so he may as well stay where we found him."

Carefully, reverently, he placed the bones in the furrow.

Clay is brother to us all.

It really is.

6

DUST

Blackness.

It reared like a solid wall passing across the land. I looked at it in terror, unable to decide whether to stand or run. It was as if the earth had risen bodily and was preparing to bury me alive.

I was standing in the middle of a huge Australian paddock, my only companions a team of skinny horses harnessed to a set of harrows. The horrible apparition that threatened us had crept up suddenly in the middle of a clear, sunny day. I had grown accustomed to tornadoes. Almost always on hot days these towering whirlwinds could be seen somewhere around. They lifted the dust and tumbleweeds high in the air. They could pick up a sheep. They could even pick up a man. Fortunately they moved rather slowly and one could avoid them.

But this wall of blackness was another matter. Escape was impossible. It stretched across from horizon to horizon. As it came nearer I felt the sensation of one about to be buried alive. I flung myself on the ground, covering my mouth and nose with my hands. A sudden wind tore at my clothes and the air became almost unbreathable. I stood up and looked around. Dust was everywhere, the sun was obscured. A few moments before I had been able to see for miles. Now I could see no further than my team of horses. I was gripped with a momentary fear that they would panic and bolt, but

they were used to dust storms. Philosophically they turned
their rumps to the wind, dropped their heads, and stood
still.

The wind died down a little, the air became slightly more
breathable. I went on harrowing, a handkerchief tied over
my face.

Later I returned to the farmhouse. I was ashamed of my
fear but could not disguise the fact that I had been frightened as that black wall advanced upon me. The farmer for
whom I worked, a war veteran used to all varieties of terror,
laughed at my fear.

"There's a poor ignorant Pommy for you!" he said.
"That's a Broken Hill dust storm. It's not as bad as it looks."

He was an intelligent fellow, not at all a bad sort. He
explained that such dust storms were common in the Broken Hill region of Australia. A sudden wind, what sailors
would call a squall line, picked up the dust and carried it
like a wall. So there was calm and sunshine on one side of
the wall, darkness and dust on the other.

My father had dumped me in a dying land. I was fourteen
years old, the victim of acute culture shock. First I had been
torn out of a proper English prep school and dumped
among rats and peasants. Then, when I had more or less
adjusted to the rats and peasants, I was dumped in the Australian outback to work for what the Australians called a
"cocky." I was, in their weird jargon, a "Pommy." It was a
term of contempt that they reserved for emigrants from England.

I did what I could. Everything was totally strange. I might
have been transferred to a different planet. In place of green
meadows there were the endless brown paddocks with mile
upon mile of barbed-wire fences. In place of the spirit-
haunted woods there was the gaunt eucalyptus, the "mallee," a scrawny growth of scrub, soulless and sere. In place
of the peasants with their dances and lovely folk songs there
were uncouth Australians, without traditions, without
roots, settled in a land to which they did not seem to belong

and which appeared to be doing its best to exterminate them.

My unfortunate employer was a good man in an impossible position. Along with a number of other returned veterans he had been allocated land beyond the Murray River in South Australia. Responsible meteorologists had warned the government that the land was not farmable. It stood on the very edge of the desert. Only the mallee scrub held the soil together.

The warnings were ignored. The White Man's greed, that deep-rooted defect of the White Man's soul, overcame all caution. Wheat prices were high after the war; and that land, given plenty of superphosphate, would grow wheat. Besides, the government had on its hands an army of returned heroes, who had to be occupied somehow before they started to tear the place apart. Let them direct their energies to "conquering the outback."

And conquer it they did—for a few years.

They plunged in boldly, cleared the mallee, tore up the soil with stump-jump ploughs pulled by huge teams of horses. They burned the brush, seeded the land with wheat and the inevitable, essential superphosphate without which nothing would grow. They strung miles and miles of barbed wire to keep in the sheep. They built houses and barns with roofs of corrugated iron, and huge cisterns, also of corrugated iron, to catch the precious rain, their sole source of water.

For a while they prospered. The rain fell. The wheat, in huge machines, was drilled into the land. Even the seed drills had to have stump-jump arrangements, for the stumps were everywhere and the farmers could not take the time to pull them out. The wheat ripened, miles of wheat. Then combine harvesters, pulled by huge teams of horses, gobbled up and threshed the heads, leaving the stalks standing. The stalks were burned.

It was mechanized agriculture at its worst—expensive, extravagant, destructive. The huge machines all had to be paid for. The huge teams of horses that pulled the machines (in those days the tractor had not replaced the horse) all had to be fed. And that flood of superphosphate, without which the land would grow nothing, also had to be paid for.

At first the rains came and wheat prices stayed high, so there was a series of fat years. The rapists of the land appeared to be prospering. But by the time I arrived in the outback, a timid bewildered teen-ager completely confused by the weird life scenario that fate had composed for me, those fat years had already ended. The rains did not fall. The land began to die. Dust was everywhere. It piled in huge drifts on the roads. It invaded the houses. The worn out, worried woman, who had borne four children, lost all her teeth and her looks, struggled to keep her house reasonably neat and clean. It was impossible. The dust got into everything. One breathed dust, ate dust, slept in dust. There was too little water for a proper wash.

The sheep were dying. There was nothing for them to eat but tumbleweed. They became paralyzed, lay down, and could not get up again. Crows descended upon them and pecked out their eyes. I had the job of riding around with a knife, cutting the throats of the moribund sheep, and taking their skins before the crows destroyed them. The few remaining cows were dying of a disease called dry bible, an impaction of the stomach caused by too dry a diet.

One day I drove the table-topped wagon loaded with seed wheat and superphosphate out to where my boss was hitching up his team to the seed drill. We poured seed into one compartment. Into the other went the acrid superphosphate, which was very acid and corroded everything. My boss swung the team around and started his seed drill toward the distant horizon.

"This is a gamble," he said. "And it's my last."

A decent man, a man at the end of his rope, but fighting to the end. The previous crop had been an almost total failure. He had borrowed money for seed and superphosphate. He had waited for rain but no rain fell. He decided to gamble on dry seeding.

Dry seeding, he told me, was always risky. You drilled
the seed and superphosphate into the bone-dry soil and
hoped for rain. If the rain was sufficient, the seed would
germinate, get its roots down, and hold on and give you a
crop. The worst thing that could happen was a light rain
followed by drought. In that case the seed would germinate,
but its shallow roots would not gain a foothold and the
plants would wither.

So we gambled. And the rain did come. I remember the
rapture with which I heard it falling onto the corrugated
iron roof. It was the first rain I had heard since arriving in
Australia. Never before had I realized how utterly dependent life was on that water from the sky. I had taken it for
granted.

The rain soaked the top few inches of soil. The acres and
acres of wheat we had seeded between us now formed a
film of green over the brown land. Flocks of pink cockatoos
descended on the rows and began, grain by grain, to devour the crop. We shot them in large numbers. They were
good in stews.

Fine weather ensued. The sky was clear and blue, the sun
was warm. Day after day of sun. The wheat was vulnerable,
tender and shallow-rooted. Already ominous patches of
brown were appearing in the carpet of green.

I watched the sky with anguish, looking for clouds.

O God, make it rain, make it rain, God make it rain.

I still believed in God. I still thought there was some old
gentleman floating aloft pulling strings and running the
show, the jealous old Jehovah we had groveled before in
those endless services in the school chapel. Groveled before
and flattered. Oh, the flattery! How many thousand Te
Deums had my childish voice proclaimed!

We praise thee, O God. We acknowledge thee to be the Lord.

Was I to get nothing in exchange for all that flattery?
Make it rain! Make it rain! This poor man has gambled all
he has. He has a wife and four children. Make it rain!

The sky remained cloudless. Then the wind returned and
with the wind the dust. It scoured the earth like sandpaper,

rasping the delicate first shoots of the wheat, leaving them blasted and dying.

My boss hunched over his cup of tea and watched. Even the children were silent. I would have to leave them; he could not afford to pay me any longer. I offered to work for nothing. I liked the man and wanted to help. No hope. He couldn't even feed me.

He drove me to the station in his battered jalopy, handed me a couple of pound notes, my last pay. I handed them back.

"You'll need this more than I will."

There were tears in his eyes. There were tears in mine. I turned away, embarrassed. On the horizon loomed a huge black cloud, another dust storm. The very earth had turned against us and was throwing us out.

"Get out, you fools, before I bury you."

The message of Mother Earth to those who had raped her.

We got out. There was absolutely nothing else we could do.

7

A
SEASON IN HELL

The large wooden pilings smelled of tar and sewage. Around the pilings, the dirty water of the harbor of Port Adelaide rose and fell, polluted with a film of oil and floating debris. It was late at night. I knelt on an abandoned dock, looking down at the water lit by a single electric light that glowed nearby. The shadowy forms of ships could be seen against the night sky, but the dock on which I was kneeling had obviously not been used for some time. The warehouse behind me was empty and collapsing into ruin. It was a symbol of the worldwide depression that had completely disrupted the economy not only of Australia but of most of the other countries on the globe.

So I knelt on the abandoned dock looking down at the oily polluted water that glistened unhealthily in the lamplight. I swayed slowly back and forth as if engaged in prayer. But I was not praying. The childish faith in the Father God instilled into me during those endless services in the school chapel had dried up and disappeared. I was without faith in anything, a friendless, bewildered derelict, seventeen years old and totally alienated.

Since the stubborn drought had ruined my first employer and compelled me to retreat from the back country, I had traveled a descending spiral into a small private hell. I was dying by inches of spiritual inanition, was ragged, smelly, and had not eaten for three days. Drifting without any aim or sense of direction I had been washed up in Port Adelaide. I lived in the ruined warehouse, searched in a desultory way for work in the docks. There was no work. The place swarmed with unemployed, hungry, ragged men with the resentful faces of the unwanted. The disruption of the economy was total. Farmers were dumping their locally grown peaches, and yet in the stores one could buy canned peaches from America. Wheat rotted unused in the warehouses while armies of unemployed had not enough to eat.

For my part, I so totally loathed my surroundings that I lived entirely in dreams. In retrospect my life in Lithuania seemed heavenly. Day after day I would return to the family ruins, would walk in the fields and forests, go fishing in the Tatolla with my friend Siegfried, work in the fields with the peasants scything hay or binding sheaves, make my magical brews in the secret power spots in the woods. These dreams so totally dominated my life that I barely knew where I was. I was entering the shadowy realm that lies between sanity and madness, a realm in which the real world becomes increasingly difficult to distinguish from the world of dreams.

When I did return to the present, I was overwhelmed with self-pity. I hated my father for having shipped me to Australia instead of giving me a college education, which I surely deserved. Timid, shy, hypersensitive, I could find no place at all in that raw land. I had been uprooted once too often, and the effect of those uprootings was deadly. The transition from peasant to farm boy in the mallee country had strained my inner resources. Fortunately my employer had been a good, understanding man and had made things easier for me. I was able to appreciate his struggle and take part in his last desperate gamble, a gamble against forces over which he had no control.

But after my employer had gambled and lost, I simply gave up. I began falling into a spiritual vacuum. I had nothing to hold onto, no friend, no adviser, no game worth playing, was totally washed up at seventeen, a piece of human debris kneeling on a deserted dock in Port Adelaide, swaying to and fro over the oily water.

I swayed further each time. Among the oil slicks I saw a face, the face of my own death. I was not afraid of it, welcomed it in fact. As I had nothing to live for, why bother to live? I leaned further forward, past the point of no return. My body rotated in the air and dropped with a splash into the water.

At this point I discovered that as a method of self-destruction drowning has drawbacks, especially if the would-be suicide knows how to swim. I did know how to swim, had learned in the covered swimming pool of my expensive prep school. It was probably the only thing of any value that I derived from that costly education. So though my mind ordered me to end it all and sink passively to the muddy bottom of the harbor, my body stubbornly refused to cooperate. I did indeed absorb a lot of water, but the water went into my stomach instead of my lungs. It tasted unspeakably foul, fuel oil with overtones of salt and sewage. The shock of the cold water seemed to awaken my almost dormant will to live. My body struck out for the shore and crawled out on a mud flat, on which, like a half-rotted skeleton, lay the wreck of an old wooden fishing boat, the water sloshing back and forth through its exposed ribs.

So I sat on that stinking mud flat like a drowned rat, soaked and shivering, vomiting the mixture of sea water, fuel oil, and sewage that filled my stomach. It was undoubtedly the low point of my career, but I was still too immature to take responsibility for my own predicament. Instead I became violently indignant, putting the blame for the mess in which I found myself on everything except myself. I cursed my father; I cursed Australia; had I still believed in God I would have cursed God. A succession of wild scenarios raced through my mind, the sort of scenarios that occur to teen-aged rebels everywhere. I saw myself as the enemy of society. I would wreak my revenge, blow up a bank, organize the unemployed, burn down the city of Adelaide, rob the rich to feed the poor, etc. They were savage, lurid scenarios, blood-red and flaming. At least they gave me enough courage to drag myself off the mud flat and clean myself up. Next day I was even brave enough to get a bowl of soup at a Salvation Army kitchen. It was no great act of courage, but I was so acutely shy in those days that I did not dare ask for a free handout even though I was starving.

That same timidity prevented me from putting into effect any of the antisocial fantasies that surged through my mind. My very first attempt to play the desperado resulted in my arrest and deportation as an undesirable alien. It was just as well. Had I continued at large I might have hurt someone. Violently antisocial teen-agers can be quite dangerous.

The long voyage back to England gave me leisure to reflect. Though still filled with passionate resentments, I did manage to reach one conclusion. Never again must I allow myself to descend into that morass of self-neglect and self-pity that had left me vomiting and half-drowned on a mudbank in Port Adelaide. Standing by the rail of the ship and gazing out across the vast expanse of the Pacific, I dimly perceived the realities of the human life game. External events could threaten us and even destroy us, but it still lay within our power to rise above those events, to be masters of our fate instead of slaves. At school I had memorized vast amounts of poetry, and now one of those poems came into my mind: "Invictus" by W. E. Henley. It was high-flown and a bit pompous, but it expressed very well my new determination. I recited it to the indifferent Pacific, over which fluttered swarms of small flying fish like flocks of sparrows.

> Out of the night that covers me,
> Black as the Pit from pole to pole,
> I thank whatever gods may be
> For my unconquerable soul.
>
> In the fell clutch of circumstance
> I have not winced nor cried aloud,
> Under the bludgeonings of chance
> My head is bloody, but unbowed.

It matters not how strait the gate,
How charged with punishments the scroll
I am the master of my fate:
I am the captain of my soul.

8

GENTLE WARRIORS

I returned to England with ten shillings in my pocket. I was officially in disgrace, the unwanted son who had been packed off to "the colonies," failed to make good, and turned up again like the proverbial bad penny. My father was not on the platform to meet me when the boat train from Southampton arrived in London. Never one to confront a difficult situation, he had dodged the issue and sent a member of an organization called the Universal Aunts who, for a fee, would take care of lost children, stray dogs, and prodigal sons returned penniless from far countries.

The Universal Aunt, a young man who looked as if he had problems of his own, handed me a letter from father. It was the sort of sermon I had become accustomed to receive from him: "shocked to hear about your behavior," "can't understand why you failed to avail yourself of the great opportunities in that young country," "unable to do a thing for you at the present time." In short, he was either broke or not interested. Probably the latter. I was not of age. He was still legally responsible for me. But my father had never had much respect for legalities and was totally lacking in what is loosely known as natural affection. He was not one to kill the fatted calf or to embrace his lost son.

I stuffed the idiotic epistle into my pocket and cursed foully and silently. That was one thing I had learned in Australia. When it comes to the use of foul language no one can equal the Aussies. However, I could hardly solve my problems by calling my father rude names. The great grey city of London seemed singularly unfriendly, and I had only ten shillings. I was beginning to experience the same panicky, trapped, hopeless feeling that had caused me to throw myself into the water of Port Adelaide harbor. Some sort of prodigious struggle evidently lay ahead, but the spirit of despair was already singing its siren song. Is it really worth it? Why don't you go off somewhere and end it all?

I struggled with the dark siren, blocked out its insidious song by proclaiming, like a mantra, the words of the poet. *I am the master of my fate, the master, the master, the master.* It helped a little, but not much.

Standing on the station platform I quickly reviewed my options. My mother had left me a little money, which was being held in trust by a shadowy entity called the Public Trustee. I visualized some Dickensian character in a frousty office in some dreary London lane. Should I go to the Public Trustee and ask for money, like Oliver Twist asking for soup? Not if I could help it. I had then, and still have, a profound distrust of officials of all kinds.

Who else was there? My grandmother was dead. My great aunt with the house in Salisbury was dead. My aunt who had married the purple colonel and rode to hounds would almost certainly have nothing to do with me. Then there was Cork.

Cork?

Of course Cork! How could I possibly have overlooked the woman who had come closest to being like a mother to me during my childhood? Cork was really Cordelia, one of the three Fisher sisters—Cordelia, Adeline, Emeline. (What names those Victorians gave their children!) One really couldn't go through life calling oneself Cordelia, dragging the whole cast of King Lear around with one like a train of bad karma. So Cordelia became shortened to Cor and further metamorphosed to Cork. Cork she became and Cork she remained to almost everyone. Outwardly she did not give the impression of being full of sweetness and light.

She could even be a bit abrasive and was prone to outbursts of righteous indignation. But under the somewhat rough exterior was the proverbial heart of gold. She would succor stray cats, old dogs, all sorts and sizes of derelict humans. If I could only locate her she would probably succor me.

I could do with some succoring.

But where was she?

She had written to me once or twice while I was in Australia. I could vaguely remember her address. The house was called Sunnyside and it was located in a town called Godalming.

I turned to the Universal Aunt.

"Would you mind if I tried to find an aunt of mine who lives in Godalming?"

The Universal Aunt would be only too glad. He obviously had no idea what to do with me and was thankful to get me off his hands. Yes, he knew where Godalming was. One could get there by train from Victoria Station.

So I arrived in Godalming. With some help from the local post office I located Sunnyside, which lay on the edge of the town, a three-story architectural nonentity with woods in the background. I trembled as I rang the doorbell. My whole future hinged on whether Cork still lived in that house. If I could not locate her, I would once again be lost, drifting around like a leaf in a storm.

Master of my fate. Master of my fate. But the words failed to carry conviction. They were clearly untrue. My fate depended on factors quite beyond my control. I rang again.

A teen-aged youth opened the door. I recognized him vaguely: Adam, Cork's son. We had played together as children in the garden of Wheatfield, her house in Oxfordshire, along with Penn and Dooley Tennyson, grandchildren of the poet. Adam, two years younger than I, was almost but not quite unrecognizable.

I stammered.

"You . . . you must be Adam."

He stared at me, puzzled. Time had evidently changed me beyond recognition. I announced my identity.

Adam's face lit up with pleasure and astonishment. He was a genial youth, full of joie de vivre, which he inherited from a charming but quite irresponsible father. I rather vividly remembered that father, because he once entertained us children in the garden of Wheatfield by balancing a fried sausage on the end of his nose. He and Cork had not managed to get along with each other. He lived in America. Cork had the custody of Adam.

"Cork, Cork, come here quickly! It's Bob. He's back from Australia!"

There followed embracings and rejoicings, and floods of questions. What on earth was I doing back in England? Over a cup of tea I told of my life and hard times in the Antipodes. Hoping to impress Cork, I put on my tough-guy expression, a mask that my fumbling persona had tried to construct to conceal an essentially timid essence. I had at the time, so I'm told, the face of a slightly shopworn angel, and the tough guy mask fitted me badly. Cork was not impressed. She laughed. It was no use indulging in heroics with Cork.

Her eyes, large and owlish behind horn-rimmed spectacles, infallibly detected the phony in my makeup as I started to describe the wicked things I had done during my outlaw phase in Australia.

"Don't be silly," said Cork. "Have some more tea."

Ah, yes, there was no fooling Cork. She was one of those no-nonsense women, forthright, and—as far as I could make out—totally fearless, who stood firmly by the things they believed in. She had seen enough genuine suffering caring for the wounded in World War I not to be taken in by displays of self-pity. So "Don't be silly," said Cork, and advised me to forget the whole stupid episode. There was nothing to be gained by weeping over the past. I had to think about the future.

So what of the future? The unfolding of my essence had by that time brought the Scientist into the foreground. The Scientist was certainly related to the Magician. Both were passionately devoted to the study of nature. The Magician approached nature with awe and reverence, trying to blend with the universe and to draw from it power. The Scientist put himself in one room and nature in another. He wanted knowledge. He wanted to find out how things worked, to observe, dissect, analyze. Clearly, from a practical stand-point, it was the Scientist who could earn a living and per-mit me to occupy a useful place in society. Our civilization was the creation of scientists.

So I would become a scientist. My decision was made and carried with it a powerful charge of emotion. I was hungry for knowledge, for the education that had been denied me. I would live in London, would starve in a garret if necessary, to gain the degree I needed to enable me to engage in scien-tific research. All this I explained to Cork, who had not much use for the idea of starving in garrets. One could not do good work on an empty stomach. Nothing could be ex-pected from my father, and my own small inheritance was not enough for me to live on. Curiously enough, neither Cork nor any other of my English relatives suggested that I work my way through college, a course of action that would have seemed quite natural to any young American. It was something that simply did not happen among English upper-class families. The parents paid for the education of their children, who in turn took care of their parents in their old age. In any case, what sort of job could I get? I was completely untrained and London swarmed with unem-ployed.

"I think," said Cork, "I'd better talk this over with Ade-line."

We all piled into Cork's battered Morris and drove from Godalming to Dorking. Adeline, Cork's oldest sister, had married Ralph Vaughan Williams, the composer. They lived in a house in Dorking called The White Gates. It was a large one-story house looking out toward the downs, chosen by the Vaughan Williamses because it had no steps at the en-trance. Adeline Vaughan Williams was crippled by arthritis and had a hard time negotiating steps.

Adeline and Ralph Vaughan Williams were Aunt Adeline

and Uncle Ralph to most of the young people who came to The White Gates. Awed young composers visiting the place for the first time would address Uncle Ralph as Doctor Vaughan Williams. He was, in fact, a doctor of music, but the title did not suit him. He was large, warm, generous, prone to tell the same jokes over and over, always with the same apology, always roaring with laughter at his "ancient chestnuts." As Haydn had been Papa Haydn to those who knew him, so was Ralph Vaughan Williams Uncle Ralph. In many ways he reminded me of one of my favorite characters in literature—the gentle, rotund, pipe-smoking Uncle Toby of *Tristram Shandy*.

Indeed the slow-paced life at The White Gates had much in common with that of Shandy Hall. After lunch Uncle Ralph would subside into an enormous armchair and, by way of settling his own digestion and everyone else's, would adjust his spectacles, open a book, and read. After a while his voice would become indistinct, the spectacles would slip down his nose, the book would fall from his hand, and a gentle snore would announce to the rest of us that we could quietly leave the room and go about our business. The rest of us included everyone in the household, including the cook, the maid, Aunt Adeline's companion, and anyone else who happened to be in the house. The servants were never treated as such, but always as equals. The Vaughan Williamses were naturally democratic.

As for the book, it was almost always by Trollope. After we had finished the inevitable *Barchester Towers*, we meandered through another of the author's numerous works. I find it touching, though not surprising, that in our restless, uneasy, inflation-ridden United States of the seventies Trollope is enjoying a revival. His works are classified among the minor tranquilizers—mild, soothing and completely free of side effects. Certainly they were soporific for Uncle Ralph. Twenty minutes of Trollope sufficed to bring on a calm sleep, which lasted for about half an hour and no doubt greatly aided his digestion.

Sheltered in this quiet harbor my spirit began to recover

from the battering it had received. I was still badly scarred, and the scarring showed in my behavior. I was ill-tempered, ill-mannered, ill-educated, still very antisocial, and prone to black moods during which I became totally unapproachable. It was a tribute to the tolerance of the Vaughan Williamses that they put up with me.

From Adeline Vaughan Williams I received my first lesson in the art of separating from the physical body. She never spoke about this art. She taught entirely by example. Her personal "season in hell" had taken the form of a crippling illness that had slowly frozen her joints and threatened to reduce her to the status of a bedridden invalid. By a superb effort of will she managed to halt the inroads of rheumatoid arthritis and to remain active. Though her knee joints were fused, she still walked with the aid of a crutch. Though her fingers were crippled, she still copied all her husband's scores and wrote most of his letters. She was always gentle and considerate toward those about her, and I never heard her complain about her illness. She was a model for me, who tended to indulge in self-pity and to brood over my sufferings.

The Vaughan Williamses were not outwardly religious. Without being openly anticlerical, they gave me the impression of harboring a deep distrust for the whole hierarchy of organized Christianity from curates to archbishops. They expressed the spirit of the Quakers without being Quakers. They respected religion without taking part in its ceremonies. Ralph Vaughan Williams, who had written one of the finest tunes in the hymnal, *For all the Saints who from their labors rest*, never to my knowledge went to church. Like Beethoven, he found satisfaction for his religious feelings in long walks through the fields and woods. He adored the English countryside. Part of his youth had been spent collecting English folk songs; and the folk song, which expressed the very soul of England, strongly influenced his early music.

For those who have ears to hear, the English countryside

sings in a special way. I think Ralph Vaughan Williams *heard* rather than saw the country. We were both fond of walking and sometimes met on our rambles. I, being dominated by my Scientist, would run around examining flowers, leaves, geological strata, the complex interactions of ecological systems. He saw none of that. He *listened* to the country and heard it as music, walking in a sort of trance, oblivious to heat or cold, rain or shine. Details did not interest him. Once I took him with me to Ranmore Common to see a beautiful bed of wild violets that grew by the edge of a beech wood. He awoke from his trance and looked. He was clearly unimpressed. He had expected an ocean of bloom, a celestial burst of color.

"But, Uncle Ralph, violets don't grow like that. They are modest flowers. You can see them poking out between the leaves."

Uncle Ralph nodded doubtfully and lapsed back into his trance.

Though liberal, generous, and broadminded in other ways, both Uncle Ralph and Aunt Adeline were bogged down in that morass of inhibitions that the Victorians constructed around all manifestations of the sexual impulse. Living at The White Gates was a very pretty girl named Honorine, who was some sort of distant relative and did the cooking. Honorine and I were not in love, but we both itched powerfully in about the same region and would certainly have ended in bed together had the slightest opportunity arisen. How nice it would be, I thought, if instead of guarding Honorine like dragons they would let us simply do what came naturally. If between us we produced a baby, they could adopt it. They were childless, and the atmosphere of The White Gates would be greatly enlivened by the patter of little feet.

Such a cheerfully Polynesian arrangement would have been unthinkable for Aunt Adeline, who was far more uptight about sex than Uncle Ralph. Unthinkable for her was another sexual scenario that would have made sense from a

purely biological point of view. As Aunt Adeline could not
have children, why did not Uncle Ralph sire a child on one
of his female admirers? He had plenty of them, referred to
them as his nymphs, had even devised a sort of scale, an
avoir du nymph, which ran, so far as I remember: Two
nymphs make one cozy, two cozies make one cuddle, two
cuddles make one orgy, and so on. There were no doubt
several of the nymphs who would have been glad to bear
him a child; and he, being sexually deprived, would have
been happy to do the fathering. But of course such behavior
was taboo. He could never have got Aunt Adeline's consent
to such a sensible arrangement. He was far too honest to
deceive her—probably could not have done so, as she was
amazingly intuitive, almost psychic, and would have
known what was happening. So, though it was one of Aunt
Adeline's great regrets that she had never had a child, she
could not break the bonds of an outmoded morality and let
her husband hand on his genes via another woman. Thus a
valuable genotype was lost.

This antiquated attitude toward sex in such otherwise liberal people as the Vaughan Williamses was all the more
surprising because just around the corner, so to speak, was
the Bloomsbury set, whose members were well in the advance guard of the movement against sexual hypocrisy.
Virginia Woolf and her husband Leonard ran the Hogarth
Press, which published, among other books, the collected
works of Sigmund Freud. Virginia Woolf was related to
Aunt Adeline. She closely resembled her physically, but
psychologically they lived in quite different worlds. Books
by various members of the Bloomsbury set—David Garnett,
Virginia Woolf, Lytton Strachey—were always lying around
in the living room at The White Gates, but none of the au-
thors ever visited the house. The nearest I came to meeting
any of them was to spend a weekend at the house of the
poet Bob Trevelyan, a fringe member of the set, whose fine
house, under the brow of Leith Hill, commanded a magnificent view of the Weald.

The Vaughan Williamses were not intellectuals. They suffered, as did many of their kind, from the effects of a lopsided education. Though Uncle Ralph was related to the Darwins through the Wedgewoods, he remained curiously ignorant of the facts on which the theory of evolution was based. I tried from time to time to explain the idea of Mendelian segregation and why mutations rather than Darwin's "insensible variations" were regarded as the raw materials of evolutionary change. Uncle Ralph could make neither head nor tail of it. He was really eager to increase his knowledge of science and bought for the purpose a popular work on the subject that he referred to as *The Child's Guide to Science* (this was not its real name). He even tried reading it aloud after lunch, but it put him to sleep even faster than did Trollope.

Though Uncle Ralph and I lived in quite different worlds intellectually, we did have one point of contact. In Australia I had possessed one book, a copy of the collected works of William Shakespeare. Because I really enjoyed Shakespeare and had nothing else to read, I had read the book frequently. Having a very retentive memory, I had an extensive knowledge of the poet's work. Uncle Ralph, who was also a Shakespeare enthusiast (his favorite poets were Shakespeare, Blake, and Walt Whitman), took pleasure in testing this knowledge of mine. So at lunch:

" '*Let the sky rain potatoes; let it thunder to the tune of Greensleeves; hail kissing-comfits and snow eringoes*'—who said that and in what play?"

Uncle Ralph looked at me, his head on one side, with an expression that said, "Got you this time!" My mind did a lightning-fast review of the works of William Shakespeare. I did not recognize the quotation, but there was only one character who could have expressed himself thus and only one play in which he would have used the words.

"Sir John Falstaff in *The Merry Wives of Windsor*."

"Bravo!" said Uncle Ralph.

My stock as a Shakespeare scholar rose several points.

Uncle Ralph had good reason to be familiar with *The Merry Wives of Windsor.* He had set the play to music in an opera called *Sir John in Love.* Excerpts from the opera were due to be performed that very week at the Dorking Musical Festival, in which choirs from all the surrounding villages took part. I attended some of the rehearsals and there learned that the amiable Ralph Vaughan Williams became a truly alarming figure when he raised the conductor's baton. Woe to the choir and especially the soloist who failed to give to the music the attention it deserved! He who was so genial and easygoing would tolerate no sloppy performances of his own music or anyone else's. An unfortunate female soloist who had failed to learn her part was summarily banished from the rehearsal hall and told not to return until she knew the music perfectly.

The actual performance went without a hitch. At the end of it the massed choirs sang William Blake's "Jerusalem," with the entire audience joining in the last verse. The splendor of Blake's words combined with the sheer volume of the sound made the experience quite awe-inspiring. It was truly an expression of the Warrior's spirit.

> Bring me my Bow of burning gold:
> Bring me my Arrows of desire:
> Bring me my Spear: O clouds unfold!
> Bring me my Chariot of fire.
>
> I will not cease from Mental Fight,
> Nor shall my Sword sleep in my hand
> Till we have built Jerusalem
> In England's green and pleasant land.

Ah, yes, I owe a great debt to the Vaughan Williamses. They put me back on my feet, gave me a game worth playing and a valid pattern on which to model my behavior. They followed what I later came to know as the Way of the Good Man or the Way of Objective Morality. They were unconscious Warriors, that is to say they never spoke of the Way and did not seem even to know about it. They never set themselves up as teachers, and if they taught anything it was purely by example. Many years later I realized that this is the only valid way to teach.

9

THE BANQUET OF KNOWLEDGE

The Vaughan Williamses, out of the goodness of their hearts, offered to pay for my continued education. The banquet of knowledge that was spread out before me was almost too much for my shrunken stomach. In Lithuania and Australia my intellect had been starved. Now I gorged myself on knowledge of all kinds. From various lodgings where I lived in squalor, I would proceed each day to the Royal College of Science, an amorphous collection of buildings that spread over a large part of Kensington. The college had none of the historic grandeur of the ancient seats of learning at Oxford or Cambridge. Its traditions were nonexistent, its social life rudimentary, its curriculum rigid, its professors underpaid and uninspired. But to me, deprived as I had been of education, it was a veritable temple of knowledge, a holy place.

In its rather shabby laboratories mystery upon mystery was revealed. I could not understand the lack of enthusiasm of my fellow students, who seemed to take everything for granted, who were bored, who made fun of the professors and misbehaved in lectures if they were given a chance—a collection of ill-mannered louts on whom the treasures of knowledge were completely wasted. I despised them and showed it, which added nothing to my popularity. I considered them unworthy to enter the temple of knowledge.

The beauty of the scientific method filled my Scientist with awe. The freedom to inquire, the freedom to investigate—how precious it was! The only loyalty that was imposed on us scientists was loyalty to truth. We recognized no authorities, no popes, no priests, no dogmas. We asked one question only: Where is the evidence? Theorize as much as you like, but find the evidence. Design the experiment. Analyze the results. If the results don't support your theory, change your theory.

Meanwhile there were techniques to master, those all-important techniques on which the whole method depended. An experimental scientist must always be part gadgeteer. If the needed apparatus did not exist, one had to invent it. But first one must know all about existing techniques.

This process of mastering techniques gave me enormous satisfaction. What a pleasure it was, in early botanical studies, to cut a perfect section from stem or leaf, stain it in safranine and hematoxylin, dehydrate it in alcohol, clear it in clove oil, mount it in Canada balsam! How delightful were the blended aromas of clove oil and xylol, the very incense of our scientific temple! And when the preparation had been mounted, what wonders it revealed: the delicate tracery of cells, the orderly arrangement of xylem, cambium, phloem!

The mysteries of the animal world were even greater than those of the plant world. Step by step we followed the pattern of evolution, from protozoa to coelenterates, from coelenterates to worms, to arthropods, to vertebrates. I dissected the earthworm, the crayfish, the frog, the dogfish, the rabbit, in a reek of formalin that made me cough. I drew pictures of embryos, embryos of amphioxus, of frogs and fish and reptiles and mammals. I noted that in its early stages the human embryo had gills and a tail. It could hardly be distinguished from an embryo fish. Shades of the past, the pathway of evolution! In our development we recapitulate the whole history of life, from one-celled protozoa to fully formed mammal. A stupendous feat, when you come to think about it.

So the Scientist kept busy, sectioning, staining, dissecting, making drawings, accumulating huge piles of notes. He had many worlds to conquer. Questions poured in from all sides and at all levels. There was the organism, man, mouse, tree, pterodactyl. It had form. It had function. What imposed the form? What held the creature together? Cells were the building blocks of life. In the cell was the nucleus, in the nucleus were the chromosomes. I had seen them with my own eyes, giant chromosomes from the salivary glands of a midge. In the chromosomes were genes, in the genes were . . .

Here the trail ended. Molecular biology lay in the future. The gene was a mystery.

There were other mysteries.

Around me, within easy walking distance of the laboratories, lay three great museums: the Science Museum, the Museum of Natural History, the Victoria and Albert. I liked to eat my lunch in a museum and meditate. The Natural History museum was my favorite. In the great entrance hall a marble statue of Darwin sat contemplating the panorama of evolution. All around spread the worlds of life, frozen in glass cases, stuffed, fossilized, pickled in spirits, copied in wax. A universe in miniature, from minerals to mammals. Dead, all dead, but conveniently assembled for the edification of those who had eyes to see.

What did I see? I saw questions and more questions. I conducted a dialogue with the dead in the shadowy region that lies between physics and metaphysics.

Who were the dead? Darwin, of course. His presence brooded over the whole scene. But there were others, many others. I read voraciously, lugging home from various libraries as many as twenty books at a time. They weren't all scientific by any means. I read Blake and Nietzsche, Keyserling and Kant. I read Lamarck, Herbert Spencer, Smuts, Lloyd Morgan, Bergson. I read Buddhist Sutras and Hindu Upanishads. I read Swift, Voltaire, Hume, Goethe, and von Humboldt. What did I seek from this dialogue with the dead?

Answers to questions. Questions that scientists are not supposed to ask. Questions relating to purpose.

The purpose of life.

Terribly wrong question. Teleological. Not scientific.

But life must have some purpose.

I asked one of my professors.

"Purpose? No. We cannot ask such questions. This is anthropomorphic thinking."

"But the evolutionary process has direction, or seems to have."

"It has no direction. All that we see is the result of the forces of natural selection acting on random mutations."

"But you said yourself that mutations are nearly always harmful."

"The ones we observe are—or the ones we induce with X rays. But think. We are dealing with a process that takes millions of years. Given enough time, quite improbable things can happen. If a hundred monkeys tapped type-writers for a few million years they would sooner or later type all Shakespeare's sonnets purely by accident."

Those monkeys and typewriters! I had heard the argu-ment before. There was a fallacy in it. What had monkeys and typewriters to do with the purpose of life?

My Scientist was content to leave the problem alone. My Magician was not. He sensed a mystery. He did not like the Natural History museum with its marble Darwin, its stuffed elephants and skeletal brontosaurus. The Magician liked better to visit the Victoria and Albert Museum, where the spoils of the British Empire, gathered from the ends of the earth, were assembled and exposed. There was a statue of Buddha in the museum. The Magician preferred Buddha to Darwin.

Tell me, Enlightened One, what is the purpose of life?

The Buddha smiled enigmatically, calm and clear.

I show you sorrow and the end of sorrow.

O Blessed One, I think I'll become a Buddhist.

I went off and assembled all my spare cash. I bought a

bronze Buddha at a curio shop. It was somewhat bashed up. It had been buried during the destruction of the Summer Palace at Peking, then dug up again, so the dealer told me. Someone had been a bit careless. There was a hole inflicted by a pickax in the Buddha's back. Apart from that and a missing finger, it was a nice bronze and genuine, and it was going cheap. I took it off to my lodging and stood it on the dressing table.

But it takes more than buying a statue to make one a Buddhist.

My inner world was turbulent. Much of my energy was expended in truly passionate resentments directed toward the Church under whose shadow I had been raised. Blake spoke to me on the subject of the vindictive Jehovah:

> Then old Nobodaddy aloft
> Farted and belched & coughed,
> And said, "I love hanging and drawing and quartering
> Every bit as well as war and slaughtering.
> Damn praying and singing,
> Unless they will bring in
> The blood of ten thousand by fighting or swinging."

What a monster, created by his worshipers in their own image! How thankful we could be that the representatives of the Age of Reason had finally dumped old Nobodaddy out of his throne. Better pure chance and a hundred monkeys with typewriters than that preposterous deity running the show. But my Magician was not happy. He read Goethe. He saw himself in the role of Faust. Faust demanded the impossible; he wanted everything:

> *Nicht irdisch ist des Toren Trank noch Speise.*
> *Ihn treibt die Gärung in die Ferne,*
> *Er ist sich seiner Tollheit halb bewusst;*
> *Vom Himmel fordert er die schönsten Sterne*
> *Und von der Erde jede höchste Lust,*
> *Und alle Näh' und alle Ferne*
> *Befriedigt nicht die tiefbewegte Brust.*

(The fool's drink and food aren't earthly. The ferment drives him far, though he's half aware of his own madness. He wants the finest stars from heaven and every high enjoyment from the earth. And all that's near and all that's far won't satisfy his deeply moved breast.)

How perfectly Goethe "spoke to my condition," as the Quakers say. He was everything: mystic, poet, magician, administrator, scientist. His *Faust* was a treasury. One could hardly open it without coming up with some gem. Faust had despaired of reaching ultimate knowledge by any of the methods available at that time. He had mastered philosophy, jurisprudence, medicine, and theology only to find that he was no wiser than before. In desperation he had turned to magic, calling up spirits in his struggle to answer the great questions.

My Magician really believed in magic. Magic involved listening to the voices that ceaselessly spoke in Nature. Magic involved finding the universal arcanum, the sacred hieroglyph inscribed on King Solomon's ring that enabled Solomon to understand the voices of the animals. The Magician was happy enough to use the scientific method as far as it went. But it did not go far enough. The basic questions lay beyond its reach.

POLITICS
IN FOG

Fog.

It crawled over London like some disgusting phantom.
The pea-soup presence penetrated everything, an aerial suspension of oxides of nitrogen and sulfur mixed with soot
that caught in the throat and caused the eyes to itch. Street-
lamps were barely visible. Buses crawled through the soup,
their spotlights focused on the curb. The whole city
coughed and choked in the foul miasma.

I turned up the collar of my coat against the chill and
shouted, without much conviction, "Smash Fascism!" All
around me were masses of dark shapes, thousands of dem-
onstrators who had flocked into Hyde Park to protest
against the antics of Oswald Moseley and his Blackshirts.
By my side was a German—a Communist, a refugee from
the Nazi terror—a student my own age, Hans by name. We
spoke in German. He looked with contempt at the ragged
masses. The British had no idea how to organize a demonstration. In Germany everyone would march in step, flags
flying. There would be bands—and weapons. In Germany
one took one's politics seriously.

The dark mob swept across the park, where a speech was
to be given by the leading light of the British Communist
Party. The theme—free Thaelmann. Thaelmann was the
leader of the German Communists, currently in jail. "Free
Thaelmann," along with "Smash Fascism," was one of the
slogans we yelled at intervals.

At Hyde Park Corner the mob came to a halt and was duly inspired by inflammatory oratory. Properly filled with loathing for Fascism, the mob now turned and made off in the direction of the Albert Hall, where Mosley and his Fascists were holding a meeting. The grey mass was now slightly better organized, for there was a battle imminent. The general plan was to attack Mosley's Blackshirts as they emerged from the hall and show them just what we thought of their brand of politics. Some of the more militant Communists had hoisted flags and lined up, more or less in order. The mob followed their example. They marched. They sang. Sounds of the "Internationale" drifted into the fog.

> So comrades come rally
> And the last fight let us face.
> The Internationale
> Unites the human race.

"Free Thaelmann!"
"Smash Fascism!"
I marched along next to Hans, trying to feel militant. From time to time a cynical little voice asked me what on earth I thought I was doing. Why was I wasting my time at idiotic demonstrations instead of studying? What earthly good could it do to get involved in an ugly brawl with a bunch of Blackshirts?

I silenced the voice and marched on, prepared for violence. It soon became apparent, however, that a major hitch had occurred. A Cockney voice out of the fog informed us of realities.

"Fuckin' police 'ave closed the bloody gates."
It was so indeed. There were gates, large and unclimbable. There were palings along the edge of the park, also unclimbable. One bold comrade tried to scale them, only to become impaled on the iron projections. He was helped down from the other side by an impassive policeman. There

were police four-deep guarding the entrance to the hall.
There were police all along the road that the procession
would traverse. Half of London's police force must have
been mobilized to protect Mosley's Blackshirts, whose un-
popularity was enormous.

The doors of the hall opened. The frustrated mob hurled
themselves at the barricades and yelled defiance. The Blackshirts unfurled their flags, took up their places, arranged
their faces in the style of Nazi storm troopers, and marched
down the road while the mob howled with impotent fury.

Hans gazed at them in disgust. In Germany there would
be a pitched battle. There would be dead in the streets.

"Pfui!" said Hans.

He spat to show his opinion of British politics.

"You have no force, no spirit," he said in German. "You
are a decaying race."

There seemed, at that dismal period, a good deal of evidence to suggest that he was right. London in the thirties
was not a place to inspire confidence. About half the population seemed to be unemployed and living on the dole, a
meager pittance barely enough to hold body and soul
together. The melancholy songs of the unemployed Welsh
miners echoed through the streets. There was no market for
Welsh coal. They had come to London hoping to find jobs.
There were no jobs. All they could do was sing.

I could not ignore these signs. My tendency had always
been to side with the rebels, to champion the underdog.
There were rebellious stirrings among the students, not
only in London University but also in Oxford and Cambridge. Children of the upper classes who had been given
everything that money could buy were turning against their
own class and becoming Communists or Communist fellow
travelers.

For a while I found myself swept up in this agitation. The
psychic energies of youth in the thirties centered around the
organization of political hatreds, as those of their forebears a
few centuries earlier had centered around the organization

of religious hatreds. The atmosphere was pervaded with fanaticism and intolerance. Young people of great spirit and high intelligence mouthed the tired clichés of Marxism-Leninism with all the fervor typical of True Believers. Though Hitler's Germany was painted blacker than hell, Stalin's Russia was portrayed as an ideal society in which muscular workers strove to liberate from their chains other less fortunate members of the proletariat.

I was introduced into this community of young fanatics by a truly beautiful girl who everyone called B.J. B.J. could have stepped right out of a Burne-Jones portrait. She was a gentle creature. Her father wrote essays for *The New Statesman*. She had received an expensive education at Oxford, the fruits of which she proposed to throw away in order to work in a factory.

It was B.J. who led me into the maze of conspiracy that hung and still hangs around the Communist movement. We read books out of the *Little Lenin Library*. We subscribed secretly to *Inprecor* (*International Press Correspondence*). We learned the techniques of subversion, of infiltration, of using deception to take over existing organizations.

Dear B.J.! The mask of a conspiratorial Communist fitted her badly. This was true of nearly all the intelligentsia who fell for the Communist con game of that period. How Stalin's propaganda machine, despite the bloody purges of that period, managed to maintain the image of the Soviet Union as a worker's paradise I will never understand. Chiefly responsible for the deception were the Fabians, Sidney and Beatrice Webb and the "celebrated buffoon," George Bernard Shaw. Many years later, in an article in the *Sunday Times*, Malcolm Muggeridge classed the "follies of the Fabians" among the great blunders of the twentieth century. Perhaps this is putting it too strongly. Certain it was, however, that the absurd credulity of the Webbs and the irresponsible clowning of Bernard Shaw helped to confuse a whole generation of earnest young people. They failed to realize that tyranny was tyranny, whether it wore a black shirt or a red shirt, and that if it came to terrorism the Russians could outdo the Germans any day.

My infatuation with Communism was of brief duration. The movement was pervaded by pedantic bores who placed theory before fact. They were as bad as the Inquisitors who had insisted that the sun moved round the earth despite Galileo's evidence to the contrary. They had a total and quite pathological disregard for truth. The Party Line was sacred, and all True Believers had to follow that line even if it maintained that black was white and wet was dry.

How any scientist could swallow the lies that were daily dished out by that propaganda machine I will never understand. But several did, and they were by no means obscure. Their faith was an extraordinary demonstration of the power of the human mind to indulge in games of make-believe. So it was perfectly possible for a scientist as prominent as J. B. S. Haldane to blind himself to the entire panorama of horrors in Stalin's Russia, even though it affected workers in his own favorite field, genetics.

Luckily for me, a deep-rooted dislike of dogmas of all kinds, whether religious or political, combined with my preference for truth to free me of the blinkers of doctrinaire Communism. My Scientist made me ask for the evidence. It looked into both sides of the question. It read books about Russia, books such as *I Speak for the Silent* by V. V. Tchernavin, in which were described all the horrors of the Stalinist labor camps.

"What do you make of this book?" said my Scientist to B.J.

Poor B.J. I really loved her for a while, but my taste for truth was stronger than love. She gazed in horror at the book. It was at the very top of the *index prohibitorum* of the Communist faithful. I began to read excerpts. The more I read, the more agitated she became. Finally she practically put her hands over her ears to prevent this frightful intelligence from reaching her brain. With something of a shock I realized that not a trace of objectivity remained in the psyche of this beautiful, highly-educated girl, whose emotions so totally dominated her intellect that she could not even listen to information that might shake her faith.

That ended my affair with B.J. It also ended my affair with Communism. I cursed the extremists on both sides, red shirts, black shirts, brown shirts, swastikas, hammers, sickles, the whole stupid rigmarole. I read Julian Benda, *The Treason of the Intellectuals*. The intellectuals, said Benda, should be objective and value truth above fiction. Since the end of the nineteenth century they had let themselves be drawn into the game of political passion. In the process they had lost all their objectivity and used their intellects for the organization of political hatreds.

In a single sentence he summed up the tragedy of those bewildered intellectuals who had so lost sight of their proper function in society.

> Although Orpheus could not aspire to charm the wild beasts with his music one could at least have hoped that Orpheus himself would not turn into a wild beast.
> (Benda, J., *The Treason of the Intellectuals*,
> Translated by R. Aldington.
> New York: William Morrow and Company, 1928.)

II

THE SMERDIAKOVS WILL TRIUMPH

I have described the professors at the Royal College of Science as underpaid and uninspired. There was one exception, at least as far as inspiration was concerned. Professor F. G. Gregory taught me plant physiology and presided over my struggle to obtain a Ph.D. He was not really Gregory. He was actually a German Jew, Guggenheim or something of the sort. He was one of the most brilliant talkers I have ever met, with a mind as swift as a humming-bird, darting from subject to subject, iridescent and a bit flashy.

From time to time he would invite me to have supper with him at his house in Hampstead. He had never married, was at heart a lonely man. He took toward me a rather fatherly attitude and frequently referred to me as "my boy."

"The first student I've had with any glimmering of original intellect."

This, from Gregory, was praise indeed.

Over a bottle of Burgundy and a plate of mulligatawny he would put on displays of intellectual fireworks that made my brain reel.

"Life," he announced one evening, "started in the soup. Please pass the pepper."

I passed the pepper and awaited the next item of this revelation. The professor was propounding his own version of creation. He shoveled down a spoonful of mulligatawny and continued.

"Yes, it began in the soup. That isn't my own idea. I swiped it from Haldane. *The primeval seas attained the consistency of hot diluted soup*. You could write a menu around the story of life. In the beginning was the soup, which occupied the whole of the Archeozoic. Next came the fish. That brings you to the Devonian. Then we have a reptile course, which brings us to the Cretaceous. Then poultry, the birds, and red meat, the mammals. That brings us to the present day."

"And the dessert?" I inquired.

"Why nothing less than the great universal ice cream. Life starts in the soup and ends in the ice. Can't help but do so. The sun runs out of fuel. The seas congeal. All water becomes solid, all life ceases. Have some more?"

I declined politely. The professor helped himself, explaining between mouthfuls how that Archeozoic soup had originated.

"Steaming hot planet. Hardly any atmosphere. Water saturated with carbon dioxide and ammonia irradiated with shortwaves from the sun. What happens? CO_2 combines with NH_3 . . . urea . . . amino acids . . . proteins. All the ingredients of life. The ocean gets thicker and soupier. There aren't any bacteria. There isn't any decay. The ocean is a vast test tube of sterile broth. Think—What a medium for life to thrive in."

"But there's a very wide gap between soup and a living creature, however simple."

"Define your terms, define your terms!" cried the professor. "What is this living creature? What is life?"

He gazed at me with an air of aggressive inquiry. His eyes sparkled in his round face. His soup spoon remained suspended halfway to his lips.

"What is life?" I repeated. "Yes, what *is* life?"

My mind groped amongst an array of textbook definitions. I could find none that would be likely to satisfy the professor. Living things grew. So did crystals. They reproduced themselves. Crystals could do that too. They burned carbon compounds for energy. So did a candle.

"I don't know that I can answer your question."

"A poor biologist . . . a sorry biologist. He studies life, he does not know what life is. Never mind, my boy. All definitions are slippery. Return to your problem of the Archeozoic soup and there you will find a definition of life."

"A self-reproducing organic molecule?" I hazarded.

"Bravo, bravo!" cried the professor. "Right on the target. Autocatalysis, my boy. Use a high-sounding word when you can. It impresses fools. *Autocatalysis*," he repeated, rolling the word round his tongue as if to extract its flavor. "There's your definition of life, the simplest ultimate living entity. A single organic molecule which catalyzes its own formation from other similar molecules. There's the beginning of nutrition, there's the start of reproduction. The Archeozoic soup begins to stir itself. Molecules transform other molecules into their own likeness. What else is life? What else is the mystery of life?

It's a very odd thing—
As odd as can be—
That whatever Miss T. eats
Turns into Miss T."

"If that theory is correct, one should be able to produce life in a test tube just by reproducing the conditions that existed in the Archeozoic."

"Ho, ho! And so one should, if one knew what they were. But the Archeozoic lasted for millions of years. The scope of the experiment was as large as the planet. But in any case, *life stirred on the face of the waters.* One molecule, several molecules, devouring and being devoured, transforming and being transformed. Oceans of free interacting enzymes. What a paradise for a biochemist! And little by little the enzymes came together in groups. What else is an organism? What are you? What am I? Moving collections of enzymes integrated into a single balanced system. We have emerged from the soup. We carry our soup within us.

"Rachel, Rachel!" he shouted, suddenly switching to German. "We are through with the soup. Bring the next dish, dear girl. Ah, *kalbsbraten!* Oh, good. Rachel, dear, meet my best student, the rising star in the biochemical firmament. De Ropp, this is Rachel, my handmaiden, comfort of my old age, solace of my declining years."

The plump old lady who had brought in the *kalbsbraten* set down the dish, wiped her hands on her apron, and took my hand. She was some sort of distant Jewish relative he had rescued from Nazi Germany. She worshiped him and always respectfully referred to him as *"Herr Professor."*

"The problem," said the professor, seizing a carving knife and assaulting the *kalbsbraten,* "is not so much how life began as how it continued. *Blind chaos brooded on the archaic seas.* No, no. That's poetry. Out with poetry! We are men of science, not poets.

> Under the wide and starry skies
> The autos autosynthesize.

Damn, that's poetry again! Rachel, dear girl, bring another bottle of Burgundy. Remember to warm it. What the hell was I talking about? That's the trouble with wine—it brings out the poet in my nature."

"May we not be poets and scientists also?" I inquired.

"No, no. They will consider you unorthodox. Tread the straight and narrow path if you wish to be well thought of. But you will never stick to the road. You have a free spirit. Mysticism is in your blood. It's in mine too. My father was a rabbi. Mix the best of religion with the best of science and what do you get? A free spirit who travels far, like Tom of Bedlam.

> By a knight of ghosts and shadows
> I summoned am to tourney,
> Ten leagues beyond
> The wide world's end,
> *Methinks it is no journey."*

The professor flourished the carving knife as though already engaged with his ghostly adversary. He swallowed some Burgundy and attacked the *kalbsbraten*.

"Orthodoxy is the curse of science!" he proclaimed. "One man beats a path, the rest follow like sheep. Beware of orthodoxy. Shun the beaten path. Change your philosophy of life at intervals. It keeps the brain elastic."

"I wish I had a philosophy of life to change."

"Abandon that wish, abandon it!" cried Gregory. "Stop looking for a hole in which to hide. Stay out on top. The air may be cold but it's fresh. Why do you want to snuggle down in some smelly little rabbit warren for the rest of your days?"

"It could be comforting."

"*Pfui!*" said Gregory, spitting generously. "At your age . . . to look for comfort. You should be ashamed!"

I swallowed some Burgundy. I was accustomed to Gregory's outbursts. It was never possible to discover what he really did believe. The provocative spirit that inhabited that plump body could assume as many disguises as Ariel. His aim was always the same: to puncture pomposity, to undermine smug self-assurance, to shake rigid orthodoxies, to question complacent assumptions. Confronted with a believer, Gregory automatically became an atheist. In the company of atheists he at once became a believer. In the presence of neo-Darwinians he would champion the theories of Driesch and Bergson; but let any student of his so much as mention entelechy and he would frown and sternly demand why the student thought it necessary to cloud a scientific problem with mystical concepts. Moreover, so nimble was his mind and so encyclopedic his knowledge that whatever position he took he could defend it effectively. Few people emerged from an argument with Gregory without the feeling of having passed through an intellectual wringer. His constant changes of position, however, had given him a reputation of fickleness. He was generally regarded as an intellectual acrobat without any sincere beliefs, interested mainly in provoking an argument for argument's sake.

"In spite of everything you say about rabbit holes," I said, "I still wish at times that I was a believer."

"A coward's wish, a coward's wish!" the professor exclaimed. "You want to crawl back into the womb, back into darkness and safety. Oh, for the comforts of a fixed belief! Oh, for the circling arms of a nice kind God! Ah, you weakling! Your intelligence has dumped you out in the cold. You shiver and want to crawl back into the warmth again."

"Quite a natural desire," I protested. "As a child I believed that a great powerful being was personally interested in my affairs. I asked his blessing at night and his aid in the morning. I was filled with the sense of his presence. But now the feeling is gone. My intellect tells me that there is no such benevolent being. No loving spirit presides over the universe. There is only a chaos of interacting molecules, a life which started in the soup and will end in the ice. Is it surprising that I sometimes look back to my childhood and regret the passing of that confident state?"

Gregory chuckled and stuffed his mouth with veal.

"That God you trusted so in childhood—what was he but consolation for your early loss? Your mother died when you were young. You sought a substitute in the form of God. Those who cling to God cling also to childhood."

"Do you feel that religious people are always immature?"

"Children, children," said Gregory tolerantly. "Lovers of heavenly Papa and heavenly Mama, they nestle in the shade of an angel's wing and comfort themselves with illusions of heavenly bliss. But we in science have put away childish things. We have left that haven and closed the door behind us. We are driven out into the storm by our coldhearted intellects. While the believers stay home with heavenly Papa, we shiver in the cold and darkness. This is the price we pay for seeing things as they are."

"Are you sure that we see things as they are? Is there truly nothing in life but natural selection working on random mutations? If only the fittest survive, why is nature so complex? There ought not to be such a profusion of variety and color. Why do birds have gay plumage which merely betrays them to their enemies? How can it help an orchid to have a flower so complex that only one species of insect can fertilize it? Why are there music and poetry? Of what use are they for survival? Have we overlooked something? We have toppled God from his throne and put a roulette wheel in his place. All is due to chance. There is no guiding mind, no plan, no purpose in life. If there is no God, no plan, no purpose, then what should be our aim? What should we live for?"

"Bravo, bravo!" cried Gregory, highly delighted. "With enough liquor inside you you talk like a prophet. Go tell that to our tedious neo-Darwinians. They wish to confine all nature to a single equation. They perform one experiment with five green and five brown grasshoppers and extrapolate from there to almighty God. But what does nature care for the neo-Darwinians? She plays with us all. We merely fiddle with the fringes of her petticoats while she watches in amusement."

"I believe that you are on the side of the angels yourself."

"Angels? Who mentioned angels? I take no sides, either with apes or angels. But this I know, and here I am being sincere and not indulging in mental pyrotechnics. Nature is vastly complex. What we know is a tiny drop, what we don't know a vast ocean. So long as we bear that in mind, there is hope for a few of us. We may yet avoid the results of our original sin."

"Original sin?" I said. "What has that to do with it?"

"It has everything to do with it. Never ignore the results of original sin. And if you want to know what it is, it's this," cried the professor as he speared a large chunk of veal and chewed it vigorously.

"I'm afraid I don't follow. What has original sin to do with *kalbsbraten*?"

"I never specified *kalbsbraten*. I refer to meat eating. Man rose because he ate meat. He will fall because he eats meat. There's the essence of it."

"You talk like Nut-cutlet Willy," I observed. It was Gregory's own term of contempt for vegetarians.

"Nut-cutlet Willy be damned," said the professor. "You don't follow my thinking. The connections are too subtle for you."

"Agreed."

"Well, well. What has happened to that brilliant intuitive intellect? Must I explain the biology of original sin?"

"Please do," I said, fascinated.

Gregory sat silent for a while, as if assembling his ideas.

"The great apes," he observed, "are vegetarians. They hunt not, neither do they slay. They live peacefully, obscurely, inoffensively. They were not involved in Adam's original sin. Do you wish to see Adam as he was before the Fall? Go to the zoo and look at an orangutan."

"I still don't follow."

"My, my, how dull you are tonight. Look at it this way. Some time back in the Pleistocene the stock from which the primates arose divided. One stream led to the great apes, the other led to man. What happened? The great apes remained in the trees and ate fruit and nuts. The hominids climbed down and stood up and started eating red meat. If you want meat and you haven't claws or fangs, what do you do?"

"You make a weapon," I said. "The deadlier the better."

"Just so, you make a weapon. Hand and brain cooperated. Tools were made. And what sort of tools were they? Tools for killing of course. So the curtain rises. Enter man the killer, clutching a stone axe, complete with original sin. He hacks and clubs his way through a million years of prehistory. He kills beasts for food and his fellows to protect his hunting grounds. He bands together with his relatives for more efficient killing. His tools are for killing, his skill is for killing, his religion is for killing. His very existence depends on his power to kill. Then he discovers agriculture, settles down, builds cities, becomes civilized. His destructive habits, far from aiding him, become a menace to the stability of his culture. But after a million years of killing how can he suddenly learn not to kill? The change in his mode of life has been too swift. He cannot adapt so rapidly. Man the killer remains a killer, even though killing no longer serves any useful purpose and threatens him with extinction as his weapons grow more potent. There's original sin for you! And the whole thing started because our ancestors craved for meat. Had we stuck to the fruit and nuts we would have been where the apes are now, without cities, science, civilization, or sin."

Gregory paused and mopped his brow. The flow of his own oratory had made him sweat. I glanced at him in admiration.

"You have worked out a good explanation for original sin. Now what about salvation?"

"Salvation? Why, my boy, it's no problem," said Gregory amiably. "Who were the saviors, the avatars, the liberators? Who were Moses, Jesus, Buddha, Krishna, Lao-Tze? They had only one message, only one aim in mind. They saw man's dilemma and offered a way of escape."

"In short," I said, "they told him that bashing one's neighbor with an axe was fine for hunters but bad for civilized beings."

"Correct, correct. There's the essence of it. What is the 'Old Adam'? Simply the heritage of a million years of head bashing. *He liveth best who basheth best*, that was the lesson which nature dinned into our ancestors during those million years. He who failed to learn the lesson failed to survive. The tendency to split our neighbor's skull was reinforced by centuries of natural selection. Now come the saviors and tell me to stop bashing. It is no longer necessary. It is folly. It can only lead to self-annihilation. Stop bashing, they say. Learn to love, not to hate. Turn your swords into ploughshares and your spears into sickles and live together in harmony. But man the killer is fettered by his past. What does he do to his savior? Why, he kills him of course. Then he makes a god out of him and fights and kills for the next two thousand years to prove that his god is better than the other fellow's. It's a thankless task, being a savior."

"It's high time we had a new one," I suggested.

"Nonsense!" said Gregory. "It would go with the new one as it did with the old. This is no time for saviors. This is the age of Smerdiakov. It was all foretold by Dostoevsky. Smerdiakov is the key figure. The world is crammed with Smerdiakovs. Nazis, Fascists, Communists—all Smerdiakovs. They have overheard the chatter of the intelligentsia. All is accident, all is permitted, and so on. They think there is no law. In the end they will destroy everything, including themselves. When fools start listening to atheists society shudders."

"Must they destroy everything? Will nothing remain?"

"Nothing, nothing," said Gregory, brandishing his fork. "It will be as was foretold by Fyodor the prophet. We toil and sweat but the Smerdiakovs inherit. The son of Stinking Lizaveta will tear down all we have built."

"But there must be some way of restraining the Smerdiakovs," I insisted. "Why should they triumph over the men of good will?"

"Because the men of good will are naive and talk too much. They give that which is holy to dogs and cast pearls before swine. They have destroyed the old law and not created a new one. They have told the Smerdiakovs that all is permitted and the Smerdiakovs have taken them at their word."

"You mean the law of God?" I asked. "Are you secretly a believer in spite of your scoffing?"

"What I believe has nothing to do with it. The concept of God is socially valuable if only to keep the Smerdiakovs in order. As you said, we have toppled God from his throne and put a roulette wheel in his place. We depict the universe as a gamble and all that occurs therein as due to the workings of chance. Very well. Perhaps this is the truth. But we ought to have kept it to ourselves and not told it to the

Smerdiakovs. Now there is nothing to restrain them. All is accident, all is chaos. There is no God, no law, no good, no evil. So these pseudointellectuals seize on a few such ideas and, on the basis of their half-baked interpretations, proceed to wreck the world. We labor to build, they work to destroy, and because they are more numerous than we are they will probably succeed. They are children of chaos, and chaos is their element. The Smerdiakovs will triumph."

12

THE SHOCK OF RECOGNITION

Seeds.

They were, when one thought about it, really extraordinary devices. I looked at one of the dry brown rye seeds in a Petri dish in front of me. There it was, a baby plant complete with its lunch neatly packaged in a seed coat and put to sleep. Soak it in water and the baby would reawaken. It would start to secrete enzymes and digest its lunch. That lunch was contained in the endosperm that made up the bulk of the grain. That same endosperm—from wheat, rye, oats, or barley—was used by man for his chief food. Whole civilizations had been built on endosperm.

We stole the baby plant's lunch bag, ground it up, baked it, and ate it ourselves.

I picked up with forceps one of the seeds that had been soaked, placed it in a sterilizing solution, transferred it to the stage of a dissecting microscope. Carefully with a tiny scalpel I dissected out the embryo and transferred it to nutrient agar in a test tube. I was skillful by then. Could set up embryo cultures rapidly. My aim was to study the nutrient needs of the embryos, especially the hormones they received from the endosperm. Plant hormones were all the rage at the time. It was fun and really instructive to place tiny cubes of agar on the sides of oat coleoptiles and watch the coleoptiles bend under the influence of auxin. The growth substance (auxin) was still mysterious in those days. There was auxin A and auxin B and heteroauxin. Het-

eroauxin was indole acetic acid, an incredibly active substance. One part in a billion would produce an effect.

It was all very exciting. I was engaged in research full-
time for my Ph.D. *The Hormone System of the Germinating
Rye Grain*, such was to be the title of my thesis. I was working in a small laboratory attached to the Chelsea Physic Garden, a centuries-old garden planted with medicinal herbs
by Sir Hans Sloane in the reign of Charles II. During the
lunch hour I would study the drug plants. I had always
been deeply interested in plant drugs, still played with the
idea of taking up pharmacology. The delicate flowers of the
opium poppy, of foxglove, belladonna, aconite, hellebore,
hemp, all represented mysteries. Why did these plants produce substances that had such powerful effects on the
chemistry of man's body?

Yes, there was plenty to look at, plenty to think about.
My Scientist was busy. My Magician, however, had other
preoccupations. In the year 1935 it was impossible to ignore
the spiritual cancer that was growing in the heart of Europe.
I read the Book of Revelation.

> And the third angel sounded, and there fell a great star from
> heaven, burning as it were a lamp, and it fell upon a third part
> of the rivers, and upon the fountains of waters;
> And the name of the star is called Wormwood; and the third
> part of the waters became wormwood, and many men died of
> the waters because they were made bitter.
>
> (Revelation 8: 11–12)

So my Magician only mocked my Scientist, whose enthusiasm for playing with germinating seeds struck him as
childish. The real problem was posed by the star Wormwood. If one intended to survive and to retain one's sanity,
one had somehow to find an antidote to the great bitterness
that was being brewed in the heart of a very sick Europe.

The Magician searched for an antidote.

In the summer of 1935 he found it. The discovery produced in me that sensation which has been described as the shock of recognition. I suddenly recovered certain knowledge. It seemed that I had had that knowledge before, but had somehow forgotten it. I had lived many times and each time, between one incarnation and the next, had lost that all-important knowledge, which I then had to rediscover.

This time around I recovered it in Hayling Island in the south of England. Cork had a house on the island to which we drove to spend a few weeks by the sea. Cork, who tended to gather up damaged creatures—which she succored in her peculiar way with a tonic mixture of honey and vinegar—had among the casualties in her collection a man called the Teagle. I think his real name was Kennedy, but to Adam and me he was always the Teagle, or the "King of the Island."

The Teagle was a Warrior. Like my Aunt Adeline he had been compelled to struggle with a physical disability that a less resolute character might have found overwhelming. As a child he had slipped on a bar of soap and injured his back. The damage could probably have been corrected, but the Teagle's parents belonged to one of the more lunatic subdivisions of the Judeo-Christian Guilt Cult. They regarded their child's injury as some sort of punishment inflicted upon them for their sins by their peculiarly vindictive God. They therefore did nothing for the boy—who, as a result of this neglect, became paralyzed from the waist down. Whenever the Teagle related the story of his childhood—which he did from time to time with pardonable pride, as if to say, "What battles I have seen!"—I would feel my gorge rise against this degrading superstition that has inflicted so much misery both on its devotees and on its foes. The words of the poet Lucretius would echo through my mind: *Tantum religio potuit suadere malorum.* (So great is the evil that religion can arouse.)

But the Teagle had the soul of a Warrior and never allowed his disability to overwhelm him. Instead of crawling into a hole to die or wasting all his powers in orgies of self-pity, he enhanced his quite formidable willpower by making his already difficult life even more difficult. Confined to a wheelchair and pushed by a devoted companion, he traveled from one end of England to another earning his living with his violin, an instrument he played with considerable skill. It was no luxury tour. He associated with tramps and prostitutes, with criminals and outcasts of all varieties. He was particularly interested in the Rom (the gypsies), whose language, Romany, he studied—becoming, in the process, almost a member of the tribe.

Emerging from this underworld, he wrote a book, which brought him a modest income. Soon afterward he met Cork, who boarded him at Wheatfield, her large country house. He was a remarkably smart mechanic, designed and built for himself a motorized wheelchair, in which he would career about the Oxfordshire countryside. Later he moved to Hayling Island—where, as it was said, he became "King of the Island" by virtue of his hypnotic personality and his ability to become friendly with practically everyone.

That hypnotic personality was the most outstanding quality of the Teagle. His face was gaunt and his nose large like the beak of a vulture. The whole vitality of his crippled body seemed to be concentrated in his eyes and in his hands. Whenever I spoke with him I was reminded of Coleridge's Ancient Mariner. "He held him with his glittering eye and his skinny hand so brown." That was the Teagle. Whether he was talking or listening, he turned on his companion a look of such intensity that one felt oneself enveloped in a sort of magnetic field. He seemed able to see into one's being and to read the deepest secrets of one's soul.

This power of the Teagle caused me one afternoon to pour out to him all the doubts that were plaguing me. I explained my sense of being fragmented. Nothing in my inner world held together. My Scientist wanted to tear everything apart to see how it worked. My Magician wanted union with nature and the inner powers that union would bring. Somehow or other I had to harmonize these two elements in my totality. What made my situation even more difficult was my feeling of being caught in a senseless circus where murderous clowns piled up barrels of high explosives and threw lighted matches. Sooner or later the clowns would blow up the world. Well, let them blow it up, damn them! I had never felt at ease on the planet earth. But I did want to find some system of knowledge that would explain why things happened the way they did. Such knowledge, I felt, would act as an antidote to the poison of the star Wormwood.

"Hum," said the Teagle. He fixed me with his glittering eye and meditated.

"I think I know what you're looking for. Don't know much about it myself but I know someone who does. It's something called yoga."

Yoga! The word echoed through my whole being, evoking as it did so all sorts of strange sensations. Yes, yoga. This was something I remembered. I had always known about yoga. In life after life I had studied its mysteries, now in the guise of alchemy, now in the guise of magic. At that time, in the mid-thirties, very little was generally known about yoga in England outside Theosophical circles. Yogis were thought of as strange beings who lived in caves eating nuts and berries or lay on beds of nails or walked on hot coals. Though the British had occupied India since the eighteenth century, they had learned very little about its inner life.

Did the Teagle actually know a yogi? Could such a rare bird exist in Hayling Island? Apparently it both could and did. The Teagle swung himself into his motorized wheelchair, we piled into Cork's old Morris, and off we went to find the wonder-worker. He did not live in a cave (hardly surprising, as Hayling Island was completely flat) nor did he eat nuts and berries. He turned out to be a mild little man in wire-rimmed spectacles and a leather apron, entirely surrounded by shoes and boots, which he repaired for a living. He did not really know much about yoga, but he had several books on the subject, including a Theosophical work called *Light on the Path and Karma*. The first sentence of this book still sticks in my mind. "Kill out ambition." It is sound advice for anyone who wants to avoid various traps on the Way.

The Hayling Island yogi did not greatly impress me, but his books whetted my appetite. Back in London I became a member of the Theosophical Society, sat in the Theosophical Library under a photograph of a large, flabby, obviously overweight Blavatsky, who gazed down at me with the pop-eyed hypnotic expression that mystics wear to impress their followers.

My Scientist had nothing but scorn for Theosophy. He mocked its mysterious mahatmas who sent letters through the ceiling, derided its tales of lost Atlantis and Lemuria, found *The Secret Doctrine* unreadable and the Great White Brotherhood implausible. If such a Brotherhood existed, why didn't its members straighten out the human mess instead of hiding in the Himalayas? The basic idea of Theosophy and its motto, *There is no religion higher than truth*, was sound enough. But the credulity of the Theosophists and the magical tricks that Blavatsky so enjoyed playing cast a shadow over the whole movement. If the Theosophists had ever possessed the key to the mystery, they had surely lost it. Only one good thing had come out of Theosophy, and that was Krishnamurti. He was a Warrior if ever there was one, had spurned the crown the Theosophists had prepared for him and gone off on his own, independent as a cat. Stand on your own feet and stop relying on gurus, that was Krishnamurti's message. My Scientist liked that message, so did my Magician, but Krishnamurti was far away in Ojai, California.

So what was to be my life game? My Magician wanted a life of seclusion, devoted entirely to the development of inner power. How could I hope to practice yoga in the middle of a great city? I might manage to impose some order on my inner chaos by half an hour of meditation in the morning but as soon as I stepped out into the London streets, as soon as I read the newspaper headlines, all my peace of mind vanished. My Magician would have been quite willing to go to India, to sit in a cave, live on berries, and practice yoga and nothing else.

For this scenario my Scientist had no use whatever. He regarded it as a betrayal of the scientific tradition of the West. It was the experimental scientists of the West, not the yogis of the East, who had ferreted out the secrets of nature. And anyway, how would I earn a living in India? I'd be one more parasite on society. India is full of parasites—holy men, holy cows—both equally useless. What India needs is scientists and engineers. Does one have to become socially useless in order to be a yogi?

That was a good question, and I did not know the answer. The Bhagavad Gita, which at that time was my bible, spoke of self-duty, the duty imposed by one's own nature. *Better one's self-duty though without much merit than the duty of another. Trying to do the duty of another produces fear.* But what was my self-duty? It was easy enough in ancient India to know one's self-duty. There were four castes only. The Brahmin was concerned with spiritual truths, the Kshatriya was concerned with maintaining order, the Vaysia was concerned with making money, and the Sudra was simply a laborer. But what was I? In our complex, fragmented, confused society where all castes were mixed and all life games confused how could I find my self-duty?

To confuse matters further there was the hovering threat of war. It pervaded our lives, poisonous and omnipresent, like those pea soup fogs that blanketed London in winter. No young man capable of thought could escape the great question: to fight or not to fight. I consulted the Bhagavad Gita. This was the very question that Arjuna had asked of Krishna, his charioteer. And Krishna's answer? Fight! Fight because that is your self-duty as a Kshatriya. Fight, but remain above the battle, taking as equal pleasure and pain, gain and loss, victory and defeat. Such is the secret of the Warrior's Way.

I could not argue with that. It was always good to remain
above the battle. But I was no Arjuna, no armed Warrior
compelled by his self-duty to maintain order. I was a humble plant physiologist trying to get his Ph.D. by unraveling
the hormone system of the germinating rye grain. Moreover, my brief flirtation with militant Communism had left
me with a deep distaste for violence. All that fist waving
and yelling, that rabid intolerance, sickening self-righteous-
ness, and total disregard for truth—what did it amount to
but the total rejection of civilized values? Could any useful
results be obtained by violence? Look at Stalin's Russia.
An even worse hell hole than Hitler's Germany. No. Violence
was self-defeating. Those who used the sword would perish
by the sword. I would not fight.

So I became a pacifist. I joined Dick Sheppard's Peace
Pledge Union. Dick Sheppard, who was Canon of St. Paul's
cathedral, had a great deal of influence in England at the
time. His followers all signed a pledge not to use violence
and studied nonviolent techniques developed by Gandhi
for use against the British *sahibs* in India. The more earnest
members of the group all tried to live lives of "voluntary
simplicity," and to eat only *sattvic*, that is, vegetarian food.
In this respect we were strongly influenced by an American,
Richard Gregg, who visited England at the time and with
whom I had several earnest conversations. After meeting
Gregg I, too, adopted the life of voluntary simplicity, eating
only vegetables, bathing in cold water, rising early to meditate. I lost weight and my studies suffered, but I felt that I
was doing the right thing.

At that time all of us in the Peace Pledge Union were convinced that the use of violence must be avoided at all costs.
We were disenchanted with militaristic heroics. *Dulce et
decorum est pro patria mori?* Pernicious rubbish! It was neither sweet nor decorous. The swarms of young men of our
father's generation who had allowed themselves to be but-
chered like sheep on the bloody battlefields of World War I
seemed to us not so much heroes as deluded fools. Better to

let the Germans, who appeared to imagine they were some sort of supermen, take over Europe or the whole world if they wanted it rather than go through that bloodbath over again. The Germans could hardly make a worse mess of things than had the victorious French and British after World War I. "We will not fight," was the message broadcast to the world by a considerable segment of England's youth. In the prestigious Oxford Union a resolution was approved: "This house will on no account fight for King and Country." Adolf Hitler and his Nazis were delighted to get the message. It confirmed them in their opinion that the British were hopelessly degenerate.

My activities in the Peace Pledge Union brought me into contact with another gentle Warrior whose battles were fought entirely in the realm of the spirit. I attended meetings for the purpose of meditation held sometimes at the Quaker meetinghouse, sometimes at Gerald Heard's flat in Portland Place. To these meetings came Aldous Huxley, a longtime pacifist and another member of the Peace Pledge Union. Aldous, the ultraectomorph, towered above us, in the thick white socks, his eyes almost invisible behind pebblelike lenses. His slender body seemed to wilt under the weight of his large head. He reminded me of those columns in Salisbury cathedral that were crushed and distorted under the weight of the spire.

Aldous Huxley was a Warrior whose battles were fought in several arenas. He was, to begin with, heavily overendowed. Intellect is all very well, but he simply had too much of it. It was a burden, an embarrassment. Its insatiable demands put a constant strain on its owner, who was gripped by the Faustian urge to know everything about everything. To make his predicament even more difficult fate's Dirty Tricks Department had dealt him a blow that could easily have crushed a man of less resolute spirit. An eye infection contracted while he was at Eton had almost deprived him of his sight. For a while it appeared that he would go completely blind.

Such a prospect for one with his passionate hunger for knowledge must have seemed almost too hard to endure. I have no doubt that he was often tempted to end the game and leave his damaged body. He was a member of a family prone to fits of melancholia. The great T. H. Huxley had suffered from depression. Julian Huxley had several nervous breakdowns. As for Trevenan Huxley, whom some regarded as the most brilliant of the Huxley brothers, he had been trapped between an absurdly high standard of sexual morality and an overwhelming passion for a young woman whose social status made her impossible as a wife. The battle proved too hard for him. The idealistic Trev, whose high standards of conduct were his own worst enemy, was found during the fateful August of 1914 hanging by his neck from a tree, dead at twenty-four.

So Aldous Huxley at an early age endured his season in hell, compounded of worry over his impending blindness, grief over Trevenan's death, and horror over the insensate butchery of World War I, into which great numbers of his friends were drawn as if into a hideous meat grinder. He did not give in. Considerably tougher than brother Trev, he managed to overcome all the obstacles fate had placed in his way. His sight improved. He read voraciously with the aid of powerful lenses. Prevented by his poor eyesight from entering the field of scientific research, a life game he might otherwise have chosen, he contented himself with reading about it, kept himself well informed on a multitude of subjects, and wrote and wrote.

He wrote easily, swiftly, and well, turning out books that combined an immense erudition with a dry humor and a capacity for portraying the less lovable aspects of human nature. In the Bloomsbury set he stood for a certain kind of rueful cynicism. He was not exactly misanthropic but was certainly not an admirer of mankind. His view of the human condition was pretty well illustrated by a scene in *Antic Hay* where Myra Viveash and Theodore Gumbril drive endlessly around Piccadilly Circus in a taxi watching the lights hop, twitch, and flicker, creating their empty illusion of jollity.

"The Last Ride again," said Mrs. Viveash.
"Golgotha Hospital, Southwark," said Gumbril to the driver.

All the characters in Aldous Huxley's early books seemed to be on a Last Ride Together to Golgotha Hospital, but they talked amusingly and were never too serious about it. In *Antic Hay* the clever young cynic exposed the absurdities of society as it is. In *Brave New World* he exposed the even greater absurdities of society as it might become. In the early thirties all of us were chuckling over *Brave New World*. It was the finest satire since *Gulliver's Travels*! A masterpiece!

But "the amused, Pyrrhonic aesthete who was the author of the fable," as Aldous described himself in the foreword to a later edition, was gradually changing. The Last Ride Together to Golgotha Hospital was all very well in theory, but it was hard to take in practice—especially when, as now seemed likely, the Last Ride would involve the whole of Europe. It is almost impossible for one who did not live through that period to imagine the sense of gloom and doom that pervaded Europe during the later years of the Dirty Thirties. It was certainly impossible for anyone as sensitive and intelligent as Aldous Huxley to remain impervious to the creeping horror. So, on June 18, 1936, there appeared a large loose novel called *Eyeless in Gaza*, which announced to anyone who happened to be listening that the "amused, Pyrrhonic aesthete" of *Brave New World* had become serious—*deadly* serious.

For many of his admirers, *deadly* seemed the right word. The book was long, diffuse; and it tangled the thread of time into as many knots as has a fishing net. But worst of all it was preachy. Aldous Huxley had turned from a laughing cynic into a man with a message. The message was delivered by James Miller, M.D., Edinburgh, who looked like a blend of Gerald Heard and Dick Sheppard, was always smiling, always had a twinkle in his eye, always was in control of himself, and preached about pacifism, brotherly love, bad physical postures, chronic intestinal poisoning, meditation, Buddhism—in short, all the things in which Aldous happened to be interested at the time.

The book produced consternation among the Bloomsbury set, many of whose members found it deliberately awful. But their criticisms were not confined to his book. Leonard Woolf, who was every bit as brilliant intellectually as Aldous, privately implored the latter to reconsider his views. Leonard Woolf had himself published a book called *Quack, Quack*. It was a most irreverent attack on the dictators, whom he compared to savage war chiefs who, to terrify their enemies, wore huge and hideous masks. Were we really going to allow ourselves to be frightened out of our last remaining wits by these murderous clowns? And could a man of Aldous Huxley's intelligence seriously imagine that a collection of thugs steeped in blood to the ears could be controlled by nonviolent methods? *Whom the gods would destroy they first make mad*. But whom did they intend to destroy and whom had they made mad—the strutting Nazis who thought they could rule the earth, or Western intellectuals who thought the Nazis could be controlled by nonviolent means?

Yes, there were bitter differences of opinion among the intellectuals as the thirties grew dirtier and dirtier. Aldous stuck by his pacifism. He contributed to a book called *Prayers and Meditations* which Gerald Heard edited, a rather dreadful compilation suitable only for bhakti yogis of an extreme kind. And of course he practiced meditation himself. We all did. It was the basis of our work. The theory behind the meditations was carefully explained by Gerald Heard, who had worked out the method. There was, so he told us, a definite force which in India was called *satyagraha* (soul force), a force that Gandhi had used with success to further India's progress toward self-rule. The force could be projected toward people who controlled world events. It could be projected toward Hitler, it could be projected toward Mussolini. If enough people projected the force toward them, the dictators would change their wicked ways. So went the theory.

So we met in Gerald Heard's flat in Portland Place and projected *satyagraha*. There was a parrot in the room. Every now and then it emitted a deafening squawk. My Scientist was awed by the thought that he was meditating with the grandson of T. H. Huxley, "Darwin's bulldog." But he really did not like Gerald Heard, who was a bhakti yogi and prone to the emotionalism that such people manifest. The devoutly religious gave my Scientist a pain. He was not at all sure that he accepted soul force either. From time to time during the hour-long meditation inner arguments would break out between my Magician and my Scientist.

"Do you really think that soul force will have any effect on those Nazi thugs?"

"Gandhi used it against the British in India."

"The British in India had moral standards. The Nazis have none. Gandhi would end up in a concentration camp."

"Do shut up. I'm trying to meditate."

"The only voice those gangsters will listen to is the voice of a gun, preferably a machine gun."

"Oh, hush! We're supposed to be emanating thoughts of love and peace."

"A fat lot of difference that will make."

"Hush!"

The parrot squawked. My legs ached. I tried to enter the silence, to fill my being with a sense of love and peace. Somewhere in the basement of my mind the Magician and Scientist continued their argument.

I continued to attend the meetings with Gerald Heard because I had no other place to go. I had less and less faith in his theories. What I sought was not a way of projecting soul force but a doctrine that would give me the courage to face the abyss of meaninglessness. I had not found it either in yoga or in pacifism. I had to look elsewhere.

13

OUSPENSKY FOURTH DIMENSION

In the spring of 1936 I sat on a bench in Hyde Park reading the newspaper. The Nazis that day had remilitarized the Rhineland. They had done so in defiance of the Versailles Treaty, marching in with banners flying and brass bands blowing. One armored division, French or British, could have chased them out, and that could have been the end of Adolf Hitler. But the French were paralyzed by indecision, and the British did not move. The darkness deepened.

Sitting there on the park bench, I tasted more strongly than ever the bitterness of the star Wormwood. Like many of my countrymen I was deeply, almost hopelessly confused. As a pacifist I could not approve of the use of violence to throw those strutting Nazis out of the Rhineland. But a deeper gut reaction told me that if we let those murderous bullies get away with it they would, like bullies everywhere, become more and more arrogant, and more and more violence would be needed to stop them eventually. The Nazi movement in Germany was a cancer of the spirit; and, like all cancers, the bigger it grew the more difficult it would be to control.

My confusion had not been helped by the meditations in which we engaged with Gerald Heard or by the activities I undertook for the Peace Pledge Union, by my life of voluntary simplicity, or by my practice of what I imagined to be yoga. What I needed was some system of knowledge that would enable me to make sense out of what appeared to be senseless, to extract meaning from a world that seemed to be meaningless. I firmly believed that such a system of knowledge existed. It was a question of finding it before the general madness drove me to despair.

At this point I met Ouspensky. He was a sort of mystery man who kept in the background and conducted very secret meetings somewhere in London. Secrecy played an important part in Ouspensky's activity. Like so many Russians he had a built-in tendency to paranoia and an almost pathological distrust of officials, especially of policemen. So the lectures he gave were hedged about with secrecy. No one was allowed to talk about the teachings outside the group. Such careless talking was the number one sin, and those who broke the rule against it were cast out.

The only way to gain entry to Ouspensky's lectures was to be introduced by someone already "in the Work." This phrase "in the Work" was habitually used by Ouspensky himself and by his followers. It referred to the Magnum Opus, the Great Work of alchemy, the process whereby adepts transformed lead into gold. This transformation, of course, was thought of as being an entirely inner process, and had no connection with metallurgy. The change, however, was definitely chemical and those who had mastered the art created in themselves energy substances that enabled them to contact higher centers than those used in ordinary life. This process Ouspensky called psychotransformism.

I happened to meet one of Ouspensky's disciples at a gathering I attended. The disciple, who was very cagey and admitted only that he was interested in Ouspensky's ideas, lent me a copy of *A New Model of the Universe*, the bible of the Ouspenskyites. I found the book very uneven; parts of it were brilliant, parts of it seemed boring. But at least it was free from those tales of magic and mystery, those improbable mahatmas, those myths of lost Atlantis and even more lost Lemuria that had given my Scientist such indigestion when he had read Blavatsky. Ouspensky was much more practical and down-to-earth than the Theosophists. I gave back the book to its owner and admitted that I had found in it much food for thought. Solemnly, as if admitting me to the mysteries of Eleusis, Ouspensky's disciple suggested that I might care to hear a series of six lectures. They were free. They were given in a house in Warwick Gardens. There was only one condition attached to hearing the lectures. One absolutely must not talk about what one heard.

I went to the lectures. For some reason I was not impressed. The person who had introduced me to Ouspensky was stiff, pedantic, and terribly orthodox. I felt as if I was once again in the presence of a True Believer who thought he knew all the answers. I faulted the Ouspenskyites for being entirely preoccupied with the salvation of their own souls. They lacked compassion. I listened to the first six lectures, then stopped attending.

I thought I was through with Ouspensky, but evidently Ouspensky was not through with me. He apparently guessed that my sponsor, whose job it was to explain those parts of the teaching that might puzzle me, had not created a very favorable impression. I was potentially valuable to the Work. I knew a lot of people, including Gerald Heard and Aldous Huxley. Ouspensky in 1936 was expanding his activities. He needed people.

So he sent after me one of his trusted lieutenants, a doctor who was as skillful at handling people as my previous sponsor had been inept. Arrangements were made for me to meet Ouspensky himself, not in London but in a country place the group maintained near Virginia Water. Lyne Place was a regular estate, one of the stately homes of England. In the center was a large mansion, with a fine garden, ancient trees, rhododendron walks, a lake, and a boathouse. At some distance from the great house was the farm with barns, outbuildings, greenhouses, a walled vegetable garden, stables, a cow barn, pigsties, chicken houses. Beyond it lay the fields enclosed by hedges.

Ouspensky himself showed me round the place. He asked me if I spoke Russian.

"I met one of your family in Petersburg," he said. "Very tall and stiff. Member of the Imperial Guard."

I said there had been a Russian branch of the de Ropp family but that they had been wiped out by the Bolsheviks. That did not surprise Ouspensky. He regarded the Bolsheviks as a gang of criminals. They had murdered not only the entire aristocracy but also the soul of Russia. Nothing would go right in Europe until Russia regained her soul and threw the Bolsheviks out.

He asked why I had stopped coming to the lectures. I said his followers struck me as lacking in compassion and did not work for peace.

"Work for peace?" said Ouspensky. "What is work for peace?"

He paused by the pigsties, where a young man was busily shoveling manure into a wheelbarrow. On the young man's face was an air of intense concentration. He was trying to remember himself. The Master was near.

Ouspensky chuckled.

"Work for peace," he said.

The connection between work for peace and shoveling pig shit was not immediately apparent to me.

"In time you will understand," said Ouspensky. "You are too impatient. You do not give yourself chance. Necessary to listen and collect material. Believe nothing. Test everything. Listen to first six lectures again. First time you did not hear anything. Give name to Madame K. Start again."

He smiled seraphically.

"Takes long time to enter the Work," he said. "One must be patient."

The interview marked a turning point in my life. I suddenly realized that here was the teacher I had been seeking. He was completely free of sentimentality and pretentiousness. He did not pontificate. Believe nothing. Test everything. It was an attitude that my Scientist accepted. "Where is the evidence?" The question every good scientist asked.

One was not expected to swallow absurd theories, stories of mahatmas who sent letters through the ceiling, stories of lost Atlantis and Lemuria. One was not expected to believe anything.

"This system is not the way of faith but the way of understanding."

I listened to the lectures again. It was most revealing. I had heard nothing the first time. My attitude of hostility, due to the fact that I disliked my sponsor, had closed off my intelligence with a wall of prejudice. Now that I actually took the trouble to listen, I realized how beautifully the teachings fitted together. They were practical and down-to-earth. They "spoke to my condition." They explained the maddening absurdity of a scientific age that was nonetheless governed by wild unreason, an age of plenty in which millions had not even enough to eat. They explained *man,* man the monster and man the angel, man the enslaved and man the truly free.

We humans talked about "I," but we had no I. Actually there were dozens of I's. Every thought, every passing desire became I for the moment. We had no real will. Our will was divided among all the different I's and was as weak as they were. We were puppets pulled here and there by external forces. We had no inner direction. We had no control, were simply biochemical machines, unstable and unpredictable.

None of this was very reassuring, but how could one argue about the correctness of the diagnosis? In any case the situation, though desperate, was not hopeless. A few, a very few, who really wanted to change their fate could do so. Nature, Ouspensky taught, had played a trick on man. She had endowed him with quite remarkable potentialities, then, as if repenting of her generosity, had introduced certain defects into his makeup. The chief of these defects was a tendency to live in a world of fantasy instead of the real world. In this world of fantasy man lied to himself. He lied about everything. Most of all he lied about his inner state.

He imagined that he was awake when actually he was walking around in a state of waking sleep.

In order to awaken fully he had first to realize that he was asleep. But this was where Nature played her trick. If you said to someone "You are asleep," he would reply, "No. I am awake." Simply by saying "I am awake," he would awaken for a moment and then immediately go to sleep again.

All the absurdities of human life, the frantic boasts and foolish words, the futile wars, the revolutions that destroyed millions in the name of progress, the religions that sanctioned burning heretics in the name of a God of love all had a single explanation: sleep. Indeed Ouspensky's whole message could be summarized in one sentence.

I show you sleep and the struggle with sleep.

How did one struggle with sleep? In this respect the teaching was strictly practical. In the beginning one could change nothing. It was necessary to observe. We were very complex machines. If you wanted to learn how to control a complex machine, you first had to understand its parts. Observe, observe, observe. But to observe correctly one needed to know certain things. And one needed help. We were in the situation of people in prison trying to escape. One person alone might not have much of a chance. Several people together would have a better one. A group of prisoners that had helpers on the outside would have an even better chance.

The so-called esoteric schools were simply organizations to help a small number of people escape from the world of fantasy into the real world. Man is a prisoner of his own lies. If he knows the truth the truth will set him free.

But why can the esoteric schools help only a small number of people? Why can't everyone escape?

The question was frequently asked. I asked it myself. The answer was obvious. Only a few could escape because only a few realized that they were in prison. The esoteric schools cannot force people to escape. Escaping involved enormous effort continued over a long period. Why should people put forth enormous efforts if they did not even realize they were in prison?

For me this was the missing piece of the puzzle. At last I could answer the question I had asked so often during my brief flirtation with Theosophy. If the mahatmas exist and constitute the Great White Brotherhood, why do they let their fellow humans make such a revolting mess of their affairs? Now the answer was obvious. Even the highest of the Initiates could not help people who had no desire whatever either to be helped or to help themselves.

That harshly unsentimental teaching answered another question as well. Gerald Heard's idea that by exerting "soul force" through meditation one might be able to influence the dictators had often aroused derisive comments from my Scientist. Now I saw clearly why such methods could not work. The dictators and their followers were totally at the mercy of their own lies. They had lied so often and for so long that they could not distinguish truth from falsehood. In them objective conscience, the voice of truth, was dead. They were, moreover, infected with the virus of various pathogenic ideas, the concept of the Master Race and "All is lawful." They had no more control over themselves or over events than rabid dogs. The only way to handle a rabid dog was either to shoot it or get out of its way. Mad dogs do not respond to soul force.

I tried to explain this to Gerald Heard and Aldous Huxley. They could not accept it. It undercut the entire pacifist position that they had supported with so much enthusiasm. I did persuade them to go to Ouspensky's lectures, and later he invited them to Lyne Place. He enjoyed meeting them. "For the first time I meet what we in Russia called intelligentsia." But he shook his head. When it came to practical matters the intelligentsia were hopeless. All talk, no action.

As for Heard and Huxley, their chief concern was to get out of England while it was still possible to do so. They strongly advised Ouspensky to do likewise. Europe was headed for a new Dark Age. Only in America might it be possible to continue living in a more or less civilized manner. Several of the British intellectuals held this view. Heard, Huxley, Auden, Isherwood all fled to the United States.

Ouspensky remained in England.

At the time I met him in 1936, Ouspensky was probably at the height of his power. He was fifty-eight years old, a point in life at which the enthusiasm of youth is balanced by the experience of age. In appearance he was massive and moved with a ponderous intentionality that at times reminded me of an elephant. This way of moving may simply have been an expression of his type, for he was very endomorphic, and this is the way in which high endomorphs often move. But we, his disciples, attributed his deliberate movement to the fact that he was remembering himself, was fully aware at all times of what he was doing—was, in short, awake. This may or may not have been true.

The massive body was surmounted by a no less massive head crowned with short-cropped grey hair. The face had considerable strength—an emperor's face, an emperor who was also a scholar and who could very easily become a tyrant. His eyes peered out at the world through a pair of thick-lensed pince-nez, which he wore so habitually that they seemed part of his anatomy. I suppose he took them off when he went to bed, but I never saw him without them.

Ouspensky was Russian to the core. He embodied both the strengths and weaknesses of that race, so much so that a saying circulated among the more objective of his followers: "One must distinguish between what is the teaching and what is just Russian." It seems to be the essence of Russianism that the Russian is either a complete slave or a complete tyrant. He must either command or obey, which explains why Russian governments will never be anything but authoritarian. Democracy does not suit the Russian character.

So Ouspensky was authoritarian. He justified his authoritarianism very simply. In esoteric schools, he informed us, the aim of the work is the transformation of people from slaves into free beings. It is the most difficult, the most dangerous, the most demanding of all life games. The neophyte who enters the school has to realize that he is asleep, that he has no will, no permanent I. He is a puppet pulled by external forces, at the mercy of casual impulses. He is a "ship of fools," without a real captain or navigator, without any idea of the purpose of the voyage.

Very well. If you don't know the Way yourself you must, at least in the beginning, put your faith in someone else who does know the Way. If your teacher gives you some task, you must accept it and perform it to the best of your ability. Such tasks may not be at all to your liking. They are given you for one purpose only, to help you to see your own mechanicalness. By the way of the slave we do only what is most comfortable. By the Way of the Warrior we do that which is most difficult, thereby building up strength and freeing ourselves from certain inner laws that keep us in bondage. The Way of the Warrior involves conscious effort and intentional suffering. But in the beginning we are far too weak and disunited to impose on ourselves the sort of discipline involved in following the Warrior's Way. Therefore it has to be imposed on us by our teacher. We have to trust him and do the tasks he gives us.

These ideas were very clearly formulated by Ouspensky in a short essay entitled "Notes on the Decision to Work" (later included in *The Psychology of Man's Possible Evolution*, New York: Alfred A. Knopf, 1974). They justified his authoritarianism. Unfortunately they conflicted with certain other principles he had stated: "Do nothing you do not understand. This is the way of understanding, not the way of faith." So suppose you don't understand the task your teacher has set you. Do you do it or refuse it? And dare we really accept the idea that our teacher is infallible? Doesn't this vow of obedience belong to the religious way rather than to the way of understanding?

So Ouspensky's teachings had a way of becoming contradictory and of placing his disciples in very difficult psychological situations that would now be described as double binds—damned if you do, damned if you don't.

Ouspensky, however, rarely interfered with the personal lives of his followers. At the time when I knew him he kept fairly aloof. There were lectures, lectures, and more lectures given in London at the house in Warwick Gardens. The material was read by one of the older disciples, often J. G. Bennett. Ouspensky was usually present to answer questions. After the lectures he was driven back to Lyne Place by a former member of the Royal Corps of Engineers who acted as his chauffeur. During the drive he always maintained a total silence, but back in the kitchen he relaxed over food and drink. He was typically Russian in his reluctance to go to bed, would sit there in the kitchen sometimes all night, until the woman whose task it was to prepare breakfast finally chased him out. Some of the men who lived in the house would sit up with him to keep him company. Never any women. This was *streng verboten* by Madame Ouspensky.

Oh, those all-night drinking parties! How many times have I sat up with Ouspensky in the kitchen drinking far more than was good for me, losing sleep waiting in vain for him to let fall some pearls of wisdom. But the pearls rarely fell. Nearly always we were regaled only with tales of Moscow and Petersburg. For this was one of Ouspensky's weaknesses. *He could not leave Russia.* Nostalgia chained him to that land to which he could never return, to the streets of Moscow, to the Nevsky Prospekt, to the nightclub called "The Wandering Dog" in which he and his journalist buddies would gather after midnight and sit up over drinks till all hours discussing every question under the sun. He would tell us how, among his friends, he was always addressed as "Ouspensky Fourth Dimension," how he knew "everyone in Moscow," how he moved in all sorts of circles, knew both the spies of the Czarist police and members of various revolutionary organizations. In his hankering for the old days he was also Russian. Russian emigrés in general seem unable to sever the umbilical cord that binds them to Mother Russia and for this reason tend to live in the past.

Nostalgia! How well I knew that particular disease of the spirit. During my season in hell in Australia I had retreated entirely into the past, had lived among the peasants in Lithuania, among the woods and meadows I had known and loved. Nostalgia practically destroyed me. It cut me off from the real world, weakened me, confused me, brought me to the edge of suicide. Nostalgia is fatal to the spirit of the warrior, whose task it is to live in the here and now, not hankering after the past or fussing about the future. So Ouspensky's preoccupation with a shadowy Russia that had passed away reduced his personal power. It also caused him, during those long night sessions, to become something of a bore.

The night sessions, however, were not always boring. I well remember one that proved very fruitful. It was terribly late and I knew that I ought to go to bed but couldn't find enough willpower to rise from the table. Ouspensky had been drinking *zoubrovka*, a fiery brand of vodka from Poland. He was not exactly drunk but he was not sober either. His speech was slurred.

Suddenly, for no apparent reason, he began to talk about what he called the "week of miracles." It was a week that he and other members of the Russian group had spent with Gurdjieff in Finland.

"I was in another room," said Ouspensky. "I heard Gurdjieff's voice speaking inside me. He told me something, something very important."

Ouspensky's eyes became glazed. He seemed to go into a

trance. The *zoubrovka* perhaps—or the memory of Gurdjieff. Hoping to restart this intriguing conversation I piped up in my prissy English voice, "He must have been a very strange man, that Mr. Gurdjieff."

Ouspensky gazed at me as if I had said something ridiculous.

"Strange! He was extraordinary! You cannot possibly imagine how extraordinary Gurdjieff was."

His eyes glazed again. He was taking a trip into the past. He was sitting with Gurdjieff in a café in Constantinople. It was late, very late.

"Suddenly Gurdjieff began to sing something in Persian. 'The Song of the Dervish.' He translated it into Russian. It was some special knowledge, very sacred. But we were both very tired. I wrote down what he said. Maybe five verses. It was already dawn. We could not stay awake any longer."

Ouspensky shook his head. He was confronting a mystery.

"At that time I felt sure I could work with him again. That was again the real Gurdjieff. But next night I tried to get him to continue 'The Song of the Dervish.' Nothing! Nothing but dirty jokes. Not even good jokes. Stupid dirty jokes!"

It was Ouspensky's contention that the "real Gurdjieff" had vanished during the flight from Russia. The Gurdjieff of the Chateau du Prieuré was no longer the real thing. This new Gurdjieff broke the rules of the Work, took advantage of the weakness and credulity of his pupils, claimed to be personally responsible for the system of knowledge he taught. Somewhere on that high and dangerous path Gurdjieff had lost his footing.

That was almost the only time I heard Ouspensky talk about Gurdjieff. For us, Ouspensky's pupils, the mystery that surrounded Gurdjieff was almost complete. Most of us did not even know whether Gurdjieff was alive or dead. He was a sort of shadow that loomed over us, not only mysterious but also vaguely sinister, for rumors circulated that certain very wrong things had happened at the Chateau du Prieuré, that Gurdjieff had either gone mad or switched over to the left-hand path and become a black magician. These rumors provided us with material for gossip, in which we indulged guiltily, for such talk was very much against the rules.

I myself was quite ready to see Gurdjieff as a monster, a cross between Rasputin and Count Dracula. I liked the idea of monsters. They added spice to life. All the same I could not forget the tone of Ouspensky's voice: "He was *extraordinary*." So many emotional elements entered into that simple statement: wonder, admiration, regret, bewilderment. I had the feeling that in his relationship with Gurdjieff Ouspensky had confronted a problem that was absolutely beyond his power to solve. He had played the great game with a master and had been checkmated, but he still could not figure out quite how it had happened.

There is a tendency today for people to regard Ouspensky as little more than an interpreter of Gurdjieff's ideas, and a rather poor interpreter at that. This view does him an injustice. Ouspensky was a philosopher in his own right, and his book *A New Model of the Universe* contains certain key ideas. In any case they seemed key ideas to me and became an integral part of my world outlook. Most important of these ideas was that of eternal recurrence. This was not a new idea. It had been developed by several other philosophers, most notably by Friedrich Nietzsche. In its crude form it seemed to me a dreary doctrine, condemning me to go round and round in the same treadmill, over and over again making the same mistakes, enjoying the same triumphs. How could one ever claim to be master of one's fate when one was locked into the cycle of repetition?

When I complained to Ouspensky that this did not seem a very encouraging model of the universe, he smiled enigmatically and insisted that there was a way of escaping from the treadmill. To understand how this was possible, he said, I would have to realize that time was three-dimensional as well as space, and that the space-time continuum had not four dimensions but six. It took me quite a while to figure this out, but I managed to do it in the end. So in four-dimensional time-space, at every moment only one possibility is realized. In five-dimensional time-space time curved back on itself, so the pattern of events was repeated. But in six-dimensional time-space all the possibilities inherent in a moment could be realized. So by flipping over into this other dimension one could in fact change one's fate.

There are only a limited number of possible world lines. If I reach a fork in the road, I can take path A or path B, but I cannot take both, nor can I take a path that does not exist. Suppose I take path B and the choice turns out to be disastrous. I die and return. Again I reach the fork. Unless I *remember*, I will again take path B and again suffer disaster. If I do remember, I will take path A and thus change my line of fate by following a different world line. But I cannot remember unless I am awake. In sleep I shall just repeat the same pattern over and over. So I must learn how to *remember* myself, to remember my whole "long body" in time. Only in this way can I become, within certain limits, the master of my fate.

So the theory offered one a nice incentive to struggle with sleep. Unless one could awaken one would never break out of the circle of recurrence. One would never be truly free. One would go on over and over again falling into the same traps, making the same wrong choices.

Remember. This was the essence of Ouspensky's teaching. He himself seemed to go over his life again and again as if to impress on his memory all that happened. "This I do not remember." "This I must try to remember." "This I do remember." He embodied his views in a rather strange book he called *Kinemadrama* later published as *The Strange Life of Ivan Osokin*. It took place in Russia and involved a young man and a magician. He was very much preoccupied with the book, rewrote it several times. It was one way of

going back to his beloved Russia. But I have no doubt that
Osokin, who repeated the same mistakes in life after life
until at last he learned the secret, was Ouspensky himself. It
was one more way of impressing on himself the great
truths:

> Next time around I must *remember*.
> In order to remember I must awaken.
> In order to awaken I must struggle with sleep.

14

HARVEST AND SUFFERING

The aim of our work with Ouspensky was to build a school of the fourth way. Gurdjieff had described four ways: the way of the fakir, the way of the monk, the way of the yogi, and the way of the Sly Man. Ouspensky referred to the latter as the fourth way. The Sly Man, it was said, was one who was smart enough to drink with the Devil and leave the Devil to pay for the drinks. In this connection there existed a rather interesting story. It was said that the Devil and the Sly Man once met and repaired to a tavern to talk. The Devil was feeling sorry for himself. Business was terrible. The quality of contemporary human beings was getting worse and worse. So feeble were they that they had even forgotten how to develop souls. How could he, poor Devil, lead them to perdition when they did not have any souls to lose? Hell was practically empty. The Devil was seriously thinking of looking for another job. Talking along these lines the Devil became more and more sorry for himself and finally got so drunk that the Sly Man slipped out of the tavern and left the Devil to pay for the drinks.

The story has several meanings, as have most teaching stories. The most obvious is that the Sly Man uses all life situations, including drinking with the Devil, to serve his purposes. The Sly Man does not retire to a cave or enter a monastery. He uses whatever material life offers, and the more difficult the life situation the greater the opportunity it affords. So it was said: *If life did not offer difficulties we would have to create them artificially.*

Followers of the fourth way worked in the world. They were active members of society. The doctors practiced medicine, the engineers engineered, the scientists did research, the farmers farmed. All schools of the fourth way had some sort of practical outward activity that provided a matrix for work. There were schools of masons, schools of potters, schools of actors, schools of calligraphers. Our own school reflected the need of the time, which was to prepare for a storm. It was quite possible that civilization would break down entirely, in which case it would be up to us to build a shelter in which physical existence could continue. We were the possessors of a very precious teaching. That teaching had to be preserved and handed on to others. To do this we had to survive.

So we prepared. This preparation was a practical activity into which I could throw myself with complete enthusiasm. I had a natural love of the soil and of farming. From the peasants in Lithuania I had learned all sorts of primitive farming techniques. I could harness a horse, use a plough, handle an axe, shear a sheep. There was a farmer in my essence.

The work on the farm was performed under the direction of Madame Ouspensky. We spoke of her simply as Madame, and many of us, myself included, regarded her as the real leader of the work. Ouspensky's contact with his pupils had become, at the time I met him, quite indirect. He gave lectures, answered questions, on rare occasions volunteered special information. He was preoccupied with creating a form within which the work would continue. To this framework he gave the high-sounding title of the Historico-Psychological Society.

Ouspensky felt sure that the material he had received from Gurdjieff represented only part of a far greater system of knowledge. He had written a book called *Fragments of an Unknown Teaching*, chapters of which were read to us now and then. It described his meeting with Gurdjieff and their work together in Russia. But Ouspensky no longer had any contact with Gurdjieff, and there were lots of missing fragments in the system. If we wished to find them we would have to discover where Gurdjieff got his knowledge and obtain the missing fragments from that source. So if Hitler would only quiet down and stop threatening war, the Historico-Psychological Society could organize trips to romantic places in India or Persia where we might hope to find the missing pieces of the puzzle.

Madame Ouspensky had not much use for Ouspensky's grand plans. I was present one afternoon when he read to us the prospectus of the society. He was sitting at one end of the long tea table, Madame at the other. As he read Madame began to laugh. She laughed till she wept, dabbing her eyes with a tiny lace handkerchief. She always laughed a great deal, but that afternoon I thought she would never stop. Poor Ouspensky was embarrassed. He took his society seriously and could not understand why she found it so funny.

I understand now very well the cause of her merriment, though I did not at the time. There we were sitting around the tea table, with our heads full of dreams about mysterious sufis and dervishes from whom we would gain some profound secret knowledge. We completely failed to realize that so far as knowledge was concerned, we already had more than enough. What we had to learn was how to put that knowledge into practice. One could not do this by running off on trips to romantic places. All the necessary conditions for *work on Being* were right there at Lyne Place in England. Work on Being was what counted. Without work on Being knowledge amounted to nothing. Knowledge without Being would produce only a wiseacring professor, a man of many words. Madame Ouspensky had not much use for professors.

Madame Ouspensky was one of the most formidable Warriors I met during my journey through time. I established with her a strong *guru/chela* relationship, which lasted over a period of several years. Such a relationship is not without its dangers and can lead to a condition of over-dependence. This overdependence, which I later described as "The Starry-eyed Syndrome," is the result of a strong emotional attachment to the teacher. Madame Ouspensky was very well able to arouse such strong attachments. Ouspensky worked on people's intellects, Madame worked on their emotions. She could, in the space of one half hour, lead the student through a whole spectrum of emotions ranging from despair to exaltation. My own feelings toward her could range from overwhelming dislike to something that came close to adoration. Of all my teachers she gave me my most direct experience of awakening and of the kind of effort that awakening involves.

To produce these effects she relied to some extent on the altered state of consciousness that can be produced in people by very hard physical work. I had a good example of this changed state one August day when we harvested our first crop of wheat. The weather was unusually hot. The sky was a deep blue, almost Australian in its intensity, and the hot air danced and rippled over the ripe wheat. We had no harvesting machinery and so were forced to cut the wheat with scythes and sickles. As I was the only person in the group who had ever harvested wheat in that way, I had been put in charge of the operation, young though I was in the Work and unworthy of such an honor.

I had attached a cradle to my scythe such as the peasants used in Lithuania for harvesting rye. It worked fairly well but added a lot to the weight of the instrument. It was three o'clock in the afternoon. My body ached. I had been wielding the scythe since early morning. With part of my attention I was trying to "observe my machine." "Observe your machine" was a very popular phrase among us at that time. It justified all sorts of actions. "I went to the party simply to observe my machine." That kind of thing.

The other part of my attention was listening for the tea

bell, the bell that would release us from our labors. I was really very tired. Theoretically, if you went on long enough, struggling with your fatigue and practicing separation, you could contact "big accumulator," a source of almost unlimited energy, which we rarely used because we did not make enough effort. I hoped I would contact the big accumulator before I dropped from exhaustion.

I heard through the haze of sweat and fatigue the sound of hoof beats. Ouspensky had trotted up on the small horse he used for riding around the estate. He was sitting on his Cossack saddle. He was inordinately proud of that saddle, obtained for him at great expense by one of the disciples. He observed the sweating harvesters and chuckled.

"Now you can understand," he said, "why Russian word for harvest same as for suffering."

We certainly did. I was very tired myself, but I was young and in good physical condition. My fellow harvesters, some of whom were neither young nor in good shape, were worse off than I was. We certainly had an odd collection in the harvest field. There was a doctor, a lawyer, a dentist, an actor, an engineer, and a former officer of the Grenadier Guards. Not one of them had ever cut wheat in his life. Now they had both to cut it and to bind the sheaves. In Lithuania no man would have tied sheaves. It was strictly woman's work. But I had learned the trick of binding the sheaves with their own straw. I tried to teach the method to my companions but they couldn't seem to learn. Finally I gave up and brought out a roll of binder twine. Even so the sheaves were too loosely tied. I could see that I would have to retie most of them later.

I worked on. It was the first time I had been put in charge of a work crew. I felt it necessary to set an example and work without stopping. The thought did occur to me that I might not look good if one of my harvesters dropped dead from heatstroke or exhaustion. However we had a doctor in the crew. He could take care of the casualties.

The doctor was my second sponsor. He was "old in the

Work." I glanced toward him, an unspoken inquiry. The
sweat was pouring down his face. He was exhausted.

"It will be teatime in ten minutes," said the doctor, fishing out a watch from his sweat-soaked pants. "Perhaps a
short rest . . ."

That was enough. The harvesters dropped like corpses.
When the tea bell rang, no one showed any sign of life. It
was very necessary to show up for tea. Madame Ouspensky
presided at the long table. It was the high point of the day.

I was wondering whether we would have to carry the
bodies in to tea when Ouspensky's chauffeur appeared.
Ouspensky's chauffeur had been a member of the Royal
Corps of Engineers, a Sapper accustomed to facing
emergencies. He had brought out a basket. In it were bottles of beer and beer mugs. He set down the basket and
himself. Gently, as if chanting a lullaby, he sang:

> And when I die
> Don't bury me at all.
> Just pickle my bones
> In alcohol.
> Put a bottle of beer
> At my feet and my head.
> And if I don't rise
> You'll know I'm dead.

At the mention of beer the corpses stirred. Mugs were
filled, froth foamed, dehydrated bodies were rehydrated. By
the time we had finished the beer, euphoria filled us. We
were sweaty, smelly, late for tea, and mildly drunk, but it
didn't matter. Madame Ouspensky, seated at one end of the
long table, took a look at our beaming faces and laughed.
She laughed so heartily that she wept. Dabbing her eyes
with a small lace handkerchief, she gasped an explanation.

"For first time I see *real people*. Not eggs."

She waved her hands, drawing a series of eggs in the air.
Normally, she explained, we stiff Britishers reminded her of

a row of eggs, each keeping himself to himself. We wrapped ourselves in our false personalities, like in egg-shells. But now we had worked until we were tired. False personality had fallen off. We were being natural.

"See Mr. de Ropp," said Madame, turning upon me that formidable look that made me feel like an insect impaled on a pin. "Usually he full of self-importance, like bishop."

She made a screamingly funny gesture, which perfectly portrayed a self-important bishop. Ordinarily I would have squirmed with embarrassment. This was part, I knew, of the process called undressing false personality, something one had to endure in the interest of inner freedom. A painful process. But that day it didn't bother me. Yes, self-important, like bishop. I had felt very self-important being in charge of the harvesting operation.

"Now he too tired to be self-important," said Madame. "He man after hard day's work, like peasant."

Yes, like a peasant. My mind was empty, my body relaxed, I enjoyed my tea and a thick hunk of coarse home-baked bread with *dvarok* made from the milk of the community cow.

Work for peace. I was beginning to understand what Ouspensky had meant.

"Your friends, Mr. Heard and Mr. Huxley, why they not come?"

"I don't know, Madame. Maybe they don't like hard physical work."

"They intelligentsia," said Madame Ouspensky, as if that explained everything.

This way, she said, was not suitable for intelligentsia. It was too practical, too down-to-earth. It involved working, doing, not sitting around meditating.

"You meditate. Stare at wall. Soon you see things. Angels, devils. Anything. This very useless practice."

She stared at me, challenging me to deny it. How many hours had I spent meditating in Gerald Heard's group, trying to project "soul force" in the direction of Hitler, Stalin,

Mussolini, and Co.? Very useless practice. I had to admit it.

She spoke of the problems of the intellectuals. Unbalanced people. They lived in their intellects. Intellect by itself had no power. Power lay in the emotional center. One could come to emotional center through the moving center. This was why hard physical work was useful. Hard work helped us to stay quiet long enough to see ourselves. We were like a zoo, full of different animals. It was necessary to know one's animals.

"What your chief animal?" said Madame, turning on me again. It was evidently my day. Up to that time she had left me more or less alone.

"I'm not sure, Madame. Probably peacock."

She nodded. Yes, peacock. Peacock showing off.

"Today you separate from peacock. You in good state. Other times you not see. You *are* peacock."

She went on to talk about personality. Personality was not all bad. It was mixed, like tar with honey. One had to distinguish between the honey and the tar. One had to know who was who. If one had a guardian at the gate, those who went in and out could be scrutinized. If there was no guardian or the guardian was asleep, anyone could enter the house. Accept or reject, this was the basis of the Work. We had a second of choice either to accept or reject an impression or thought. The inner work was not heroic effort like climbing Mount Everest. Most of the time it was simply a matter of inner stop. Stop thoughts. Thoughts ran round and round "like squirrel in wheel." It was necessary to put a stick in the wheel. To do it again and again. Gradually this would create a change, like drops of water wearing away hard stone. We would fall down again and again and have to pick ourselves up. Never despair. Never indulge in self-pity. Self-pity was the worst of sins, along with self-importance. Once we realized our own nothingness, we could emerge into the real world.

"Real world very big, we very small. When small becomes big, big disappears."

This account gives a general idea of the method used by a

really remarkable Warrior to arouse in others the urge to struggle with their inner slavery. Her efforts were fairly effective, at least for a time. It was difficult to sleep comfortably in her presence. It was almost impossible to be pompous, self-important, verbose, or theoretical. Showing off one's knowledge was a process she called "singing." Singing was characteristic of professors who were all knowledge, no being. She regarded such people as quite useless, mechanical as phonographs. You wound them up and they droned out an endless succession of theories about higher consciousness, the nature of nirvana, satori, samadhi, enlightenment, and so on. It was all words and totally worthless, like a parrot saying a prayer.

Under the circumstances it was hardly surprising that Gerald Heard and Aldous Huxley did not feel inclined to join our group. They were quite unpractical, could never have managed the physical work, and were too fond of their own opinions to work under the direction of someone else. Madame Ouspensky showed them around Lyne Place, even displaying the secret stores of food in the basement. She and other members of the Russian group had almost starved when escaping from Russia. The group would not starve again if she could help it. From the visit to the basement Aldous Huxley emerged to declare that Madame's teachings consisted of a mixture of nirvana and strawberry jam. It was the sort of airy witticism one expected from the old cynical Aldous, who continued to exist under the skin of the earnest being who was trying to take his place.

Actually Madame never mentioned nirvana, and the strawberry jam was incidental. What she taught was the importance of simple awareness, of struggling with mechanicalness, of keeping on the alert, of relating to a force larger than oneself, which the religious call the practice of the presence of God. Aldous wrote at length about all these subjects when he later assembled, with his usual erudition, an anthology he called *The Perennial Philosophy*. But it is one thing to write about these methods, another to put them into practice.

15

LION
INTO RABBIT

Fear.

It hung like a poisonous fog over London, penetrating everywhere, inescapable, enervating. In the mild September sunlight of the year 1938, sweating laborers dug shelters. The green turf of Hyde Park was scarred with trenches. A battery of antiquated antiaircraft guns, hastily dug up from somewhere by a fumbling government, poked their snouts vaguely skywards. In the warm streets citizens queued for gas masks.

I queued with the rest of them, duly received the gas mask in a cardboard box, took it home, and tried it on. I looked at myself in the glass. The mask had transformed me into a monster, a cross between a pig and a gargoyle. As I breathed the mask emitted loud, fartlike noises. I glanced at the wall. On it hung a cartoon by David Low that I had cut out of *The Evening Standard* and framed. It showed a large pig confronting across a trough a naked man on all fours with his face in a gas mask. "They kill me for food," said the pig, "but you, poor sap, they kill you just for your own good."

"God!" I said. "This place is a mess. Can't you tidy it up?"

I was in a foul temper. The crisis was wearing me down. The remark was addressed to a girl who stood by the bed looking worried. I had picked her up the previous spring during a visit to the Indian museum. Together we had plunged into that morass of lust, hate, fear, confusion, shame, attraction, repulsion that is loosely referred to as young love. I called her E. She was a refugee from a lower-class household in which a tyrannical father had made life intolerable. She worked for a manufacturer of remedial foot-wear, who spent much of his time trying to seduce her. Now she lived with me in my tiny flat over a garage, which had once been a stable with tiny rooms over the stable to house grooms and coachmen. Princes Mews in Notting Hill Gate. A place of my own.

E. started to clean up. Newspapers covering every stage of that endless crisis were strewn all over the floor. The London newspapers were indulging in an orgy of horror stories. The most gruesome of these was that the *Luftwaffe* would attack in force and blanket the whole of London in poison gas. We believed it. It never occurred to anyone, in the government or out, to perform a few simple calcula-tions, which would have quickly shown that it was abso-lutely impossible for the *Luftwaffe* to drop that much gas on London, or even a hundredth part of the required amount. Fear of poison gas had attained hysterical proportions, fanned by an imbecile government that issued gas masks for everyone, even babes in arms.

"Look," I said to E., "there's no point in your staying here. They may attack London at any time. Why don't you go into the country and try to get a job. Take this with you in case you need it."

I unfastened a money belt and took out of it two crisp five-pound notes. I had sold some shares in Imperial To-bacco that I had inherited, withdrawn from the bank one hundred pounds in five-pound notes and put them in a money belt. From a marine supply house in East India Dock Road I had purchased two heavy fisherman's sweaters and sundry other weighty garments. We visualized ourselves living in bomb shelters like troglodytes. Warm clothing would be nice.

Having sent E. into the country I proceeded to flee from

London myself. I locked up the flat and took a train to Virginia Water. There was plenty of work to do at Lyne Place. No point in staying in London to be asphyxiated in the great gas attack.

As the train left the station I tried to understand what was happening. I had really allowed myself to get into a disgustingly bad state. I was constantly tense, couldn't eat, couldn't sleep properly. In this respect I was no different from thousands of my fellow Englishmen. The country was in a state of panic, shameful, inexcusable, inglorious panic, shaking in its collective shoes, shitting in its collective pants.

The British lion had turned into a rabbit.

Why?

Why had these people who had built a huge empire, ruled half the earth and most of the oceans, so utterly lost their nerve that they trembled before a murderous little gangster with a toothbrush moustache? Ouspensky, during a recent lecture, had clearly defined the situation. We were facing, he said, a criminal government. Criminal activity was one of the destructive triads and it had definite characteristics. These were reliance on violence, defiance of law, and total disregard for truth. The war of 1914–18 had produced nothing but evil fruits. It had left what remained of the civilized world facing not one but two criminal governments, the Bolsheviks in Russia and the Nazis in Germany. The Nazis were a collection of gangsters. The more we trembled before them, the more impudent and aggressive they would get.

What could we personally do about it?

"Nothing," said Ouspensky.

Very large forces were at work. We were like mice under the feet of a mad elephant. All we could do was to try to avoid getting crushed. For that we had to keep cool and have our wits about us.

"But I can't keep cool," said somebody. "No matter how hard I try I keep worrying about the crisis."

Ouspensky launched on a description of negative imagination. It was a perfect example of wrong work of centers.
The intellectual center imagined all sorts of horrors, the
emotional center overheard the intellectual center and got
terrified, the intellectual center then imagined still more
horrors, the emotional center got still more terrified. And so
on, a vicious circle. There was only one remedy. Stop
thoughts. We had no direct control over emotions, but we
could stop thoughts.

Could we really? I had tried again and again to stop my
thoughts, not to read the scary newspaper headlines, not to
be influenced by the general panic. Hoping to quiet my
fears, I would repeat the words with which Shakespeare's
Julius Caesar replied to Calphurnia when she warns him
not to go to the Capitol:

> Cowards die many times before their deaths;
> The valiant never taste of death but once.
> Of all the wonders that I yet have heard,
> It seems to me most strange that men should fear,
> Seeing that death, a necessary end,
> Will come when it will come.

It didn't help. I was, by Caesar's definition, simply a coward, tense, nervous, prone to anxiety. My type was melancholic-choleric. My imagination swarmed with dark
thoughts. That was my nature.

Evidently I was not the only person in that meeting having problems.

"I find during this crisis," someone said, "that I have difficulty eating and sleeping. What can I do?"

Ouspensky gave a seraphic smile.

"Human machine gets used to anything. In time you eat
again, you sleep again, if there is anything to eat or any
place to sleep."

He went on to describe how, while they were escaping
from Russia, they became caught between the Bolsheviks

and the Cossacks. Shells passed overhead and exploded on
either side of them. They had managed to buy some dried
onions, out of which they made soup. They ate the soup as
the shells screamed over. There was nothing else to eat.
There was nothing else to do.

"The more difficult life becomes the greater the opportunity for inner work, provided that you always remember
your aim."

By the look of things we were going to get plenty of
chances to work on ourselves.

At Lyne Place the passion for digging bomb shelters that
had become the national obsession was also operative. I
discovered my friend the doctor somewhat disconsolately
wielding a pick in the bottom of a shallow trench. He had
hit stony ground. The going was slow.

"I don't know if this will do much good. Madame said
make preparations. I suppose she meant bomb shelters."

I joined him in the ditch. It was hot. We sweated. The
doctor had blisters. He suggested a pause.

"Why has this crisis happened?" I asked.

The doctor thought in medical terms. Certain ideas, he
said, were pathogenic, like pathogenic viruses or bacteria.
Ideas were machines of enormous power and destructive
ideas could wreck whole nations. The idea of the Master
Race was truly pathological. The idea "All is permitted"
was equally bad. These ideas had taken charge of the German people. It was like a streptococcal septicemia.

The doctor sighed. He had good reason to think about
strep infections. One of his closest friends, a well-known
surgeon, had just died of one.

"Pricked his finger doing an autopsy. Hemolytic strep.
Extraordinary. Couldn't fight it at all. Dead in a few days."

The doctor meditated. It took two to make a disease, the
parasite and the host. If the host reacted, the infection could
be stopped. (This was before the days of antibiotics.) The
reaction might look terrible—inflammation, swelling, floods
of pus. But this at least showed that the body could re-

spond. The trouble was that we were not responding, or not responding soon enough. And the longer we delayed the worse would be the infection.

"These are gangsters," said the doctor. "Criminals armed to the teeth. They have taken over Germany. They plan to take over the world. If we don't react soon they *will* take it over. That would be the end of civilization as we know it."

We climbed back into the trench and wielded our pickaxes again. Ouspensky rode up on his horse and watched us.

"What do you think you're doing?"

The doctor mopped his brow and looked sheepish.

"Digging a shelter," he said.

"Fill it in."

"But, Mr. Ouspensky, that is a bomb shelter."

"Fill it in!"

We filled it in.

Actually Ouspensky was quite right. The outdoor bomb shelters that the British people were feverishly digging were completely useless. They filled with water in the wet weather and turned into swimming pools. If one didn't drown in them one was likely to catch pneumonia. This was discovered later, when the real bombing started. The mania for digging holes that obsessed us that summer was only one more symptom of the sorry transformation that had afflicted us.

Lion into rabbit.

16

AN
EVENING
WITH THE BARON

Among the strange events of that hectic period was a meeting with my father. I had sent him, purely out of vanity, a notice of a paper I was to present at a Cambridge meeting of the British Ass (officially the British Association for the Advancement of Science). The paper had to do with the artificial culture of plant embryos. I also told him that I was well on my way to getting a Ph.D. No thanks to him, of course.

Games of one-upmanship.

At the height of that Czechoslovakian crisis, when we expected to be slaughtered by the *Luftwaffe* at any moment, I got a call from him. He wanted me to dine with him at the Savile Club. He had belonged for years to the Savile. It was a vital component of his persona. Despite the often desperate state of his finances he always managed to pay his dues. I think it gave him the feeling that he really was a genuine Englishman, not a naturalized Baltic baron whose mother had been a Cossack.

Well . . . It would hardly be sporting to turn down an invitation from one's own father. When had I last seen him? It was on a station platform in Berlin. I was on my way to exile in Australia, the exile he had imposed to save himself the expense of giving me an education.

It occurred to me that I hardly knew the man. As a boy I had been afraid of him. Later I had hated him for shirking his responsibilities and messing up my life. My English relatives regarded him with a sort of amused disdain. They called him the Baron, as if he belonged in some sort of Graustarkian musical comedy. I too thought of him as the Baron. I had seen very little of him, had only the vaguest idea what he looked like.

Perhaps a man should get to know his own father. Besides, he was connected with the British Intelligence Service, and rumor had it he knew Hitler. As Hitler seemed on the point of making all our lives extremely precarious, I felt bound to learn as much about the Führer as possible.

I dressed in my best and headed for the Savile Club.

So that was my father. Short, sandy hair and eyebrows, nothing very impressive. Why had I ever been so scared of him?

We had a drink. He had a fondness for Italian vermouth. He drank a lot of it that evening. He had been under considerable strain. So had we all. In order to show my manliness and independence I felt compelled to match him drink for drink and was soon floating in an alcoholic haze. Out of this haze there slowly emerged the character of the Baron, the active cause of my arising, the father I had never known.

It was really a shock to discover that this man I had disliked so heartily was very like me. He had, for example, a certain facility with words that I shared. His intellect ranged over many subjects. As he spoke and read four languages, his knowledge was wide. Intellectually he was really quite outstanding. Emotionally he was almost moronic. He had abandoned me among the rats and peasants of Lithuania, then shipped me off like a convict to Australia. It had never really occurred to him that such treatment of a sensitive boy might be damaging. He was totally incapable of understanding the emotional needs of another. I had to admit that I resembled him in that respect.

I wondered if he had been permanently damaged by his experiences in World War I and by the loss of my mother. I wondered why, with his obviously brilliant intellect, he had accomplished so little. He had no staying power, no capacity for application. Brilliant but fickle, that was it—brilliant but fickle.

Having to my satisfaction analyzed the character of the Baron, I sat back and listened. He talked and talked, as if to make up for all those years of noncommunication. I listened with astonishment. He knew Hitler quite well, had known him for a long time, since the days when the future Führer had been a shabby little character in a cheap raincoat with nothing much going for him but a dream of grandeur.

"You may not believe this," said the Baron, "but Hitler could be quite charming. As long as you kept him off the subject of Jews and the Versailles Treaty he could be really *gemütlich*. Polite, very polite. I remember a meeting I attended. I was doing the translating. There was one chair too few at the table, and Hitler trotted off next door and brought another. He was already Chancellor, the head of the Reich. Can you imagine a Prussian doing that?"

The Baron gazed into the depths of his vermouth as if pursuing a vision. He raised his eyes and looked at me.

"In the beginning, you know, he had a program that made sense. *Drang nach Osten.* Hold Europe against the great gray mass of the Slavs. Push them back. Hold the Ukraine, the breadbasket of Europe. It was the original dream of the Teutonic Knights, *our* forebears. It makes sense. If the Russian avalanche ever gets moving it could overwhelm us all."

The Baron paused again. He was evidently following a difficult train of thought through some intricate maze of conjecture.

"In the beginning the German aristocracy expected great things of Hitler. He seemed able to protect them from the Dark Force, the force that has taken over in Russia. People in this country have *no idea* what is happening in Russia. They think Stalin is a rather nice old boy who has to cope with traitors in the Party. The left-wing intellectuals! They'll believe anything! Actually Stalin is one of the greatest mass murderers since Genghis Khan. If he dared he'd let the Red Army loose and have it roll right across Europe to the Atlantic."

Europe's nightmare. The barbarians from the east. Only two things held Stalin back. First, he had so demoralized the Red Army that he could not trust it to fight an offensive war; second, he was afraid of the *Wehrmacht*. It was Germany's great opportunity. All the nations of northeastern Europe—Poles, Finns, Lithuanians, Latvians, Estonians, and Ukrainians—would flock to the German banner and embark on a holy war to crush the Bolshevik menace.

"The Germans can do it now. It's their great opportunity. They could become masters of Europe. They could drive back the Slavs and hold a line east of the Ukraine. They could impose the *Pax Germanica*. But I think they will miss their chance. They always do."

The Baron shook his head. His eyes took on a conspiratorial expression. He was about to share with me some vital secret.

"Something," he said, "something is working against us."

He tried to define more clearly that sinister something. It was a force that worked in the soul of Adolf Hitler, that compelled him to deviate more and more from his original program.

"He trusts all the wrong people. He has surrounded himself with the scum of the earth. Himmler, Bormann, Heydrich, Streicher! Monsters! Absolute monsters! He has alienated the aristocracy and the responsible elements in the *Wehrmacht*. They are only waiting for an opportunity to bring him down. But you know the Germans. Sheep. Obedient to authority. Even the aristocracy . . ."

He was silent again, looking back.

"Whatever happened to us?" he said.

I was in no position to answer the question. Nor was the Baron. It was simply a fact. The European aristocracy, German, Russian, French and British, had totally lost the will to

power and the will to govern. The Russian aristocracy had
let themselves be exterminated without even putting up a
serious fight. The German aristocracy, all those Counts and
Barons with pedigrees a mile long, watched like rabbits
hypnotized by a snake while Hitler steered the ship of state
straight for the rocks.

"It's incredible," said the Baron. "Loss of nerve, total loss
of nerve. No one dare lift a finger. And to think that, in the
early days, I could have put an end to little Adolf myself.
One well-placed bullet . . . It might have changed the history of Europe."

"Is it still too late?" I inquired.

"To assassinate him? No. But no one in Germany has the
nerve. They are waiting for us to give them a sign. One
strong gesture from the French and British will give them
courage enough to throw Hitler out. But the French are
shaking in their shoes and the British are as bad. All we
have is an elderly ostrich with an umbrella who knows
nothing, absolutely nothing, about the situation in Germany. Neville Chamberlain! Ugh."

The Baron made the gesture of one about to vomit. He
was rather a good mimic. He returned to the subject of
those sinister forces that were leading all the nations of
Europe into a trap.

"It's incredible, really. Here we are in the twentieth century, the age of science, totally at the mercy of the Dark
Force. If I were a religious man I suppose I'd call it the
Devil. Something compels us to make all the wrong moves.
The British and French are weak when they should be
strong. The Germans are confused and arrogant. They know
it is their big moment but they can't play it right."

He paused, seeking an explanation. The Germans were,
he said, quoting Kipling, a lesser breed without the law.
Which meant that they had never learned how to use power
with moderation. Arrogance and brutality, the curse of the
Prussian. And sentimental! And romantic! But always,
always unbalanced. They were, he said, quoting Vansittart,
either at your feet or at your throat.

"Right now, they seem to be pretty well at our throats," I observed.

"No," said the Baron. "You are wrong. They are not at our throats. They are desperately, desperately looking for a signal. They are like naughty children who know they are being bad and really expect to be spanked and put in the corner. We could still spank them. It isn't really too late. And if we do they will start behaving themselves. The *Wehrmacht* will throw out Hitler or kill him. There are still intelligent people in Germany who see the signs.

"But if we miss this chance, then it really will be too late. The German people will believe Hitler is infallible. They will follow him to the end.

"Of course I could be wrong. Neville Chamberlain may not be quite as stupid as I think. But my guess is that he'll betray the Czechs and let Hitler get away with it. In which case, as Pitt said in the days of Napoleon, we might as well roll up the map of Europe."

What a strange evening! We talked until two in the morning. No buses were running when I finally emerged from the Savile Club. I had to walk all the way to my flat in Notting Hill. I did so, glad to work the alcohol out of my system. I was aware, as never before, of the tragic farce in which we were all involved, of the utter powerlessness of men to control their destinies. The drama of Europe boiled down to a species of Wagnerian slapstick, with a megalomaniac in the role of Harlequin and a sad old ostrich in the role of Pierrot. Columbine (the dream of world domination) flitted to and fro like the whore she was. The music was from the *Götterdämmerung*, played on a barrel organ.

Millions and millions of lives, including my own, depended on the outcome of this farce.

The prospect was depressing enough to make one wish, once and for all, to leave the planet. It was some consolation, though not much, that I knew the secret. As I walked home through the London night, the words of Ouspensky echoed through my mind.

Man is asleep. He has no permanent I, no real consciousness, no will. He is a helpless puppet in the hands of outside forces. He is a being that Nature has only half created. If he wishes to be complete he must complete himself.

But this is the one thing that he refuses to do.

17

IF
FAULT
OF PLANETS...

"Look! One, two, three . . . sixteen German bombers! Let's get the children into the shelter! Hurry!"

War had been declared. The air raid warning had sounded. At Lyne Place preparations had been made. Sensible ones this time. No trenches in the garden. A room in the basement had been heavily reinforced. It would hold up under anything short of a direct hit.

The man who had spotted the German bombers was very nervous. Stress shows us who we are. The chief fireman (we had our own section of the Auxiliary Fire Service with our own portable pump) was a veteran of an earlier war and a good deal more cool.

"Calm down," he said. "Those 'bombers' are the barrage balloons over London."

So they were. We were close enough to London to be able to see them when conditions were right, silvery specks hanging in the sky. The air raid warning was also a false alarm, a product of nervous tension. The all clear sounded. I changed out of my fireman's uniform and went back to my work, which was gathering and drying apples. We had built a large fruit dryer of which I took care. It was possible that we might be reduced to living on dried apples.

The war we had awaited so long had finally started. German tanks were overrunning Poland. The gangsters of Europe had made a pact. Hitler and Stalin were dividing Poland between them.

Had I not met Ouspensky, I would probably have chosen
that moment to hand back my entrance ticket. There
seemed every reason to resign from the human race. Everything that could go wrong had gone wrong. For one who by
nature tended to misanthropy this spectacle of large-scale
human idiocy was really too much.

Ouspensky's teachings prevented me from taking the
easy way out. If one accepted the idea that the man-mass
was asleep, that it had no control over its destiny, was the
helpless plaything of external forces, then obviously it was
useless to lament over what had happened. Hitler was no
more responsible for his actions than the virus of influenza
had been responsible when it killed 20 million people in the
pandemic of 1918–19. The spiritual virus that Hitler and
Stalin represented would probably kill far more people than
had the influenza virus.

Ouspensky taught that there were two cultures, the culture of civilization and the culture of barbarism. Always, at
all times, the culture of barbarism stole from the culture of
civilization and poisoned its fruits. The whole history of
man could be viewed as a struggle between these two
forces. There were creative periods when the culture of civilization predominated. The sciences flourished, great works
of art were created, magnificent cities were built. But all the
while the other culture grew like a cancer and finally overwhelmed the culture of civilization. So all the buildings
were destroyed and the works of art with them.

We had entered such a phase of destruction. How long it
would continue was anyone's guess. But I wanted to be
around to see what would happen.

I had another reason for wishing to survive. The reason
was still enclosed in E.'s body, a new being that kicked and
squirmed and was due to be born at any time. An accident
of the night! I was then and am still appalled by the ca-
sualness with which a human life can get started. I had
never been seriously interested in E. The bond that held us
together was 90 percent sexual lust, and maybe 10 percent

the other interests we shared. But the tiny presence within her body was confirmed by tests. Four weeks old and already equipped with gills and a tail, it was busily growing in the warm wet dark.

Together we had managed to land ourselves in the world's oldest fool trap. War was obviously on the way. It was certainly no time to start a family. But the family had started itself. To stop it was incredibly difficult in those days. Abortion was hedged about with an absolute jungle of obstacles. It could not be performed in England. The girl had to go to France. There were endless problems.

And after all there were other considerations, besides our personal convenience. Here was someone evidently waiting to get incarnated. How could one tell who it was? It might be another Einstein, a second Beethoven, or even the new avatar we so desperately needed. Dared we, purely to avoid the problem of raising a child, cut off its life while it was still in the form of a fish?

The answer was that we dared not. We were discreetly married in a church near Princes Mews. On September 18 E. went into a nursing home to produce the baby. I stayed home. In those days it was unthinkable to admit the father into the delivery room to support and encourage his mate in the process of parturition. The whole process of birth was hedged around with mystery. How greatly we have progressed since those times!

So I was left alone in the cottage while E. struggled through labor. My thoughts were not cheerful. Poland had collapsed. A blitzkrieg of unprecedented ferocity had torn the country to pieces in less than a fortnight. The Soviet jackal had moved in from the east to claim its share of the spoil. Two gangster governments had split the country between them. There was no more Poland.

I put a record on our portable gramophone. Paderewski playing Beethoven's *Moonlight Sonata*. As the calm melody flowed from the instrument, I found myself weeping. Paderewski, the master pianist, had once been president of

Poland. Now there was no more Poland. But I wept not only for Poland but for all the millions still to die in the struggle that had just started. I had an intuition that it would last a long time and bring appalling destruction. Would anything survive?

The blitzkrieg versus Paderewski playing Beethoven—the culture of barbarism versus the culture of civilization . . . No doubt Ouspensky was right in his pessimistic assertion that the culture of barbarism would always come out on top. But why? Why did we humans have to behave in this disgusting fashion? Why had the nation that had produced Beethoven placed its destiny in the hands of the criminal Adolf Hitler? Why had the nation that had given us Tolstoy and Dostoevsky fallen into the clutches of the criminal Stalin?

The Smerdiakovs will triumph.

They had indeed.

But it was useless to weep. I had other things to think about, a little bundle in a Shetland shawl. There lay the little creature curling its tiny fingers and its tiny toes, totally unaware of the manmade mess that hung over us all in the gloomy autumn of 1939.

> My mother groan'd! my father wept.
> Into the dangerous world I leapt:
> Helpless, naked, piping loud:
> Like a fiend hid in a cloud.

I had not been present at the birth, but I hoped my first-born had entered in a Blakean rather than a Wordsworthian ("trailing clouds of glory") mode. Certainly the world was dangerous, and a fiend had a better chance to survive than an angel. The child's arrival added a new dimension to life. They are poor indeed who have never had children. Our children are our teachers. In them we see repeated the fall of man, the lapse from innocence, the growth of the false ego clouding the essence, the corrosive effect of what passes for education, the poisonous influence of our collective bad karma.

Verily I say unto you, except ye be converted and become as little children, ye shall not enter into the kingdom of heaven.

According to Ouspensky there were twenty-five different ways of interpreting this saying. It contained the ultimate secret of the inner work.

Meanwhile life continued. I had just managed to complete my research and write my Ph.D. thesis before war was declared. Now I lived as best I could on a little money I had saved, bicycling daily to Lyne Place to work the fruit dryer. I gathered a basket of apples and sat down by the fruit dryer to core, slice, and string them on drying rods. Helping me was a Russian called Ephraimov, one of several refugees who hung around Ouspensky. He was, as we used to say, "old in the Work," and reputed to be wise. I had a problem. Ouspensky had suggested that the orientation of the planets had an influence on the behavior of mass-man. My Scientist intensely disliked this "planetary influence" idea. It smelled of that old astrological delusion, that mishmash of pseudoscientific nonsense that we had inherited from the Babylonians and is still taken seriously in some circles. How could the planets influence human behavior? Where was the evidence? Was the idea supposed to be taken seriously, or was it just a roundabout way of saying that man had no control over his fate?

I asked Ephraimov.

"Mr. Ephraimov"—we were always very formal in Ouspensky's group, Mr. this and Mrs. that—"do you think this war is due to the influence of the planets?"

Ephraimov laid down the knife with which he had been cutting apples. His English was not very fluent. Carefully, painfully, he put together his reply.

"If fault of planets . . . then nothing to do. But if fault of man . . . then it is shameful."

18

THE
SINKING SHIP

Compost heaps.

We built them regularly out of all the waste material we could find and watered them lavishly with liquid from the communal cesspool. I had, as chief composter, responsibility for seeing that they heated properly and were turned regularly. A well-made compost heap steams like a tea kettle and gets hot enough to destroy all pathogens that may be present when one uses human sewage. An extraordinary device when one thinks about it. Thermophilic bacteria. Bacteria that can live and flourish in temperatures hot enough to cook an egg. How can they survive in such heat?

Truly the tricks of nature are extraordinary!

We had passed a strange winter, snowbound and bitterly cold. *Blitzkrieg* had turned into *Sitzkrieg*. A phony war. It was very confusing. The bombing of London that we had so confidently expected had not taken place. The hordes of Civil Defense workers, who had trotted around looking heroic in tin hats emblazoned with all sorts of designs, had nothing to do. They had lost their sense of dedication and lapsed into a state of total boredom.

My friend the doctor shook his head. According to his view of things the great struggle should be at its height, civilization desperately trying to cope with its pathogens. There should be inflammation, swelling, fever, buckets of pus. The illness should be progressing toward a crisis. But nothing happened. Throughout the bitter winter of 1939–40 the armies on the Western Front sat and looked at each other.

It was all very puzzling.

We did not stay puzzled for long.

In April the Nazi troops suddenly poured into Norway, aided by the local traitor, Vidkun Quisling. In swift succession they overwhelmed Norway, Denmark, Belgium, Holland, France. We began naming compost heaps after the fallen cities. The first was Narvik, followed by Copenhagen, Rotterdam, Amsterdam. By June we had a compost heap called Paris.

Would the next be called London?

Really it was extraordinary! The whole of Western Europe, riddled with traitors, rotten with fifth columns, crumpled like so much paper before the German advance. The vaunted Maginot line, on which the French had lavished millions, might as well have been made of cream cheese for all the good it did. By late May the entire British army was driven back to Dunkirk. The world was treated to the extraordinary spectacle of 335,000 soldiers being snatched out of the jaws of destruction by everything that could float, from warships to dinghies.

Heroic days. Tragic days.

Winston Churchill, who had at last replaced the doddering Neville Chamberlain, offered us nothing but blood, toil, tears, and sweat, but assured all who might be listening that we would fight to the end. The British people, not without a certain perverse satisfaction, discovered that they were completely alone, facing a foe that had occupied every port in Europe from Norway to the border of Spain. Immediate invasion was expected. Every household in the country received a pamphlet entitled *If the Invader Comes*. I still have mine. It recommended calm. It even made elephantine attempts at humor.

The sort of report which a military or police officer wants from you is something like this—

> At 5.30 P.M. to-night I saw twenty cyclists come into Little
> Squashborough from the direction of Great Mudtown. They
> carried some sort of automatic rifle or gun. I did not see any-
> thing like artillery. They were in grey uniforms.

Everyone was obsessed with the idea of paratroopers falling from the skies in all sorts of unlikely disguises. A town
in Belgium had been captured, so rumor had it, by paratroopers dressed as nuns. The pamphlet offered reassur-
ance.

> Remember that if parachutists come down near your home
> they will not be feeling at all brave. They will not know where
> they are, they will have no food, they will not know where
> their companions are. They will want you to give them food,
> means of transport and maps. They will want you to tell them
> where they have landed, where their comrades are, and where
> our own soldiers are. The fourth rule, therefore, is as fol-
> lows—
> 4) DO NOT GIVE ANY GERMAN ANYTHING.

(Nice polite Germans, of course, wouldn't think of taking
anything they weren't given.)
The pamphlet went on to announce a few more rules:
Stay put, Stay off the roads, Don't listen to rumors, and
Don't panic. It concluded on a heroic note—

> Remember always that the best defense of Great Britain is
> the courage of her men and women. Here is your seventh
> rule:—
> 7) THINK BEFORE YOU ACT. BUT ALWAYS OF YOUR
> COUNTRY BEFORE YOU THINK OF YOURSELF.

Well . . . We were ready to do our best. A sense of
unreality pervaded those summer days. The Local Defense
Volunteers (LDV's, who later became Home Guards) rushed
about madly looking for enemy paratroopers. As all the
army's weapons had been left on the European mainland,

the LDV's might be armed with anything from shotguns to pitchforks. They were really quite dangerous. It was as much as one's life was worth to wander around after dark.

Signposts were torn down, names of stations were blotted out, weird contraptions consisting of tree trunks and cart-wheels were placed in position to close roads. A huge trench was dug across southern England. Concrete pillboxes sprouted everywhere like mushrooms. Haystacks were built in the middle of open fields to prevent the landing of enemy planes.

June passed, July passed. It was a lovely summer. All the while the sense of unreality persisted. We were ready for the invader, but no invader came. There was a curious pause, as if the forces developing that lunatic scenario had momentarily run out of ideas.

Then, on August 15, the show started again. Furious dog-fights raged over the south coast of England as waves of Heinkels, Junkers, and Messerschmitts ran into the concentrated fire of Spitfires and Hurricanes. The blue sky was crisscrossed with white vapor trails. The rattle of machine-gun fire sounded from the sky and spent bullets fell to earth like hail. I looked up from my job of hoeing turnips as a solitary Spitfire with a gaping hole in one wing flew unsteadily inland. As I watched the damaged wing fell off the plane and drifted down to earth like an autumn leaf. The rest of the plane crashed in a wood nearby. I rode to the place on my bicycle, thinking maybe to rescue the pilot. The wrecked Spitfire did not even catch fire. No petrol left. No bullets either. In the cockpit lay a blond young man of my own age, shot to pieces. He must have been dead before the plane crashed. I thought of the motion that had been passed by the Oxford Union: "This house will on no account fight for King and Country." I thought of Dick Sheppard's Peace Pledge.

We had certainly changed our tune since those days.

Dulce et decorum est pro patria mori.

Then the night bombing started. On September 6 the

Luftwaffe dropped over four million pounds of bombs on the London docks. We stood on the roof of Lyne Place looking toward the city. The entire sky was lit up, a vast crimson backdrop. Streams of tracer bullets rose like flights of red birds. Searchlights combed the sky, which constantly sparkled with bursting shells. Every now and then huge explosions added fresh splashes of light to the infernal scene. We of the Auxiliary Fire Service expected to be called to help fight what must have been the biggest blaze since the Great Fire of London in 1666. We were ready for some lively action. Rather to our disappointment we were not called. The firemen, fighting up to their waists in crude oil from exploded storage tanks, had no water left. The docks blazed on, and there was little anyone could do about it.

Ouspensky watched the fiery sky and shook his head. He was obsessed with the idea that he had lived before, had been endlessly recycled along the curve of eternal recurrence. He was always trying to remember events before they happened. But he shook his head over the Great Fire of London.

"This I cannot remember," he muttered. "This I cannot remember."

Perplexing.

It was not the only perplexing element in life at that time. We at Lyne Place were a tightly knit group working under Ouspensky's direction, first, to survive and second, to preserve the teaching. Life had certainly become difficult, but it was not really very dangerous. Every night each of us spent some time on the roof watching for fire bombs, which the Germans had a habit of scattering over the countryside. So we had less sleep than usual and, as there weren't many of us, had to work hard during the day.

Those conditions, it seemed, should have been perfect for what Ouspensky called intensive work. He had referred several times to this intensive work. Gurdjieff had organized such work while the group was escaping from Russia. They had had a house in Essentuki on the northern slopes of the Caucasus mountains. There this intensive work had been performed.

I believed in those days that some sort of supereffort was needed if one was ever going to break the bonds of one's mechanicalness and become a liberated being. The idea was reinforced by Madame Ouspensky, who frequently talked of the great difficulties she had been forced to overcome during the flight from Russia. It was therefore with great consternation that I heard the news. Both Ouspensky and Madame Ouspensky were leaving for America.

This information produced in me a howl of righteous indignation. I had always been prone to indignation. It was my chief feature, the central psychological weakness around which my false ego was constructed. The indignation remained unspoken, for so brainwashed were we and so accustomed to the authoritarianism of the Ouspenskys that we dared not criticize them openly. The indignation was no less heated for being unspoken. I simply could not accept the idea that the Leader of the Work would abandon us at that point. It was true that, in the winter of 1940–41, the outlook did seem bleak. Despite Churchill's heroic oratory one could not see how we could possibly win the war. We had, however, managed to survive the first assault, and the nightly air raids, though highly unpleasant, could hardly by themselves bring the country to its knees. Was it really right for the Ouspenskys to desert their followers, who had, after all, provided them with every creature comfort?

It was a difficult moment. Slowly, sadly, I began to realize that my teachers were not superhuman. They were limited by their personal laws, just as I was limited by my personal laws. They were not particularly heroic. They wanted peace and quiet.

Well so did we all want peace and quiet. If the aim was to form a new group in the States why hadn't Ouspensky moved there in 1936? Gerald Heard and Aldous Huxley had both urged him to go. In 1936 all of us could have gotten out. Now the trap had closed. Ouspensky said we should follow him to America. How? How could a young man of military age possibly get out of England? What would Ouspensky do in America anyway? Give lectures, lectures, and more lectures? What was the use of all those lectures? Why didn't he work intensively with the small group he had at Lyne Place?

"Hush!" said my True Believer, a starry-eyed dope, as they all are. "He is a man of higher knowledge. He knows what he is doing."

"I don't believe he knows at all," said my Cynic. "He's out to save his skin. He's ratting on us. So is Madame."

"Hush! You can't judge their motives. You can't judge people at a higher level of Being than yourself."

"I know what I see with my own eyes and I draw my own conclusions. The captain is supposed to be the last to leave. If there isn't room in the lifeboats it is only proper that he go down with the ship."

19

KEEP CAREFUL NOTES

Night and fog.

The gun I was carrying was cold and clammy. My battle dress, which fitted badly, rasped my throat and irritated my skin. I had always been allergic to wool. My "British Warm," in spite of the cozy name, seemed unable to keep out the chilly damp. Around me was an empty meadow, nothing to be seen, nothing to be heard. Above, just visible through the fog, a solitary star looked down indifferently on the earth.

Circumstances had compelled me to leave Lyne Place. I had a wife and two children (a second one had shown up, just as casually as the first). I had to earn a living. I was a biologist with a Ph.D., and as such considered too valuable to be used as ordinary cannon fodder. The Agricultural Research Council needed a bacteriologist to assist in a program designed to eradicate Bang's disease in cattle. The disease was also known as contagious abortion. In cattle it produced abortion, and it cut down the milk supply of a country that needed all the milk it could get. In humans it produced undulant fever. It was caused by an organism called *Brucella abortus*.

So I became a bacteriologist. I also became, not because I wished to but because I had to, a member of the Home Guard. There was not, at that time, much need to guard the home. Hitler had finally double-crossed his noble ally Joseph Stalin, so Europe's chief gangsters were now at each

other's throats. The Teutons had torn into Russia, the Slavs
had retreated and retreated and retreated. The Germans
were advancing on Odessa.

Meanwhile we had Home Guard exercises. Retired majors
and colonels who had nothing better to do wasted other
men's time and energy playing soldiers. The research institute in which I worked was located in the little village of
Compton on the Berkshire downs. This village was now
supposedly under attack from "the enemy." Home Guards
from another village were supposed to sneak in and capture
something or other.

I shivered and peered into the darkness. I was not a good
soldier. Despite the fact that I really believed we were fighting in a good cause, that it was absolutely essential to defeat Hitler and his gangsters if any sort of civilization was to
survive, my body seemed to balk at soldiering. Perhaps the
pacifist teachings that I had absorbed while in the Peace
Pledge Union had become an integral part of my subconscious.

The Warrior's Way for me involved a spiritual struggle, a
battle with the forces that keep us in sleep. But the actual
business of destroying my fellow men seemed to me utterly
repulsive. The heroic aspects of the soldier's life did not
impress me. I saw it stripped of its gaudy trappings as the
most idiotic activity ever devised by the mind of man. As I
shivered in the damp meadow, the appalling thought struck
me that all over the earth—in Europe, Africa, and the remotest corners of Asia—millions of young men of my own age
had been forced by fate to play this lunatic game—not as I
played it, with an unloaded rifle and dummy hand gre-
nades, but with deadly weapons of every shape and size
from bazookas to flame throwers.

It was beginning to grow light. The assumption of our
war game was that the enemy would attack at dawn. I
peered into the fog. There was indeed a vague shape moving toward me. The enemy? What on earth was one expected to do? Shoulder one's rifle and shout "Bang, you're

dead!'' as we used to at school when playing cowboys and Indians? How silly could you get?

Fortunately the vague shape turned out to be a cow, a large black and white Ayreshire. It contemplated me with dewy eyes. Turning away from me it raised its tail and plopped out a round pad of shit on the damp grass as if to express its opinion of war and warriors.

I seconded the motion.

We were called together in the dawn's early light to analyze the results of the night's maneuvers. I managed to slip out of the meeting, ran to the place where I lodged, changed out of my battle dress into normal clothes, and hastened to the lab. It was all very well for retired colonels to play war games, but I had work to do. A lot of it. It was not particularly glamorous research, but my Scientist took it seriously. We were experimenting both with cows and with guinea pigs, testing the efficacy of a vaccine made from a strain of living organisms, of attenuated virulence. There are always problems when one uses a live vaccine. Will it regain its virulence? Will it be excreted in the milk and cause human disease? Undulant fever in humans was a most unpleasant infection. It lasted for months, even years, a chronic disease, with a fever chart that went up and down like the edge of a saw. It was very debilitating. One did not die of it. It just made life not worth living.

That day I had to terminate one experiment and start another. I put on a clean lab coat and assembled my guinea pigs. I had grown accustomed to slaughtering guinea pigs. It was hardly a proper occupation for one who considered himself more or less a Buddhist, but at least it was better than killing my fellow men. From frequent practice I had developed extraordinary speed. I grabbed the animal, which uttered little shrieks of alarm and despair, and cracked its skull on the concrete edge of the sink. Blood poured from the creature's nose and I collected it in a test tube. I plunged the body in a bath of disinfectant, pinned it like a crucified Christ to a dissecting board, peeled back the skin, cauterized the abdominal wall, opened the abdomen, plunged in with sterile forceps, and removed the spleen.

The chief sign in *Brucella abortus* infection in guinea pigs was an enlarged spleen. This normally small purple organ could attain truly fantastic sizes in badly infected pigs. The spleens were weighed and placed in sterile test tubes, homogenized with a measured amount of sterile saline. The homogenate was diluted and a measured amount was placed on blood agar plates. By counting the number of bacterial colonies that developed, I could rate the level of infection. I also spun down the clots in the tubes of blood, removed the serum and tested it for agglutinins. If the animal was infected, its blood, even at very high dilutions, would react with a killed suspension of *Brucella abortus* and precipitate the organisms.

A neat in vitro test for Brucella infections.

All this I did swiftly and irritably, for my sleepless vigil of the night before had left me on edge. Lack of sleep always has a disastrous effect on my nervous system. I am an extreme cerebrotonic as far as sleep patterns are concerned.

The first part of my experiment was completed. I prepared to start another. A series of new vaccines had been made and I was testing them on guinea pigs. The procedure was simple enough. One injected a group of animals with the vaccine, then challenged their immunity by injecting them at different intervals with a suspension of virulent Brucella organisms. This suspension had to be freshly prepared each time.

I entered the large walk-in incubator and took out a bell jar full of Petri dishes. It was one of the pecularities of *Brucella abortus* that it could only grow in an atmosphere of 10 percent CO_2. So all cultures had to be grown under bell jars in which this special atmosphere had been introduced. The cultures were pretty. Small clear bacteria colonies like dewdrops showed against the red satiny background of the blood agar. I washed the bacteria off the plate with sterile saline, drew up the suspension in a Pasteur pipette, and transferred it to a sterile test tube. I compared its opacity to that of a standard, diluted it until the opacities looked the same, marched off to the animal room followed by my technician.

The next step was to inject both vaccinated animals and controls with the suspension of bacteria. I was tired. My hand was unsteady. The third guinea pig gave a sudden kick and wriggle. My technician lost control of the beast just as I was about to press the plunger of the syringe. The needle of the syringe came loose. A spray of virulent *Brucella abortus* organism hit me in the face.

"Damn!"

I swore so loud that my technician dropped the guinea pig.

"I've got about ten trillion of those blasted bugs in my eyes! Here, hold this syringe while I wash. And catch that damned pig before it gets out of the room."

My technician rushed around like a flustered hen while I soused my face under the tap. Getting the organisms in one's eyes was one of the very best ways of becoming infected. I felt irritated and stupid. Before starting my work with *Brucella abortus* I had received special training from Dr. G. S. Wilson, coauthor of Topley and Wilson's *Textbook of Bacteriology*. He was an authority on Brucella.

"You must bear in mind," said Wilson, "that this is a bad organism to work with. Brucella and the organisms of tularemia and typhus all have a tendency to produce laboratory infections. I speak from experience. I became infected with Brucella myself. It was over a year before I felt reasonably well again. Fortunately it was *Brucella abortus. Melitensis* and *suis* are worse."

Brucella melitensis was endemic in the goats of Malta and produced in humans a disease called Malta fever. *Brucella suis* infected pigs.

I finished washing my eyes, completed the inoculation of the guinea pigs, and told my flustered assistant to go home. A stupid blunder. That was what one got for playing soldier all night before trying to do serious experiments with pathogenic bacteria. I had been clumsy and careless. When you worked with an organism as infective as *Brucella abortus* you had to watch every move. Even Wilson, a meticulous worker, had made a mistake. He had been ill for a year. Chills, fever, headaches, general malaise. Well, bacteriology had its own list of martyrs. Ricketts and von Prowazek had died of typhus. Adrian Stokes had died of yellow fever. I had no intention of joining the martyrs if I could help it.

But how could I avoid it?

A new wonder drug called penicillin had just been prepared in pure form. The work had been done at the Institute for Experimental Pathology at Oxford, the very institute at which I had received my training from Professor Wilson. They were growing the mould in flasks. The place swarmed with spores of *Penicillium notatum.* One could hardly open a Petri dish without its becoming contaminated.

Rumors were rife in scientific circles about the amazing efficacy of the new drug. It was said to cure almost any infection. But its purification had proved fantastically difficult. More than thirteen years had elapsed since Alexander Fleming had first noticed the activity of penicillin. By February 1941 there was just enough of the drug to test on one human, a policeman dying of staphylococcal septicemia. He made a recovery that seemed nothing short of miraculous, but the penicillin ran out before the infection was fully controlled. He died just a month after the treatment had been started.

Yes, in 1941 penicillin was priceless. There certainly was not enough available to treat a young bacteriologist who had managed to expose himself to virulent *Brucella abortus.* Also, the drug was mainly active against gram-positive organisms, especially those members of the great family coccus, the streptococcus, the staphylococcus, the pneumococcus, and the gonococcus. *Brucella abortus* was gram negative. It had a nasty habit of getting inside one's cells, from which it was very difficult to dislodge.

I debated with myself. Should I ask advice of the Chief? The Chief was Director of Research. He was a nice old boy called Major G. W. Dunkin, whose main claim to fame was that he had developed, with P. P. Laidlaw, a vaccine for the control of canine distemper. The discovery was of interest to more than dog lovers, for canine distemper closely resembled human influenza.

I went up to the Chief's office and somewhat nervously informed him of what had happened.

"I wasn't properly in control," I said. "I was up all night on that Home Guard exercise. How can people be expected to do good work if you keep them up all night playing soldiers?"

I looked at him accusingly. He was an officer in the Home Guard, one of the enthusiasts who developed those futile exercises.

"Well, well," said the Chief. "So you got Brucella in your eyes. Too bad."

He gazed at the ceiling, lit a cigarette.

"I suppose we could inoculate you with the vaccine, but it's only meant for cows and I don't know how a human would respond. Besides, it's probably too late. You wouldn't develop antibodies soon enough."

He continued to gaze at the ceiling. A dreamy look came into his eyes. He was elderly, tended to live in the past. He was especially fond of anecdotes about his old friend Laidlaw, "a great scientist and a great man."

"Did I ever tell you the story of Laidlaw and Lipsky? We had this Russian refugee, Lipsky. Terrible worker. Sloppy. Shouldn't have been allowed in the lab. But we wanted to help him. He had a brilliant mind. Just sloppy technique. Well, Lipsky was working on yellow fever. It's a virus, you know, transmitted by a mosquito. Well, Lipsky was wandering around looking terribly gloomy, so Laidlaw asked him what was up. 'Why are you wandering around looking like a wet hen?' It seems that Lipsky had spilled a fresh preparation of yellow fever virus and got some on his hand

and his finger had a cut in it. He was thinking he'd die of yellow fever. It's not a nice way to die. There was no vaccine available. Nothing to do. So you know what Laidlaw said? 'Keep careful notes,' he said. 'Keep careful notes, Lipsky. It's bad luck for you that you're your own experimental animal. The only thing you can do is be objective about it.'

"And that," said the Chief, "is about all I can say to you. Just keep careful notes. Check your blood for agglutinins and keep a record of the titer. We need to know more about the course of the disease in humans."

"What happened to Lipsky?" I asked.

"Lipsky? Oh, nothing. Just a scare. Never developed yellow fever. And quite likely you won't develop undulant fever either. But keep careful notes."

I did. Regularly I watched for aches, pains, fever. I checked samples of my own blood for antibodies against Brucella. Nothing. I shall never understand why I didn't get undulant fever as a result of that accident. But it brought home to me very forcibly the truth of the saying: It takes two to make a disease, the parasite and the host.

20

MAD SONG

In February 1944 various forces operated to change my line of fate. At the beginning of the month everything seemed to be going well. I had been offered and accepted a position at Rothamsted Experiment Station, the oldest agricultural experiment station in the world. It had been started by J. B. Lawes and J. M. Gilbert in 1843, and some of the experiments on the farm had been in progress for more than one hundred years.

The research I planned involved a study of the physiology of leaf growth. I intended to use tissue culture, a technique with which I had become familiar during my study of the growth of plant embryos. The transfer to Rothamsted made sense. I was a plant physiologist by training and my main interest was in the mechanism of plant growth. My studies on *Brucella abortus* had been purely a wartime project. I was not really a bacteriologist and had no wish to spend the rest of my scientific career in a remote research station on the Berkshire downs.

So I went to Rothamsted, leaving E. and the children in the little house we had bought near Lyne Place, which remained, despite the vicissitudes of war, my spiritual home. In the greater world the enormous forces of destruction that the Germans had unloosed were now turning against them. British and American troops were advancing on Rome. The Russians were already in Estonia and rapidly advancing toward Lithuania. I thought of Daudzegir, damaged and battle-scarred even when I had lived there. What would be left of our old family home? A pile of rubble, most likely.

Anyway, things were improving, and one could begin to make plans to live a more normal life. The winter had been very warm, and green shoots of daffodils were showing in our little garden. Though I returned home only on weekends, I planned to grow most of our own food for the coming year. I rented a piece of ground near our little house and carefully drew up my crop plans: green peas, potatoes, broad beans, string beans, summer squash, Jerusalem artichokes. I was an enthusiastic gardener. Still am.

At this time E.'s behavior underwent a change. She had become very vague and out of touch with the real world. She read incessantly—mostly *Gone with the Wind*, that vast, panoramic, utterly romantic novel that everyone seemed to be reading at that time. E. had always been dreamy. Now she was neglecting the children and her household duties. She was in love, she told me, with another man, a man already married, whom I knew quite well and who had no interest in her whatever. I was angry and disgusted. I had always secretly despised the poor girl and considered her beneath me, a sort of encumbrance inflicted on me by fate. She had borne me two very fine children in whom I took great delight, and those children plus the sexual bond might have sufficed to hold us together. But now this idiotic fantasy of hers, the product of an imagination overheated by too much reading about Scarlett O'Hara and Rhett Butler, soured me completely. I treated her not so much with violence as with contempt, told her she had the soul of a romantic housemaid, that she was an utter fool, that she was wrecking our home for the sake of a man who had no interest in her whatsoever.

In addition to my reproaches E. found herself upbraided by the elders at Lyne Place. Madame Ouspensky had been strongly opposed to our marriage and given E. a hard time. She could be extremely drastic in her treatment of her pupils, especially the younger women, toward whom she seemed to feel a certain dislike. The elders in the Work who had taken Madame's place after she left us took much the same attitude toward E. She had no real business in the Work at all, was there under false pretenses. Now she was behaving in a manner unworthy of any candidate for the higher life. So E. received no support, no sympathy, nothing but disapproval.

How unkind we all were, how utterly lacking in insight! Looking back now with all the knowledge of mental illness that I have so painfully acquired, I find it appalling that those "spiritual directors" of ours presumed to guide others when they were almost totally ignorant of the sicknesses of the mind. E. was quite obviously a potential schizophrenic, as anyone familiar with the illness could have seen. She had had a nervous breakdown in her teens. She appeared to have recovered, but all the warning signs were there for those who knew how to read them.

But our spiritual directors did not know. Madame Ouspensky, who played the role of the tough guru, never really knew her own strength. She was a fine teacher for the strong, who could cope with her attacks; but fragile psyches, which were barely held together by a weak ego, were apt to disintegrate under the sort of assaults she was prone to launch. She certainly was far too rough with E., whose diary, discovered later, showed how seriously she had been affected by a treatment that had been intended to strengthen her but had actually had the reverse effect.

It could, of course, easily be argued that those who choose to tread the Warrior's Way do so at their own risk, that the Way is full of dangers and difficulties, and the higher you climb the further you can fall. I argued in this way myself, citing a sentence from the writings of Eliphas Levi: "Magic, which men of old denominated the SANCTUM REGNUM, the Holy Kingdom, or kingdom of God, REGNUM DEI, exists only for kings and priests. Are you priests? Are you kings?"

Most emphatically E. was neither a priest nor a king, but

a confused young woman whose bad luck it was to encounter a way of life not at all suited to her real needs. So she wallowed out of her depth in ideas that were beyond her comprehension. And those who were said to be "old in the Work" and ought to have realized what was happening did nothing to help her, but only, by their reproaches, made a bad situation worse.

I was as blind as the rest. I left her alone, went back to my work at Rothamsted, planned my experiments, returned the following weekend. I found E. in a chair, rocking herself back and forth. She was singing to herself the words of one of our exercises, "I must try to remember myself." Over and over again she sang the words. Her eyes were unnaturally bright, her face was flushed, and there was a strange smell about her that I learned later is characteristic of schizophrenia. Now and then she stopped singing and laughed. There was nothing to laugh at. That weird merriment, so inappropriate, so uncanny, is also typical of the disease. I further learned that during the last three nights she had not slept at all. Another symptom.

But then I knew nothing. I had barely even heard of schizophrenia. I attributed E.'s weird behavior to some sort of hysteria. I had heard that a sudden shock would stop hysterical attacks. I slapped her face. Shook her. She felt strange. Flexible, as if made of wax. She appeared to feel nothing. Was not even aware of my presence. A horrible suspicion began growing in my mind, so horrible that I tried to exclude it. It kept coming back.

This was not hysteria. The girl had gone mad.

I shook her again, struggling to bring her back into some sort of contact with reality. No response. Whatever strange land she had entered, it was beyond my reach.

I was totally at a loss. What does one do with a girl who has gone out of her mind, who cannot be reached by any means at all? What does one do, in the middle of a major war, with two small children aged one-and-a-half and four-and-a-half? How does one get help when one has no phone and dare not leave the mad girl alone with the children?

I put her to bed and hoped she would stay there. A more or less sleepless night followed. In the morning I fetched the doctor, who mumbled about *dementia praecox.* Psychiatry was not his specialty. He admitted himself nonplussed.

Schizophrenia.

I was destined to see so much of this disease that now I can pronounce the word without horror. But the horror was there in the beginning. There are few experiences more devastating than watching someone with whom one has been very intimate go mad. I had not much faith in benign providence anyway, and this experience shattered what little I had. E.'s madness posed a threat to my own sanity. It opened an abyss into which I peered in terror, terror that was not unmixed with fascination. I knew that there existed in the mind a strange territory full of distortions and illusions, a land of fear, a land of nightmares and phantoms. I knew there were forces in the mind that could draw one toward that land, voices that called, strange shapes that beckoned.

Was it the land of the mad or the land of the dead?

I could not tell. I can only say that I stood on its edge. My situation was made worse by the fact that I had endless decisions to make just at the time I was least in a position to make them. What to do with E.? In the year of her madness (1944) only insulin shock was available for treating schizophrenia. It was a fiendishly expensive and somewhat dangerous treatment. It worked by lowering the blood sugar until the patient went into convulsions. It was effective in some cases, not in others.

I decided I could not possibly afford it. Out of the welter of emotions that filled my being, a dark irrational anger began to emerge. In that black mood I cursed the girl. Why had she let go? It was an easy way out, a sort of quasi-suicide. If she wanted out of the game, why didn't she end it cleanly instead of leaving me with a living corpse on my hands? It was the old fear and resentment that the ostensibly sane feel toward the mad. The mad are guilty of bad faith. They desert their posts. They shirk their responsibilities, etc. Always lurking in the back of my mind was the idea that E. could emerge from that other world if she wanted to. She was simply indulging in madness to escape responsibilities.

The situation was made worse by various relatives who began, as relatives will, to try to find someone to blame for E.'s collapse. This tendency to allocate blame is very common, but it is also quite disastrous. Any man or woman who has to cope with a schizophrenic is under quite enough stress and strain without having to cope with criticisms from relations. The same is true of that breed of meddlers who call themselves psychoanalysts, who also have a tendency, in the name of some half-baked theory, to allocate blame and thus arouse feelings of guilt. If the wife goes mad they blame the husband, if the husband goes mad they blame the wife, if the son or daughter goes mad they blame the parents. In this way they make a bad situation worse. It was my fate to study schizophrenia from the biochemist's standpoint and I learned a lot later about the illness. At the time of E.'s collapse I knew nothing except that fate had played an unusually dirty trick. I felt sorry for myself and resentful toward her. I had never really loved her, had been trapped into marriage by her unintentional pregnancy. I could not call her back from the unknown region into which she had strayed. My main preoccupation was to avoid straying into it myself.

I held on as best I could and tidied up the mess. My sister took care of the children. E. was dumped into one of those large institutional garbage cans that society maintains for the criminal and for the mad. Her illness was one of the most malignant of all the many varieties of schizophrenia (for the illness takes many forms, is not one disease but several). The extreme form of catatonic schizophrenia leaves its victims corpselike. They do not move for hours on end. They do not communicate. From time to time the catatonia

gives way to attacks of violent rage, at which time the patient can become acutely dangerous. (The last time I saw E.,
she was locked in a padded cell, having tried to strangle one
of the attendants and nearly succeeded.) Then the catatonia
settles in again and the patient resumes his role of living
corpse.

No doubt it was incorrect to blame external forces for E.'s
illness. She was the victim of a hereditary defect, a faulty
biochemical mechanism that caused her body to create a
substance that poisoned certain centers in the brain. Perhaps under less stressful circumstances she might just have
kept her balance on the wobbly tightrope she traversed over
the abyss. How could one tell? In any case, she had fallen,
and how terribly insecure her madness made me feel. It was
as if the earth had opened under my feet. Surely it could
happen to anyone. I remember at the time reading a passage from *The Varieties of Religious Experience*. In it William
James, surely one of the sanest and clearest minded of philosophers, described his own descent into the abyss. He
had found himself obsessed with the image of an epileptic
patient he had seen in an asylum, a black-haired youth with
greenish skin sitting on one of the benches as motionless as
an Egyptian mummy. That shape am I, thought James, at
least potentially.

> Nothing that I possess can defend me against that fate, if
> the hour for it should strike for me as it struck for him. There
> was such a horror of him, and such a perception of my own
> merely momentary discrepancy from him, that it was as if
> something hitherto solid within my breast gave way entirely,
> and I became a mass of quivering fear. After this the universe
> was changed for me altogether.

It became similarly changed for me. I was plagued by a
horrible awareness of the insecurity of life. What becomes
of our lofty spiritual aims in the face of this fact that one
small error in the chemistry of the body can plunge us into

madness? We humans are close to madness anyway. Our
badly made, disharmonized nervous systems are subject to
all sorts of derangements. At the time E. went mad almost
the entire population of the so-called civilized world was
busily trying to destroy itself simply because certain pathogenic ideas had taken hold of the minds of a few fanatics.

I began to question the basic assumption of the Work.
This assumption was that if you realized you were asleep
and sincerely wished to awaken, you could do so. You
could make great efforts, you could get help from "the inner
circle of humanity," you could change your fate. But now I
could no longer accept this reassuring belief. I began to
wonder if there was any freedom at all. We are at the mercy
of our genes. We are at the mercy of our biochemistry. One
error at the molecular level can wreck our lives and turn us
into lunatics.

21

TO THE
NEW WORLD

The troopship, drab, battle-grey, rolled gently in the swells of the North Atlantic. In a previous incarnation she had been the luxury liner, *Île de France*. Now, stripped of her ornaments, she was transporting Canadian veterans to Halifax. Among the veterans was a small group of specialists, scientists, and engineers on their way to America for various special purposes. I was one of them, on my way to the Rockefeller Institute in Princeton, New Jersey, to learn the techniques of tissue culture from Philip R. White.

It was June of the year 1945. The war in Europe was over. After that ghastly interruption it appeared as if civilized life might once again become possible. Though my faith in the Ouspenskys had been severely shaken by what I considered their desertion of their followers, I had nonetheless a strong desire to continue working with them. The Work had become to such an extent the focal point of my existence that I could not live without it. Our group in England had managed to stay together during the war, but it was somewhat lifeless and lacked direction. It was a school without a teacher. The center of the Work was now in America.

Before leaving for the States, Ouspensky had given us the task of joining him there as soon as we could. It was not an easy task. One could not simply go to the nearest travel agent and buy a ticket to New York. The Atlantic swarmed with U-boats. There was little shipping available. Every able-bodied man and woman under the age of sixty was

needed for the war effort. In spite of this, many members of
our group managed to arrange to be sent to America on
government business of one sort or another.

I too managed to be sent to America. The technique of
plant tissue culture was not well understood in England at
that time. I was one of the few botanists using the method.
I was able to persuade my superiors that it would be a good
idea to send me to the Rockefeller Institute in Princeton,
where studies were being done in this field. Working at the
Rockefeller Institute would be an education in itself. It had
at that time quite a formidable assembly of first-class
brains, and any young scientist eager to learn could profit
by working there.

I had other personal reasons for wishing to leave England. The madness of my wife was a constant source of
anguish and frustration. It involved me in a morass of negative emotions that poisoned my inner life. I hated visiting
her and did so as rarely as possible. What was the use of my
sitting there by a female body that, for all the signs of life it
displayed, might as well have been fashioned in wax?
When not held in a catatonic trance, E. was dangerously violent, so much so that she spent most of her time in a padded cell. She refused to eat and had to be fed. She soiled
herself and had to be cleansed like a baby. My Scientist, an
unsentimental creature, could see no sense in these labori-
ous efforts to keep her alive. What the poor girl really
wanted was to die. But a hopelessly muddled culture,
which had just finished butchering millions in a stupid
war, would not allow poor E. to leave her demented body,
but continued elaborately to feed and cleanse it as if it was
some sort of precious relic.

I do not wish to give the impression that I was totally
heartless. The hope still existed within me that somehow or
other contact with E. could be reestablished, that I could in-
fuse into her the spirit of the Warrior, enabling her to fight
her way out of that trap into which she had fallen. I remember being urgently summoned to the hospital because

she was seriously ill with a staphylococcal infection, which showed signs of turning into generalized septicemia. As sometimes happens in cases of schizophrenia the other, more acute illness had induced a partial remission of the schizophrenic process. For the first time since the beginning of her illness, she was able to talk to me, inquired about the children, about the little house in which she had taken so much pride in the old days. I remember taking her hands in mine and imploring her, with tears in my eyes, to come back to us.

"Come back! Come back! Fight your way out of this mess. Come back to us."

She looked at me with the frightened, haunted eyes of a trapped animal.

"I cannot come back. I'm dead. I cannot come back."

It was a frightful moment. I really had the sensation that I was talking to a corpse. My grief turned to anger.

"Why don't you fight? Either fight or die. Anything is better than continuing like this."

But E. was drifting in dreams, talking in fantasy to one of the children, out of touch with her surroundings. There was nothing to hold on to, no way of infusing into her the Warrior's spirit. I thought of Henley's defiant lines about captains of fate and masters of souls. But Henley had been battling with tuberculosis, not schizophrenia. How can one fight a disease that undermines the very foundations of the soul?

I left the gloomy asylum secretly hoping that the staphylococci would gain the upper hand and release poor E. from her damaged organism, a burned-out hulk, adrift on a sea of delusions. But penicillin, which by then was freely available, conquered the staphylococci, and E. survived. She had lost the will to live without acquiring the will to die.

Meanwhile her presence, stuck in that limbo between life and death, enormously complicated my existence. In order to be nearer to Lyne Place and still have a job I had persuaded my employer, the Agricultural Research Council, to let me work at Kew Gardens. That ancient botanical garden, justly famous for its taxonomic knowhow, was still, as far as physiological research was concerned, stuck somewhere in the eighteenth century. It had absolutely no modern equipment or modern facilities. The plan was that I would work there and set up a laboratory combining the fine resources of the garden with modern methods of research and up-to-date equipment.

So in May of the year 1945 I found myself in Kew walking across the gardens from the rhododendron grove to the Jodrell House where my laboratory was to be located. The gardens were truly beautiful in May, bursting with blooms of lilacs, rhododendrons, azaleas. They had been well kept up in spite of the war. The flying bombs that had been dropping on London had left undamaged the enormous greenhouses.

I was reflecting on this fact as I approached the arum house when I caught sight of a girl. She was dressed in worn working pants and a rather ragged sweater and was carefully shoveling compost into a wheelbarrow. She was a slender, blonde, very English girl with the complexion of a slightly faded rose (rationing was tight and I guessed she was undernourished). She looked about eighteen.

I stopped dead in my tracks, my whole body trembling with the shock of recognition. There she was, my soul mate, body mate, life mate, the girl I had met and loved again and again through heaven alone knew how many rotations of the wheel of recurrence. She looked up, shy as a fawn, uneasily aware that something had happened, an ominous something. From the very start I noticed that there was an air of sadness about her. I put it down to bad diet and the generally heavy atmosphere of those days at the end of the war, for though technically the British were victors there was no great joy in victory. The war had lasted too long and cost too much. We were exhausted, physically and spiritually.

Even before I spoke to her, my literary imagination gave

her a name. She was Tess, as in *Tess of the d'Urbervilles*, or
she was Tessa, the Tessa of *The Constant Nymph*. It did not
escape my notice that both Tess and Tessa had come to
early and tragic ends. Perhaps this explained the air of
sadness that hung about her.

I could not continue to stare at her like an enchanted oaf,
so I asked her the way to the Jodrell House. Gravely the
nymph gave me directions. All sorts of signals crackled between us, like sparks between high-voltage electrodes, but
she was virginal and shy, and I was confused. My instincts
clamored for a prompt and lasting union. I was naturally
monogamous, and this was one of the very few girls I had
met who really attracted me. But my reason demanded caution. I recalled an equally casual meeting in the Indian museum, which had led to my disastrous marriage to E.
Though I refused to take responsibility for E.'s madness, I
could not escape certain feelings of guilt. I had dragged her
out of the social niche where she belonged and exposed her
to ideas and practices that were way above her head. I had
not been kind to her, treated her more as a sort of sexual toy
than a woman with emotional needs of her own. Now her
dead-alive remains hung round my neck. Though in my
prevailing mood of self-pity I cursed my fate, a hard, realistic spirit somewhere within me informed me that I had
deserved it.

So while the part of me from my heart to my gonads
flashed signals saying "Go, Go, Go," my head flashed
others saying "Caution" or even "Stop." Besides, there was
no reason to plunge in wildly. I could afford to take time
out to think. I knew that Tessa worked in Kew Gardens in
the arum house, a steamy microtropical environment full of
giant foliage and rich earthy smells. I could always find her
again if, after mature deliberation, I really felt that it was
right to seek her out.

Mature deliberation? I have to smile even as I write the
words. What chance did sober reason have in the ensuing
argument? The gonads shrieked, the blood called, the emo-

tions surged. In the midst of all this instinctive tumult
my poor "sober reason" was helpless, like a cautious old
gentleman swept up in a Dionysian orgy. Of course I saw
Tessa again, and again, and again. I was in love with her. It
was not the casual love of a heartless lecher seeking to
deflower an innocent virgin. My intentions were entirely
honorable. I desperately needed a mate and a new mother
for my children, was perfectly willing to bestow on her all
my worldly goods, to put a ring on her finger, to care for
her, feed her, house her, look after her. She certainly could
do with some care and feeding. She was twenty-one and I
was thirty-two, an eleven-year difference. It explained why
I felt a bit fatherly as well as loverly toward her.

So my impulse was to take Tessa to the nearest church or
registrar's office and turn her into the second Mrs. de Ropp,
a transformation she would have welcomed, for she was really lost among the aroids. She would have much preferred
to lavish her attentions on a husband than on those vaguely
sinister enormous plants whose strange flowers smelled like
a mixture of rotten meat and feces. But the marriage was
impossible. I was married already. Moreover it was a marriage I could not terminate. How could E. in her stuporous
catatonic state agree to a divorce? She was *non compos men-
tis*. Even if she could sign documents, they would not be
legally binding.

I cursed my fate, wriggling and threshing about like a
fish in a net. If only E. would have the decency to die instead of inhabiting that shadowy limbo and messing up the
lives of the living. What could I offer Tessa? At best the
prospect of marriage in four years time. Insanity became
grounds for divorce, according to the newly passed Herbert
Act, after either spouse had been five years continuously
under care. Was I going to waste four years of love and
pleasure? Not if I could help it. What was a marriage certificate? A license to copulate without the disapproval of society. Well, I could do my copulating without a license. As
Robert Burns put it:

The Kirk an' State may join an' tell,
To do sic things I maunna;
The Kirk an' State may gae to hell,
And I'll gae to my Anna.

I broached the subject with Tessa. We could either wait about four years to marry each other or do the sensible thing and live, as was then said, "in sin." Tessa was quite willing to try sin. Though she looked like a pretty maid straight from the pages of Kate Greenaway, she had the soul of a rebel.

But news of our proposed flouting of the conventions reached the ears of relatives, hers and mine. The shrieks of indignation that ensued were so uproarous that in the end, if only to escape the clamor, I felt thankful to board the troopship for America. Perhaps it was as well that we should be separated for a time. In the interval the various relatives would have a chance to calm down, and Tessa could think things over and come to a decision based on reason rather than emotion.

So I stood by the rail of the *Île de France* as the liner raced westward with its crowded human cargo. Beside me stood a Canadian veteran with whom I had become friendly. He was actually quite young but appeared middle-aged. His hair was grey. His hands trembled constantly. He was one of a group of men who had landed early on the Normandy beaches. For six days they had fought without food, without sleep, without respite. Of the 189 men who had disembarked only nine had survived.

"I'm supposed to be going back to the family farm," said the veteran, "but I don't know what use I'll be as long as I'm like this."

He looked down sadly at his trembling hands.

I felt ashamed. I had been feeling sorry for myself because fate had saddled me with a lunatic wife, preventing me from marrying the girl I loved. But at least I had passed a quiet war. A fuse cap from a bursting antiaircraft shell had dropped uncomfortably close to me. A fire bomb had dropped near our house but burnt itself out without damaging anything. That was all. But here were these Canadians, many of them shattered for life; and Penn and Dooley Tennyson, with whom I had played as a child, both dead; and Neville and Charlie, Admiral Fisher's sons, both dead. And pretty Honorine, after whose body I had lusted in the old days at The White Gates, crushed to death in the ruins of a bombed house in London. As for my German relations, heaven knows what had happened to them. I thought of my cousins, the von Stralendorfs, on whose estate near Rostock I had once spent Christmas. They were an earnest God-fearing family, full of the graces and pieties of old Prussia. Now the Russian armies had poured across Prussia and by all accounts behaved about as savagely as the troops of Genghis Khan. What a price for that idiotic conflict!

Well, it had finally ended, at least in Europe. The Germans had sown the wind and were reaping a tornado. Meanwhile there to the west lay America, the fabulous New World, unbombed, undamaged, the hope of ravaged Europe. A fragment of Walt Whitman drifted through my mind.

> Not wan from Asia's fetiches
> Nor red from Europe's old dynastic slaughterhouse,
> (Area of murder-plots of thrones,
>   with scent left yet of wars and scaffolds everywhere,)
> But come from Nature's long and harmless throes,
>   peacefully builded thence,
> These virgin lands, lands of the Western shore,
> To the new, culminating man, to you, the empire new,
> You promised long, we pledge, we dedicate.

A prophetic verse if ever there was one! It came from *Song of the Redwood Tree*, a poem that celebrated the rugged grandeur of northern California that I later came to love. But at that moment it stood for the whole of the New World, untainted by the militaristic madness that had wrecked Europe. As the *Île de France* neared its journey's end and I stood looking westward at the coast of Nova Scotia, the same excitement filled me as must have possessed the souls of millions of immigrants who, standing on the decks of various vessels, caught their first sight of the New World.

22

MORBIO INFERIORE

The train which carried me from Halifax to New York wound its way through the rocky farms of Nova Scotia, crossed into New York State during the night, and reached its destination on the following morning. In the cathedral-like immensity of Grand Central Station I stood confused, caught up in the strange sensation of not being able to believe that I was where I was.

Monstrous New York. From the very beginning the city terrified me, a steel and concrete madhouse without a soul. But the power of the place—the raw, savage, pulsing, incredible power! Leaving the station I stood on Forty-second Street while the crowds of the morning rush hour surged around me. They poured from the subway exits as if the earth were vomiting them from its guts, a rushing, tense, preoccupied multitude, the men already in shirt-sleeves with their jackets over their shoulders (the heat of the city was rapidly increasing), the girls spotless in their summer dresses, bearing with them, like a cloud of incense, the aura of various perfumes and deodorants. Off they rushed, this way, that way, like swarms of fish flowing along the can-yonlike streets, always, it seemed, in a hurry. (Was the whole city late for work that day, or was that the way New Yorkers always behaved?) I stood there gaping, like a bewildered yokel, wondering how to find my way to Fifth Avenue and the Rockefeller Center, where my old friend Rodney Colin Smith had a job in some government office. In

London, if one was lost one asked a policeman, but where were the police in New York? Finally, too shy to stop any of those hurrying citizens, I bought a map of the city at a news kiosk, found Fifth Avenue, and set off along it. At least there was nothing complex about the New York streets. As long as one could count and knew east from west one could find one's way through the city.

Good God! Is this really possible? I stood by the fountain in the Rockefeller Plaza gazing in awe at the towering slabs of masonry that rose up around me. One would have to be a clod indeed not to be impressed by Rockefeller Center, a vertical city, its roots deep in the granite of Manhattan, its branches towering into the sky, thousands of offices stacked on top of each other, buzzing with activity by day, completely emptied by night. In its terrifying way it was beautiful. The buildings, carefully spaced and of graded height, created a sense of balance and harmony. Flags waved, fountains played, flowers bloomed in neatly tended beds, people sipped drinks under brightly colored umbrellas, and pigeons, completely unawed by the towering slabs of masonry, waddled around seeking crumbs.

I stood there and gasped. The sheer size of the place created in my soul a feeling of awe, as if I had found myself standing in the midst of a great cathedral. A monument to Mammon? Yes. But what a monument! What courage, what power, what know-how had been needed to raise those enormous slabs of steel and concrete. And yet it was soulless, a gigantic termitary, where thousands of telephones and typewriters chattered and rattled in a frenzy of activity to accomplish—what? I did not know. An uneasy thought crossed my mind. Was this enormous, beautiful, awe-inspiring, soulless structure a symbol of America?

But no. There were other Americas. I had been warned in advance. Don't judge the United States by New York City. And Rockefeller Center, which seemed so blatantly to advertize the Rockefeller wealth, was only one aspect of the activities of that remarkable family. A very different aspect was the Rockefeller Institute, both the one in New York and the one in Princeton, generally conceded to be the finest centers for scientific research in the world.

I plunged into the great termitary and found Rodney Colin Smith. Large and genial, he exuded a certain fervor which I later came to associate with all True Believers. We were old friends, had both belonged to Dick Sheppard's Peace Pledge Union. After I had discovered Ouspensky, I brought him and his wife into the Work. She was quite wealthy, had helped the Ouspenskys to get started in America. They were devoted to Ouspensky.

The new center of the Work was at Franklin Farms, near Mendham, New Jersey. It was larger and showier than Lyne Place. The house, built of grey granite by stone masons specially imported from Italy, had once been the residence of the governor of New Jersey. Along the drive that led to the farm buildings were aviaries that had once housed ornamental birds. The aviaries were now empty and decaying. The farm was large with silos, barns, outbuildings. There were no neat fields separated by hedges, such as I had known in England, but rolling vistas of land planted on the contour with crops that to me seemed exotic: corn, which I called maize or Indian corn (in England corn meant wheat), and soybeans, which were completely new to me.

I worked on the farm for three months. There had, it seemed, been a major muddle back in England due to delays in communications. A message had reached my employers only a day after my departure urgently requesting that I arrive no sooner than September. July and August were apparently dead months at the Rockefeller Institute at Princeton. So unpleasant was the heat at that time that all those who could either went away on vacation or fled to the Oceanographic Institute at Woods Hole where many of the senior scientists rented laboratories for the summer. There, cooled by ocean breezes, they worked in a condition of happy informality, investigating such phenomena as the behavior of biological membranes in sea urchin eggs.

So I had a chance to do as I liked for three months. What did I want? I wanted or thought I wanted to reestablish contact with the Ouspenskys, to work on myself more intensively than I had in England. I still cherished the illusion that some sort of supereffort was involved in following the Warrior's Way. It was the Heroic Myth, the "Climb Mount Everest" fallacy. It took me years to get it out of my system.

So there I was, all eager to conquer the heights, to complete in myself those alchemical transformations that I had failed to bring about in England. Undeveloped man, I told myself, is like a crucible containing a mixture of components, iron and sulfur for instance. You can shake them together as long as you like, but they will not combine. They can still be separated by mechanical means. But if you apply sufficient heat to the mixture a change takes place. The substances interact chemically to form a new compound with properties totally different from those of the parent elements.

This analogy between the inner work and a chemical reaction of the endothermic variety had been made by Gurdjieff and was described in one of the (to me) most fascinating chapters of the then unpublished *Fragments of an Unknown Teaching*. In man, said Gurdjieff, the heat needed to bring about inner fusion is generated by the struggle between Yes and No, the force affirming and the force denying. The explanation satisfied me. It was an example of that practical alchemical thinking that distinguished Gurdjieff's teachings from the more woolly pronouncements of the Theosophists. Struggle and effort, these were the essential components of the Warrior's Way. So I would struggle and make efforts. I set off with Colin Smith, a hoe over my shoulder, to work in the vegetable garden, full of excitement over making contact with the soil of this new world.

"I feel like a Pilgrim Father," I declared.

"By the time you've finished you'll feel like a Pilgrim Grandfather."

How right he was! Nothing I had heard or read or

thought about America had prepared me for the debilitating effect of the East Coast climate. It seemed to drain all the vitality out of my system. One lived in a permanent bath of sweat. I had known heat in Australia. I had even, though rarely, known heat in England. But that East Coast heat was different, oppressive, heavy, even frightening, culminating as it so often did in savage thunderstorms with downpours of rain that carved channels of erosion in the vegetable garden and battered helpless seedlings into a sea of mud.

That climate, I felt sure, had had a disastrous effect on both of my teachers. Neither Ouspensky nor Madame Ouspensky had ever been really healthy even in England. Both had the pale flabby faces of those who spend too much time indoors, who eat food not suited to the needs of their bodies, who get far too little exercise. But at least in England Ouspensky had his horse and his Cossack saddle and could get some exercise by daily rides around the estate. There was nothing to prevent him from doing the same thing at Franklin Farms, but he seemed to have lost all interest in physical activity. He gave lectures in New York, so dull that after hearing a few I absolutely refused to attend any more. Between lectures he sat in his study. I sat up with him on several occasions but was saddened by what I found. He was quite obviously ill, drinking far too much, and still wandering in imagination through the streets of Moscow and Petersburg.

Furthermore, his mental state was far from good. His paranoid tendencies had become more pronounced. He was apt, at the slightest provocation, to throw people out of the Work. One of his oldest pupils, J. G. Bennett, had been excommunicated, along with all the people who studied with him. We were forbidden to see or communicate with Bennett or with any of the people in Bennett's group. I was reminded of the Stalinist purges and of the words of one of the elders in the Work who had always had reservations about Ouspensky: "One must distinguish between what is the teaching and what is just Russian."

I kept silent. The Ouspensky regime was well and truly

authoritarian and no criticism was permitted. I even nodded agreement when Ouspensky began berating Bennett
for, as he put it, "dealing in psychological blackmarket," by
which he implied that Bennett had stolen his ideas. What I
saw in Ouspensky was truly frightening. Here was a man
who had one of the best minds of anyone I had met indulging in really ridiculous fantasies. The resentment I felt toward him for leaving us during the dark days of 1940 now
increased. I was not at all loyal, had always considered loyalty a mixture of sentimentality and stupidity. My interest,
as a scientist, was in observing reality. I could see what was
happening very clearly and made no attempt to hide from
the unpleasant knowledge. Ouspensky was no longer a
teacher. He had lost his power and wrecked his health by
indulgence in two poisons, alcohol and nostalgia. The only
honest thing for him to do at that point was to face his own
weakness, send all his disciples packing, close down that
ostentatious house, and either die or, by a supreme effort,
recover his lost power.

Actually he did neither. The situation was out of his control. The Work carried on because it had attained a certain
momentum, but it was still really Work without a teacher.
Madame Ouspensky, always prone to withdraw to the privacy of her room, no longer had direct contact with the
group. She remained for the most part invisible, running
the house by sending messages via two of the pupils,
whom I called Madame's Archangels.

The Archangels were brother and sister, Brother Archangel and Sister Archangel. They were really too young in the
Work to play the roles they had been given. They trampled
heavily on the egos of those who were as old or older in the
Work than they were. It was one thing to receive direct
from Madame those often withering comments on one's
weaknesses that she was so fond of making. It was quite
another to receive those same comments, always offered
publicly and with a certain note of satisfaction, by Brother
or Sister Archangel.

I received such a message myself, delivered by Brother

Archangel at the tea table before all the assembled students.
"I disappointed in him. He harmful idiot." To Madame
Ouspensky we were all idiots of one sort or another. She
had borrowed the word from Gurdjieff and used it freely.
The message came at a time when I was in a particularly
low state. The initial enthusiasm that I had felt on arriving
in America had by then evaporated. I was entertaining
grave doubts about the wisdom of my teachers. I was having trouble adjusting to the climate and I was tormented by
the pangs of disprized love.

Yes, disprized love. My nymph of Kew Gardens, Tessa of
the Aroids, had not answered any of my letters. I could not
tell the reason for her silence. Had she rejected me, become
interested in someone else, been bullied into silence by her
mother? I wrote again and again, but no answer. Absolutely
nothing. How was it possible? She had been ardent enough
when I left, ready to live with me in sin, as the laws of England made marriage impossible. Now she had evidently
completely changed her mind.

Then came more bad news. The old "friend of the family"
who was looking after my children had discovered, hidden
in the children's toy box, a diary of my wife's. She had read
the diary and communicated the contents to the Vaughan
Williamses. Evidently some of the diary dealt with E.'s
treatment by Madame Ouspensky, which had, as I knew,
been quite drastic (far too drastic in view of E.'s very weak
ego and schizophrenic tendencies). There resulted from all
this some stormy correspondence, on the subject of what
would now be called brainwashing. To my English relatives
the Ouspenskys appeared as a pair of power-crazed religious fanatics who took advantage of the weakness and
credulity of their followers, reduced them to the condition
of slaves, and drove poor weak girls crazy by putting them
under stresses they could not endure.

It was a familiar story. Those who do not understand the
spiritual hunger that leads people to work with such
teachers as the Ouspenskys are always highly suspicious of

the teacher-pupil relationship. We in the West do not have
the *guru/chela* tradition that is so much a part of life in the
East. So when this relationship is established, it tends to be
regarded with disfavor. The teacher is looked upon either as
an out-and-out con artist only concerned with getting
money out of his dupes or a power-hungry fanatic, a sort of
Svengali, who enjoys manipulating human beings like puppets. All too ofen these suspicions are well justified. The
teacher/disciple relationship is a dangerous one and does
lend itself to abuse. I think, however, that the accusations
that my relatives started hurling across the Atlantic were excessive. E. had gone mad two years after Madame Ouspensky had left England. She was really devoted to the
group at Lyne Place, which she regarded as her spiritual
home. As for her diary, it may have been written at a time
of despondency. We all went through such times.

In my days of faith when I was a True Believer, I would
have dismissed all these accusations as absurd. But my own
faith was shaken. I could no longer maintain, as I had done
previously, that my teachers could not make mistakes. Obviously they both could and did. Their worst mistake had
been deserting their group to take refuge in America. Now
they were compounding the mistake by trying to run a
school of the fourth way by remote control. They had lost
that special power that the Sufis call *baraka*, but were either
unaware of the fact or not honest enough to admit it.

Looking back over that difficult time I can see how very
easily a teacher of the Way can become trapped by his own
followers. It is a very common occurrence. At one point in
his life the teacher has power. That power attracts to him
followers who, as often happens, confuse the teacher with
the teaching. The pupil's admiration and obedience feeds
the teacher's ego. Gradually he comes to regard himself as
infallible. The more authoritarian he grows, the more impossible it becomes for any of his pupils to suggest to him
that all is not well. Generally, however, they do not even
notice that anything has gone wrong. They sheepishly in-

terpret all the teacher's weird behavior as being consciously designed to test them. Or if that fails, they take refuge in what they call loyalty, which amounts, in most cases, to a sentimental refusal to face unpleasant facts. This situation tends to develop into a closed system with a highly authoritarian leader exerting complete dominance over his followers. In such a system there is no feedback and the errors multiply until the whole organization blows up or falls apart.

My growing loss of faith in my teachers plus the debilitating effect of the climate had the effect of plunging me into the depths of that spiritual wilderness which Hermann Hesse called the *Morbio Inferiore* (see *Journey to the East*). All followers of the Warrior's Way sooner or later find themselves in that deep and desolate gorge where all inspiration fails, all visions are lost, all enthusiasm dies.

Sacred enthusiasms! How right was Louis Pasteur in calling our attention to the derivation of that word. For enthusiasm comes from the Greek *en theos*, the "god within." "Happy is he," wrote Pasteur, "who bears within himself a god, an ideal of beauty, and obeys it; ideal of art, of science, of patriotism, of the virtues symbolized by the Gospels. These are the living sources of great thoughts and great acts. All are lighted by reflection from the infinite."

By the same token miserable is he whose inner god dies or deserts him. This is what happens to all those who lose themselves in the Morbio Inferiore. Once they were eager members of the League, engaged in the Journey to the East, clearly aware of the high aims of the journey and ready to face any hardship or difficulty. But in the rocky desolation of the Morbio they lose that awareness. The bright and lovely vision fades into a grey shadow. They even lose the League ring, with its four precious stones that symbolize the Four Spirits and the Four Elements. All that they have left is a memory. "Once I took part in a great and glorious enterprise. It seemed very important to me then. Now I can hardly remember what it was. Some sort of youthful foolishness. Some idealism. Some spiritual quest. Ah, well, I was young and foolish in those days. It all seems unreal to me now. I can't even remember what the excitement was about.''

Morbio Inferiore! To every follower of the Warrior's Way the term has an ominous sound. And there was I, who had set off so hopefully to the New World expecting to be reunited to my teachers and journey with renewed vigor on the Way, hopelessly trapped in that accursed place, disenchanted, discouraged, disconcerted. And there was Ouspensky drinking himself into a stupor, and there was Madame, the teacher I most loved, remote and bedridden, trying to run the show through the Archangels. A fine old mess!

Well, if one intends to go on living, one has to find a game worth playing. If one game fails one must discover another. Any game is better than no game. So, as the Journey to the East had lost its glamor, I found myself turning for consolation to the Science Game. That, at least, I could play with confidence. There was only one question one had to ask: "Where is the evidence?" If you don't have the evidence, what experiment can you design to provide it?

My work with Philip R. White at the Rockefeller Institute had brought me face to face with one of the basic problems of biology. From him I had learned that plants, like animals, suffer from tumors. The tumors could be caused by insects (galls), by viruses, and by a very peculiar bacterium called *Agrobacterium tumefaciens*. Yes. Puncture a plant with a needle infected with the bacteria and a tumor would develop at the site of the wound. It was extraordinary. Something went wrong with the growth pattern of the plant cells. They refused any longer to follow the general design imposed on them by the plant's organizer. Even stranger, one could by suitable means eliminate the bacteria, but the cells continued to grow abnormally. One could grow them in tissue culture, graft them back into the plant, and again they grew as a tumor. They were permanently changed, permanently malignant.

So there I was, face to face with the problem of cancer. I

approached it not, as a doctor might, as a widespread and terrible disease that took many lives, but as a biologist with a deep interest in the phenomenon of growth. For the laws of growth are very mysterious. Somehow the organism as a whole imposes order on its parts so that they grow in a definite pattern. The pattern is imposed by a mysterious force we call the organizer. All normal cells in the body obey the organizer. Cancer cells do not. They are anarchists. They have rejected the higher law. Their uncontrolled growth tends to destroy the organism of which they are part. So in the end the cancer cells destroy themselves.

But what exactly takes place in the cancer cell to cause it to rebel against the higher law? Is the cancer cell a victim of a virus infection? Several members of the Rockefeller Institute were inclined to believe this, and the virus etiology of cancer was often discussed at those very tasty lunches that were served to the senior staff at Theobold Smith House. Peyton Rous had clearly shown that a certain cancer of chickens (the Rous sarcoma) was caused by a virus. There was an inclination on the part of several students of cancer to generalize from this finding, to see all cancers as virus diseases, though the presence of the virus could not be demonstrated.

This problem became for me so fascinating that it began to assume the proportions of an obsession. I had been sent to the Rockefeller Institute to learn the techniques of plant tissue culture. These I had learned. They were easy. Anyone with a training in bacteriology could master them. But beyond the techniques lay the basic problems that those techniques might be used to study, the problems of growth and organization, specifically the problem of malignant growth.

My newly developed obsession with the cancer problem plunged me into further difficulties. My employer, the Agricultural Research Council in England, had not sent me to America to study cancer. It was really not their concern. After some rather acerbic correspondence I faced a choice. I

could return to England to work on problems that had a
practical bearing on agriculture, or I could change the direction of my career and try to get a job that would enable me
to study some aspect of the cancer problem.

I was tormented by indecision. It was unfair, disgraceful,
not to return to England. I had been sent out by the government at considerable expense, paid a bonus to cover the
extra cost of living in the States. I had a laboratory waiting
for me at Kew Gardens. I was morally obligated to return.

And yet I couldn't. Something, some twist in my line of
fate, some force over which I had no control, made it absolutely impossible for me to return to England. To this day I
don't understand what the force was. I liked England and
did not particularly like the United States. The climate was
terrible. New York City, where I proposed to get a job, was
alarming. The cost of living was high. My esteemed
teachers had lost their way and could no longer be trusted.
Why not return to England?

I could not. There was something about America that
pulled me like a gigantic magnet. Perhaps it was the sheer
size of the place, the awe-inspiring immensity of the continent that stretched all the way from Atlantic to Pacific. Perhaps it was dread of returning to a country that seemed,
despite its valiant war effort, to be slowly dying. Perhaps it
was fear of confronting the mess I had left behind, the poor
madwoman in her padded cell, the disapproval of my relatives, the broken affair with Tessa of the Aroids. In any case
I could not return. Somewhat ashamed of myself, but
thankful at least that a decision had been made, I sneaked
off to Canada to exchange my visitor's visa for an immigrant visa and to take a job in the research department of
the New York Botanical Garden, studying the problem of
abnormal plant growth with funds provided by the American Cancer Society.

So I lived in the Bronx in one room and walked to work.
At weekends I went to Franklin Farms and helped care for
the vegetable garden. My life was pervaded by a strong

smell of hypocrisy. I was mechanically repeating a pattern that had become habitual. From 1936 to 1945, every week-end I had worked at Lyne Place. From 1945 on, every week-end I worked at Franklin Farms. All my friends were there. A thousand associations bound me to the place. Moreover, though I deplored the way in which the Work had deterio-rated, I could not abandon hope. Somehow, surely, Ou-spensky could find his way out of the trap into which he had fallen and give to our enterprise once again the sense of direction it had had in the past. He was, after all, if not con-scious man, then at least a cut above the ordinary sleepy types who went mechanically through their routines on the world's major treadmills. What had become of those fine fantasies, those trips we were to make to romantic places in search of the "custodians of the Tradition"? What had hap-pened to the Historico-Psychological Society? Could not Ouspensky somehow make those superefforts he so often spoke of and get himself moving again? Did he never listen to his own lectures?

23

PRAYER
OF THE HEART

Ouspensky did indeed make his supereffort. On January 18, 1947, I stood with other members of the group watching while Ouspensky walked slowly across the hall and settled himself in the corner of a waiting car. He had decided, against doctor's orders and the pleas of his wife, to tear himself out of those for him debilitating surroundings and return to England. He was pale and unwell and walked very slowly. I was overcome with a sense of grief with which was mingled a curious feeling of hope. I felt sure that I would not see him again in my present life but that, through the working of the wheel of recurrence, we would meet in some other part of the time-space continuum. As the car drove away, I caught one last glimpse of my old teacher, and a voice inside me said, "Till next time."

Though Ouspensky, during the last phase of his life in America, had not lived like a Warrior, he certainly died like one. Back in England the man who had spent so much time lecturing and explaining refused to explain anything. His old followers flocked about him, expecting once more that the old pattern of lectures would be resumed. "You taught us—" began one of them.

"I never taught you anything," said Ouspensky.

Rodney Colin Smith was with him to the end. He described to me the superhuman efforts Ouspensky made to fix in himself some kind of memory that might enable him, next time around, to avoid making certain wrong decisions.

By almost complete silence he insulated himself from the distracting forces of life. Though he was in great pain and extremely weak, he insisted on being driven day after day to all those places in England that had, at one time or another, formed the center of the Work.

"Next time I must remember." This, I feel certain, was Ouspensky's reason for making those excursions. By a supreme effort of will he threw off the inertia that had held him powerless during the fatal last years in America. His body was dying, and he made no attempt to prolong its life. He neither ate nor drank. Though hardly able to set one foot in front of the other, he would force his dying body to walk for hours at a time through rough lanes and along country roads. He would rise in the small hours of the night, dress, walk, observe, *remember*. Often he would remain all night sitting in the car in the darkness and cold. On the day that he knew would be his last, he rose from his bed, dressed, pushed aside all who tried to restrain him, went downstairs, and assembled his closest followers and spoke with them. I do not know what he spoke about, but can guess that the subject was remembering—that special kind of remembering which enables a few developed souls to carry something from one life to another across the chasm of death. After this last conversation Ouspensky died.

I can understand Ouspensky's feeling of urgency. In the book to which he devoted so much time at the end of his life, Ouspensky wrote about the secret of eternal recurrence.

> A man who has begun to guess the great secret must make use of it, otherwise it turns against him. It is not a safe secret. When one has become aware of it one must go on or one will go down. When one finds the secret or hears about it, one has only one or two or three or in any case only a few more lives.
> (*The Strange Life of Ivan Osokin*,
> London: Penguin Books, 1947.)

The death of Ouspensky activated in me a dormant aspect of my persona. It had been kept in the background by the ban Ouspensky had placed on talking about that collection of ideas we called the System. Now that Ouspensky was dead, the creature crawled out of the burrow in which it had been confined and began to preen its plumage and prepare to play the role of teacher. After all, this character assured me, I had worked for twelve years with Ouspensky, surely a long enough apprenticeship. Ouspensky himself had worked for only two years with Gurdjieff and had then set himself up as a teacher in his own right—becoming, as the years went by, more and more authoritarian.

This personality, which I later came to call the Missionary, was a manifestation of the False Messiah disease. This affliction causes its victims to imagine that they have some vitally important message to give to mankind. I was not the only one to be afflicted with this sickness at the time of Ouspensky's death. My old friend Rodney Colin contracted it in an even more virulent form, became convinced that the spirit of Ouspensky was working through him, and rushed off to Mexico to found his own school. As for me, I had contacted a meditation group that derived its inspiration from Gerald Heard, who had founded a monastery of a sort called Trabuco in Southern California. My Missionary had designs on that group, planned to take over the leadership. He was a crass, domineering creature with a taste for power. He had been kept in abeyance for so long that he found its sudden freedom quite intoxicating.

My Missionary, however, did not have things all his own way. Years of ridicule and putdowns by Madame Ouspensky had left their mark. A voice informed me that the Missionary was a jackdaw in peacock's feathers, a member of my personal ship of fools whose influence could not be anything but harmful. I had enough sense to realize that he who tries to teach and guide others creates around himself many hostile forces that, unless he is strong, can easily destroy him. After all, look what happened to Ouspensky. He had become a prisoner of the organization he himself had created. Only at the very end, when it was already too late, had he broken out of the cage in a final bid for freedom.

Moreover, though Ouspensky was dead, Madame was not. She was still lurking up there in the best bedroom and sending down messages by the Archangels. Madame Ouspensky was my real teacher. Everything I knew that was of practical value I had learned from her. Ouspensky worked in the realm of knowledge, Madame worked directly on one's being. She did this in ways that were drastic and often painful, but they were certainly effective.

A voice, the spirit of truth, my objective conscience, told me that the honest thing to do would be to expose my Missionary and his ambitions to Madame Ouspensky. I knew perfectly well what her reaction would be. She would laugh till she wept, call me various kinds of idiot. And because I was so unsure about the Missionary, I would probably laugh with her. I might be honest enough to admit that I was stuck in the Morbio Inferiore and had no idea how to get out.

But I no longer had contact with Madame. Brother and Sister Archangel guarded her door like Fasolt and Fafner guarding the Rhinegold. I could not bring myself to ask for an interview. The poison fermented within me. My Missionary schemed and plotted and gradually assembled around him a group of followers. All he wanted was to escape from the influence of his old teacher and give more time to running his own little show.

The break, when it did occur, was sudden and unexpected. In the restless state that prevailed among the various members of the crew of my ship of fools, any unpleasant incident would suffice to provoke a mutiny. A schizophrenic break now provided the catalyst. Such breaks cannot justly be blamed on anyone. They result from some sort of chemical malfunctioning to which certain people are prone, but I did not know this at the time. So the break, which involved a girl in whom I was interested, sufficed to set off a full-scale mutiny. Violent and critical protests resounded in my mind. The organization to which I had belonged for so many years was not so much a school of the fourth way as a

group of starry-eyed believers, brainwashed fools who allowed themselves to be dominated by a teacher who no
longer had direct contact with her pupils and who did not
know what was really happening. So it was perfectly possible for a pupil to sink into the morass of schizophrenia
without anyone even noticing that all was not well.

Looking back now, thirty years after the event, I see
clearly the perils inherent in the guru game. Mentally unstable people are so often attracted to teachers who, despite a
certain charisma, are usually totally ignorant of the first
principles of psychopathology. Fragile psyches are thus
subjected to stresses that, far from being salutory, are dangerous in the extreme. When such weaklings fall apart
under the strain, the resulting shit-storm breaks over the
head of the guru. Which is really what he or she deserves
for practicing psychotherapy without a license. There is an
old Persian saying: *May God kill him who himself does not
know but presumes to guide others to the doors of his kingdom.*

So . . . filled with righteous indignation and various
other brands of negative emotion, I finally left the group of
which I had been a part for so many years. I wanted out and
I was out. I noted the date in my diary. August 26, 1947.

For over eleven years every weekend and most of my
vacations had been spent either at Lyne Place or at Franklin
Farms. Now, suddenly, the link was severed. I was an outcast by my own decisions. I had, as we put it, "left the
Work." The sudden change added to my sense of inner desolation. The part of my being that was strongest and most
honest told me that I had acted like a coward. I had sneaked
out and written a nasty letter to Madame accusing her of
misusing her power. It would have been worthier of one
who was trying to follow the Warrior's Way if I had
brought the whole problem out into the open, demanded ex-
planations, made a regular pest of myself. The teacher had
surrounded herself with stooges who said nothing but Yes,

yes, yes. It was time for someone to get up and shout No,
no, no. If they threw me out for shouting No, that would be
their business. It would prove that the organization had
become so locked in a pattern of blind obedience and
teacher worship that no dissenting voice could be allowed.
But I had taken the weakling's way and slunk out secretly.

I spent a wretched Christmas. For all those years I had
always joined the group to celebrate the birth of Christ.
Now I was completely alone. My children were far away.
My wife was mad. The woman I had hoped to marry had
apparently rejected me. In my squalid little room in the
Bronx I sat like Scrooge in his lonely lodgings while the
ghost of Christmas Past paraded before my inward eye.

Oh, those ghosts! No wonder lonely people with nothing
left to look forward to have a tendency to commit suicide at
Christmas time. The echo of distant carols, the memory of
tinsel, colored lights, and the scent of Christmas trees, the
gay shouts of children and their happy laughter as they
unwrap their presents—all such remembered scenes haunt
the lonely ones and curdle into a poison that can be lethal.

Moreover I was paranoid. I feared some sort of spiritual
reprisal for having left the Work. I had noticed this sort of
paranoia in people I knew back in the thirties who, having
been ardent Communists, had become disillusioned and
left the Party. It was a reaction common to all those who
had belonged to very authoritarian organizations, from ex-
Communists to lapsed Catholics. As long as one remained
in the bosom of the Church, the Party, or the Group, one
was protected and cared for. But if one left, then those formerly protecting forces turned sinister and hostile. So great
was my paranoia that I hardly dared venture into down-
town New York for fear of meeting some member of the
group.

Then came Easter. In Ouspensky's group, dominated as it
was by the spirit of old Russia, Easter was a much holier occasion than Christmas. It was celebrated in style, with eggs
elaborately painted, with *pashka* and *kulich*, with the tradi-

tional greeting "Christ is risen." We had even learned the Easter music of the Greek Orthodox Church, singing in Church Slavonic or Greek the ancient hymn that expresses the whole mystery of death and rebirth.

> Christ is risen from the dead.
> He has conquered death with death.
> And given life to them that were in tombs.

I woke early on Easter morning. The Easter hymn was echoing somewhere in my mind, and with it an awareness of life renewed. Could it be that I was at last emerging from the Morbio Inferiore? In any case there was hope where there had previously been nothing but emptiness. Some voice was trying to speak in me, but I could not hear the message. It had to do with love, the sacred *karatas*. Opening my worn copy of the New Testament, I turned to the thirteenth chapter of the Epistle to the Corinthians.

> Though I speak with the tongues of men and of angels and have not love, I am become as sounding brass, or a tinkling cymbal.
> And though I have the gift of prophecy, and understand all mysteries and all knowledge; and although I have all faith so that I could remove mountains and have not love, I am nothing.

That was it! There was a flash of insight within me, a spiritual explosion. I remembered how Gerald Heard had dismissed Ouspensky and his work.

"He is certainly a strong character and *knows* a great deal. There is just one thing wrong with him. He seems to be totally lacking in compassion."

Surely that was what was wrong with us all. We lacked compassion. We lacked love. We had become an isolated, self-satisfied little group, prone to teacher worship, dominated by authority, cut off from the mainstream of life, guardians of a mystery we ourselves did not understand.

At once the resolution formed in me. I must then and there return to the group, make up for my cowardice and state clearly what I saw. I was called to do battle. Battle with what? First of all with my own cowardice. Second, with the sycophantic tendency of the group, its slavish dependence on the teacher, its lack of love—a lack that had allowed that poor girl to sink into madness without help, without anyone even noticing what was happening.

I took a train from New York to Mendham, New Jersey. At Franklin Farms I walked into the house, ready for anything. Almost at once I encountered Sister Archangel.

"What do *you* want?"

The words were thrown at me in the tone used by butlers in mansions to beggars in rags. No rejoicings over the return of the lost lamb, no Easter greeting, no kiss, no "Christ is risen." I was tempted to return Sister Archangel's scorn with some powerful denunciations of my own. But that was not the way it happened.

Suddenly my whole being was flooded with light. It was light so blinding that I was almost physically bowled over. In that harsh pitiless light every detail of my inner life was revealed. How could I have the impudence to reproach others for their lack of charity? I was totally lacking in charity myself! When had I clothed the naked, fed the starving, comforted the sick, visited the prisoners, consoled the dying? What right had I to talk of charity? In that sudden state of clarity I observed myself with total objectivity. The pettiness and meanness of my own inner life was revealed to me in the form of a decaying corpse, a maggot-ridden heap of putrefaction. It stank. At the same time there was born in me the realization that by some means, if I could only find it, I would be able to rise out of that rotting mess. That was the ultimate mystery of the Great Work.

I was still standing in front of Sister Archangel, whose glance of contempt was so intense that (to borrow a phrase from Gurdjieff) flies that encountered the radiations of her hate dropped dead. Without another word I turned away and walked out of the house. I looked up at the mild spring sky. My vision of my own putrefaction suddenly brought the words of the Pilgrim's Prayer into my mind.

Lord Jesus Christ, have mercy on me.

For more than a year I had tried repeating that prayer, hoping to bring it out of the head and into the heart. I had not succeeded. Now, suddenly, the prayer began repeating itself. It was no longer a string of words in my head but a living fountain playing in the heart. It was wordless, pure feeling. The thought crossed my mind: If I could only maintain that prayer, I would be one of the happiest men on earth, for nothing could harm me. At the same time I realized that the prayer was not repeating itself in my physical heart but in another body, whose existence I had known of in theory but which I had not been able to contact.

I walked down the drive past the decaying aviaries to look at the kitchen garden. There I was overtaken by Brother Archangel, who had been sent with some sort of message to deliver. I listened with only half an ear. He was talking about sentimentality. His voice seemed preachy and self-satisfied. I listened in silence to Brother Archangel. The prayer bubbled in my heart. It was pure feeling. It was light, a living fountain. Brother Archangel, sensing that he was not making much of an impression, wound up his sermon and left me. I walked toward the village of Mendham, proposing to buy myself a lunch at the Black Horse Inn.

Halfway there I was overtaken by Lornia, Madame Ouspensky's grandson. I had always liked Lornia. He was the "all-licensed Fool" at Franklin Farms, permitted by a doting grandmother to do anything he liked—an outrageous character, very Russian, quite impossible, but the possessor of certain insights that might have made him, had he lived, a rather unusual player of the great game. From him I received another message from Madame Ouspensky. "If you want to say how wrong you are and how sorry you are you may stay."

So that was it. Madame in the right. Always infallible! I did not feel particularly repentant, nor was I at all sure that I was wrong; but if my old teacher wanted apologies, let her have them.

"Tell her that I was wrong and that I'm sorry."

As if it mattered!

So instead of going to the Black Horse Inn I returned to the great house and had lunch with the disciples. Some regarded me with dislike, some with indifference, some with kindness. My old friend the doctor observed that I was getting fat. I probably was. Not getting enough exercise.

But the prayer continued to splash and bubble in my heart, and I cared very little about what the faithful thought of me. An extraordinary secret had been revealed to me, and my only concern was how to remember what I had learned. I had been shown mysteries of bhakti yoga. Normally I distrusted bhaktis. I regarded them as sentimental and often ridiculous. They were Starry-Eyed Believers who would swallow any old tale, worshippers of faith rather than reason, apt to become self-righteous and fanatical. My old friend Gerald Heard had been a typical bhakti, and the news that reached me from Trabuco in California convinced me that something had gone very wrong over there.

But the prayer of the heart was bhakti yoga pure and simple, and when it worked it produced the most astonishing results. But how could one persuade it to work? The transfer of the prayer from the head to the heart had taken place within me. But I myself had had nothing to do with it. I had not even been thinking of the prayer. It had just happened.

Could I now maintain it? This was the question that haunted me as I sat eating lunch among the True Believers. I realized that the Prayer of the Heart went far beyond the limits of sectarian religion. The same effect could be obtained if one repeated *La Ilah Illa Allah* or *Hare Krishna* or *Om Mani Padme Hum*. The words were unimportant. When the prayer entered the heart it became wordless anyway. It

produced a turning away from the personal self and a turning toward a source of light and joy. One underwent a species of resurrection.

Rebirth? Illumination? That was it. For a brief time I had
been illuminated. If I could learn to remain turned toward
that source of light, I could continue my Journey to the East
and escape from the Morbio Inferiore. I could learn the
mysteries of the Archives of the League. And I would need
no teacher. The light itself was the teacher.

24

HUNGERS
IN CONFLICT

Games and aims . . . What shall I play? How shall I play?
With whom shall I play? These questions bubbled in my
mind as the year 1948 unfolded. During that spring new elements had entered the game. Tessa of the Aroids, after
receding so far into the background of my life as to be almost forgotten, had suddenly reappeared. A letter informed
me that she had left Kew Gardens. She had taken a job on a
farm in Cornwall planting strawberries. It was wet, muddy,
backbreaking work planting strawberries. She was sick of
it. She was sick of England. She was migrating to Canada.

All the pieces in my personal game were suddenly rear-
ranged by this information. Two aspects of my totality
glared at each other across the board. There, on the one
hand, was the Domestic Oaf, a creature no different from a
million other domestic oafs whose idea of bliss is a mate, a
home, and some children. Opposing the Oaf was the Missionary, who now had a new exciting scenario, for the
working of fate had brought him into contact with Wym
Nyland, and Wym Nyland was the representative, in
America, of Gurdjieff himself.

Yes, after all those years of hearing about Gurdjieff there
was now the possibility that I might meet him. This was really extraordinary, as if some mythical figure, Hermes Tris-
megistus or Asculapius, were suddenly to put on flesh and
appear in real life. Only then, when I had a chance to meet

him, did I realize how much of a myth Gurdjieff had become for me.

Ouspensky had hinted that Gurdjieff was mad. He was represented to us as a great master who had lost his way and failed to fulfill his mission. Ouspensky always seemed to assume that he would outlive Gurdjieff, that after Gurdjieff's death he would publish *Fragments* and the great search would begin for the origins of Gurdjieff's knowledge. But fate had arranged things quite differently. Ouspensky was dead. Gurdjieff was alive. He had spent the war years in Paris and kept his work going in spite of the Nazi occupation. Gurdjieff was not one to run away and seek safety in America.

But who was Wym Nyland? It took me a while to understand his place in the scheme of things. That mania for secrecy that characterized all of Ouspensky's activities had left us younger members of his group completely in ignorance about the Work in America. We never knew that A. R. Orage, an Englishman who had been with Gurdjieff at the Prieuré, had had a large group in America, that several members of that group had worked with Gurdjieff himself. People I had worked with at Franklin Farms and been inclined to treat rather disdainfully as mere neophytes were actually far "older in the Work" than I was and had worked with the Master himself. Never once had they spoken of this or given me reason to suppose that they knew far more than I did. Presumably they were allowed to work with Ouspensky only on condition that they never mentioned Gurdjieff.

Oh, those paranoias! How silly and irrelevant they seem to me now, how unworthy of what we called the "inner circle of humanity," whose members supposedly are completely objective and therefore cannot misunderstand each other. As I look back on the Ouspensky-Gurdjieff squabble, it seems to me that there were nothing but misunderstandings. And later, after both Gurdjieff and Ouspensky were dead, the misunderstandings were perpetuated by their followers. Members of one group refused to have anything to do with members of another. Everyone seemed engaged in the silliest games of one-upmanship: "I am better than you" or "My authority is greater than yours." They resemble the Fathers of the Church endlessly squabbling over doctrinal details. Some inner circle of humanity!

Anyway, Wym and Ilonka Nyland were in touch with Gurdjieff and would have nothing to do with Ouspensky or with Madame Ouspensky. I found them a refreshing change. Wym Nyland was a genial Dutchman, a master builder, a chemist, a man of integrity. Ilonka was a dark Hungarian, an artist who painted covers for *The New Yorker* and designed wallpaper. They had two children, thirty cats, and an extraordinary house they had built themselves. That house, near Brewster, New York, was a miniature village, an organic growth that had multiplied by budding. As room after room was added, it had spread over the rocky hillside, enclosing a patio, where, on a vine-covered trellis, Concord grapes struggled to ripen under a glistening load of Japanese beetles. Ilonka was an excellent cook and there on the patio would serve meals to various guests, mostly members of the old Orage group who visited the place at weekends.

My last visit to Franklin Farms had convinced me that the place was dead, a school without a teacher that did not have enough honesty to bury itself. Now the home of Wym Nyland became for me a new center of the Work. The place offered a refreshing change from Franklin Farms with its paranoia and authoritarian atmosphere. The Nylands did not give themselves airs. They did not pretend to be inspired teachers whose word was law. They were friendly and encouraging. My ego, shrunken from endless putdowns by Madame Ouspensky, began to expand again.

It was at Wym Nyland's house that I first made acquaintance with Gurdjieff's writings. None of them had been published at the time. We read them from the manuscript. Here was something new indeed! *Beelzebub's Tales*, a *lego-*

minism with a quality all its own, impressed me far more than had any of the writings of Ouspensky. Here was evidence of the workings of an extraordinary mind. Though the style was complex, the subject matter obscure, the neologisms unpronounceable, the jokes dated, and many of the statements preposterous, the impression persisted that hidden in those tangled skeins of verbiage was a group of very significant ideas. The fact that the style was so difficult as to make *Finnegan's Wake* easy reading by comparison did not lessen my admiration for the work. Clearly the writer did not intend to make things easy for his readers. The book unfolded like an incredibly complex Rorschach test. What one saw depended on what one had in oneself.

Very different from *Beelzebub's Tales* was the second series of Gurdjieff's writings, *Meetings with Remarkable Men*. Written in a simpler style, with a great wealth of picturesque detail, the book had all the qualities of a spiritual thriller. Against a background of ancient cities, Egyptian pyramids, horrendous deserts, snow-capped mountains, and the enormous empty spaces of Central Asia, Gurdjieff and his companions, the "Seekers after Truth," proceeded from one adventure to another. These were not chattering intellectuals sitting around discussing metaphysical problems. They were Warriors of the spirit, willing to sacrifice comfort and risk their lives to discover secrets relating to the inner transformation of man. The story of their efforts made me feel ashamed of myself. How poor, how trivial my strivings had been compared with theirs.

Wym Nyland, impressed by my apparent enthusiasm, had voiced the opinion that I might be a second Orage. There was talk of my going to Paris to work with Gurdjieff. The Missionary was all in favor of such a move. He still thought in terms of sacrifice and supereffort, and a trip to Paris would involve both. I would have to give up my job, put off any idea I might have of marrying Tessa, of building a home, of having my children over from England. My Missionary considered the sacrifice worthwhile, imagining that

the effort involved would bring about a fusion of all those
conflicting elements I called myself. There would emerge
one big powerful I, which would have complete control
over my ship of fools and be able to keep that unstable vessel on a steady course.

But it was one thing to dream about superefforts, another
thing to make them. We are the playthings of our hungers.
When the chips are down, it is the most powerful hunger
that wins. My Missionary, with his dream of being a Man
with a Message, confronted my Domestic Oaf, who wanted
nothing more than physical comfort and sensual gratifica-
tion. The Oaf had had more than enough of both messages
and messengers. He wanted no more to do with high-
powered authoritarian gurus, or with suffering, sacrifice, and
supereffort. The Oaf wanted a girl to couple with, a house
to live in, home-cooked meals, and the company of his children. He wanted to marry Tessa. His hungers were plain
and simple: Eat, drink, and copulate, have your mate and
your children around you, grow your own food, be independent.

At that point in my life it was the Oaf who had the
power. All the Missionary had was imagination. So I did
marry Tessa and bought some land near the Nylands, just
over the state line in Connecticut. There I set to work to
build a house. I had never built a house before, did not
know a joist from a rafter, but was willing to learn. This
dream was an old one, embodied in the title of a book I
greatly enjoyed reading, *Five Acres and Independence.* It was
a very old dream and one shared by many other young
Americans. Most of those who have this dream discover
that there is a tremendous gap between the dream and the
reality. I was no exception. I struggled to build a house, to
grow food on five stony acres, to hold down a job in the
Bronx that involved three hours of commuting each way.
All this consumed most of my energy and left little over for
higher things.

My Missionary wrung his hands over this squandering of

energy and furiously accused the Oaf of selling our spiritual birthright for a mess of domestic pottage. As for the Oaf, he called the Missionary a hypocrite, a phony guru, a crow in peacock's feathers. "Look at you," said the Oaf, "how much longer will you keep up this pretense of being a follower of the Way? All you do is talk about it or dream about it. I'm just an honest peasant with no lofty pretensions. You are a fraud." Meanwhile the Pilgrim yearned for peace and quiet. In my Easter experiment I had discovered that it really was possible to transfer the prayer from the head to the heart. Through it, I began to understand the technique that the Sufis called *zikr* and certain Christian mystics called the "practice of the presence of God." It was a form of remembering, a method of relating to something bigger than the personal self. My pilgrim considered it unnecessary to seek any more teachers. The teacher-pupil relationship was full of pitfalls and often proved more harmful than useful. Why bother with teachers if one could, by the practice of interior prayer, maintain a constant awareness of one's creator, preserver, and destroyer?

But there were problems. It was true that for a short time that Easter the prayer had suddenly bubbled up in my heart. This, however, had resulted from the stress of an exceptional situation. By placing myself intentionally in a very difficult position I had suddenly been forced to *see*. That *seeing*, involving an emotional realization of all the contradictions in my inner world, had evoked a genuine cry of contrition, which had taken the form of a Christian prayer, "Lord Jesus Christ, have mercy on me." Under the ordinary conditions of life, however, I was powerless to evoke that emotion, could at best repeat the prayer mechanically, and most of the time forgot about it completely.

In the midst of all this my Scientist—who, as breadwinner, was a very important member of my traveling circus—remained aloof and went on with his experiments. His concern was with a central problem of biology: How does the organism as a whole exert control over a universe of 10^{13}

cells, and why, from time to time, do certain cells break away from the control to form those malignant lumps of tissue we call cancers? My Scientist could manage very well without gurus and without prayers. He just wanted to be left in peace to design the critical experiments that might help to solve this riddle.

By November of 1948 it became clear that Gurdjieff himself would be coming to America. The various components of my totality reacted in different ways. The Domestic Oaf wanted no contact with this disturbing person, whose reputation was very peculiar to say the least. The Pilgrim was distrustful. The Scientist was mildly intrigued. He regarded Gurdjieff not as a teacher but as a fellow scientist who used human beings in place of experimental animals. He had adopted this view after reading an obscure work of Gurdjieff's called *The Herald of the Coming Good*, in which Gurdjieff spoke of "these human guinea pigs allotted to me by Destiny for my experiments." The Missionary, of course, was full of eagerness to meet the Master, seeing in Gurdjieff a possible source of power. The Missionary had gathered his own modest "tail of donkey," namely a small group of followers to whom he played the teacher. He now wished to bring his little flock to the Master and maybe get something for himself in the process.

So the various elements in my totality pulled me this way and that; the force affirming struggled with the force denying. The upshot was that though the force affirming was certainly not strong enough to take me to Paris, it did suffice to take me to the Wellington Hotel on Sixth Avenue. It would, after all, be a shame not to meet the man and find out what he had to offer.

25

FAIR-WEATHER
SAILOR

Gurdjieff . . .

Even now, nearly thirty years after his death, the name
has for me a certain magic. He was, without doubt, the
most extraordinary human being I have ever met. There he
sat on the sofa in the hotel room, a red fez slightly askew on
his totally bald head, and on his lap a lap organ from which
he now and then squeezed a few notes. Immediately I felt,
as Ouspensky had done years earlier on first meeting Gurdjieff in Moscow, that this was a man in disguise, a king in
exile, far from the place of his arising both in space and in
time. Gurdjieff, like his own creation Mr. Beelzebub,
seemed not only a being from a different planet but also
from a different solar system. He had been around for centuries, observing the strange behavior of the human inhabitants of the planet Earth, who—through no fault of their
own, but due to the lack of foresight on the part of certain
cosmic individuals—had been afflicted with that accursed
organ Kundabuffer, the properties of which continued to
distort the workings of their psyches. They were poor creatures, more to be pitied than blamed. He had watched their
antics over the centuries, seen the Pyramids raised, heard
the chariots in the streets of Babylon, seen the armies of
"the arch vainglorious Greek" pour into Asia, seen the
hordes of Genghis Khan threatening Europe. Above all he
had seen that in all those many centuries nothing
changed—that just as the inhabitants of Babylon had be-

haved "in a manner unbecoming to three centered beings," so did the modern inhabitants of Paris, of London, of New York.

We sat at his feet, a motley bunch, for on that first day after his arrival the floodgates had not opened and the mob scene had not begun. So there were relatively few of us in the room: my own "tail of donkey," the Nylands, some other member of the old Orage group, various members of the group from Paris, that was all. From time to time Gurdjieff took from a bag by his side a lichee nut, a chocolate, a candy of some sort. It was near Christmas time. With his protuberant belly and his white moustache he had a certain resemblance to Santa Claus. He tossed the goodies to the people sitting at his feet as if feeding the animals at a zoo. All the while those strangely observant eyes traveled from face to face as if looking for something. His look was strange, sad, old, utterly objective. What was he seeking?

After supper and numerous toasts to idiots—round idiots, square idiots, zigzag idiots, hopeless idiots, all drunk in Armagnac—he sat back again on the sofa, declaring it was "necessary settle tapeworm," took up his lap organ and looked at us. The look was intense, hypnotic. I could see that he had once been a master hypnotist, though he now intentionally abstained from using his powers.

"This music I play you now come from monastery where Jesus Christ spent from eighteenth to thirtieth year."

A strange melody flowed into the room. It produced a quite extraordinary effect, as if I were listening to an echo of a ceremony from the remote past. Was there such a monastery? Where had that mysterious teacher Jesus of Nazareth obtained his knowledge and power? Not from the Pharisees or Sadducees. He lambasted them both right heartily as hypocrites, blind leaders of the blind. That left the Essenes. Jesus never criticized the Essenes. Was he one himself? Had there been an Essene monastery perhaps in Egypt, perhaps on the shores of the Dead Sea, in which the Galilean initiate had gained his power? In a chapter in *Meetings with Re-*

markable Men Gurdjieff stated that Bogachevsky (or Father Evlissi as he later became) was assistant to the abbot of the chief monastery of the Essene Brotherhood, situated not far from the shores of the Dead Sea.

Were there still Essenes in Gurdjieff's time? I had always assumed that that cult, so admired by Josephus, had vanished from the face of the earth after the occupation of Judea by the Romans. But why should they have vanished from the face of the earth? They were quiet, secretive, unobtrusive people, bound by oath to hold all things in common and to give to any member of their sect whatever he needed. They kept their beliefs secret, accepted neophytes only after a three-year period of probation. Though some lived in monasteries in the desert, others dwelt in cities. Indeed they were scattered far and wide throughout the Roman Empire, and were doubtless very numerous in Alexandria, where there was a large Jewish community.

Was Gurdjieff himself an Essene? The thought crossed my mind as the strange music evoked all sorts of peculiar impressions. But if he was an Essene, he was certainly a very odd one. He really did not fit in that pigeonhole. He didn't fit in any pigeonhole. He was unclassifiable.

In a rented studio in Carnegie Hall we thumped and bumped through those various exercises that were Gurdjieff's specialty. Since the old days at the Prieuré he had devised a whole set of new movements. They were taught by a fervent young Frenchman with the nervous intensity of one whose inner fire is too hot for a frail body and who is destined to die young. The new movements were jagged, staccato, even militaristic. They lacked the depth of the old ones I knew so well. I disliked them immediately and intensely. Gurdjieff must have sensed my dislike. He attended one of the classes, banished me from the front row to the rear. He was irate and eyed the whole class balefully.

"You move like worms in shit!"

He grabbed a chair. Holding it to maintain his balance, he demonstrated certain leg movements. He was no longer the genial Santa Claus who had dispensed goodies on the occasion of our first meeting. With his bald head, his flourishing moustache, and his fiercely commanding presence, he reminded me of a Prussian colonel, a von something or other, I had met at the house of my uncle Friedrich von der Ropp when I had spent a year there during the 1920s.

The class livened up. In fact we made such a racket that a worried functionary appeared at the door imploring us to be quieter. We were ruining a concert that was being given in the main hall.

It was odd. That night I walked back with Gurdjieff along Sixth Avenue to the hotel. He who was usually surrounded by people had for some reason been left alone. He was a very unusual figure, wearing an astrakhan hat that gave him the appearance of a Cossack. I walked on one side of him, Tessa on the other. The thought occurred to me that that would be the right moment to ask the key question. But what was the key question? I could not remember it. We walked in silence all the way to the hotel.

Later the floodgates opened, and it became increasingly difficult to get anywhere near Gurdjieff. Madame Ouspensky had finally given her disciples permission to meet Gurdjieff. They flocked to do so. Brother Archangel, as usual, put himself in the limelight and took over the reading of the Beelzebub book. Bennett reappeared, the anathematized Bennett to whom we had been forbidden even to speak. The elaborate system of prohibitions that Ouspensky had so carefully constructed crumbled totally. In a rather mocking spirit I turned to one of the Ouspenskyites and remarked that he didn't have much loyalty to his old teacher. The Ouspenskyite regarded me with contempt.

"You don't have loyalty to anyone," said he.

Touché. I could not deny it. I was interested in learning the truth, not in loyalties. That evening at supper I found myself seated at Gurdjieff's table right next to Sister Archangel. We were quite close to Gurdjieff, who was stirring up a salad, adding various ingredients from a collection of bottles. All sorts of unspoken signals crackled between me and Sister Archangel. I felt sure that she loathed and despised me, but I did not reciprocate. Really I owed her a debt. She had been responsible, without intending to do so, for bringing me into a very unusual state. Gurdjieff raised his eyes from the salad and looked at me. It was a very odd look. It seemed to tell me something. But I could not really understand its significance. He said nothing and returned to his salad making.

Later we drank toasts to the two and twenty categories of idiots. Every idiot represented a certain type, or a certain level on the Way. The toastmaster proclaimed the toasts loudly and distinctly. One in particular stuck in my mind:

To all hopeless idiots, that is to say, to all those who are candidates for honorable deaths and to all those who are candidates to perish like dogs.

I asked myself, What kind of idiot am I?

Hopeless idiot?

Quite possibly. The argument between my Missionary and all the other parts of my totality started again and grew furious. Everyone except the Missionary wanted out. They loathed the whole atmosphere that Gurdjieff created about him. Why did this king in exile choose to hold court in a New York hotel, squeezing his admirers into one small room "like herrings in barrel," stuffing them with more food than they could digest? Why did he seem to place so much reliance in those hoary old poisons alcohol and tobacco? The air in the room was almost unbreathable. And why did this master surround himself with such a mob of sycophants, scrambling over each other to get his attention? Guinea pigs? Yes. He experiments. He is interested in types. He comes, so to speak, from a different solar system, is "a spy of God," has to report back to the source. But do I want to be a guinea pig in his experiment? I had my fill of guinea pigs when I worked on the Brucella problem during the war. Guinea pigs are stupid creatures. None of mine ever survived the experiment.

I looked at Gurdjieff. He seemed old and tired and sad.

He was obviously not well. I found myself appealing to him to live more healthily, speaking to him in my mind, as if such a silent petition could make any impression.

"Master, this isn't the proper setting for your teaching. What did they call your group in the days of the Prieuré? The Forest Philosophers? Surely that's more like it. Move your court back to the Forest of Fontainebleau. We would have contact with the forces that give us life—the sun, the soil, the biosphere. Let's leave this dreary hotel and go where there's some fresh air. The forest is a fine place for a king in exile. How many of these starry-eyed dopes who flock around you will stay when there's nothing but roots and berries for breakfast and a cup of cold spring water to wash it down with? It would be better for you too. Even my unpracticed eye can see that your body is sick. You smoke too much and don't get enough fresh air and exercise."

Vain fantasy! It was not merely my dislike for alcohol, tobacco smoke, and crowding that kept me from working with Gurdjieff. I had neither the strength nor the courage that was needed to follow that particular branch of the War-rior's Way. Nor was I at all sure that even if I did violate all the laws of my essence and force myself to work under those very unnatural conditions, the results would be worth the sacrifice. It is dangerous to violate the laws of one's being. It is necessary to recognize one's limitations. My feelings toward Gurdjieff formulated themselves in nautical terms. *If you're only a fair-weather sailor, you'd best not put to sea in a gale-force wind.*

Was I only a fair-weather sailor? All the evidence seemed to point to such a conclusion. If one wanted to travel with Gurdjieff, one had to be prepared to put up with storms. He was not so much a gale-force wind as a self-perpetuating hurricane. I thought of that young Frenchman who had taught us the movements. He had spent part of the war in a concentration camp. His body was permanently damaged. But he had the soul of a Warrior, never spared himself, put up with all the stresses inevitably encountered by those who worked with Gurdjieff. And he did indeed die a few years later, worn out by his own efforts. I admired him. Compared with him I felt like a coward. And yet . . . And yet . . .

Does one have to kill oneself to follow the Warrior's Way?

Something is not quite right here. To follow the Way one must learn to prolong one's life, not shorten it. We have all too little time even at best and need every day we can get.

Something here is not quite right.

This was my personal conclusion. Shortly after Christmas I contracted a form of gastric influenza. The attack was so violent that I thought I was dying. It drained me of all my remaining energy and took from me any appetite I might have felt for working with Gurdjieff. Ten months later Gurdjieff was dead, and the chance of working with him was gone forever. The Gurdjieffians went their own ways, doing what they could to keep his work alive. I gradually lost touch with them. But still the feeling persisted: Something here is not quite right.

Nearly thirty more years had to elapse before I realized what that something was.

26

KING
IN EXILE

On the morning of October 31, 1949, I found myself on the New York subway headed for the Greek Orthodox Cathedral on East Seventy-fourth Street. I planned to attend a memorial service for George Ivanovich Gurdjieff, who had died two days earlier. Ordinarily I shun memorial services, seeing in them one more example of the priestly hocus-pocus that has confused mankind for centuries. But the thought had occurred to me that in the quiet of the cathedral I might be able to focus my awareness on a being whose teachings had greatly influenced my life—who was, moreover, a master player of the great game, and so far removed from the human average as to belong almost to a different species.

The life of Gurdjieff represented a special aspect of the Warrior's Way. More than any other man I have met, he lived by self-imposed rules and pursued intentional aims. In the fullest sense of the word he was inner-directed and lived strategically, knowing what he was doing and why he was doing it. He cared nothing for the artificial laws that confine weaker people to narrow patterns of behavior. He made his own laws and played the game by his own rules. Because these laws and rules were very different from those that ordinarily govern human behavior he seemed like an enigma to some and like a madman to others.

My impression that Gurdjieff was a king in exile, that he had been displaced not only in space but also in time, needs some qualification. He was no ordinary king. In him were combined no less than four sacred archetypes, all of them rare and all of them powerful. These four archetypes are represented in the Book of Fate by the signs of the Magus (Juggler), Hierophant, Emperor, and Hanged Man. The odds are high against a human being having even one of these archetypes strongly developed in his essence. The odds are astronomical against anyone having all four. Such *overendowment* puts the individual under fearful stresses and exposes him to dangers and temptations that the average human being cannot even imagine.

Gurdjieff made his appearance on that part of our planet's surface where the continent Europe meets the continent Asia. It is a stormy area. Between the Black Sea and the Caspian Sea is a region of rugged mountains, thrown up by the grinding collisions of great land masses, snow covered, jagged, and harsh. Mount Ararat is there, and other peaks towering to 15,000 feet. Out of this region, from a watershed 7,000 feet above sea level, flow two ancient rivers, the Tigris and the Euphrates, that cradled civilization between them and enclosed the original Garden of Eden.

These rugged mountains, themselves the product of geological collisions, were also the scene of endless human struggles. In that area the hordes of Asia met the peoples of Europe, and the whole region resounded with the clash of armies—Romans and Persians, Armenians, Tartars, Mongols, and Turks all met there in battle at one time or another. Genghis Khan was there, and so was Tamerlane, who had so much trouble breaking through the region that he had to bring up a second army. Right into the nineteenth century this carnage continued as the Russian Empire clashed with the Turkish Empire. In October of 1877 the town of Kars, where Gurdjieff spent much of his youth, was taken by the Russians and almost totally destroyed along with most of its population.

Though the region was physically poor, it was spiritually rich, pervaded by relics of all sorts of ancient wisdom.

Traces of Babylonian, Zoroastrian, and Mithraic mysteries could still be found there. The Aisors (descendants of the Assyrians) and the Yezidis still retained some of their old beliefs. There were the traditions of the Armenian Church as well as those of Greek and Russian Orthodox Christianity. In addition there was a strong element of Islamic mysticism brought there by the Turks. There were many dervish communities in that part of the world.

Gurdjieff was exposed at a very early age to influences coming from the very remote past. His father, a Greek, was one of the last of the *ashokhs*. Those *ashokhs*, Gurdjieff informs us (in the second chapter of *Meetings with Remarkable Men*), were preservers of a very ancient tradition. Though often illiterate, they had such powers of mind and memory that they could sing or recite lengthy narratives and poems and improvise various melodies, choosing appropriate rhymes and changing the rhythm of their verses with astounding facility. Among the stories that Gurdjieff's father recited was the legend of Gilgamesh, in the twenty-first song of which was related the story of the great flood that destroyed the land of Shuruppak. He explained to his son that the legend came from the Sumerians, a people more ancient than the Babylonians, and that from that legend came the story of the Flood in the Hebrew Bible. Gurdjieff remembered the words of the twenty-first song. Years later he came across a translation of the legend of Gilgamesh. It had been found and deciphered from clay tablets by modern scholars. The words were almost identical to those that he had heard from his father. The legend had been handed down by the *ashokhs* for thousands of years and had reached our day almost unchanged!

It was his contact with these ancient traditions that gave to Gurdjieff his quality of great age. He knew things that most people had forgotten, knew them not in the purely intellectual manner of scholars who have laboriously ferreted out the meaning of dusty clay tablets, but directly, as if he had been present when the events took place. It seemed as if he had really known Babylon in the days of its greatness, and watched the emergence of that doctrine he called Babylonian dualism, which exerted so baneful an influence on the thinking of Western man. Much of that knowledge he obtained from his father and other *ashokhs*, for he often was taken to gatherings of these bards in which they competed, improvising and singing, before a great throng of people.

A second influence that moulded the character of the young Gurdjieff was exerted by his grandmother. When dying at the age of a hundred and some years she placed her hand on his head and, as he tells us in the first chapter of *All and Everything*, pronounced in a whisper, but very distinctly, the following words:

"Eldest of my grandsons! Listen and always remember my strict injunction to you: In life never do as others do."

This advice must have made a deep impression on the child, for he acted upon it at once. Instead of standing solemnly by the grave of his dear grandmother, over whose mortal remains the usual requiem service was being performed, he started to skip round the grave as if dancing and sang:

> Let her with the saints repose,
> Now that she's turned up her toes,
> Oi! Oi! Oi!

This must be one of the most original tributes ever offered by a loving grandson to his newly deceased grandmother!

And so it went. Never, in the course of a fairly long life, did this truly extraordinary man forget the advice of his esteemed grandmother. He who was a master player of the most difficult of all the life games played it in such an original fashion that even those who considered themselves experts on the subject could not classify him. Was he black magician, white magician, "rascal guru," avatar, saint, madman, prophet—or just, as he put it himself, a master of dancing? Vain speculations! He resists all attempts of the spiritual taxonomists to label him. He was a mystery at the start and he remained one to the end. The advice of his dying grandmother must surely have become embodied in his essence: "In life never do as others do."

One other feature of Gurdjieff's upbringing should be mentioned. He was trained by his father from a very early age not to be afraid of physical discomfort. His father always forced him to get up early in the morning, "when a child's sleep is particularly sweet," and go to the fountain and splash himself all over with cold spring water and run about naked till dry. In later years Gurdjieff thanked him for this harsh treatment, declaring that had he not been raised in this way, he could never have overcome the hardships he encountered during his travels.

He needed to be tough and he was tough. Three times during his travels he was wounded, almost mortally, by a stray bullet. Twice he was practically destroyed in automobile accidents. Several times he "played host," as he put it, to such "delicacies" as "Armenian dysentery," "Ashkhabadian bedinka," "Bokharian malaria," "Tibetan hydropsy." Any one of various accidents that befell him would have sufficed to end the career of a weaker man. The fact that he lived a fairly long life (1872–1949) indicates the power he possessed over his own organism. His bashed and battered body was held together by his will long after it should, by all the rules of medicine, have disintegrated.

It is the chief characteristic of an impeccable warrior that he lives strategically, never does things by halves, prepares meticulously in advance, and enters the battle knowing what risks he is taking. These patterns of behavior were characteristic of Gurdjieff. He planned, he prepared, and when the time came, he acted. There were always risks involved in the journeys he made, for they often led into forbidden places. He took all possible steps to minimize those risks. When he decided that to find a certain esoteric brotherhood he had to penetrate forbidden Kafiristan, he and his friend Professor Skridlov spent a year in the ruins of Old Merv learning various Persian chants and instructive sayings. They planned to enter an area in which all foreigners were treated with suspicion and apt either to be enslaved or disposed of in various quite unpleasant ways. Members of the wild tribes of the area, however, had an inborn respect for those who devoted themselves to the service of God. So Gurdjieff planned to pass himself off as a direct descendant of Mohammed (a Seid) and the professor disguised himself as a venerable Persian dervish. The slightest errors in playing these roles could have had disastrous results for them both.

Such expeditions—and Gurdjieff made many of them—called for a special combination of skill and daring. They created conditions so challenging that only people of exceptional ability could survive. In the period during which Gurdjieff made his search for hidden knowledge (about 1885 to 1910), there were regions both in Central Asia and in the Middle East in which an ancient way of life persisted. This old way of life defined the duty of man in terms of growth of being rather than growth of possessions. Hidden among the external practices of various religions were more or less secret traditions relating to the transformation of man. To bring together these traditions and unite them into a single system was the self-appointed task of the Seekers after Truth, a group to which Gurdjieff belonged, several members of which are described in *Meetings with Remarkable Men*.

Many attempts have been made to discover the sources from which Gurdjieff collected his knowledge. It appears that some of it came from the Sarmoun Brotherhood, whose monastery, deep in Kafiristan, he visited with Professor Skridlov. Some of it came from Tibet, some from the Naqshbandi Order of dervishes, whose center of activity is in Bokhara. Other elements seemed to be derived from the Pythagoreans and from Rosicrucians of the sixteenth century such as Robert Fludd. We have reason also to believe that he found certain important material in Ethiopia.

I myself was quite interested at one time in such speculations and hoped that Ouspensky's Historico-Psychological Society would organize trips to various distant places in search of hidden knowledge. I now realize that such trips would have been a waste of time and money. The important question was not where Gurdjieff got his knowledge but how that knowledge could be transformed into understanding. For knowledge and understanding are quite different. This was one of the key ideas that Gurdjieff and Professor Skridlov learned during their stay at the monastery in Kafiristan. Knowledge can indeed be transmitted without much difficulty, provided two people speak the same language. But understanding depends on a person's level of being, on his past experience, on his type—on a whole host of factors not easily described. This makes it impossible for one person to give understanding to another. And knowledge without understanding is quite useless, a mere rhapsody of words.

In the year 1913 Gurdjieff evidently considered that the time had come to hand on the system of ideas he had collected. These ideas related to the transformation of man from a slave at the mercy of external circumstances to an autonomous inner-directed being who understood and consciously performed his role in the scheme of things. But merely to explain the ideas would not produce results. The process of psychotransformism demanded the participation of all the five functions of man: instinctive, moving, emotional, intellectual, sexual. Unless all of them were involved, development would be lopsided.

In order to avoid such lopsided development Gurdjieff created in Russia the Institute for the Harmonious Development of Man in which students could work on all the aspects of their being. Gurdjieff was a very astute businessman and capable of turning his hand to almost anything. By the year 1913 he had amassed a fortune of a million rubles and two very valuable collections, one of rare carpets and the other of Chinese cloisonné. This wealth enabled him to create the Institute. It had barely been founded, however, before that outbreak of mass psychosis now known as World War I made continuation of the Work in Russia impossible. Gurdjieff moved his group to the Caucasus. There, in the midst of such chaos as can hardly be imagined (for the Bolsheviks, the Cossacks, and the White Army were all at each other's throats), he organized, of all things, a scientific expedition into the Caucasus Mountains to investigate certain dolmens which existed in those parts.

Anyone who doubts that Gurdjieff's powers were truly extraordinary should read the account he has given of that expedition (it will be found in the last chapter of *Meetings with Remarkable Men*). At a time when, owing to the constant movement of troops, it was almost unthinkable even for one man without luggage to travel by train, he managed to procure from the Bolshevik government two railway wagons. Nor was this his most remarkable feat. He had in his possession a permit to carry a revolver. On one side it was signed by General Heyman of the White Army and on the other side by Roukhadze of the Bolsheviks. His ability to move among (as he put it) "infuriated beasts of people, ready to tear each other apart for the slightest booty" was due to a capacity to play upon the slightest changes in the weaknesses of people caught up in that kind of mass psychosis. Moreover, although the people with whom he had to deal were in the grip of a psychic state in which the last grain of reasonableness vanishes, the instinct inherent in all human beings for distinguishing good from evil in the objective sense was not completely lacking. Guided by this instinct, they did what they could to further Gurdjieff's aims.

As the roadbed of the railroad had been destroyed beyond Maikop, Gurdjieff's party was forced to proceed on foot into the uninhabited territory beyond Kumichki. For two months the party struggled through the wilds of the Caucasus, suffering from hunger and exposure in a region of hot days and freezing nights. It was, as Gurdjieff put it, a "Way of Golgotha" and served to separate the strong from the weak. From Sochi on the Black Sea the party proceeded

to Tiflis and from Tiflis to Constantinople. There Gurdjieff
began again to construct his Institute, but because the activities of the Young Turks began to "have a particular smell,"
he again felt compelled to move, settling finally in the Chateau du Prieuré near Fontainebleau in France.

From this point on the development of the Institute might
have gone fairly smoothly, had not Gurdjieff, on his way
back to Fontainebleau from Paris, driven his car into a tree
at a speed of 90 kilometers an hour—from which prome-
nade, he says, he emerged looking like a picture entitled "A
Bit of Live Meat in a Clean Bed."

After the smash Gurdjieff changed his tactics if not his
strategy. Determined to remove from his sight all those
who, in one way or another, made his life too comfortable,
he gradually drove away from him all his oldest pupils and
closed the Institute. His time was occupied in writing, and
he produced the three books that have now been published
(*All and Everything, Meetings with Remarkable Men* and *Life
Is Real Only Then, When "I am"*).

The production of these books cost Gurdjieff a fantastic
amount of effort. A great deal of the material he wrote he
later destroyed. The so-called "third series" suffered particularly from Gurdjieff's impulse to destroy everything he
found unsatisfactory. The material that has been published
is little more than a fragment, though a very informative
fragment for those who know how to read it. But the books
by themselves could hardly provide a substitute for the balanced program of work that had been offered by the Institute for the Harmonious Development of Man. So once
again, in the mid thirties, Gurdjieff tried to create the Institute.

The gods were not with him. No matter how hard he
tried to recreate the Institute, something always happened
to frustrate his plans. In 1935 Senator Bronson Cutting became greatly interested in Gurdjieff's ideas and was prepared to raise the money to restart the Institute, but the
senator died in a plane crash only a few days later. In the
same year Gurdjieff applied to the Russian Embassy for per-

mission to return to Russia and teach his system there. Needless to say the rulers of Soviet Russia had little use for one who taught methods whereby man may escape his inner slavery. "He may return to the Soviet Union," came the message, "only if he will accept work where he is assigned, but he must not teach anything."

Finally, after World War II, when communications were reopened and members of his former groups in England and America were flocking to Gurdjieff's apartment in Paris eager to work with him again, a very real possibility existed of recreating the Institute. Conditions seemed favorable. There was a lull in the series of storms that had convulsed humanity during the first half of the twentieth century. Many people were tired of the materialistic life games and ready to learn from a master how to attain real freedom. Gurdjieff had, moreover, a group of assistants who had worked for a long enough time with him to understand the methods and hand them on to others. So in 1949 the outlook for recreating the Institute was very promising. But it did not happen. Gurdjieff was running out of time. As a developed man he presumably knew the secret of what in some circles is called "the art and science of balancing the yin and the yang." This, as every good Taoist knows, enables the sage to enjoy his full permitted life span—which, at the present stage of human development, is about one hundred years. Gurdjieff probably expected to live far longer than this.

He had some very peculiar ideas about life spans. Quoting, in the third series of his writings, from what he calls "a very ancient manuscript," he states that in people who have consciously perfected themselves to the so-called "all centers awake state," certain factors continue to form until the age of three hundred years in man and until the age of two hundred in woman. Such life spans are, as far as we know, quite impossible. But a hundred years is well within the reach of anyone who knows the methods of maintaining inner balance.

So Gurdjieff, in the year 1949, should have had at least

twenty more years to live, years that would have been relatively free of those large-scale upheavals and disasters that
had frustrated all his earlier plans. He should, by rights,
have died in the year 1972. But either he had forgotten the
science of balancing the yin and the yang or his body had
been so damaged by accidents and illness that maintenance
of inner balance was impossible. He himself expected to
live the full permitted span. One of his pupils who rashly
prefaced his remarks with the statement "When you die,
Mr. Gurdjieff . . ." was furiously interrupted. "I am Gurdjieff. I *not* will die!" But Azrael, the Angel of Death, was not
listening. He took Gurdjieff's soul a short while later, on
October 29, 1949.

What lessons did I learn from G. Gurdjieff? I learned that
the Short Path, the most difficult aspect of the Warrior's
Way, demands of all those who would tread it both conscious effort and intentional suffering. Intentional suffering
is very different from the sort of suffering a person experiences as a result of the casual workings of fate. Intentional
suffering involves opposing the mechanical tendencies of
one's being. It involves the creation of certain reminding
factors that will help the follower of the Way not to fall
asleep in the midst of the hypnotizing influences of ordinary life. What these reminding factors are will depend on
the nature of the individual.

Gurdjieff created such a reminding source by intentionally refusing to use that exceptional power based upon
strength in the field of "hanbledzoin," which most people
would call the power of telepathy and hypnotism. In addition to his refusal to use these powers, he imposed on himself the task of discovering in any new or old acquaintance
whatever his social standing, his "most sensitive corn," and
of pressing it rather hard. This procedure undoubtedly provided Gurdjieff with plenty of opportunities to endure voluntarily other people's negative emotions. It also strengthened a capacity, intentionally developed in him in his early
youth, which consisted in his being able not to identify
with the external manifestations of others.

In his book *Gurdjieff: A very great enigma*, J. G. Bennett speculates that Gurdjieff followed what is known among the Sufis as the way of *malamat*, or way of blame. Those who follow this way deliberately present themselves to the world in bad light and act in such a way that their conduct attracts blame rather than praise. The method is or at least was used by those who, on account of their special powers, were likely to attract to themselves swarms of starry-eyed believers. This special spiritual power was described by Gurdjieff in *The Herald of the Coming Good* as *Hvareno*. In the old Zoroastrian teaching this word referred to the mark of kingship. One who had this power had the royal touch, was a natural king, and was recognized as such by the people. It is significant that in the Gospels we read that the Jews wished to take Jesus by force and make him king but that he withdrew and hid himself. Jesus evidently had plenty of *Hvareno*.

Gurdjieff had it too. It gave him the quality of a king in exile. His kingdom was neither in our time or our place, but he could, had he wished to, have used his *Hvareno* to draw great numbers of people to him. He could have had a following of thousands.

He refused to use his power for this purpose, preferred, by following the way of blame, to set all sorts of stories going which were not at all to his credit. This certainly involved much intentional suffering, but it also gave him a measure of inner freedom inconceivable to those whose behavior is governed by a love of praise and fear of blame. I was surprised, when I myself experimented with the way of blame, to discover how much I depended on approval by other people. To place myself intentionally in a situation where I looked foolish or contemptible was exceedingly difficult. It was also very profitable. It enabled me to observe both the mechanicalness of others and the extent to which my own ego depended on praise and approval. Following the way of blame is one of the best ways I know of separating from the ego.

Gurdjieff was, for me, the last link with a world that has

vanished, a world of mysteries and secret powers. In that world the sacred knowledge was protected, and those who wished to find it had to exert themselves. It was a world, moreover, that preserved living links with the past, in which the *ashokhs* could entertain the people with recitation of the epic of Gilgamesh, a world in which the omnipresent boob tube had not spread over everything a blanket of universal inanity. It was a world in which a Magus could develop his power and use that power.

Was Gurdjieff the last Magus? In moments of pessimism I think perhaps that he was. I visualize our enormously overgrown man-swarm as a degenerate product of the biosphere, consisting of more or less identical dolls stamped by a machine from a sheet of plastic. A man-swarm of four billion plastic dolls . . . Can such cheap, mass-produced entities do any more than follow the way of the slave, wasting their time on trivia, greedily guzzling the last of earth's remaining resources, playing the lowest of the low games, Hog in the Trough?

But then again I reflect that we are all products of the Old One and that we cannot hope to understand its workings. The resources of the Old One, who is the mind and soul of the biosphere, though not unlimited, are nonetheless very great. It has been said that the human organism has power to draw from the general cosmic alembic energy-substances of various potencies. The soggy man-mass uses a heavy fuel, comparable to crude oil. A more vital minority uses a slightly purer fuel comparable to kerosene. A still smaller group uses fuel still more potent, like gasoline of various octane levels. Finally there is a minute group of exceptional individuals that uses a fuel so powerful it can only be compared to dynamite.

These rare individuals can exert very powerful effects on their fellow men. Depending on whether they use their power creatively or destructively, they can be for their fellows either a blessing or a curse. Just as they are dangerous to their fellows, so they are dangerous to themselves. Because they use such powerful fuel, they are liable to suffer from explosions in the fuel tank.

Was Gurdjieff the victim of such an explosion? There were some who thought he was, who maintained that the explosion had damaged his machine, distorting his activities, causing him to attribute to himself the power of a group of ideas that were, in fact, the common property of all initiates who had reached a certain level. Such critics objected to Gurdjieff's repeated use of the phase "followers of my ideas," insisting that esoteric ideas cannot be anyone's personal property, that they belong rather to that body of hidden knowledge that Hesse referred to as the *Archives of the League*.

I do not pretend to know whether such criticisms are justified. I could not work with Gurdjieff myself. First I did not understand his method of teaching. Second I did not have enough personal power to take what he had to offer. I recognized my limitations and this awareness prompted me to stay out of his way. For the intelligent and the strong he could provide the inspiration of a lifetime. But for the stupid and the weak he could be dangerous, even deadly. You have to be a pretty strong player to be able to play games with such a master.

27

TAKE FATE
BY THE THROAT

My Domestic Oaf had won a victory of a sort, and my Missionary had suffered a corresponding defeat. There could be no hiding from the fact that a challenge had been offered and declined. I was no longer a follower of the Warrior's Way. I had accepted the blessings of domesticity as a worthwhile substitute for the struggle and sacrifice involved in following the Way. I felt entitled to some peace and quiet and the elementary joys of raising a family.

Tessa wanted a baby. She was full of maternal impulses and demanded biological fulfilment. My Oaf was quite willing to concede to her demands. He had the soul of a peasant, and peasants see children as riches. Besides, I could hardly expect Tessa to stay with me if I denied her the experience of motherhood. She would leave me and seek a more cooperative mate. She would be right:

> From fairest creatures we demand increase,
> That thereby beauty's rose might never die.

My Missionary, who still had vague dreams of becoming the Man with the Message, groaned at the prospect of more babies. Had I not already given enough hostages to fortune and paid a high enough price for so doing? "Won't you ever learn? Look what happened before." But the Domestic Oaf dismissed the Missionary as a gloomy spoilsport and went ahead anyway. Why should I assume that history would repeat itself? I would give Tessa the child she needed for biological completion. Instead of a dyad we would become a triad. It was natural, after all.

Certainly it was natural, but I had failed to take into account the fact that nature has maleficent aspects. Tessa's pregnancy was terrible. She and her fetus seemed poisonous to each other. She kept vomiting and became very thin. The birth was difficult also. For twenty minutes the baby failed to breathe, twenty fatal minutes during which brain cells vital to the child's functioning were irreparably damaged.

So we had a brain-damaged child on our hands. The diagnosis of cerebral palsy was confirmed by a specialist. The baby screamed all the time. The specialist seemed to take it as a personal affront and announced roughly and brusquely that the child was badly brain injured and should be put in a home. Tessa was in a state of shock. I was furious. Really there are some members of the medical profession who should be barred from practice, not because they don't know medicine but because they don't seem to know anything about human beings.

We were, like all parents of cerebral palsied children, faced with a horribly difficult decision. What should we do? CP's at times developed quite extraordinary powers. By careful training they could learn to use parts of their body that were unaffected by the brain damage. They could use their feet instead of their hands. They could even learn to paint pictures holding the brush between their teeth. How could one tell the extent of the damage if one did not attempt to educate the child? Put her in a home and forget about her? It was easy enough for a tactless specialist to make such a suggestion. The child was barely a year old. How could one tell at that stage what possibilities were hidden in the damaged brain?

So we made pilgrimages to various clinics, hoping to discover just how extensive the damage was. In an imposing clinic in New Haven white-coated specialists put Sally through various tests, but the tests showed only that she was very retarded. The motor cortex, that part of the brain that governs voluntary movement, had been seriously damaged. She was spastic, which meant that certain muscles were in a state of chronic contraction. Her feet, instead of resting on the ground, were pulled into a state of constant extension, so that she walked on her toes. Braces were necessary to hold the feet in a normal position and prevent them from becoming permanently deformed.

Unable to make up our minds to put her in a home, we struggled with the child's problems, laboriously strapping her into braces, which she had to wear even at night. She could not feed herself. She could not talk. She did finally learn to walk on crutches, but if she fell over she could not get up again. However much we tried to help her, the child could never be more than half alive.

The commuting involved in our highly artificial way of life was becoming too much. First a long drive to the station, then a train ride to White Plains, then another train ride to 125th Street, then a subway ride to the Botanical Garden. I was spending six hours a day to get to and from my house in Connecticut to my place of work in the Bronx. An absurd way to live.

Five acres and independence . . . It was just a dream. There was no independence to be got from those five stony acres. (Actually I had six, but the sixth was a swamp and no good for anything.)

What does one do when one loathes cities and absolutely has to live in the country, but cannot make a living except in a city? How many millions face this dilemma? And how many cherish the dream of the tiny homestead, all self-sufficient, eggs from one's own hens, bread from one's own wheat, milk from one's own cow, bacon from one's own pig, a little house one has built with one's own hands from trees or from stone gathered on one's own place? Surely this is one of the oldest of dreams. Our huge, unwieldly, fragmented society is full of unhappy souls cut off from the soil, imprisoned in steel and concrete, deafened by noise, sickened by bad air, poisoned by bad impressions. Their one longing is to own a little piece of land, enough to satisfy the simple needs of a man, a woman, and maybe a couple of children.

But how to get it and still have money to pay for the doctor, the dentist, the taxes, the clothes and shoes, things one cannot make. Cannot make? What am I talking about? I have lived among peasants. They wove the linen from flax, the tweed from wool; they ate the products of the soil; their cabins were of logs from the forest. Self-sufficient. But oh, how precarious! One bad harvest and they faced starvation.

They call it the simple life. It isn't so simple.

By the autumn of 1951 it became clear that I would have to move. I had a choice. There was a possibility of working at the University of California at Davis or of taking a job in industry at Lederle Laboratories just across the Hudson near Pearl River in New York State. California called. It had been calling ever since I had settled in America. I had visited the state only once, but its special magic remained with me: the magic of rocky seacosts and tawny hills, of orange groves, vineyards, old missions, redwood trees, and mild winters. I longed for California with an essence longing.

But California was very far away. The job was a poor one. I did not feel strong enough to make the big move. Instead we crossed the Hudson and settled in New York State near New City in Rockland County. We bought thirteen acres of land. There was a stream, a huge black walnut tree; Lady Slipper orchids grew in the woods. Thirteen acres, but not independence. A regular job, eight to five, with an hour for lunch.

So I entered industrial research. At that time those in academic research tended to despise those who worked for industry. It was considered belittling. The ivory tower boys wanted to stand aloof from the lesser breed who tried to apply the fruits of scientific research. There was pure science and applied science.

The division was quite artificial. The condescending attitude of the "pure" scientists was a form of snobbery, not unmixed with envy, because in those days industrial scientists earned more money than academic scientists. As for me, I was thankful for any job that would give me a chance to do research and live in the country. Lederle Laboratories offered that opportunity to its workers. The place had been founded by old Dr. Lederle, who needed a farm on which to make diphtheria antitoxin. He bought a farm near Pearl River, New York, back in the 1900s. For $5,000 he got 999 acres and a farmhouse. He had a stable, horses. The horses were injected with diptheria toxin in increasing doses. They developed antitoxin, were bled, and the serum used to protect children from the disease. In the early 1900s children died like flies in New York City, and diptheria was one of the chief killers.

So there was Dr. Lederle's farm, all 999 acres of it, now a major center for the manufacture of pharmaceuticals. In those days the place basked in the sun of prosperity. It was the sole possessor and producer of a wonder drug, first of the "broad spectrum antibiotics," a golden substance produced from a mold *Streptomyces aureofaciens*, the mold that made gold. It really did. Aureomycin earned millions and the earnings were reflected in the lavish building program then underway.

So I entered the industry at a time when it was doing very nicely and could afford to be lavish in its support of research. I would work in the field of tissue culture. Great things were expected from tissue culture. There were dreams in several people's heads of growing special animal cells in large volumes and harvesting rare and special products, insulin for instance. How nice it would be if the specialized cells of the pancreas that produce this vital molecule could be trained to grow in thousand-gallon tanks and make insulin by the ton! It was perfectly possible to grow the mold that produced penicillin in thousand gallon tanks; and that precious antibiotic, which had been worth its weight in gold, was now so cheap that it barely paid to produce it. If penicillin could be produced in this way, surely insulin could be too.

An attractive line of reasoning. At that time I knew little about the special conditions required to grow animal cells. I was only familiar with plant cells, which grew fairly well if offered the right growth factors. My immediate job was to help isolate a growth factor for plant cells present in coconut milk. But I itched to know more about animal cells and proceeded rapidly to learn how to culture such cells, so much more exacting than the cells of the plant.

Meanwhile Tessa and I had to build our own house. In Connecticut we had built our own house and learned a lot of lessons. We had built casually, from sketches on the backs of envelopes. We made mistake after mistake. There was not enough room for the stairs. The bathroom did not have proper ventilation. The septic tank was inadequate. The hand-dug well gave out during the summer. Emphatically, working from sketches on the backs of envelopes was not the proper way to build a house.

The second house was developed more deliberately. Everything was planned. I had acquired a book: *Your Dream Home: How to Build It for Less than $3,500*. (Back in 1951 it really was possible, if one did all the work oneself, to build a home for about that amount.) I planned everything—full basement, three bedrooms, double garage with breeze-way—a typical suburban house. It was early November by the time we finished the basement. With help I managed to frame the place and put the insulation sheathing on the walls. Then the help disappeared. In December I was laying asphalt roofing shingles in weather so cold we had to heat the shingles over an old kitchen range to prevent them from cracking as I nailed them in place. To lay the bricks around the fireplace, I had to add antifreeze to the mortar to keep it workable.

Building a house in midwinter in New York State has nothing to recommend it. We did, however, manage to get

a roof over our heads, and in spring made ready to plant a
garden. I had a ten-minute drive to work instead of more
than two hours commuting. My condition appeared to be
improving.

This apparent improvement did not last long. I was oppressed by a sense of guilt and inadequacy, ashamed of
having abandoned the Way and settled into a mere domestic routine. Once again I was lost in the Morbio Inferiore,
lost far more seriously than I had been before. Both Gurdjieff and Ouspensky were dead. No one was left to whom I
could turn for help. I did not deserve help anyway. For
those who fail to accept the challenges of the Way, life becomes more and more difficult. Like mountaineers who
have severed their link with the other members of the
group, they tend to slip further and further until finally they
lose the possibility of reascending. My position was
summed up by the aphorism: *Strength exerted equals more
strength, weakness indulged equals greater weakness.* Nor
could I forget a second aphorism: *All possibilities exist only
for a limited period.*

The second aphorism scared me whenever I thought of it.
It referred to what Gurdjieff called the Merciless Heropass,
the inexorable passage of time. The Warrior's Way, to be
sure, was never a nice straight path like a Roman road. It
went up and down and around, was full of detours, traps,
deluding signs, dead ends. One had to expect ups and
downs. But the fact remained that those who would follow
the Way had only, in the course of one lifetime, just so
many hours, days, months, years. They were permitted to
make just so many mistakes, to waste just so many years
wandering down the wrong roads. At any time death could
end the game and sweep all the pieces from the board. Even
a full life span of a hundred years would not suffice if one
wasted too many opportunities. Every challenge one failed
to accept reduced one's personal power and increased the
likelihood that one would fail in the next test. Nothing suc-
ceeds like success, nothing fails like failure.

My Domestic Oaf, by trying to take refuge from the strains and stresses of the Warrior's Way, had merely involved me in other strains and stresses that were much less spiritually profitable and much harder to accept. Our inability to decide whether to put Sally in a home created a constant tension in our household that was wearing down all its members. My two older children were now with us and found themselves also involved in the daily struggle that centered around Sally, the endless fastening and unfastening of braces, the struggle to attend to those needs that she could not cope with herself.

The burden began to prove too much for Tessa. It gradually became clear to me that she was going to break under the strain. She was showing the same symptoms as E. had shown before her breakdown: inability to sleep, inability to concentrate, total lack of motivation, heavy feelings of guilt, paranoid delusions. I had the sensation of being trapped in some lunatic circus in which everything was being managed by a malevolent ringmaster. Was it possible that I had really let myself in for two schizophrenic wives in succession and a cerebral palsied daughter into the bargain? Did some basic defect in my sex center attract to me only schizophrenics, fragile beauties who could not cope with stress, who would retreat from reality into the shadow world of schizophrenia? From the very start I had noticed around Tessa a certain aura of sadness, as if she knew that she was doomed to a tragic life. Now the tragedy was unfolding. She was unable to endure her own feelings of guilt for having produced a hopelessly damaged child. She was haggard, sick, and becoming madder every day.

As Tessa became increasingly paranoid, the strain under which the household was laboring became intolerable. I had to take action before we all went collectively insane, so I shipped Tessa off by air to England to stay with her parents for a while. The hope was that a change in scene might bring her back to her senses.

So I was left with Sally. What to do? The thought crossed

my mind as I watched her painfully struggling across the lawn on her crutches that she might be better off dead. In a more primitive society than ours she would be dead. She had been kept alive only by the interference of a misguided medical science, which seemed to think life was always worth preserving, however hopelessly deranged that life had become.

My Scientist, harsh and unsentimental, saw the child as a violation of nature's laws. She had no right to exist. Our society, cursed with a sentimental ethic that regarded all life as sacred, was overburdened already with a huge accretion of human vegetables, of imbeciles, hopelessly retarded beings, all of whom had to be cared for at enormous expense.

And yet this same society that cherished every imbecile, no matter how hopeless, would send off the flower of its youth to face mutilation and death, would bomb "enemy" cities until not a soul survived, spent billions each year on death-dealing devices so frightful that only a totally amoral lunatic could contemplate using them!

Once again I had the sensation of belonging to a species that was fundamentally insane.

My Scientist continued its dark mutterings about putting Sally out of her misery, liberating her from her hopelessly damaged body. It would be simple enough. An overdose of insulin discreetly injected in the perianal fat would put the child into a coma. Convulsions and death would follow. No one would be any the wiser. If there was a soul trapped in that damaged body, surely it should be thankful for its release. And if there was no soul, what did it matter?

But despite the harsh promptings of the Scientist, I knew I could never take that step. It was easier to put her in an institution. Out of sight, out of mind.

"If you keep her at home," observed a medical friend, "you will have both headaches and heartaches. If you put her in an institution you will get rid of the headaches and the heartaches will heal in due course."

Still I hesitated. I was violently prejudiced against institutions. I saw them as soulless places where paid workers full of professional heartiness put human wrecks through various training programs. I knew, as far as I was concerned, that such an environment would be equivalent to hell and that death would be preferable. But would this apply to the child? Would she, with her much reduced brain capacity, find that existence so hellish?

How much can the healthy be expected to sacrifice for the sake of the crippled? The burden had proved too heavy for poor Tessa, who had cracked up under the strain. The burden could also prove too heavy for me. I had the other two children to think about, also my job. Reluctantly I decided to place her, at least for the time being, in a nearby rehabilitation hospital, a large hygienic building with a magnificent view of the Hudson River. There were not very many people being rehabilitated in the hospital. Most of the neat beds were empty. I left the child in the hands of a starched and smiling professional.

The child looked bewildered, betrayed.

I fled, feeling like a criminal leaving the scene of the crime.

Alone in the house I felt desolate. An awful emptiness surrounded me, a sort of psychological vacuum. Nothing any longer seemed worth doing. My scientific work was insignificant, my domestic life was a mess. The will to live, never strong, flickered like the light of a lamp that is running out of oil. I had always had suicidal tendencies. Now, in that empty house, I vividly remembered that other occasion when I had seen my own death looking back at me from the oily water of Port Adelaide. I regretted that, on that occasion, I had failed to let myself sink to the bottom of the harbor, thus bringing to an end a very senseless existence.

Now once again I felt the urge to end the performance. I could send the two older children back to England. The old friend of the family who had looked after them and regarded them practically as her own would be only too glad to have them back. I could sell everything, send the money to England, leave the game, leave the country, leave the planet. I regarded myself as such an inept player, such a total bungler, that I could hardly face the prospect of continuing to live. I had failed to accept the challenges of the Warrior's Way and settled for a life of plain domesticity, only to find I had landed myself in a mess far worse than the one I had confronted during the war.

My Domestic Oaf, who was responsible for the mess, had nothing much to offer in the way of consolation. Instead he indulged in an orgy of self-pity. Why does this happen to me? I have done the best I could, worked hard, saved my money, built this house with my own hands, sweated and struggled to give my children a better start in life than I had myself. Why does fate keep kicking me? Why won't it leave me in peace?

I wandered from room to room through the empty house. Tessa's room empty. Sally's room empty. What desolation! I was emotionally exhausted and began to weep. Eros and Thanatos, the will to live and the will to die, confronted each other across the chasm of my life. Eros had not much to say. What could he offer me, poor little naked love god? But Thanatos had a very soothing line of talk. Lay down your burden, said Thanatos, the dark angel. All games are futile. All aims are senseless. Even that tough old Stoic Epictetus allowed that if one grew sick of the performance, it was always permissible to leave the theater.

Leave it I could and would. My laboratory was well stocked with various poisons. And yet . . . and yet . . . Would it really solve anything? I thought of Ivan Osokin, hero of Ouspensky's last book. Osokin had rushed out into the street, a revolver in his hand, with the intention of blowing out his brains. On the street he met a magician, who spoke to him. "As you don't seem to want your life, give it to me." Osokin was so fascinated by this request that he went to the home of the magician and asked him for a favor. "Send me back to the beginning," said Osokin. "If

I can have my life over again I will avoid the mistakes which have driven me to despair." So the magician put Osokin right back in his cradle. But at each critical point in the development of his life Osokin forgot himself and made the same mistake again. And finally? Finally Osokin rushed from the house brandishing a revolver. He met a magician. The magician said, "As you don't seem to want your life, give it to me."

Da capo. Once more with feeling. Suppose I did lay my burden down, hand back my entrance ticket, leave the theater? Would I have rest and nothingness, or would the operation of the wheel of recurrence merely carry me back to that day in February 1913 on which I had first set out on my voyage through space-time? Might I not, like Osokin, discover that I had only put myself back at the beginning of the maze? I would have to traverse the whole thing again— and, as all suicides travel on the descending path, I would surely repeat all my former mistakes, and probably make a few new ones.

At that point a ghostly melody sounded in the empty house. I am sure it really sounded in my head, and yet it seemed external. I recognized it at once. The challenging theme in the horns from the first movement of Beethoven's *Eroica*. I had been reading, at that time, a biography of Beethoven and noticed how close the composer came to suicide. The *Heiligenstadt Testament* was Beethoven's cry of despair when he finally realized that he was incurably deaf. Obviously at that time Beethoven had decided that the game was no longer worth playing and was prepared to commit suicide. Think what it would have cost us had he done so! His crisis occurred in 1802, before he had found his voice. He would have left us only two symphonies, mere juvenilia that sound like warmed-over Mozart. All the mature works of Beethoven would have been lost.

But something intervened. Beethoven was at heart a Warrior, and he followed the Warrior's Way despite deafness, loneliness, illness, and all the other misfortunes fate threw at him. In a letter to Wegeler he voiced his defiance.

I will take Fate by the Throat; it shall not wholly overcome me!

That sudden upsurge of power found musical expression in the *Eroica*. The symphony pulsates with force, with defiance, with the will to live in spite of fate's dirty tricks. What dirtier trick could fate play on Beethoven than to rob him of his hearing? But he accepted the handicap. Perhaps it even added to his power. As Nietzsche put it: That which does not destroy me strengthens me.

For me that echo from the *Eroica* tipped the balance. I had slipped a long way and almost fallen over the precipice. Now, if I was ever to return to the Way, I would have to begin the slow process of self-renewal. Lying down and wallowing in self-pity was the worst possible reaction to the challenges life had offered. Don't give in, don't slobber, don't pity yourself. Take fate by the throat! Only by such an attitude can one once again become capable of following the Warrior's Way.

28

DRUGS
AND THE MIND

In the winter of 1955 I stood in the cavernous customs shed in New York as the *Liberté,* pride of the French Line, was nuzzled into place at the dock by a retinue of tugs. Tessa had returned, defying advice and warnings. It was my opinion, expressed in several letters, that she would do well to stay in England. Stay there, said my Yogi, who was now trying to run my ship of fools, and wanted to attain some sort of higher consciousness. Marry a good solid Englishman who owns a farm in Sussex, wears tweeds, smokes a pipe. What's a nice girl like you doing with a crazy mixed-up character like me, half mystic, half scientist, with all sorts of monsters crawling around in his subconscious, the legacy of a heritage that mixed Cossacks with Baltic barons? Stay in England. Catch yourself a fish you can fry.

Words to that effect.

Wasted advice. Tessa wanted to return. She had acquired a taste for spacious America, found England grey, cramped, damp, and generally awful. She wanted to come back to the house we·had built together. She didn't want an English squire with tweeds, pipe, and pigs. She wanted me.

Tessa, the constant nymph.

My Yogi sighed and called her a fool. The silly moth, not content with singeing its wings once, now had to fly toward the flame a second time. But the Yogi deferred to the Domestic Oaf, who wanted his mate back. The Yogi argued from the head, the Oaf from the heart and balls. When it came to a showdown, the lower organs carried the power. So there was Tessa back in America, no longer a thin, haggard, poisoned schizophrenic but a pretty love-girl with English roses blooming in her cheeks.

"Guess what!" said Tessa. "I ate *snails* and *frog's legs* on the way over."

Well, what can you do? Tessa was a child. Suddenly the truth dawned on me. She had never grown up. And I, because of some peculiar quirk in my nature, found just such child-women irresistible. She was a very beautiful child. When oppressed by her madness and guilt she was silent and paranoid, but when well she never stopped talking. So on the way back she prattled on about the snails and the frogs and the *Liberté* and how dull England was and how exciting it was to see New York again. Reborn, I thought. A resurrection. Truly a miracle.

I had never really expected that she would recover.

Would she stay well? None of my medical friends dared answer my question. In schizophrenia the prognosis is guarded. This was one way of saying that they had not the remotest idea what caused the disease and that if they managed to cure it, it was largely a matter of luck. Perhaps there were as many forms of schizophrenia as there were of cancer, some of them very malignant, some quite mild. I thought of poor E., still locked up and mad as ever after twenty years, a victim of the disease at its most malignant. But here was Tessa in perfect health, ready again to play the games of life, her joie de vivre restored. Was this the basic cause of schizophrenia, a poison brewed in the brain that attacked the pleasure center and made life not worth living? I had no doubt that the schizophrenic was poisoned. The pallid, frightened appearance, the strange brightness of the eyes, the inability to sleep, the peculiar characteristic smell all indicated a toxic state. But how could one find the poison?

My Scientist was determined to seek this poison. His interest in the cancer problem had diminished. There was indeed a strong program of cancer research at Lederle, but it consisted almost entirely of screening compounds for anticancer activities. It was the old hunt for the "silver bullet" that Ehrlich had started at the beginning of the century. But even Ehrlich had despaired over the cancer problem. It was indeed a frustrating hunt. Nearly all the compounds that destroyed cancer cells destroyed normal cells also. The cure could be almost as deadly as the disease. In any case it was technicians' work; graft cancer tissue into mice, inject the mice with the compound to be tested, measure the rate at which the tumor regressed. It was not real research at all. Merely mechanical screening.

But the hunt for a drug with which to treat schizophrenia was a much more exciting affair. One confronted the enormous complexity of the chemistry of the brain. One came face to face with basic problems, the interdependence of mind and matter. At that time Albert Hoffman of Sandoz had just discovered the extraordinary effect on the mind of a derivative of lysergic acid that later became notorious as LSD (lysergic acid diethylamide). A mere trace of the compound distorted the chemistry of the brain, and this distortion was reflected in the workings of the mind. It was thought at the time that LSD produced a condition similar to schizophrenia. The drug was labeled *psychomimetic*, that which mimics a psychosis. It did not really mimic a psychosis, but the term was thought-provoking. How easily one could vizualize some error in body chemistry, either in the liver or the brain itself, that would produce a poison having effects similar to those of LSD. Find an antidote for that poison and you would have a cure for schizophrenia.

A nice problem. A problem moreover that I had very personal reasons for wishing to solve. There were not too many people working at that time in the field of brain biochemistry. I determined to become one of them. But how? I had been trained originally as a plant physiologist, had worked during the war as a bacteriologist, was competent in the field of plant and animal tissue culture, but knew absolutely nothing about the chemistry of the brain.

Fortunately, as a botanist I was able to interest my em-

ployers in the properties of drugs of plant origins. Sophis-
ticated pharmacologists tended to despise these humble
herbal remedies, but since the isolation of reserpine from
the Indian snakeroot, *Rauwolfia serpentina*, they had suddenly developed a new respect for folk medicine. I suggested that I might profitably collect and screen folk remedies for their effects on the brain. I knew that there was a
very elaborate herbal lore in Jamaica. The herbal lore was
the secret of the *obeahs*, who corresponded to the voodoo
sorcerers in Haiti. If my employers would allow me to visit
the island, I might be able to collect some plants of interest.

My employer, rather to my surprise, agreed to this plan.
Leaving the two older children to take care of the house
(they were in high school already and quite independent), I
flew off with Tessa to Kingston, Jamaica, plunging in one
swoop from grey, snowy New York into blue skies and hot
Caribbean sun. There among the hibiscus and humming-
birds Tessa and I mated with the careless abandon of Poly-
nesians, and she conceived a new child to replace the one
she had lost. More hostages to fortune! "Whatever you do,"
said my cautious doctor friend, "don't get her pregnant."
Wasted advice. Someone was around who wanted to be
conceived. And was. And was duly born, normal and
healthy, nine months later. Tessa had a chance to enjoy the
fruits of normal motherhood. It was her right, after all.

Ah, Jamaica! What lessons it had to offer. We stayed for
part of the time with a member of the great white plan-
tocracy. His plantation was enormous. He raised coconuts,
sugar cane, bananas. The plantation had been in the hands
of the family since the days of Lord Nelson. High up on the
hillside with a magnificent view of the ocean stood the
Great House. It had been built during the sugar boom,
when Jamaican plantation owners became millionaires. The
house was empty now. My plantocrat friend did not live in
it. He was a bachelor. What would a bachelor want in a
house with ten bedrooms?

Nonetheless all those bedrooms were luxuriously furnished and supplied with double beds, as if awaiting the conjugations of a whole swarm of lovers. But no one came. Only the termites bred. They had eaten most of the books in the bookcases. They were starting to devour the house.

What a contrast! What a lesson for a biologist! In the Great House on the hill were ghosts and termites and shabby remnants of old riches. In the shacks at the bottom of the hill were laughing blacks who danced and sang calypsos and starved and bred. The incidence of syphilis was horrendous. The poverty was fantastic. But who would survive? Who, in the end, would own the island—the wealthy plantocrats, who did not even replace themselves, or the cheerful blacks, who multiplied at random and cared so little about money that they could hardly be bothered to earn any?

Survival of the fittest. Darwinism in action.

What is fitness anyway?

We journeyed through the Jamaican mountains gathering information about herbal remedies, listening to songs, watching dances. Why is it that dirt poor blacks have so much more fun than hardworking whites? Compared with them we seem stiff and awkward, only half alive. And the songs were really remarkable. One of the most beautiful folk songs I have ever heard, "Linsten Market," was sung quite casually in a little Jamaican village. It was in the tradition of the finest English folk songs, yet purely Jamaican. I wished Vaughan Williams could have heard it.

Meanwhile it was necessary to find the *obeah* lady. For this my plantocrat friend was no help. He was a magistrate, had a real fear of *obeah*. The very word was unmentionable. Fortunately I had a friend in the Jamaica Institute who knew a lot about *obeah*. The *obeah* men and women, he assured me, were not necessarily sorcerers. They were more often equivalent to the *curanderos* of Mexico and South America. *Obeah* was a collection of pagan practices that the black slaves had brought with them from Africa mixed with knowledge of hypnotic techniques and of herbal remedies.

We found the house of the *obeah* lady on the outskirts of Kingston. The place was dusty and decrepit, guarded by mangy dogs and ghostly objects, a rag on a piece of stick, a crudely carved human figure, a bashed skull with all its teeth missing. The *obeah* lady at first refused to show up for the interview. One of the dogs had stolen her shoes. She wanted to wear shoes to talk to the learned doctor from America.

She found her shoes at last and appeared wrapped in a gaudily colored bedspread, a real African queen. I was glad that my friend was with me. Jamaican English ranges from a singsong dialect that can be understood quite easily to a strange tongue that is practically meaningless to the uninitiated. The *obeah* lady's English was of the latter variety. I arranged for her to collect plants for me and send them to the Jamaica Institute, which would see to their further shipment.

The plants, when extracted and tested in mice, did not offer much that was new and exciting.

"These are the most hepatotoxic substances we've tested in a long while," said a pharmacologist. "I'd be sorry for anyone who took them regularly. They knock the liver for a loop."

"Perhaps they work differently in men from mice."

Perhaps they did. But you could hardly expect to screen hundreds of compounds in human schizophrenics. You had to use mice. There was only one drawback to this arrangement. Mice did not suffer from schizophrenia.

29

SLY MAN
AND SUPERMAN

Those who would follow the Warrior's Way must generate in themselves certain high-energy substances. This truth had become particularly clear to me during my trip to Jamaica, when my mind had been much preoccupied with such subjects as *obeah*, voodoo, and sorcery. They are not subjects with which a respectable biochemist is supposed to concern himself, but I was not a respectable biochemist. I was, if anything, more alchemist than chemist, concerned with the inner transformation that converts man from a slave into a Warrior.

Everything is material. Thoughts are material; feelings are material; emotions are material. But there are more levels of materiality than the chemist recognizes. Higher levels of materiality could be studied only alchemically. The alchemist used his own body as the alembic and transformed, by certain intentional efforts, the raw materials that nature provided into spiritual gold.

Which did not mean that an alchemist could not avail himself of chemical aids if he could find them. Surrounded as I was by all manner of drugs that influenced in one way or another the workings of the psyche, I naturally tended to try them. I had at my disposal tranquilizers, psychic energizers, and psychedelics, some of botanical origin, some synthetic. What effects did they offer that might be of value to an alchemist? Could any of them function as what Gurdjieff called the Sly Man's pill?

Yes, the Sly Man's pill. That curious entity had intrigued me ever since I had first heard of it. In the alchemical process the struggle between yes and no generated heat and lit the fire under the alembic. By means of this fire the high-energy substances were created and refined. It was, as chemists would say, an endothermic process (one requiring an input of energy, like the splitting of water to hydrogen and oxygen). But the alchemist had at his disposal various ways of generating this energy, some of them crude and some of them refined.

These methods of generating energy could be related to what Gurdjieff had called the four ways. The way of the fakir was the crudest of these ways. The fakir, using self-torture, might take a month to generate the needed energy. He would do this blindly, without understanding aim, method, or results, simply in imitation of another fakir. A follower of the way of the monk would know what he wanted a little better and would need only a week to generate the energy, using fasting, continual prayer, and privation. A follower of the way of the yogi would know a lot more than the monk. He would generate the needed energy in one day by a certain kind of mental exercise and concentration of consciousness. But a follower of the fourth way, the "Sly Man" who could "drink with the Devil and leave the Devil to pay for the drinks," knew far more than the yogi. The Sly Man would simply prepare and swallow a little pill which would contain all the energy substances he wanted.

Well, it was certainly a nice idea, but it did not seem to work in practice. None of the drugs available to me even remotely resembled in their effects that mysterious entity Gurdjieff had described. I was becoming very skeptical about the Sly Man's pill. Was it only another example of the Gurdjieffian sense of humor? Or had he been speaking allegorically?

Anyway my observations suggested that not much was to be gained by the use of drugs. They were unreliable and unpredictable. Perhaps, if used under special conditions and after long and careful preparation, they could be of value. But I did not know enough about those special conditions to be able to use the drugs constructively. Under ordinary conditions they robbed me of energy and left me feeling more or less depleted.

A different approach was required.

I began to experiment with a combination of *raja* yoga and *hatha* yoga. They offered, I believed, a means of modifying the circuitry of one's brain in such a way that one could contact the two higher centers that existed in the brain but were not used. One had somehow or other to find one's way around in that complex device that the neurophysiologist John Lilly called the human bio-computer. Large segments of that computer were totally out of our reach. We could not, by conscious effort, alter our temperatures, change our rate of metabolism, enhance or decrease the production of certain hormones, slow down the heartbeat or the rate of peristalsis. Nor could we, as every hummingbird did at night, allow our temperatures to drop to that of our surroundings, thus inducing a state of temporary hibernation.

I was especially interested in hibernation. It was, I believed, one way in which our lives could be prolonged. Several students of the human condition had observed that man almost always dies before he is really mature. This is particularly true of followers of the Warrior's Way. By the time a Warrior has made all the usual mistakes, taken all the usual detours, wasted the usual amount of time, he is too old to make further progress. Old age, as Don Juan observed, is the last enemy of the man of knowledge.

The capacity to hibernate would probably prolong life, because it enormously reduces the amount of work demanded from such vital organs as the heart. It would drastically reduce the metabolic rate of the body. It could aid, I believed, the cure of a variety of stress-induced disorders. Indeed hypothermy, the lowering of the body temperature, was already being employed to facilitate certain forms of surgery.

Learn to hibernate. Learn to lower heart rate, blood pressure, metabolic rate. An arctic squirrel can let its temperature drop to a few degrees above freezing. What an arctic squirrel can do, a man can surely learn. Are we not more ingenious than arctic squirrels?

So during this period of my life I began to explore the techniques of *hatha* yoga, striving to obtain mastery over functions that normally lay beyond the reach of the human mind. Vain attempts! *Hatha* yoga was incredibly difficult. To gain the requisite mastery, one really had to give up everything and work on nothing but *hatha* yoga day in and day out. I was in no position to do this. I had a job, a family to support. But could not the gadgetry of modern science offer shortcuts to the results that the *hatha* yogi attained by such arduous efforts?

At this point I became interested in cyborgs. The cyborg (cybernetic organism) was man redesigned by man. The term was invented by Manfred Clynes, who, with Nathan Kline, worked on brain research at Rockland State Hospital, not far from Lederle Laboratories. I had problems to discuss with Nathan Kline that had nothing to do with cyborgs. He was a leader of the new, biochemically oriented school of psychiatrists who were introducing scientific methods into psychiatry. Officially I was supposed to discuss with Kline a group of drugs called psychic energizers, which he had been largely instrumental in discovering. I hoped in addition to obtain further insights into the nature of cyborgs.

So I drove across Rockland County to the huge mental hospital where Kline and Clynes worked—wondering, as I did so, what marvels those two wizards were producing. The cyborgs were rather hush-hush. The Department of Defense as well as NASA were supposedly interested in these cybernetically modified men. Were cyborgs the wave of the future? Were they the next thing to the Nietzschean superman? Or were they merely updated versions of Frankenstein's monster?

I arrived at Kline's office. We talked of psychic energizers, of antidepressants, of monoamine oxidase inhibitors. Above his office was a room full of disturbed patients who made as much racket as a small army of poltergeists. Kline carried on two telephone conversations at once while at the same time composing a preface for the first edition of my book *Drugs and the Mind*. He was one of those beings capable of functioning with complete efficiency in an atmosphere of bedlam.

And what of the cyborgs?

A cyborg developed for space travel would have truly supernatural powers. First, it would be able to live without breathing. An artificial organ would function in place of the lungs, remove CO_2 and replace it with oxygen. Second, it would neither shit nor piss. The by-products of its metabolism would be removed and recycled artificially. Third, it would be able at will to turn off its thoughts and sink into a trance. On a space trip lasting weeks or months a normally conscious person would probably go insane as a result of sensory deprivation. Not the cyborg. It would pass out of space-time into a sleep far deeper than Rip van Winkle's, while never-sleeping computers took care of navigating the spaceship. Finally the cyborg, following the example of the arctic squirrel, would allow its temperature to fall until its metabolism almost came to a halt. This would enormously reduce the wear and tear on the organism. During the long journey through space the cyborg would be in a state of suspended animation. Once arrived at its destination, the cyborg—with its built-in-computer, its jet-assisted takeoff, its artificially reinforced sensory organs—could cope with strange environments in a manner quite impossible for an ordinary man.

How nice to be a cyborg!

Well, maybe. It was well within the power of modern neurosurgeons to give to any human being the power to stimulate directly various centers in the brain. The pleasure centers, the centers controlling hunger, thirst, sexual desire, sleep and waking, temperature, anger, fear, were all accessible. Place a thin wire in any of those centers, equip the patient with a small battery and a sort of keyboard allowing him to activate any center at will, and behold a being with almost superhuman control over his functions. All the advantages of *hatha* yoga with none of the hard work!

But who wants to go around with wires sticking out of his head like a porcupine? And how many neurosurgeons would be willing to implant electrodes in normal healthy brains? Such an operation would surely be considered unethical, even if the subject of the experiment gave his consent. No. The conclusion was unavoidable. There were disadvantages to becoming a cyborg and they outweighed the gains. But although the idea of having myself converted into a cyborg with electrodes permanently implanted in my brain seemed to me rather repulsive, I continued to seek in the realm of science some shortcut to the sort of inner mastery that *hatha* yoga could give.

The subject in which I was so interested was later defined as biofeedback and explored very thoroughly by such scientists as Elmer and Alyce Green. But all that lay in the future. At that time there was only one scientist I could think of who might perhaps have studied the problems I had in mind. That scientist was Alexis Carrel.

I had always been an admirer of Carrel. Not only had he helped to lay the foundations of the technique of tissue culture, but he had also (in his book *Man the Unknown*) confronted the problem of man's inner transformation. Carrel had read and reflected upon the words of Nietzsche's Zarathustra: *Man is something to be surpassed. What have you done to surpass man?* He had honestly tried to answer that question, was one of the very few scientists to make the attempt.

I wanted to learn more about Carrel. He had been a mystic as well as a scientist and was rumored to occupy a high position in the Roman Catholic hierarchy. It was also rumored that he had conducted a series of secret experiments on an island he owned called Saint Gildas off the coast of

Brittany. Those secret experiments had supposedly been concerned with the forces involved in man's spiritual evolution. I could not communicate with Carrel directly. He had died in 1944. But there was one person who had worked with him on the island of St. Gildas who would surely know his secrets if he had any. That person was Charles Lindbergh.

Lindbergh was a complex and extraordinarily gifted man, a Warrior in his own right. To most Americans he was the "Lone Eagle," the aviator whose solo flight across the Atlantic had produced a wave of hysterical hero worship in 1927. But Lindbergh was far more than an aviator. Like Carrel he was both a scientist and a mystic. His knowledge went far beyond flying machines.

I decided to write a book on Carrel. The man's scientific work was familiar to me. I knew many of the people with whom he had worked at the Rockefeller Institute. But a mere recapitulation of his studies on chicken heart fibroblasts would be pointless. His work had long been superseded and was only of historical interest. What I wanted to do was to update *Man the Unknown*.

Accordingly I wrote to Lindbergh. Knowing his dislike of any sort of publicity, I did not really expect an answer to my letter. I did in fact have to wait several months before I received a reply. Lindbergh was not an easy man to contact. The fact that I had worked at the Rockefeller Institute certainly helped. Finally I was invited to visit his home on Scott's Cove in Connecticut.

Lindbergh seemed very happy to talk about Carrel. He had obviously admired the man, but his admiration was tempered by an amused awareness of the scientist's limitations and peculiarities.

"He was never very popular at the Rockefeller Institute," said Lindbergh. "An individualist, you know. Didn't conform. He ate alone in the dining room for the senior staff or entertained quite outlandish people. I remember once he had lunch with a man who trained camels. This man trained this camel to walk backwards. Apparently it's very difficult to train a camel to walk backwards. Carrel was like that. Interested in the oddest things. An unusual man."

Lindbergh paused and gazed out across Scott's Cove, over which floated seagulls.

"Odd, very odd," he mused. "Carrel collected the strangest things. They found an Egyptian mummy stuffed away in a cupboard in his lab at the Institute. He had tried to dissect it. It was so hard he had to work on it with a hammer and chisel. After he left the Institute the directors were puzzled to know what to do with it. They couldn't bury it because they didn't have a death certificate. In the end they chopped it up and fed it to the furnace. The Negro janitor came down while they were doing it. Couldn't believe his eyes. There were the top brass of the Institute feeding a dried-up human corpse into the furnace."

I laughed. Lindbergh told the story in a most amusing way. I could well imagine the dismay of the solemn directors of the Rockefeller Institute when confronted with the problem of disposing of Carrel's mummy.

"How did you first get to know Carrel?" I asked.

Lindbergh reflected. It had been in the summer of 1930. A member of the family had been dangerously ill with heart disease. Growths were forming on the heart, interfering with its function. Unless those growths were removed the patient would die.

"In those days it was quite impossible to operate on the heart. Surgeons didn't even consider it. But the heart is only a pump after all. I was a mechanic. I knew something about pumps. Why not invent a pump which would take over the role of the heart while it was being operated on? So I started trying to invent such a pump."

Lindbergh quickly discovered that pumping blood was no easy matter. The stuff had a terrible tendency to form clots, and a clot in the circulating blood could easily be fatal. In the course of trying to devise a heart pump he was introduced to Carrel. For twenty years Carrel had been interested in methods of circulating blood through isolated organs. He escorted Lindbergh through his laboratories and showed him the procedures he had used.

After this meeting Carrel and Lindbergh worked together. Lindbergh, cursed with a fame that had brought him more sorrow than joy, would enter the Institute by a side door, disguised with a large pair of dark glasses. Over a period of five years he worked with Carrel to devise what later became known as the Carrel-Lindbergh pump. It was not immediately used as an artificial heart. The time was not ripe for open-heart surgery. It did, however, provide a basis for an extraordinary study conducted jointly by Carrel and Lindbergh, on the culture of organs separated from the body.

I had, of course, heard plenty about the artificial culture of whole organs. It was even thought to have commercial possibilities. Cultivate the pancreas and you get insulin, cultivate the adrenals and you get all the adrenal hormones, cultivate the pituitary and you get the pituitary hormones. So ran the script. In practice it never worked out. The isolated organs never lived long enough to make such experiments worthwhile.

Even stranger experiments were being discussed. Rare and special individuals with powerful brains might be kept alive long after they were technically dead by perfusing their brains with an artificial blood aerated by an artificial lung, purified by an artificial kidney, enriched by injections of sterile nutrients. It was the sort of semi-science-fiction scenario that imaginative scientists enjoyed envisaging. Could an isolated brain be kept alive independently of the body? For how long would it live, and so on?

Such experiments, however, had been far beyond the reach of Carrel and Lindbergh on their mysterious island. Indeed I hoped they had been interested in more serious problems than this sort of biological gadgeteering. I began talking to Lindbergh about *hatha* yoga. Yes, he had been much interested in the subject, had in fact flown all over

India with Theos Bernard looking for a *hatha* yogi who could really be buried alive for a long period and survive the experience.

"Of course there have been several cases reported, but they always put the yogi in some sort of coffin or box and then buried the box. Well, I happen to know from experience that one can learn to survive on very little oxygen if one breathes in the right way. I made experiments on the effects of anoxia during the war—nearly died, in fact, when my oxygen supply gave out at 42,000 feet. I don't think these yogis really hibernate. They do go into a sort of trance and breathe very lightly. And they can survive in the box for a long time. Several hours, maybe a day. But not for months as has been rumored. India is full of tall tales, you know. Indians want to oblige. They tell you tall tales so that you won't be disappointed."

Lindbergh continued to talk about Carrel.

"He used his Nobel Prize money to buy this island off the coast of Brittany. It was called St. Gildas. We bought another island nearby called Illiec. We saw a lot of him. He had a little laboratory on the island. Did a lot of experiments. He used to hypnotize the shepherd dogs. He studied psychic phenomena. What he really wanted was to found an institute entirely devoted to the study of man. Institute of Man. He considered man very degenerate. Wanted to remake the creature."

Lindbergh rose and left the room. He returned with a copy of *Man the Unknown*, inscribed it with a flourish, and gave it to me.

"If you're going to write a life of Carrel you will have to study that. The last chapter is the most important. 'The Remaking of Man.' All the work we did with the pump and on organ transplants was just technical fiddling. What Carrel really wanted to do was to recreate man."

Shades of Gurdjieff and the Institute for the Harmonious Development of Man! What did Carrel have to say on the subject of man's transformation?

To progress again, man must remake himself. And he cannot remake himself without suffering. For he is both the marble and the sculptor. In order to uncover his true visage he must shatter his own substance with heavy blows of his hammer. He will not submit to such treatment unless driven by necessity. While surrounded by the comfort, the beauty, and the mechanical marvels engendered by technology, he does not understand how urgent is this operation. He fails to realize that he is degenerating. Why should he strive to modify his ways of being, living, and thinking?

An ascetic and mystic minority would rapidly acquire an irresistible power over the dissolute and degraded majority. Such a minority would be in a position to impose, by persuasion or perhaps by force, other ways of life upon the majority.

We must single out the children who are endowed with high potentialities, and develop them as completely as possible. And in this manner give to the nation a non-hereditary aristocracy.

We must rescue the individual from the state of intellectual, moral, and physiological atrophy brought about by modern conditions of life. Develop all his potential activities. Give him health. Reestablish him in his unity, in the harmony of his personality. Induce him to utilize all the hereditary qualities of his tissues and his consciousness. Break the shell in which education and society have succeeded in enclosing him. And reject all systems. We have to intervene in the fundamental organic and mental processes. These processes are man himself. But man has no independent existence. He is bound to his environment. In order to remake him, we have to transform his world.

(Man the Unknown,
New York: Harper and Bros., 1935.)

We must . . . we must . . . we must!
Who must?

Driving back from Lindbergh's house, I thought about these blueprints for the remaking of man. I remembered that some of my German cousins, in the early days of Hitler, had also thought in terms of an ascetic and mystic elite who would take over the world from the degenerate democracies. Why do these movements start out so nobly and end so disastrously? Why do the worst come out on top?

Those phrases of Carrel's brought back the special flavor of the thirties. It had been, from one point of view, a degraded decade, the Dirty Thirties. But from another point of view it had been strenuous, almost heroic. I thought of things my father had told me about the Dark Force and the terrible power this force had attained in Germany. How much had Carrel known? Had he really been one of the secret princes of the Church who had entered that confused struggle on the side of the spiritual hierarchy? It was entirely possible. Wilton Earle, the eminent tissue culturist, who knew of my interest in Carrel, had asked me in all seriousness if Carrel had been a "prince of the Church." I knew little about the Roman Catholic hierarchy, had always assumed that the princes of the Church were cardinals. But were there hidden princes of the Church, and was Carrel one of them?

The thirties had seen a clash of rival elites. The Black Order headed by the Death's Head SS in Germany had clashed with the White Order, a secret organization within the Roman Catholic hierarchy. There had been a real struggle between magicians, a very confused struggle because the White Order did not really regard the Black Order as the enemy. The real Antichrist was Stalin and his Communists.

So the members of the White Order—which included statesmen, scientists, and engineers, as well as many members of some religious orders, chiefly the Jesuits—hoped to win over the members of the Black Order and direct their energies to the destruction of Stalin's Communists. Both the Black Order and the White Order were elitist. Both took the view that the ordinary man was quite incapable of managing his own affairs, needed direction from a spiritual elite. Both Orders spoke of the new man who would emerge like a phoenix out of the ashes of the old. But the White Order envisaged a gradual gentle transformation, whereas the Black, dedicated to destruction, planned a mass sacrifice. Their Man-God would arise out of an ocean of blood. (For more details see Pauwels, L., and Bergier, J., *The Morning of the Magicians*. New York: Avon Books, 1968.)

This all sounds a bit fantastic today, but in the thirties such scenarios were taken seriously. The Satanic force, which is a very real force and very deadly, had suddenly erupted into the conscious life of man and started to dominate the affairs of an entire nation. Right in the middle of what was supposed to be an age of reason there emerged a Satanic Order, totally governed by the destructive force, totally mad and totally dedicated.

The Satanic Order certainly had its own ideas about the Warrior's Way and the remaking of man. Hitler had dreams of biological mutations, of the Man-God, the superb Nietzschean blond beast, the flower that would emerge from the human dunghill. What other function did that mass of "half men" have but to provide the compost from which the Man-God could grow? And if, to get enough of that compost, a few million "half men" had to be slaughtered, what did it matter? They were expendable.

The Black Order was designed to provide the Ring of Power within which the Superman would be generated. There would be a regular hierarchy, a series of initiations. The Man-God would emerge from among the second-stage initiates. It was all worked out in astonishing detail. Black Magic of the blackest kind flourished in the midst of a country that had given to the world Goethe, Beethoven, and Kant!

What had all this to do with Carrel? A great deal. He was a devout Roman Catholic. He was an elitist, a believer in hierarchy. He was authoritarian, even dictatorial, in his attitude to life. He was convinced that only with the help of an ascetic and mystic minority could any sort of tolerable existence be created for the "feeble, unruly, incomplete, empirical creatures created in jest" that constituted the bulk

of the human man-mass. There had to be such an elite, and
they had to have authority. If no elite emerged to control
the man-mass, it would certainly wreck the planet. Without
the elite nothing could save us from the "anarchy of the
masses." Millions of human hogs all screaming for more
swill would squander the resources of the planet. There
would be runaway inflation, total breakdown of law and
order, complete destruction of the social contract. Without
the guiding elite man would return to the Stone Age.

And what organization could provide the guiding elite?
Only the Roman Catholic Church, with its centuries of experience, its powerful hierarchy, its trained religious orders, its strength both spiritual and material. But the
Church, in that foggy epoch, was in a terrible quandary. It
confronted not one but two versions of the Antichrist. Soviet Communism seemed a worse threat than the Satanic
Order that had arisen in Germany. The black monks of the
SS had cast off Christianity to revert to the ancient pagan-
ism. But at least they were at heart religious. Stalin and his
murderous henchmen were mere materialists who had sold
the soul of holy Russia for a mess of Marxian pottage.

What a tangle! As I gathered my material for the life of
Carrel, I gained more and more insight into that weird
epoch that brought death and ruin to almost the whole of
Europe. The Catholic hierarchy never could make up its
mind whether to openly oppose Hitler's Satanic Order or to
try to convert it back to Christianity.

Carrel confronted the same problem. Returning to a de-
feated, prostrate France, he began with remarkable courage
to plan the creation of his Institute of Man. Not only did he
plan it, he actually got it started, which was no small feat
considering the circumstances. On November 17, 1941, *La
Fondation française pour l'étude des problemes humains* was officially created by the collaborationist regime of Marshal
Pétain.

Carrel, in order to keep his institute going, had to keep
on good terms with the victorious Germans. Did he secretly

admire them? There were many who, after the liberation, accused him of being a Nazi in disguise. He was called a racist, an apologist for the Nazi theories, a Nazi eugenist and other unflattering things. Certainly, in *Man the Unknown* he had openly declared that the Nordic races were superior, that Western civilization was ruining itself by its sentimental practice of encouraging the survival of the unfit. He had written, "We must help the strong: Only the elite makes the progress of the masses possible." During a shipboard interview in 1935 he had stated: "There is no escaping the fact that men were definitely not created equal, as democracy, invented in the eighteenth century, would have us believe." He had proposed drastic methods for dealing with crime, suggesting that those who had murdered, robbed while armed, kidnapped children, despoiled the poor of their savings, misled the public on important matters, should be "humanely and economically disposed of in small euthanistic institutions supplied with proper gases."

Did this make him a Nazi, or was he merely stating clearly certain views that liberalism had made unmentionable?

As for his Institute of Man, it offered nothing new or startling. It simply demanded a return to a healthier pattern of life and a more balanced style of education, education of the whole man, not merely of his intellect. "The task of the professor of integral education in every school will be to build up complete human beings." It was essential for a new elite to remind their fellow man of the challenges of the Warrior's Way, to lead them toward a cleaner, more strenuous life-style. He wrote poignantly of the decline of France:

> The young Frenchman of the defeat, rude, slovenly, unshaven, slouching about with his hands in his pockets and a cigarette in the corner of his mouth, was all too representative of the anemic barbarism on which the France of those years prided herself. She had destroyed her own ability and

strength. Her fate was inevitable, for she had committed the unforgivable sin. Nature annihilates those who abandon themselves. Suicide often takes a subtle and pleasant form such as an abundance of food, soft living, complete economic security and absence of responsibility. No one realized the dangers of the comfort we enjoyed in the years before the world war. Neither did they realize the dangers of the excessive eating and drinking to which everyone was addicted from infancy to old age. To have a safe position, exempt from responsibility, in some government department seemed to most people highly desirable. Yet this sort of existence is as dangerous as the drug habit both for the individual and for the nation.

(*Reflections on Life*,
New York: Hawthorn Books, 1952.)

He implored his countrymen to live strenuously, to avoid idle chatter, silly novels, the lies and absurdities of the radio and the movies. How many precious hours are frittered in activities worthy only of demented fools? What is the point of living if it consists only of dancing, driving about in cars, being a slave to one's appetite, pursuing fantasies instead of realities? Instead of pampering ourselves, we should learn to endure heat and cold, walk, run, climb in all sorts of weather, avoid as far as possible the artificial atmosphere of offices, flats, motor cars, eat sparingly, sleep neither too much or too little, develop our bodies, our minds, our aesthetic ability, and find satisfaction for our religious urges. People who have the strength and courage to order their existences will be magnificently rewarded. "Life will give herself to them as she gave herself to the inhabitants of ancient Greece, in her full strength and beauty."

Who would lead the French people to the way of regeneration? Carrel envisaged a new order.

To teach men how to conduct their lives, we need guides who combine a knowledge of the modern world with the science of the doctor, the wisdom of the philosopher and the conscience of the priest; in other words, ascetics who have experience of life and are learned in the science of man. Perhaps a religious order whose members possessed a character at once scientific and sacerdotal should be founded for this very end. These men, when they reached the threshold of old age, would be qualified to serve as guides to the vast flock of those who wander in universal confusion. It would be incumbent on such men to adjust the general rules of the conduct of life to the needs of each individual.

It was all good, stirring stuff, but Carrel's clarion call would have sounded a lot better had it come from the camp of General de Gaulle. By setting up his institute under the auspices of the despised Pétain, Carrel seemed to accept the Nazi domination of Europe. He certainly did not regard Nazism as a spiritual cancer that had to be excised at all costs if any sort of civilization was to survive. He was confused, as were most of the members of the White Order, who could not understand the truly Satanic quality of the Black Order and still hoped somehow to use it against Soviet Communism.

Carrel's confusion cost him dearly.

As the war continued and feelings grew increasingly bitter, any organization having to do with Pétain and his collaborationist regime became suspect. After the liberation Carrel's Institute of Man was regarded with disfavor. Carrel found himself accused of harboring racist ideas, of being antidemocratic, of secretly dealing with the Nazis. He had indeed dealt with them, but only to ensure a more adequate diet for the seriously malnourished French population, especially for the children. "I would collaborate with the devil himself to save the children."

But the spirit of the age was against him. France swarmed with superpatriots thirsting for vengeance, eager to ruin anyone who had worked with the hated enemy. On August 21, 1944, the new Minister of Public Health, Pasteur-Vallery-Radot, published a brief statement:

Dr. Alexis Carrel, director of the French Foundation for the Study of Human Problems, is relieved of his post.

The shock of this announcement killed Carrel. Already ill with heart disease, he now found himself reviled as a traitor and deprived of his institute, cast out, rejected, despised. He had sacrificed his easy life in America to return to occupied France. He had suffered cold, hunger, illness, struggling to help his countrymen and to get more food for their children from the victorious Germans. All he received from the people of France was hatred. He had nothing left to live for. He died on November 5, 1944, aged 71, and was buried on the island of St. Gildas. In 1945 his Foundation for the Study of Man was dissolved.

30

IN
DUBIOUS BATTLE

If only . . .

These words expressed my reactions to Charles Lindbergh. They recurred again and again as I thought about him and his life. I had acquired at that time a habit of looking for someone with that special power that Gurdjieff described by the word *Hvareno*. I was still obsessed by the idea that the Work needed some kind of charismatic leader to create the Ring of Power. A Ring of Power consists of a group of men and women firmly united by a common aim and motivated by a common will. Within a Ring of Power the forces produced are far greater than those that any one member of the ring can generate.

But the Ring of Power can be brought together and held together only by a being having the special quality *Hvareno*. Such beings are natural leaders and natural Warriors. They are endowed so richly by the life force that they seem like a race apart. They combine in themselves the intellectual, emotional, and physical qualities necessary for one who must function both as a thinker and as a man of action.

At the time I met Lindbergh, all my teachers were dead, and I had no intention of looking for new ones. I did not need more knowledge. What I needed was growth of being. But to bring about such growth of being, interaction with others was needed—not the ordinary interactions that take place in everyday life, but the special interactions that can only happen between members of a Ring of Power. The members of such a ring strengthen each other in accordance with the law "One hand gives, the other hand takes." They do not lie to each other. They are essence friends and comrades in the struggle with sleep.

If only . . . As I listened to Lindbergh talking about Carrel's plans for the Institute of Man, a peculiar sadness invaded my being. Those two, Charles and Anne Lindbergh, had all the qualities needed to create a new Ring of Power. They were both Warriors of the first order. They had met Ouspensky and knew enough about the Work to understand all its basic principles. They were so prominent that they could make contact with anyone in society from the President down. They could attract to themselves others who were as strong as they were, not dropouts, little lost lambs, or borderline schizophrenics, but men and women of the Warrior type, strong people who could play the ordinary life games very successfully and still have energy left to play the master game.

If only those two would use their power to draw toward them a group of creative spirits! With the resources such a group could command, we could once again organize the Seekers after Truth. For the conviction still persisted in my mind that there existed somewhere an inner circle of initiates who held the missing fragments of the teaching. I was convinced that Gurdjieff had not taught all that he knew. Perhaps there were several things he had not known. After all, I had no reason to suppose that he was omniscient. But a group would need to be very strong and very determined to get results. They would have to be members of a spiritual elite, capable of using knowledge to develop being. Only through work on being could knowledge be transformed into understanding.

The sadness that I felt as I thought about the Lindberghs was due to the realization that they could not play the role I envisaged. Though they had so many of the right qualities, they could not create a Ring of Power. Something that I could not understand had happened in the course of their lives that prevented them from playing a leading role in the great game. There was nothing I could do about it.

Nothing except study the web of cause and effect that had shaped their lives. As always I was eager to understand the laws of fate. Few people had been treated more dramatically by fate than had Charles Lindbergh. Even today, several years after his death, I cannot contemplate Lindbergh's life without a feeling of amazement. It reveals so much, not only about the fantastic complexity of human beings but also about a disastrous period of history.

To begin with, there was Lindy, the Lone Eagle. He had flown alone from New York to Paris in a small plane called *The Spirit of St. Louis.* It was a pretty heroic feat in those days. The distance from New York to Paris, 3,400 miles, was thought to be beyond the range of the planes then in existence. Lindbergh was called the Flying Fool by certain newspaper men who knew little about flying and less about Lindbergh. A flyer he certainly was, a barnstormer, an air-mail pilot, survivor of several crashes, and about as fearless as any man could be. A fool he was not. He understood from the beginning the meaning of the aphorism "You'll be more of a simpleton than a warrior if you let yourself in for a battle against hopeless odds." He had calculated to the last gallon the fuel he would need to make the trip. He had no intention of committing suicide.

He took off at dawn on May 20, 1927. The weather was awful. Rain poured down from a leaden sky. The mud on Roosevelt Field sucked at the wheels of the small plane as if determined to hold it to the earth. Burdened with five thousand pounds of gasoline the little plane struggled into the air at the last possible moment. Watchers on the ground thought it would never clear the telephone wires that stretched above the end of the runway. It did—just. The plane vanished into the clouds.

It is hard for us now, surfeited as we are with space spectaculars, to understand the emotions Lindbergh's flight aroused. As his biographer Leonard Mosley points out, he had appeared out of nowhere in a tawdry world of booze and gangsters where the frenzied couples of the Jazz Age danced their way toward the coming crash. He was clean, young, handsome, and untainted by the frenzy of the twenties. He had arrived without fuss or fanfare, stayed aloof from the shabby carnival that swirled round him during his stay in New York.

He coolly ignored the jibes of those self-appointed experts who called him the Flying Fool and foretold his certain death. So confident and godlike was his aspect that he seemed like a veritable messenger carrying the Word. He was challenging the standards of a cheap, flashy, cynical, corrupt world by a single act of superb courage. For millions of people he became a symbol of all that was highest in the spirit of man, the willingness to adventure beyond the horizon, to go to the utmost limit, to challenge and dare and die if necessary. On that grey morning in May he offered the American people a living emblem of the Warrior's Way.

For Lindbergh also the flight was far more than a trip from New York to Paris. When he was alone over the Atlantic, after nearly forty-eight hours without sleep, his state of consciousness began to change. As he stared at his instruments, desperately struggling to stay awake, the fuselage behind him became filled with ghostly presences. He felt no surprise at their coming. They appeared to pass in and out through the walls of the fuselage. Familiar voices conversed and advised him on his flight, discussed problems of his navigation, reassured him, gave him messages of importance unattainable in ordinary life.

As the plane droned on, both time and space disappeared. There was no longer any weight to his body, the feeling of flesh was gone. He was on the borderline of life and the greater realm beyond. He was being acted upon by powers incomparably stronger than any he had ever known. The enormous stresses he had endured preparing for the flight, the constant challenges of fog and rain and ice, the struggle with sleep, a struggle so fierce that he had to hold his eyelids open with his fingers, were bringing him to one of the supreme experiences of the Warrior's Way, the experience of death without dying. He wrote:

> Is this death? Am I crossing the bridge one sees only in last, departing moments? Am I already beyond the point from which I can bring my vision back to earth and men? Death no longer seems the final end it used to be, but rather the entrance to a new and free existence which includes all space, all time.
>
> . . . On this fantastic flight, I'm so far separated from the earthly life I know that I accept whatever circumstance may come. In fact these emissaries from a spirit world are quite in keeping with the night and day. They're neither intruders nor strangers. . . . I live in the past, the present, and the future, here and in different places, all at once.
>
> (*The Spirit of St. Louis,* Charles A. Lindbergh. New York: Charles Scribner's Sons, 1953.)

Here was no ordinary aviator. Here was a mystic, a poet, a spiritual Warrior, entering that mysterious region between life and death that few dare to penetrate. He was one of the elect, the twice born. He had gone through death without dying and had seen mysteries hidden from all but a few.

But he had to return to earth. He had to return to play the role of hero, to be wined, dined, feted, decorated, pawed over, and gaped at, pestered by newsmen, plagued by cranks. The faceless man-swarm reached out its arms like the myriad tentacles of some gigantic polyp, as if it intended to swallow him whole. Everywhere it was *Lindbergh, Lindbergh, Lindbergh.* He who loved privacy had become, practically overnight, one of the most public figures in the world. He hated it, hated especially the hounds of the press who never gave him any peace, pursuing him endlessly with their cameras. "Smile," they would say as he stood beside his plane. "What for?" he would snap and glower at them.

Ordeal by fame.

In May 1929 he married Anne Spencer Morrow. Despite her small size and frail appearance, she was as much a Warrior as he himself. Lindbergh had no use for the type of wife who sits at home knitting socks for the coming baby while her man goes off and has adventures. Where he went she would go too. So she learned to fly a plane, to navigate, to send messages by Morse code (the only means of communication between air and ground in those days). She went with him on a record-breaking trip across the American continent. She was radio operator, navigator, and spare pilot on a truly hair-raising expedition across the polar cap to China. When their plane tipped over in the flooded Yangtze River, she jumped when he said jump. He rose to the surface spluttering, to see, as he put it later, "little Anne Pan, perfectly happy paddling along like a little mud turtle."

She was a Warrior all right, and she needed every bit of her Warrior's spirit.

On February 29, 1932, a carpenter from the Bronx called Bruno Richard Hauptman kidnapped the Lindbergh's first child. The kidnapping plunged Anne and Charles Lindbergh into a ghastly circus. There were gangsters who claimed to know where the child was. There were politicians and film stars who announced they had important clues and wanted to be photographed with the Lindberghs for publicity reasons. There were 38,000 letters, of which about 5,000 were from cranks who announced that the misery of the Lindberghs was a sign of the wrath of God and a punishment for the sins of arrogance and affluence. Others found the private number of their telephone and would call at night to say they had the child, then would jeer and cackle and mouth obscenities. There was the boat builder John Hughes Curtis, who took Lindbergh out to sea to rendezvous with the boat that was holding his child—then, when news reached them that the dead body of the child had been found, burst into floods of tears and admitted his story had been a tissue of lies. He had hoped to "become famous."

Later, during the trial of Bruno Hauptman, the same obscene performance was repeated. The little town of Flemington, New Jersey, where the trial was held, had a carnival atmosphere. There were even people who offered a "certified veritable lock of hair from Baby Lindbergh" sealed in small envelopes. All the filth that lies at the lowest level of American life seemed to become stirred up by the kidnapping. All that Nietzsche expressed in the disdainful phrase "human, all too human" was demonstrated by the reaction of the man-swarm. It was a truly disgusting performance and provoked in the minds of the Lindberghs some serious questions. Was this vulgar, sensation-seeking, gloating, repulsive mob the logical end-product of the American dream of democracy? Was America a civilized country at all? The doubts were very real and they went deep, so deep that the Lindberghs left the United States and set sail secretly for England. They were far out on the Atlantic before the American public learned that their hero had left them. The New York *Herald Tribune* mourned their departure:

> Nations have exiled their heroes before; they have broken them with meanness. But when has a nation made life unbearable to one of its most distinguished men through a sheer inability to protect him from its criminals and lunatics and the vast vulgarity of its sensationalists, publicity-seekers, petty politicians and the yellow newspapers? It seems as incredible as it is shocking. Yet everyone knows this is exactly what has happened. . . .

The Lindberghs expected to live peacefully in England. They arrived there in December 1935 and settled in Long Barn in Kent, renting the house from Harold Nicolson and his wife, Vita Sackville-West. Their privacy was respected. There were no reporters, no crowds, no flashbulbs, no receptions. They did not need to fear that their second son,

Jon, would suffer the same fate as their first. At last they could feel reasonably secure.

But the Lindberghs seemed to be the objects of a special experiment by fate. A relentless force seemed determined to test their spirits, challenging both of them again and again, refusing to allow them to sink into obscurity. In June 1936, a letter reached Long Barn from the United States Embassy in Germany. It was signed by the military attaché, Major Truman Smith. It extended to Colonel Charles Lindbergh in the name of General Goering and the German Air Ministry an invitation to visit Germany and inspect the new German civil and military air establishment. Lindbergh accepted the invitation.

It was a fateful decision. Lindbergh was dazzled by the power of the Nazis. An extremely truthful person himself, he could not understand the method of the Big Lie, which was Hitler's favorite weapon. It was used on Lindbergh with devastating effect. Every effort was made by Goering and his minions to impress their American visitor with the strength of the *Luftwaffe*. He was shown all the latest military planes. He was given grossly exaggerated figures concerning aircraft production in Germany, figures he accepted without question. He made several other trips to Germany, and with each trip his admiration for the Germans increased, as did his conviction that the German air force was invincible.

So in the dismal month of September 1938, when the whole fate of Europe hung in the balance, we find Lindbergh writing a letter to Joseph P. Kennedy, the American ambassador to London. Kennedy, like Lindbergh, was convinced that Germany was insuperable and was determined to use his considerable influence to keep Britain out of a war. Everything he read in Lindbergh's letter reinforced his views.

> Without doubt the German airfleet is now stronger than that of any other country in the world. . . . I feel certain that Ger-

man air strength is greater than that of all other European countries combined. . . . I believe that German factories are capable of producing in the vicinity of 20,000 aircraft each year. . . . I do not believe civilization ever faced a greater crisis. Germany now has the means of destroying London, Paris and Prague if she wishes to do so. . . . It seems essential to avoid a general European war in the near future at almost any cost. . . . I am convinced that it is wiser to permit Germany's eastward expansion than to throw England and France, unprepared, into a war at this time.

There was much more to this effect. It was hardly the sort of stuff to encourage the already terrified British prime minister, Neville Chamberlain, or the no less terrified French prime minister, Edouard Daladier. At Munich on September 29, 1938, Britain and France forsook their ally Czechoslovakia. Influential Germans, many of whom were ready to dump Hitler at that point, became convinced that the Führer really was infallible.

Strange destiny! Lindbergh, one of the most honest men alive, had become a special channel through which the fog of lies within which the Nazis operated was generated. They were masters of the art of deception, and Lindbergh, without in the least intending to do so, aided them enormously. His prestige, his knowledge of aviation, his status as official world hero gave to his reports a devastating impact. Those reports were false. All the facts that came to light after the war show that the strength of the *Luftwaffe* in 1938 was grossly overrated. Udet, director of the Technical Department at the German Air Ministry, was making a complete mess of Germany's aviation program. Had Britain stood firm, France would have plucked up courage and the Soviet Union would have come to the aid of Czechoslovakia. Against the combined forces of Britain, France, Czechoslovakia, and Soviet Russia, the *Luftwaffe* in 1938 would not have had a chance.

Goering knew this. Many other responsible Germans

knew it too. But the Nazis were always willing to bluff, and in this case the bluff worked. It worked in that it deferred war for a year and gave the *Luftwaffe* a victory it could not have won in the air without its even having to leave the ground. That victory, of course, turned out in the end to have been a disaster. It led to the ultimate ruin of Germany and the devastation of Europe. One of the contributors to that disastrous victory was Charles Lindbergh.

How did it happen? How could a man of Lindbergh's spiritual stature allow himself to be used by that bloodthirsty gang of thugs that had managed to dominate Germany? Had he, following Carrel's teaching, accepted the concept of the spiritual elite who would, by force if need be, impose a nobler, more strenuous way of life on the degraded man-swarm? Did he see Hitler's gangsters as representing this spiritual elite? Did he admire the tubby Goering, from whose hand he accepted in 1939 the Silver Cross of the German Eagle, a decoration Anne Lindbergh designated "the albatross," and which did indeed hang round his neck as heavily as did the albatross round the neck of the Ancient Mariner?

It is hard to answer these questions. The confusion that prevailed during the Dirty Thirties was so complete that many honest people lost their bearings. Lindbergh was one of them. From 1939, when he returned to the United States, to December 1941, when the Japanese bombed Pearl Harbor, he struggled to keep America out of the European war. His isolationist stand was not popular. The hero of the 1920s was becoming the villain of the forties, the sworn foe of Franklin D. Roosevelt and of all those who believed that it was high time for the United States to come to the rescue of the British, who had fought off the *Luftwaffe* and disposed once and for all of the myth of German invincibility. Colonel Henry Breckenridge, once Lindbergh's attorney and one of his closest friends, expressed the feelings of many when he wrote: "Norway has its Quisling, France its Laval. The United States has its equivalent. He who spreads the gospel of defeatism is an ally of Adolf Hitler." He did not mention Lindbergh by name, but those who read the passage knew whom he meant. The once impeccable hero was now being classed with the despised traitors Vidkun Quisling and Pierre Laval!

He was a stubborn man. After the war was over, he was sent out as a civilian to a starving and ruined Germany to study German developments in aircraft and missiles. He sympathized with the Germans and insisted that the whole struggle had been in vain. Most of the prophecies he had made were coming true. The British Empire was disintegrating. Half of Europe had come under the domination of the unspeakable Stalin. The rest of Europe stayed free only because the American possession of the atomic bomb made Stalin afraid to advance. The powerful German army, which could have held him at bay, was destroyed. America was in greater danger than ever before.

But the times were changing. In the late 1940s a ghostly presence seemed to be whispering advice to those members of the human race attentive enough to hear it. "Little man, how about a change in behavior? How about a little less arrogance, a little less boasting, a little less talk of war and the 'conquest of nature'? How about some second thoughts on the subject of technology? How about calling a halt to the rape of the planet? You are only a part of the biosphere, little man. Who told you you own the earth? Now put your house in order and start cleaning things up or you're apt to go the way of the dodo and dinosaur."

Anne Lindbergh was one of those who heard that ghostly adviser. She had spent some months alone on Sanibel Island off the coast of Florida and there reestablished her links with the Old One, the soul of the biosphere, which speaks in all nature for those who have ears to hear. The product of her retreat was a book, *A Gift from the Sea*. It was a plea for solitude and meditation, an expression of gratitude for those marvels of life which our hasty, almost insane life-style leaves us no time to appreciate.

Charles Lindbergh also heard that voice. In a little book called *Of Flight and Life* (New York: Charles Scribner's Sons, 1948) he set down his thoughts. The quality of civilization depended on the balance of body, mind, and spirit in its people. If we were to survive, we had to keep this balance. If we were to progress, we would have to improve it. A naive faith in science had led us to accept false values and stupid life games. Day after day scientific man had to serve the mechanistic utopia he had developed, because if he failed to do so his world would collapse.

In turning his back on the gifts of nature he was born with, in replacing grass with concrete and sun with artificial sunlight, in making himself a superman of earth, scientific man loses contact with both the qualities of life and the truths essential to his own survival. He goes on amassing knowledge and power until he creates weapons with which he can destroy himself at will. Neglecting body, enthroning mind over spirit, dabbling with superhuman powers, striving to compete with God, the ruins of Europe and the new spectre of the atomic rocket at last bring him face to face with his own frailty. Discovering, complicating, theorizing, quarreling, he approaches the terrible devastation of an atomic-biologic war—as though God had set a final limit to his sins.

It should now be branded on our consciousness that unless science is controlled by a greater moral force, it will become the Antichrist prophesied by early Christians. If we are to keep it from destroying that part of our civilization which is left, if it is to be the great benefit to mankind that we have hoped, we must control it by a philosophy reaching beyond materialism, a philosophy rooted in the character of man and nourished by the eternal truths of God.

Charles Lindbergh, now one of the directors of Pan American Airways, found his old beliefs and life games challenged as never before. He had been a Cold War Warrior, motivated by hatred and suspicion of the Russian and Chinese Communists. He had been a fervent admirer of technology, especially as it applied to aircraft. Now he had doubts, both about the Cold War and about technology. His technological doubts were focused on the Concorde, that supersonic monster of a plane which the French and British had combined to inflict on mankind. Could he sincerely advise his fellow directors on the board of Pan American Airways to plan to build such a monster or to purchase the Anglo-French Concordes? No, he could not. He saw nothing but danger to man and his environment from fleets of supersonic airliners. The accursed machines would merely add to the pollution of the biosphere, waste the planet's dwindling oil resources, and add to the already excessive noise levels prevailing in the neighborhood of airports. Besides, why was it necessary for human beings to travel at speeds approaching that of a rifle bullet? Why the hurry?

To escape from the clamor that surrounded the Concorde controversy, he fled to Africa where he went on safari with a camera instead of a rifle. Resting under an acacia tree with the sounds of dawn around him, he reflected that the construction of an airplane was simple compared to that of a bird. Airplanes depended on advanced civilization; and where civilization was most advanced, few birds existed. He realized that if he had to choose, he would rather have birds than airplanes.

He had found, as Don Juan would put it, a "way with heart." He continued to follow that way to the end of his life. And, as always happens to one who finds a way with heart, he was at peace. "I have not seen Charles so happy or excited for years," Anne Lindbergh told her friends. He was always a man of action, but now his activity was concerned with restoring the ecological balance that man had so grossly upset. He exerted himself on behalf of the threatened whales, the polar bear of Alaska, the one-horned rhinoceros of Java, the tamarau of the Philippines. He campaigned on behalf of the gentle Tassadays, a race of people still in the Stone Age who lived in the dense jungles of Mindanao Island. The Tassadays had no words for war, enemy, murder, or even for indicating that someone was bad. They were a smiling, peaceable tribe. Now they were threatened by "civilization," gun in hand and murder in its heart.

Lindbergh was determined to save them from such a fate. He dropped into the forests from a helicopter and befriended the Tassadays. The Tassadays, who were about the size of pygmies, must have regarded him as some sort of towering god who had specially descended from heaven to protect them. His intervention was effective. President Marcos announced that 46,299 acres of Tassaday country would henceforth be a reserve.

Lindbergh's interests, however, went far beyond saving the one-horned rhinoceros and protecting the Tassadays from so-called civilization. In July 1969, amid enormous publicity, the United States prepared to launch Apollo XI, which would take three astronauts to the moon. If all went well, they would actually walk on its surface. The event was heralded by a special issue of *Life* (July 4, 1969), to which Lindbergh was asked to contribute. He refused, but wrote a long letter explaining why, which *Life* considered important enough to publish.

Years ago, wrote Lindbergh, he had decided to stop writing about aviation and astronautics. The very improvements that had made flying so much safer and easier, the radios and automatic pilots, had helped to turn him away from flying. It had become too easy. It was no longer a challenge. He explained how he had met Carrel and how, between them, they had studied certain basic problems of biology. Could longevity be extended? Was death an unavoidable part of life's cycle, or could physical immortality be achieved by scientific means? Could a severed head be kept alive apart from the body? He explained that he had become disenchanted with this kind of biological gadgeteering and set off to India in 1937 with the hope of gaining insight into yogic practices.

He further explained that when the Apollo program began, he felt an almost overwhelming desire to reenter the field of astronautics. After all, he had been a longtime friend of Robert Goddard, the pioneer of rocket technology. But he knew that return to that field of research was impossible. He saw too clearly the limits imposed on technology by inescapable laws of biology and physics. Mars and Venus marked the limit for spaceship travel. The great space adventure was really a dead end. Far greater journeys beckoned, but they would not be accomplished by means of rockets. Through his evolving awareness, and awareness of that awareness, man could merge with the miraculous—"to which we can attach what better name than God?" In that merging, long sensed by intuition but still only vaguely perceived by rationality, experience would be able to travel without the need for accompanying life.

> Will we then find life to be only a stage, though an essential one, in a cosmic evolution of which our evolving awareness is beginning to become aware? Will we discover that only *without* spaceships can we reach the galaxies; that only *without* cyclotrons can we know the interior of atoms? To venture beyond the fantastic accomplishments of this physically fantastic age, sensory perception must combine with the extrasensory and I suspect that the two will prove to be different faces of each other. I believe it is through sensing and thinking about such concepts that great adventures of the future will be found.

He had traveled far. He had known fame and obloquy, been called a hero and a traitor, been worshipped and reviled. Now once again, as he had done during his lone flight to Paris, he was venturing toward the outer edge, the unknown region. He had followed his own version of the Warrior's Way, and now the path was vanishing into the vastness. In March 1974 his body began to fail. He was suffering from lymphatic cancer and had not long to live. Refusing to die in a hospital bed, he had himself flown to his property on the island of Maui overlooking the sea. He had always been methodical, planning his flights with meticu-

lous care. Now he prepared for the last one, arranging his
writings, going over his will. His coffin of plain eucalyptus
wood had been prepared. He even planned what he would
wear at the burial (a simple drill shirt and pants) and what
would be said and sung at the funeral. On August 25, 1974,
he said good-bye to Anne, who had been his comrade on so
many adventurous journeys. Next morning Charles Lindbergh took off on his last flight.

31

I
HAVE BEEN
HERE BEFORE

> I have been here before,
> But when and how I cannot tell:
> I know the grass beyond the door,
> The sweet keen smell,
> The sighing sound, the lights around the shore.
> —I knew it all of yore.

This poem, *Sudden Light* by Dante Gabriel Rossetti, had been a favorite of Ouspensky's. It described the strange sensation that comes to certain people at certain moments in their lives. *I have seen this before.*

Ouspensky took this sensation as evidence of the reality of eternal recurrence. Time, like space, was curved and had three dimensions. Eternal recurrence represented the second dimension of time and the fifth of the time-space continuum. But for us, in our ordinary state of consciousness, the second dimension of time was inconceivable. Time sped like an arrow in one direction only, from past to future.

These thoughts passed through my mind as I drove with a realtor from Sonoma up the narrow curves of Sonoma Mountain Road in northern California. I had reached, in that year 1961, another fork in my personal line of fate. They are mysterious, these forks. They occur at intervals, and one's personal fate depends on which road one chooses. Do we in fact choose, or is the choice made for us? Do we shape our own fates, or are we programmed like mechanical toys?

Idle questions, purely philosophical, unanswerable. Stick to the facts. Here I am, employed already for nearly ten years by a large manufacturer of ethical pharmaceuticals. I have risen slowly to a position of moderate responsibility. I am a group leader in the biochemistry department. My work is fairly interesting, concerned with the effect of various drugs on the biochemistry of the brain. There are, without a doubt, fascinating problems to be explored in the realm of brain biochemistry. We already know that the anterior pituitary is the source of the arousers and awakeners, of the hormones that stimulate glands to produce other hormones, gonadotropin which awakens the gonads, thyrotropin which awakens the thyroid, adrenocorticotropin which awakens the adrenal cortex. But above the pituitary is the hypothalamus, that potent segment of the old brain that regulates hunger, thirst, temperature, sex, rage. We have reason to think that the hypothalamus produces even more potent hormones than the anterior pituitary, that it generates the arousers of the arousers, the awakeners of the awakeners.

These mysterious substances are almost certainly peptides or small proteins. To extract and purify them would be very tricky and very challenging. Quite possibly in the course of such research one might gain an insight into the nature of those "twisted molecules" that cause schizophrenia. I have no doubt that some chemical process goes awry in the brain of the schizophrenic and that only by chemical means can that condition be cured. It is an attractive line of research, difficult but fundamental. I now know enough biochemistry to be able to pursue it. Why then am I seized with this strange restlessness that makes me reluctant to embark on such exciting research?

I did not know the reason, but some agitation had begun in my personal ship of fools, not exactly a mutiny but something very like it. An element was missing from my inner life that the Scientist could not supply. At that time the Scientist had become predominant. He was, after all, the breadwinner. He had done fairly well, and might do better in future. He was flexible, always ready to learn new methods, and when really interested in a problem, prepared to work very hard to solve it. He enjoyed mastering the rather elegant technical tricks that were constantly being introduced into biochemistry: gel-electrophoresis, immunoelectrophoresis, various fancy versions of chromatography that made possible the purification of proteins. The introduction of radioactive elements into biochemical research was another development that greatly pleased my Scientist. He loved to stand in front of the large scintillation counter and watch the machine rolling its electronic eyes and printing out its data on yards of tape. He enjoyed such gadgets, was as happy with them as a child with a new toy.

So far as my Scientist was concerned, there was nothing wrong with working at Lederle Laboratories. The ivory tower boys in academic research tended to look down on scientists in industry as mere commercial hacks. So what? We worked for a company that was in business to produce compounds that would cure human disease. We had practical aims in mind. The company had to sell pills to stay in business. The ivory tower boys could dream rather more freely, and follow their fancy a bit more skittishly. But I had been given quite a lot of freedom in industry, more perhaps than I could have found in the groves of academe.

So my restlessness had nothing to do with dissatisfaction with my job. It arose rather from a growing disgust with my environment. I had arrived in Rockland County, New York, in 1951, while the Korean War was still raging and Truman was president. I had found it rural and very much to my taste. The house we had built was quiet and isolated. The garden produced enough vegetables for our needs. A stream, unpolluted, ran through the property. There were huge oak trees, black walnuts, tulip trees. Lady's-slipper orchids grew in the woods. Outside the house, narrow Vanderbilt Road had little more than a trickle of traffic, and the children could safely walk to school at Chestnut Grove, about a mile away.

But in less than ten years what a change had swept the

county! A huge bridge had been flung across the Hudson River at Tappan Zee. Most of the town of West Nyack had been bulldozed aside to make way for an east-west expressway. Another gigantic expressway (north-south) chewed into the county connecting it, via the George Washington Bridge, to the New York megalopolis. Along these expressways, like rats leaving a sinking ship, poured thousands of refugees from the horrors of Manhattan. A rash of subdivisions devoured Rockland County, bulldozers roared, chain saws screamed, streams were polluted, great oaks felled, the fragile orchids crushed under the treads of huge machines. Traffic along our little country road grew steadily more raucous. Soon they would widen it to make a four-lane highway. Brats on bicycles and tricycles, the spawn of suburbia, swarmed everywhere, trespassing freely, uprooting fences built to keep them out, destructive and undisciplined. Taxes quadrupled. Land prices soared.

The writing on the wall.

Said Tessa, "Why don't you spend your vacation in California?"

Ah, yes, California. Who would live in the east if he could possibly move west? California was calling. California, cradle of the new root race, a land flowing with wine and orange juice, a land of mild winters and clear summers, a golden land. From San Francisco, in a hired Volkswagen, I traveled north under the brilliant sky to the vineyards and tawny hills of Sonoma County. In the quaint little town of Sonoma, with palm trees growing around its sleepy plaza and ducks waddling around a pond, I walked into the office of a realtor.

"I am a refugee from a suburban cancer. I want a quiet little place away from it all with vines and redwood trees and a running creek."

The realtor reflected.

"I think I have just the place."

It was pure luck, he explained. The realtor who normally handled the place was away in Europe. It had just been put in his hands. The man who owned it, a retired dentist, had

had a slight stroke while driving to Santa Rosa, had driven his car into the ditch, barely escaped with his life. He could not drive anymore. Up there on the mountain one depended entirely on one's car.

A chain of karma. A series of seeming accidents. The realtor and I drove north to Glen Ellen, up past Wake Robin, once the house of Jack London. Already, under the huge bay trees that overarch that part of Sonoma Mountain Road, the feeling was growing on me. I have been here before. All this I have seen somewhere. These bay trees, these towering redwoods, these clucking California quail with their comical topknots, these mountain vineyards, this incredible expanse of sky, these smooth tawny hills crouching like lions. I know it all. It is my spiritual home. This is the place where I shall die.

We stopped in front of a massive redwood gate. The house was partly hidden among oaks and bay trees. From the patio one looked out across a vineyard, where luscious bunches of Golden Chasselas ripened under their canopy of leaves. The house was at the bottom of a natural amphitheater, facing a semicircle of tree-covered hills. Great redwoods, dark and solemn like cowled monks, rose on the far side of the vineyard. There was a spring house hidden among enormous bay trees, a trickling creek shrunken in the July heat. The owner was brokenhearted at having to leave the place.

"I'm not allowed to drive anymore and my wife can't drive. This is a rather remote neck of the woods. I suppose one could live up here without a car. The early settlers did. They went into Santa Rosa with a horse and buggy. It took them most of the day to get there and get back, with time out for a chat with neighbors along the way. Those were leisurely times. But try driving to town with a horse and buggy nowadays. It would be as much as your life was worth."

It certainly would. Sonoma Mountain Road was steep and tortuous, and motorists did not always drive carefully.

I admired the old man's garden. He had orange trees,

lemons, ginger, apricots, almonds, figs, grapes. This was truly a land of abundance. The little place was in the thermal belt. On frosty nights the cold air drained into the valley.

"I believe if one found a sheltered corner one could raise avocados up here," said the old man. "This is a warm pocket."

A warm pocket. I thought of the previous winter. Snow five feet deep. Endless snow. No sooner was the driveway cleared than it snowed again.

"Does it ever snow up here?"

"Just now and then, a sprinkling. Sometimes Mount St. Helena will be snowcapped for a few days. It melts almost at once."

Thank you for those kind words. I really don't mind if I never see snow again, but a distant snowcapped mountain is always scenic. From the back of the house one could look across the Valley of the Moon to distant Mount St. Helena, where Robert Louis Stevenson had written *The Silverado Squatters*. And Glen Ellen in the valley below was pervaded by the ghost of Jack London. Literary country.

I bought the place, just like that. Didn't even bother with a termite inspection. I paid cash. No mortgages for me. I wrote a letter to Tessa from San Francisco.

"I have bought you a ranch." (In California anything larger than an acre is a ranch.) "It has oranges, lemons, ginger, apricots. A large redwood gate."

I looked at that large redwood gate. On one of the posts supporting it was a string of plastic letters of the kind that glow in the dark. Read from top to bottom they gave a message: DUNROMIN.

Had I really done roaming? Was this my journey's end? It seemed that way.

Back at the lab my boss was incredulous. You're really leaving? A good job, an assured pension. What do you have in California? Nothing. We were just preparing to give you a raise. $15,000 a year. (It was not bad money in those days,

1961. Now they pay more than that to a San Francisco garbage collector!)

Leaving the lab, all that money, all those intriguing research problems! You must be crazy. We can offer you . . . Oh, those offers! Money, money, money. But I have only two possessions, my personal power and my time, the time still unused between this moment and the hour of my death.

I sent out Tessa and our child by plane, followed them later, driving across the country. Before me unrolled the enormous expanse of the North American continent. I had always thought of Chicago as being in the middle, and now it turned out to be only one-third of the way across. My elderly Dodge broke down in Last Chance, in the plains of Colorado. A complete engine job cost me eighty dollars and lasted only as far as Kremmling, Colorado (elev. 7322 feet). I traded the Dodge for a 1954 Chevy and crossed the Rockies. I arrived exhausted. It took me a week to recuperate. And to think that only a hundred years earlier people were making the trip in covered wagons! And had no nice house with telephone and electricity to welcome them, nothing but a wilderness, thinly occupied with Pomo Indians. Those early settlers must have been tough. "The cowards never started, the weak died on the way." Natural selection at work.

Not any longer, alas! Anyone now could enter California, and without a struggle, either. They poured in over the passes in an unending flood. Fortunately the state was enormous and could absorb a lot of people. But the madding crowd did nothing to improve the environment.

Meanwhile my oldest, fondest dream came back with renewed vigor. Five acres and independence. I did not have five acres. I had little more than three, but the land was exceedingly fertile. Thistles as high as my shoulder grew on the land, which had once been cleared but later been neglected. I cleared it again, hacking my way through brush and poison oak. The rich black adobe soil was ten feet deep in places. Incredible soil, sticky and unworkable when wet, brick hard when dry. And yet, when in just the right state—not too wet, not too dry—it could be worked into a beautiful tilth. It accepted organic matter avidly and opened up in proportion to the organic matter it received. It took me years of trial and error to learn how to handle that soil, but the struggle was well rewarded. The black earth fed me and my wife and child, and fed us well.

Health-giving California! I was now fifty years old, and the first grey hairs were appearing. But the glorious climate, the quiet atmosphere, the fog coming in from the Pacific, all this infused my being with extraordinary vigor. Only after moving to California did I realize how debilitating, at least for me, had been the East Coast climate. In the muggy days of summer, when the thunder clouds hung heavy over the land, my body would be wracked with rheumatic pains. But in California I never felt a twinge of rheumatism, and my body seemed to take on a new lease of life.

This upwelling vigor showed itself in my treatment of my little estate. I planted fruit trees, apples, pears, peaches, plums, grapes. I dug ponds for fish and raised silver carp. I even grew a small crop of wheat, harvesting it by hand as I had learned to do in Lithuania. I stomped out the grain and winnowed it in the wind, ground it in a hand mill. I had beans and squash, tomatoes, potatoes, chard, carrots, beets, and onions. I could live almost entirely off my three acres. A happy state.

32

THE GREAT PSYCHEDELIC FREAKWAY

In 1962 I met Aldous Huxley again. It was in a house high in the Berkeley Hills. The huge expanse of the Berkeley-Oakland man-swarm lay below us in the darkness transmuted into fields of sparkling light, a feverish, energy-guzzling glitter. Beyond lay the waters of San Francisco Bay, and beyond that San Francisco itself, also glittering and guzzling.

It was strange to meet Aldous again. He had forgotten all about our earlier meetings in London, the uncomfortable meditations with Gerald Heard, our half-baked attempts to use soul force to restrain mad dictators, the pathetic efforts of the Peace Pledge Union, which had only served to hasten the coming of war. He had aged and was already carrying within him the cancer that was to kill him. But the enormous intellect, the beautifully modulated voice, the gentle objectivity, all were unchanged. He was one of the most highly civilized human beings I had ever met.

Aldous Huxley, prophet and seer . . . He had certainly forseen the psychedelic age. It was an integral part of *Brave New World*. Soma. "All the advantages of alcohol and Christianity, none of their drawbacks." Since that time he had been turned on to mescaline by Abram Hoffer and written of his experiences in *The Doors of Perception*. He had followed this with a second book, *Island*, describing an imaginary community in which the use of psychedelics to induce altered states of consciousness was an accepted part of everyday life.

Aldous Huxley was the senior member of a group of scientists and doctors interested in studying the mode of action of drugs on the mind. Among the more active members of the group was Timothy Leary. Leary, who had just been thrown out of Harvard, was then in the process of launching IFIF (International Federation of Internal Freedom). I attended a small private meeting in Palo Alto to hear him describe the project.

Seated among a mixed collection of psychologists, psychiatrists, and other members of the Bay Area intelligentsia, I listened while Leary described his tropical utopia. It would be located, he said, in Zihuatenejo, a tropical village one hundred and eighty miles north of Acapulco. There, in the Catalina Hotel, Leary would open his Psychedelic Training Center. The happy inhabitants of that Mexican paradise would drift in and out of higher states of consciousness, taking their trips along the Great Psychedelic Freakway under the guidance of experts. They would explore their own and one another's psyches and spend endless hours engaging in that form of spiritual masturbation that passes for self-study in psychological circles.

I listened with growing skepticism to Leary's colorful fantasies. It was so typical of those wordy intellectuals to imagine that a combination of drugs, talk, and lolling about under coconut palms would bring about some sort of inner growth. Talk was truly the curse of the intellectuals. They indulged in endless analyses of themselves and each other, thereby dissipating what little higher energy they possessed. When would they learn to shut up and do something useful—dig soil, plant beans, herd goats, catch fish, shovel shit—anything rather than indulge in this endless jabber? The essence of the Warrior's Way could be expressed in one short sentence: *Stop thoughts as often as possible and for as long as possible.*

Leary finally stopped weaving his Mexican romance.

Questions were called for. A struggle began between various elements in my psyche. I felt an urge to protest. Leary was doing everything in the wrong way and was bound to run into trouble. The kind of operation he contemplated required the utmost discretion. Never once should the real aim of his group be revealed. Its members should move invisibly, like the fighters in a guerilla war, taking the advice of Chairman Mao to be as shy as virgins and quick as rabbits. The group should disguise its aims, never mention LSD or psychedelics, let people think it was down in Mexico to enjoy the fishing or the climate. It should follow the example of the old alchemists, who, fully aware of the menace of the Inquisition, concealed their true aims under the pretense that they sought the Elixir of Youth or the Philosopher's Stone.

But here was Leary, who seemed to think of himself as an alchemist of sorts, madly proclaiming the aims of his group from the rooftops, inviting *Time, Life, Newsweek, Saturday Evening Post* and even CBS television to observe his marvelous experiment. It was obvious to any normally intelligent being that Leary's group in Zihuatenejo would bring down upon itself the wrath of the establishment, both in Mexico and the United States. By calling attention to the power of LSD, they would certainly rouse the zeal of the Cross-eyed Crusaders who make it their business to enact prohibitive legislation. This would make it difficult or impossible for serious students to obtain the drug.

But this was not all. LSD was really a potentially dangerous substance. It could, taken under the wrong conditions, induce a frightening paranoia. A person already balancing on the edge of the abyss of schizophrenia might easily be pushed over that edge by the strange experiences the drug was apt to induce.

I looked at Leary, struggling to be objective. Here was a man with very real possibilities. He was a natural Warrior, courageous to the point of recklessness. He was extremely intelligent, had a sense of humor, the Irish gift of the gab, considerable charisma, and a very deep insight into the sicknesses of our technological civilization. In spite of this he was wildly plunging down one of the most dangerous detours on the Warrior's Way, a detour that was clearly marked Dead End.

Why did he insist on taking it?

Timothy Leary was the very embodiment of the Man with the Message. He had the missionary disease in its most virulent form. What is the missionary disease? An overwhelming impulse to impose one's personal beliefs on others. Leary had this impulse. His message: Start Your Own Religion. How? By dropping out, turning on, and tuning in. "Drop out" means detach yourself from the fake prop, TV-studio games that Americans call reality. Quit school. Quit your job. Don't vote. Avoid all politics. "Turn on" means refocus on the natural energies within the body. To turn on you go out of your mind. To turn on you need a sacrament, which is an external thing that turns the key to the inner doors. LSD is such a sacrament. "Tune in" means start your own religion. You must form that most ancient and sacred of human structures—the clan. A clan or cult is a small group of human beings organized around a religious goal. You are God—but only you can discover and nurture your divinity. No one can start your religion for you.

There was a lot more than this to the message. Leary could talk about it for hours on end. And did. He was a great talker. Which did not answer my own inner question: whether to rise and denounce this psychedelic nonsense or simply keep quiet and let the inevitable happen. For it was clear to me then that Leary craved martyrdom and would probably get it. And why not? Perhaps this was his karma, his own peculiar method of following the Warrior's Way. Was he perhaps really a master player, staging an elaborate masquerade for purposes of his own? Was he purposely following the Way of Outrage in order to shine his spirit and go beyond praise and blame? How much did he really understand about the game?

The Way of Outrage, the Way of *malamat* . . . yes, it was
certainly one of the most difficult of ways. Warriors who
follow this way place themselves *deliberately* in situations
that bring down upon them the wrath, contempt, disapproval of most members of society. "He was despised and
rejected of men, a man of sorrows and acquainted with
grief." Yes indeed, the followers of the Way of Blame had to
be real heroes. But they had to understand what they were
doing and why they were doing it. The Way of Blame could
easily become a fool trap. A fool could follow that way simply to show off, to shock the "squares," to attract attention,
to stir up trouble. A fool would confront, out of sheer bra-
vado, challenges with which he was unable to cope. A Warrior, living strategically, would avoid if possible embarking
on a battle he could not win. The difference between a Warrior and a fool was simply this: A Warrior knew his limitations, a fool did not.

Was Leary a Warrior or a fool? I weighed what evidence I
had. It was not sufficient to give me an answer. There was
only one way to get more evidence, and that was to challenge Leary and observe his reaction. If he was really a master player, he would show me this by his reaction to criticism. So I rose to my feet and poured a stream of cold water
on Leary's Mexican fantasy. I said exactly what I thought.
He had talked too much about his plans. His experiment in
Mexico would be closed by the police after a week. He had
placed far too much reliance on psychedelics, which could
play only a very limited role in the process of psychotransformism. And so on and so forth.

Leary was rather deaf. After listening to the first part of
my tirade, he turned off his hearing aid. It was a gesture
whose meaning was not lost on me. I sat down. He had answered my question.

The Great Psychedelic Freekway! It was odd how many
otherwise intelligent people plunged down this detour during the sixties despite the fact that it was plainly labeled
Dead End. Allen Ginsberg, Alan Watts, Tim Leary, William

Burroughs, Dick Alpert, Ralph Metzger, Ken Kesey, all set out full tilt along this dead-end road and drew large numbers of trusting followers after them. The scenarios they evolved were often thrilling, sometimes tragic, always interesting.

Consider Tim Leary. His tropical utopia, as I had foretold, was closed by the police a few weeks after it had started. All those who had hoped to join the group were deported from Mexico. But it is impossible to stop the activities of a religious fanatic except by throwing him into jail or killing him. A fanatic sees himself as 100 percent right and his opponents 100 percent wrong. He lives in a black and white world with no shades in between. (Leary, despite his sense of humor and high level of intelligence, had all the hallmarks of a fanatic.)

So, undaunted by the Mexican fiasco, he immediately created another utopia, using as a base the old Millbrook estate outside Poughkeepsie, New York. In the ugly old mansion with sixty-four rooms the new League of Spiritual Discovery was started. It contained elements borrowed from Hermann Hesse's *Bead Game*. Leary's Castalia Foundation was no doubt intended to reproduce, more or less, that brotherhood of scientist-scholars in Hesse's novel who used the bead game as a means of weaving together poetry, music, mathematics, and science. Leary was a great admirer of Hesse; indeed, if Leary could be said to have a teacher, Hermann Hesse was the man.

Certainly, by creating the Castalia Foundation, Leary was providing a very interesting matrix for any players of the game *who knew what they were doing*. Hesse's bead game is a version of the Master Game formulated by a wise old player who understood a great deal. Leary also understood a great deal, but only about certain aspects of the game. There were other aspects about which he understood absolutely nothing. "I'm very fond of Tim," said Aldous Huxley, "but why does he have to be such an ass?"

Why indeed? To Aldous Huxley, old and wise, the antics

of Tim Leary were those of the braggart schoolboy whose urge to show off takes the form of constantly breaking school rules and defying authority. Leary could not resist the temptation to tickle, ridicule, and provoke the establishment rhinoceros. The establishment rhinoceros is certainly a very stupid beast, thick-skinned, shortsighted, ill-tempered, and unwieldly. It is also a very dangerous beast; and when it puts down its head and charges, those who stand in its way are apt to get hurt.

Leary stood directly in its way and it charged him with a vengeance. The Castalia Foundation at Millbrook—which could have provided a real training ground for players of the great game—managed, by bungling its public relations, to give the staid burghers of Poughkeepsie the impression that it was a cross between Frankenstein's laboratory and Dracula's castle. All sorts of horrors were thought to take place in the old mansion. It was, accordingly, raided by the police at one-thirty in the morning. They arrested four people on various charges but could not make the charges stick.

Undaunted, Leary again provoked the rhino. This time he was arrested in Laredo, Texas, on the charge of importing marijuana from Mexico without paying the tax. To that charge was added a second charge of possessing marijuana in California. The federal district judge in Texas sentenced him to ten years in jail. The superior court judge in Santa Ana sentenced him to another ten years. He faced twenty years in jail for possession of less than an ounce of marijuana.

He had really riled that rhinoceros!

The rest of Leary's career was strictly on the Keystone Kops level. At the Vacaville Prison he swung through the air on a cable, dropped down a utility pole, was picked up by the Weathermen, smuggled out to Algeria to join forces with Eldridge Cleaver's Black Panthers, was imprisoned by Eldridge Cleaver (the Black Panthers proved more intolerant than the White Rhino, and a lot more violent!), fled to Switzerland, fled to Afghanistan, was abducted by American agents, who snatched his passport and returned him to jail in California. There he was thrown into Folsom Prison to serve up to fifteen years for possession and escape.

By that time the Sober Seventies were well under way. The whole Zeitgeist had altered. To a new and more cynical generation of young people his old siren song, "Drop Out, Tune In, Turn On," sounded like the ravings of a lunatic.

What went wrong? Why, I asked myself, did a man who seemed to be a born Warrior play out this rather sorry farce? For surely it was a sad waste of time and energy to spend all those years playing Keystone Kops with a bunch of narcs. It was Charles W. Slack who answered my question for me. Slack, a psychologist himself, knew Leary well. He wrote a book about him (*Timothy Leary, the Madness of the Sixties and Me*. New York: Peter H. Wyden, 1974). Leary, said Slack, lacked objectivity. He was strongly, even passionately *anti*-middle class. "The middle class is awful, of course," wrote Slack, "but you are not class free if you are constantly fighting the middle class. Head-hunting is awful, but you can't be an objective anthropologist if you are constantly fighting against head-hunting. You are a missionary, not an anthropologist."

Leary made the same mistake as did the Communist intellectuals I mixed with back in the thirties. He sacrificed his objectivity in order to engage in the game of political hatreds. No follower of the Warrior's Way can afford to do this. The Warrior's aim is to awaken, to enter the real world, to *see*. How can you *see* if you indulge in personal prejudices? Gurdjieff and his group escaping from the Russian revolution perfectly exemplified the proper attitude of the Warrior:

> The epidemic of fanaticism and mutual hatred, which had seized all the people around us, did not touch us at all: one might have said that I and my companions moved under supernatural protection.
>
> Just as our attitude towards each side was impartial, as if we

were not of this world, so their attitude towards us was the same—they considered us completely neutral, as in truth we were.

Surrounded by infuriated beasts of people, ready to tear one another apart for the slightest booty, I moved amid this chaos quite openly and fearlessly . . .

(Meetings with Remarkable Men, p. 274.)

There speaks a real master of the game! The true Warrior understands the art of becoming invisible, just as a good anthropologist blends with the culture he studies so completely that he seems part of that culture. Leary did not understand this. He ranged himself on one side against the other. Despite such amiable slogans as "Make love not war," the whole hippie movement was heavily loaded with hostility. It was Freaksville versus Squaresville, the counter-culture versus the establishment. Leary got caught in the crossfire, and having made himself a very conspicuous target he was duly shot down.

The most spectacular trip down the Great Psychedelic Freakway was that made by Ken Kesey and his Merry Pranksters. Kesey was a big man and did things in a big way. He drove down the Freakway in an International Harvester school bus, decorated with Dayglo, filled with Pranksters in all states of dress and undress, piloted by Neal Cassady in a way no school bus had ever been driven before or since. Some trip!

For Kesey's group the emphasis was on action. It was not, as are all predominantly intellectual enterprises, "sicklied o'er with the pale cast of thought." Kesey was a wrestler, an athlete, a man of action, and his trip was an action trip from start to finish. It was bumpy, risky, scary, fantastic, outrageous. Ken Kesey had read his Nietzsche. *Live dangerously.* It was dangerous all right. One thinks of Neal Cassady piloting the school bus down a windy road in the Smoky Mountains, never using the brakes, barely touching the steering wheel, probably high on amphetamines, with

Kesey on the roof taking a movie of the whole wild whooshing descent. The bus was practically airborne. *Live dangerously.*

The whole crazy episode was preserved like a fly in amber by Tom Wolfe in *The Electric Kool-Aid Acid Test*, a book that captures the essence of the Shrieking Sixties, and Kesey's special contribution to those shrieks. The shrieks were made up of a mixture of agony and ecstasy, of the indignation of young men compelled to risk their lives in a futile war, of the raptures or agonies of those turned on (or off) by psychedelics, of the blare of "acid rock," the roar of the motorcycles of Hell's Angels, the anguished yelps of the "guardians of public morals" convinced that the country's youth was going collectively insane.

A noisy decade. And of course the noise was loudest in California, and Ken Kesey and his Merry Pranksters contributed a special scream to the general cacophony, which would not be of any interest to a student of the Warrior's Way were it not for the fact that Ken Kesey almost achieved something of great value.

Almost.

He had the personal power. He had the integrity. He had the courage and the sheer physical toughness one needs to stand the strains and stresses of the Way; he had intelligence and, more important, a sort of intuitive awareness about certain aspects of the game. He was not handicapped, like Tim Leary, by a tendency to become involved in games of political passion, and he was relatively free of the missionary disease. For a time it appeared to certain objective observers that this wildman from Oregon would become a burning and a shining light.

It was a light that failed. It failed because the game Kesey played was unbalanced. The Merry Pranksters really abused the psychedelics. Not content with taking enormous overdoses themselves, they poured them into the systems of the world at large, as in the Electric Kool-Aid Acid Test in Los Angeles, where Kool-Aid heavily laced with LSD was served to about two hundred unsuspecting people who attended the gathering to meet the Merry Pranksters—minus Kesey, who had fled to Mexico. The Electric Kool-Aid Acid Test ended, as might have been expected, in a scream—the scream of a girl on a bad trip, out of her mind. The scream announced the demise of the Merry Pranksters. It was their last prank, and not a very funny one.

Kesey certainly riled the establishment rhinoceros, but he had the wit to sidestep when the beast charged. He even charmed it into behaving more or less reasonably by talking of a "new message." What was the new message?

Graduate from acid.

That made sense. As Kesey put it, acid is only a door. When you've gone through the door you're through. You don't go on going through the same door. You go on beyond acid, beyond drugs.

What lies beyond acid?

It was Steward Brand, one of the Merry Pranksters, who offered the clearest answer to this question. Beyond acid lies the real world.

Reality: Love it or leave it.

This became the slogan for the New Realists. They emerged from the psychedelic fog to offer practical guidance to a very mixed-up generation. They recognized the signs of the times. The old hectic squandering life-style could not continue. It could not continue because we were rapidly running out of practically everything. We were close to bankruptcy both spiritually and materially, and neither Squaresville nor Freaksville offered a solution to the problem. If you loaded yourself with possessions like a packhorse and spent your entire time struggling to pay for them, you merely became a slave.

So much for Squaresville.

If you dropped out, contributed nothing to society, neglected your body, your mate, your children, passed your time in a drug-induced stupor, you were merely a parasite.

So much for Freaksville.

A different life-style was called for.

What is the ultimate reality for us humans? The ultimate reality is the Whole Earth. How can one approach that reality? By trying to take everything into account. Yes, everything. Everything affects everything else. If you can't blend in with the biosphere, the biosphere will dispense with you. For the White Brother, always boasting about conquering nature, a new philosophy of life was needed. How can you conquer nature? You are part of nature, you poor swaggering fool, and had better realize it before nature squashes you like a bug.

America needs Indians, said Steward Brand.

Which meant that the White Brother might do well to learn from the Indian Brother some of the latter's reverence for the Great Spirit. An awareness of totality and his place in that totality. A picture of the Whole Earth.

So the *Whole Earth Catalog* emerged. It was far more than a catalog. It was an entire philosophy of life, centering around the ideas of access to tools. The message was made still more explicit in the *Coevolution Quarterly*, in which Steward Brand and the other New Realists (Dick Raymond of the Portola Institute, Michael Philips of Point, John Todd of the New Alchemy Institute) demonstrated in various practical ways the realities of the post industrial age.

Those realities were a very far cry from Tim Leary's "Drop Out, Tune In, Turn On." Trips down the Great Psychedelic Freakway had demonstrated one great truth. We are part of a cosmic process and can play in that process the role of Warrior or slave. One does not, by fuddling one's awareness with psychedelics, decrease one's slavery or come closer to reality. One merely depletes one's energies and increases one's confusion.

The new way of life would be based on voluntary simplicity. Eliminate the frills, simplify the design, occupy some modest ecological niche, "live in the cracks." And be ready to sidestep when the Tower of Babel crashes. As for spiritual development, the simple tasks of everyday life, performed conscientiously in a spirit of nonattachment, could provide everything needed. Nirvana and samsara were one and the same.

> Before enlightenment
> Chopping wood, carrying water.
> After enlightenment
> Chopping wood, carrying water.

33

RELUCTANT
GURU

"If Leary is on the wrong track, show us the right one."
This challenge, thrown at me by a psychologist after the
meeting with Leary in Palo Alto, confronted me with a
question. I was fifty years old that year (1963). Twenty-
seven years had passed since Ouspensky showed me round
the farm at Lyne Place on that foggy winter afternoon. I
could remember his words, his smile: "It takes a long time
to enter the Work. One must be patient." What had I
learned in twenty-seven years? That the processes of neo-
alchemy are very difficult. That many start but few arrive.
That the Way is full of traps, and that even those who might
be considered advanced can go astray. That it is better to
sleep soundly than to become half awake. How did Gurdjieff put it? *Blessed is he who has a soul, blessed is he who has
none, but woe and grief to him who has it in embryo.*

So then . . . would it not be better to keep silent? The
Bay Area swarms with self-styled gurus. Send these seekers
to someone else. But then again there are those sacred laws:
*From him to whom much has been given much shall be required.
In order to give you must get, in order to get you must give.
One hand washes the other.*

So went the debate. Two opposing members of the crew
of my ship of fools were struggling to grab the steering
wheel and direct the vessel. On the one hand there was the
Missionary, on the other the Recluse. I knew the Missionary
well. He had tried to dominate my life before, filling my

head with dreams of being a leader in the Work, trying to force me to go to Paris to work with Gurdjieff, encouraging me to live in a manner totally contrary to the needs of my essence.

The Recluse had no use for the Missionary's fantasies. He wanted only to be left in peace to practice *hatha* and *raja* yoga and seek out the secrets of the universal arcanum. He despised and distrusted the Missionary, a talkative fool obsessed with the craving to inflict his personal beliefs on others. The Recluse took his stand behind the sayings of Lao-Tze.

> Who knows speaks not.
> Who speaks knows not.
> The virtuous do not show off.
> The show-off is not virtuous.
> Therefore the sage does not reveal his wisdom.

So shut up and cultivate your own garden, said the Recluse. The battle raged.

In the end the two came to a sort of truce. There was a large abandoned chicken house on the property I had bought. It was infested with rats, overgrown with weeds, and the roof leaked. All the same it was a very well-built structure, twenty feet by sixty, and would provide, if we chased out the rats and relaid the floor, a place where people could practice the exercises. Surrounding the chicken house was about an acre of land, obviously fertile but smothered in brush, poison oak, and thistles.

Very well, let us see what will happen. Can these would-be students who ask me to show them the Way stop their endless chatterings and self-analyses and get down to work? Can they clear the brush and plant a garden, repair the chicken house, relay the floor, get rid of the rats, turn it from a ruin into an ashram? If they can do that, it will at least be a positive achievement. If they cannot, it will be no great loss. In the process I shall learn some things about myself. For instance, whether this character who wants to teach others is merely a fraud or based on something genuine.

Members of the first group, all intellectuals, were not very useful. They wanted to debate and discuss, to turn our gatherings into what they called an encounter group, a phenomenon that was just starting to emerge at that time and that reached its full flower later in the Esalen Institute. Encounter groups offered their members unlimited opportunities for expressing negative emotions, bullying each other, and being rude to each other. Above all they involved talk, endless talk. So any energy that might be developed as a result of hard physical work was frittered away in clouds of verbiage.

The intellectuals all left; but others, not so intellectual, came in their place, and the work went forward slowly. The chicken house was repaired, some of the ground was cleared, a fence was put up to keep out the deer, and a garden was planted. I adapted the de Hartman music of the Gurdjieff movements to such instruments as we had: guitars, oboes, clarinets, drums, cymbals. I taught some of the movements to a few of my students, warning them that they must on no account perform them in public or show them to others. The movements were sacred. They were designed to generate certain energies in the body. They were not to be used as a vehicle for showing off.

To clarify my ideas, I assembled all that I knew in a book, *The Master Game: Beyond the Drug Experience.* It was designed to put psychedelics in their place. Psychedelics might give one a glimpse of the high places of the spirit, but climbing those peaks was another matter. One could ascend only by following the Warrior's Way, which called for effort, knowledge, courage, and a guide who knew the way. One could try to climb by oneself, but it was safer to climb with a guide.

My ideas crystallized around the concept of Creative Psychology, which I described in *The Master Game.* It was not a new idea. It was, in fact, an exceedingly old one. Again and again in the literature of religion and philosophy one came across references to this aspect of the science of man. Man is a prisoner in a cave. He mistakes shadows for reality. If he wants to enter the real world, he must leave the cave. Man is a mad king. He has a magnificent palace at his disposal but lives in the cellar. If he wants to enjoy the treasures that are his by right, he must regain his sanity and start living in the palace. Man is the prodigal son. He has wasted his substance on riotous living in a far country and been reduced to eating husks with the swine. If he wishes to live in a more worthy fashion, he must return to his father's house. Man is enveloped in a veil of illusions centering around the idea of "I" and "mine." To escape these illusions he must get rid of his sense of separateness. Man is a victim of an error in brain formation, endowed with a new brain that conflicts with his old brain, half angel, half savage. To develop his full powers, he must learn to harmonize his conflicting brain systems.

Harmonize the brain systems. This was the essence of Creative Psychology. The most important single idea I had learned from Gurdjieff and Ouspensky concerned the education of the five centers. I had learned during all those years of study and experiment that my five centers functioned with hideous inefficiency. The intellectual center created fantasies that prevented my making contact with the real world. The emotional center took these fantasies and charged them with fear, anxiety, hatred, envy, or vanity. The combination of negative fantasies and negative emotions affected both the moving and the instinctive centers, producing needless muscular tension and various more or less destructive autonomic responses. Even the sex center was poisoned by these malfunctionings of the other centers. The result was disharmony and unhappiness, an inner disease, which made life hardly worth living.

I had found that no improvement in my inner state was possible unless the malfunctioning of the various centers was corrected. Gurdjieff, in one of his parables, had portrayed the situation of underdeveloped man with admirable clarity. Man could be thought of as a conveyance: horse, carriage, driver. In our usual disharmonized state the horse was unruly and ill cared for, the driver drunk or asleep, and the carriage in poor repair. As for the Master (higher consciousness), which ought to ride in the carriage and tell the driver where to go, it was not there at all. Instead the conveyance was for hire like a cab. Any passing I could take over and tell it where to go. So it traveled now here, now there, creaking and groaning, with its unoiled wheels, its starved horse, its drunken or dreaming cabbie. It was not surprising, with millions of such crazy conveyances careening around on the surface of our ill-starred planet, that horrendous collisions and catastrophes kept happening. The wonder was that a creature so out of touch with the real world had managed to survive at all.

So Creative Psychology could be defined as that branch of the science of man concerned with the correction of his inner disharmony. It was not enough to correct the malfunctioning of one center. One had to correct them all. This called for careful observation, a lot of self-study. We are very complex machines, and we do not know ourselves. Our little island of consciousness rests on a submerged base of instinctive functions that we cannot control and of which we are not even aware. Our overall state is influenced by the amount of certain vital energy substances, the level of which is kept permanently low by the wasteful way in which our organism operates. We squander these substances in useless talk, daydreams, muscular tension, and above all in anxiety—anxiety that has no cause, a sort of generalized angst, a fear of our own being. Obviously, with an energy system so depleted, we cannot attain those higher states of consciousness which are our birthright. We are kings who live in the cellar because, even if we know that our palace exists, we do not have enough energy to climb up into it.

So Creative Psychology would deal in a practical way with the creation and destruction of psychic energies on which our level of functioning depends. Without power we can do nothing. We develop power through the struggle between yes and no, through the sacrifice of our favorite daydreams, our pet negative emotions, our habit of doing the easy rather than the difficult, our vanity and self-importance. This struggle is "the moral equivalent of war"—the Warrior's Way. We become, through this struggle, the creators of ourselves. We become food for a higher level of the cosmic process, "food for archangels." We enter the way of return, which is an uphill path and leads to that level of being that is rightly ours, which we do not enjoy because we waste our energies on inessentials.

The kingdom of heaven is indeed within us, but we cannot reach that kingdom if we insist on living in squalid little hells of our own creating.

So my intention was to build an Institute of Creative Psychology in which those who seriously wanted to raise their level of being might find conditions suitable for such an endeavor. The conditions would have to be strictly practical, aimed at bringing the student into contact with those fundamental forces on which life depends. It was essential to get away from that overemphasis on talk which constitutes the most depressing feature of most systems of psychotherapy. Keep talk to a minimum. Encourage action. Dig, plant, sow seeds, make boats, go fishing, perform plays, sing songs, and dance. Anything rather than indulge in those endless gabfests that form the stock-in-trade of clinical psychologists and psychiatrists.

I dreamed at that time of using the label Institute of Creative Psychology to disguise a modest school of the fourth way. On the fourth way one did not retire to a cave, live on nuts and berries, spend endless hours in uncomfortable postures, trying to meditate. One took part in life, engaged in the struggle, contributed to society, paid one's dues. One was, in short, a *householder*, able to cope with the struggles

and challenges that life offered and at the same time to
follow the Way. The inner work, to be of any real value, had
to be practiced under all sorts of conditions easy and difficult, pleasant and unpleasant.

A teacher can create conditions favorable to work and
hold up a mirror. That is all.

Hold up a mirror. Look at your own image. Separate from
it. Separate from all the manifestations of your machine: intellectual, emotional, instinctive, moving, sexual. Only in
this way can you escape the stifling embrace of the personal
ego. Only in this way can you find the great self, the *atman*,
which lies outside time-space and is not under the law of
birth and death.

Separate.

How could the practice of separation be mastered?

Well, there were tricks. The oldest trick and one of the
best was the practice of Outer Theater. Epictetus, noblest of
the Stoics, knew and practiced it in the days of the tyrant
Domitian, when life in Rome was dangerous, brutish, and
short.

> Remember that you are an actor in a play, and the Play-
> wright chooses the manner of it: If he wants it short it is short;
> if long it is long. If he wants you to act a poor man you must
> act the part with all your powers; and so if your part be a
> cripple, a magistrate, or a plain man. For your business is to
> act the character that is given you and act it well; the choice of
> the cast is Another's.
>
> (*The Manual of Epictetus.*)

An actor is expected not to identify with the role. Love,
hate, anger, rapture, exaltation, depression, the actor por-
trays them all. But the emotions do not affect the actor.
They are put on and taken off like so many masks—comic
masks, tragic masks, pretty masks, ugly masks. The actor
remains separate from the masks.

The techniques of Outer Theater are hard to master. It is

one thing to act on a stage, quite another to act in life. We become identified with the role we play, lose ourselves, lose control. Events play us, we do not play them. It is no simple matter to separate from the personal ego, to watch, as if one were manipulating a puppet, one's very *personal* self—face, arms, legs, the whole machine. Even Yama, King of the Dead, who taught Nachiketas (in the Katha Upanishad) the ultimate secret of the after-death state, admitted that separation was very difficult: "As a razor's edge is hard to pass over so is the path to the higher self difficult to tread."

Well . . . one had to start somewhere. A play would help, a play dealing with this problem of lesser and greater self. I wrote such a play, drawing material from the Katha Upanished and the Tibetan Book of the Dead. Members of my group performed it in Berkeley, in the open-air theater. They had fun, dressed up, danced, sang. They may even have learned a few things about the after-death state.

But a play is always an artificial situation and has very little to do with real Outer Theater. It does not bring about separation from the little self, is more likely to strengthen than weaken ego-centered illusions. Were this not so, our leading actors and actresses would all become liberated beings. Real Outer Theater calls for extraordinary control on the part of the teacher, who must be able to grab any fleeting opportunity to play a role with a pupil in such a way that that pupil is put in a position to *see*. This seeing is the essence of the alchemical process called *nigredo*, "the blackening." It involves confronting those forces in oneself that are mainly responsible for one's inner slavery, forces referred to as the chief feature. One who has seen his chief feature and learned to separate from it is on the way to real liberty (the whitening or *albedo*).

But this work of discovering the chief feature can be as rough on the teacher as it is on the pupil. The teacher has to maintain a role that may be unpleasant and difficult. He must put up with abuse from the person he is trying to help. For few come easily to the meeting with their chief

features. It is a real showdown, at which Dr. Jekyll meets
Mr. Hyde, at which all the rotting monsters in one's personal cesspool come crawling out into the light of day. The
process is not without its dangers, and with my experience
of schizophrenia I was well aware of those dangers. The
aphorism of Hippocrates was present in my mind: *If you
cannot do good at least do no harm*. Besides, there was the
backlash: the screaming, the abuse, the tears, coun-
tercharges, indignant denials, excuses, justifications.

Oh, those justifications! You confront "seekers after
truth" with the mirror of karma, in which they should
surely be able to see their own faces. Not a bit of it. This is
not me at all. This I did because, because, and because. I
was perfectly justified in behaving in such a way. So would
you under the circumstances . . . and so on and so forth.

Well, if they don't want to see, you can't force them. You
can lead a horse to water but you can't make it drink. Perhaps they could use the technique of Inner Theater. In Inner
Theater one evokes one's own cast of characters and lets
them perform their little piece while one sits back and watches. Inner Theater can be fun. And of course it spares the
teacher, who plays no part and so escapes the shit-storm
that Outer Theater is apt to evoke. The practitioner can dis-
solve the whole performance if it becomes too unpleasant.

> These our actors
> As I foretold you, were all spirits and
> Are melted into air, into thin air.

Shakespeare understood. But of course the inner performance, because it can be turned off at the flip of a psychological switch, is never likely to result in those shattering rev-
elations like the taste of blood in one's mouth. Those
insights can only be earned in actual combat. I thought of
that Easter day when, full of righteous indignation, I had
confronted Sister Archangel, only to find myself struck
dumb by a revelation so devastating that it blew me com-

pletely out of my ordinary self and gave me a taste of separation that I have never forgotten. That was real Outer Theater, a response to a difficult, challenging situation that I had intentionally imposed on myself.

But it was one thing to impose that sort of stress on oneself, another thing entirely to impose it on others. How could one be sure that the stress would be salutary, that the conflicts would not tear an already unstable psyche to pieces?

So what should I do? Follow the easy way? Stick Band-Aids on spiritual cancers? Avoid seriously upsetting my students, in case the poor darlings came apart at the seams? What sort of a school would that be? A drawing-room debating society, a factory for generating mystical hot air and comforting illusions. Certainly it would not be an aspect of the Warrior's Way. Too easy. Too comfortable.

But I had to face my limitations. To force on others those devastating confrontations that led to real self-knowledge was too hazardous and too unpleasant a procedure. I wanted no shattered psyches on my hands or conscience. I would play the safe game as a mild but ineffectual guru. I would teach the few who chose to work with me the art of gardening. I would follow in the steps of Voltaire, Warrior of the enlightenment. What were Voltaire's final words of advice? *Il faut cultiver notre jardin.*

Cultivate your own garden. No one else will do it for you. Separate weeds from flowers. Grow your own food. Worship the Father Sun and the Mother Earth and the countless spirits that move within the biosphere. Here in the garden we witness the magical transformation that makes life tick. Here macrocosm meets microcosm, the two being intertwined like the two triads of the hexagram. Look about you. Learn to *see* alchemically. The green leaf eats the body of the sun. We eat the green leaf or its products. So we eat the sun at one remove. And what do we do with that sun substance? Fritter it away in dreams, in needless tension, in silly worries, in pathetic hopes and fears. Stupid, is it not?

And really unworthy. So what could we do with this energy? Transmute it into higher consciousness, thereby becoming a part of the mind of the biosphere. In developed man the cosmic process becomes conscious of itself. So how can we afford to waste time in the state of dreams, when by exerting ourselves we can enter the real world?

Consider the other sacred symbols from monad to enniagram. What do they tell us? Each symbol is a device for helping us to activate higher mind. Higher mind can show us the relationships of all things. "He shall know the laws of the immortal gods and of men," as Pythagoras said to his adepts in the old school in Crotona.

Only one who knows the inner and outer laws is in touch with the real world. Only such a one knows what is possible and what is impossible and how far he may go and in what direction. Only such a one can emerge from the jungle of illusions, climb beyond the mountain of power, and ascend the mountain of liberation. Only such a one is truly free.

34

WARRIORS
IN THE
TREE HOUSE

Meanwhile the flower children were pouring into San Francisco and pouring out of it again, appalled by the crime and violence that was making the city environment intolerable. I sought the refugees from Haight-Ashbury, filled with a mixture of curiosity and hope. What did they represent, these flower children? Were they a modern version of the disastrous Children's Crusade, or the forerunners of a new spiritual elite? Was the way of life they had embraced a peevish revolt against the bourgeois life-style, or was it a new aspect of the Warrior's Way? Were they spiritual heroes or irresponsible tramps?

I was all in favor of the alternate life-style. Simplify, simplify, simplify. It was, of course, nothing new. Thoreau had spelled out the message a century earlier. Now it was more urgent than ever that as many people as possible should hear that message. We lived under the shadow of the coming collapse. After frantically guzzling our own resources and doing our best to guzzle everyone else's, we faced a time of scarcity. It made sense to prepare to return to the family farm. In rural California one could still find plenty of old-timers who remembered the days of self-sufficiency. They had had a garden, ran some sheep and cows, had a vineyard and an orchard. It was no big deal. They had been self-sufficient then, we could be self-sufficient now.

The family farm . . . better still the *expanded* family farm. If several families could learn to cooperate and pool their resources, they could buy a larger place than any single family could afford. I spoke about this to the group that had assembled round me. We had to stop talking about higher states of consciousness and interact directly with the forces that gave us life: the sun, the soil, the biosphere. We had to be gardeners and fishermen, carpenters, electricians, engineers. We had to learn to work together and put up with each other. We had to find "soul glue," the mysterious adhesive that holds a group together.

What is soul glue? I had to admit I did not know. In Ouspensky's group the power of the teacher had held us together. Authoritarianism was glue of a sort, but not the kind of glue I had in mind. I had the impression that the young people everywhere were in revolt against authoritarianism. The emphasis was on doing your own thing. But could a group hold together if all its members insisted on doing their own thing? I had my doubts.

Perhaps the flower children knew about soul glue. They formed communes of sorts. What held their communes together? Seeking an answer to this question, I drove over to Graton, where Lou Gottlieb had established a commune on his Morning Star ranch. He had even offered to give me the ranch for the use of my group.

So I visited Morning Star ranch, thirty-one acres of redwoods, abandoned chicken houses where thistles and nettles grew as high as one's head, a large wooden cross on which a previous owner had been in the habit of suspending himself from time to time to do penance for his sins in a decaying apple orchard.

Generous Lou showed me round the place. He was a musician, a former member of the Limeliters. He was also a prophet, a beaming, bearded, patriarchal mesomorph, full of energy and benevolence.

Lucky Louis Love Divine. And the thirty-one acres of Morning Star might indeed have provided a home for my group. Only one thing prevented me from accepting the offer.

"It must be land to which none are denied access," said Lou.

"You're kidding, Lou."

"Why should I be kidding?"

"Because land access to which is denied none will attract all those who are denied access everywhere else. You will collect a bunch of outcasts."

"Wonderful," said Lou. He evidently found the prospect delightful. In his vibrant prophet's voice he recited a poem.

> Give me your tired, your poor,
> Your huddled masses yearning to breathe free.
> The wretched refuse of your teeming shore.
> Send these, the homeless, tempest tossed to me,
> I lift my lamp beside the golden door!

"Do you know where that comes from?" asked Lou, turning upon me his glowing seer's eyes.

"Of course I do. I'm an immigrant myself. It's carved on the Statue of Liberty in New York Harbor. But no one expects America to live up to it, not in this year of grace 1967."

"We live up to it," said Lou. "We offer a place for the technologically unemployed. They have to go somewhere. It is better they come here than clutter up the jails. Besides, why should one go to prison because one can't find a place in a society that has no place for one?"

"You have a point there, Lou. But I'm afraid it will make your neighbors unhappy. In fact, from what I hear, it has already made them unhappy."

"We love them," said Lou. It seemed as if he really did. It was powerful, aggressive, overwhelming love. But the neighbors didn't seem able to reciprocate.

The flower children were full of hope and dope. They dreamed of a new society based on something finer than the lust for possessions. They had emerged from comfortable middle-class homes to reject all the values their parents cherished. They wanted a better, more meaningful life game. They wanted to measure values in terms other than houses, swimming pools, cars, yachts, televisions. They would willingly live in domes; tipis, tree houses, if they could be left in peace to smoke pot and dream.

Unfortunately, they had overlooked the fact that they had to share the earth with the Squares; and as the Squares were dominant, it made sense not to offend them. The flower children were sloppy and inconsiderate. They shat all over the place, kept dogs that killed sheep, lit fires in the open during the dry season, played noisy rock and roll music at all hours. Clearly a major clash in life-styles would soon take place in Sonoma County. I did not wish to become involved in the clash.

Even so, there was much to be learned from the flower children. They had a sort of inner freedom that one did not find in the average bourgeois. If they could combine that freedom with respect for their neighbors and learn to observe a few simple health rules, they might indeed become a vivifying force in our soggy society. But could they learn? Could they listen to the voice of experience?

I sought out Sita, the star of Morning Star. Sita was really turned on. She came from a wealthy New York family, a tribe of Jewish superachievers, rich enough to afford yachts and Cadillacs. And here was Sita refusing to own anything. She had even shed her name, adopting in its place the name of Rama's consort, Sita Morning Star. Only eighteen and in rebellion against everything her parents stood for. Usually she wore nothing but a necklace of prayer beads, but her nakedness was so natural that one hardly noticed it. Mother Eve before the Fall.

"I had it all," Sita told me. "I was at the top of everything in my scene. Private school in Westchester, editor-in-chief of the school newspaper, vice-president of the student government, honor roll student. My life was quite beautiful, but I knew I had to find something else."

"Like what, Sita?"

"Like independence, freedom, God, happiness. I knew I couldn't find it there."

So Sita took the money she had earned working for the Anti-Defamation League the summer before, boarded a plane for California in December 1966, arrived in San Francisco with flowers in her hair and a few dollars in her pocket, and found herself in Haight-Ashbury.

"It was different in those days," said Sita. "The crime and violence hadn't started. I didn't know anybody. I just had the name of one friend there with whom I could stay. The first day I was walking down Haight Street just digging my new life, just digging the world. Do you know what happened?"

"You were propositioned by some elderly lecher."

"No. Someone handed me a chocolate eclair. All for free. I didn't know what to make of it. I'd just come from New York. Paranoid New York. You know New York?"

"To my sorrow."

"Well, my first reaction was, 'This must be poisoned.' Typical New Yorker. But I ate it anyway. I grokked it. It was free. It was beautiful. So I was directed to the Free Frame of Reference. It's the Digger's free store. They had free clothes and free food for anyone in need."

So Sita got an apartment in San Francisco. She was, she admitted, still a Square at heart, and enrolled in high school to continue her education. She worked on the *Berkeley Barb* and the *Oracle* to make money. She worked as a cocktail waitress but gave it up because, as she put it, "they expected you to turn tricks on the side." In January there was the great Be-In in the Golden Gate Park, and Sita was there, stoned out of her gourd on LSD.

"There were thirty thousand people at the Be-In, all in union with each other and God. They handed out three thousand tabs of Owsley 500s."

Wow, what a dose! Five hundred micrograms of bottled madness! Enough to take you to hell and back, or leave you there if you couldn't find energy to return. But Sita had had a good trip. Quite celestial in fact.

"I didn't see much of what was happening because somehow I found myself under the stage. It seemed there was the most room, the most air to breathe under there. There were so many people outside. But everything that went down at that Be-In—the love, the sharing, the oneness—it penetrated my soul. It was like nothing I'd experienced on the East Coast. The people I met—hippies, flower children, children of God—they all wanted to turn each other on to love and sharing. I dug all those ideas."

But the spirit of love was leaving Haight-Ashbury. More and more people were turning on to speed. Speed kills. Sita had found that out for herself. She had tried speed once, stayed awake for five days and five nights, then crashed on New Year's Eve. It drained her totally and made her so uptight that she could not bear to be in the same room with speed freaks. But the whole Haight-Ashbury seemed to be turning to speed, and she knew she had to get out.

"I had this friend Larry. He was the best friend of the man I was living with. He was my lover too. We had some fine orgies in the Haight-Ashbury. He had a wife and baby but it didn't matter. Well, he moved out and started living at Morning Star in a tree house. He told me to come out because I needed to cool my head. I was really uptight. I'd had an STP trip in the city about a month before. I hadn't been able to smile for a month. STP was a grey trip. My hallucinations were grey, the day was grey, my mood was grey. I walked up to Morning Star and it was bliss. As soon as I set foot on the land I could smile for the first time in a month."

"What have you been doing since you came?"

"Nothing much. I've stopped eating meat and I eat what God provides. I've been healthier and happier. Morning Star is a beautiful place where I can freak out. I can go naked and enjoy the sunshine, go down to the brook and bathe. Truly in heaven, truly in heaven! We go out and gather blackberries and we come back with flowers in our hair dancing like angels to all the people and giving them blackberries to eat. I don't do much work; I didn't do any for the first few months. I just think I've got it all out of my system. There was a lot to get out. Everyone loved me, they didn't care that I didn't do any work, it didn't matter. People were beautiful, there was plenty of pot which I enjoyed, and the rest didn't matter. I was learning about God."

Dear Sita! It did my cynical old soul good to talk with her. So full of enthusiasm! Enthusiasm, *en theos*, the god within. What are we without this inner god? Mere hunks of meat.

Which didn't alter the fact that Morning Star was doomed, as were both Olompali and the Wheeler ranch. Lou Gottlieb, Don McCoy, Bill Wheeler, idealists all, had made the same error as did Tim Leary. They had riled the establishment rhinoceros and were not nimble enough to sidestep when the beast charged. And charge it did. Morning Star was raided by the police. Sita, who had been attending classes at Sonoma State College, returned to find the place deserted.

"They busted twenty-two people. I was very upset that I missed the bust. I felt like the father of Anne Frank coming back home after the Gestapo had taken all his family."

The trial that followed must have been one of the oddest in the history of Sonoma County. From all sides the flower children converged on the Santa Rosa courthouse. They had jackets daubed with Dayglo. They wore beards, beads, they carried bells, they chanted mantras. *Make love not war*, said the Dayglo. They smoked pot openly and shamelessly. When hassled by the cops they siad "God bless you." It unsettled the police quite a bit. The police weren't used to such treatment.

Beaming Lou Gottlieb, finding himself accused of conducting an organized camp without a license, indignantly denied the charge.

"If I'm conducting anything it's a disorganized camp," said Lou.

"It was a drag," said Sita. "It went on about three days.

The Health Department kept talking about shit. We found this piece of shit, they'd say, x feet from this tree in a northerly direction and another piece y feet from the fence. All solemn and silly. It was truly a bore. The jury was mostly women, I remember. They found about half the people guilty and half not guilty. I don't know how they decided. Lou got fifteen days for letting us live at Morning Star and Don got five for contempt of court. That was good because Lou and Don got a chance to meditate and talk together which they both needed.

"The jails aren't full of criminals, you know. About half the people in jail just can't make it in the Great Society. They put them in jail because they can't think of anything else to do with them. Lou said he ought to get the Nobel Peace Prize for running Morning Star and that the county should award him a medal. So they put him in jail. He ended up paying about fifteen thousand dollars in fines.

"We went back to Morning Star after the bust, although we weren't supposed to. The cops continued to wake us at five A.M. with their joyful head counts. The cops were quite friendly. We used to say 'God bless you' to them and finally a couple of them would even say 'God bless you' to us. Morning Star had a rather small population by that time. The police were really very beautiful. They dug us."

The police may have. The neighbors didn't. They were determined to abolish Lou Gottlieb's commune. I drove over to the place again a few years later with our beautiful blond Ceres, goddess of increase, carrying her newest baby in her arms. Ceres was a member of my group and interested in the counterculture. We thought we might do a book on it together. *Revolt in the Tree House*.

We looked for Lou. No Lou. We looked for Sita. No Sita. The upper house was a wreck, the courtyard filled with rubble. We struggled through the garbage and entered the house. On the walls were crude drawings and slogans. "Fuck a bunch of Fuckyous." "Love each other." We climbed through a window into the remaining functional part of the house.

In sleeping bags or under blankets on the floor were three boys, fifteen or so. Two boys and a girl were sitting on an old sofa. The room was a wreck. Everything was in disrepair and dirty. There was a large hole in the ceiling, and the underside of the roof was exposed.

"This place is sure a mess," said one of the kids. "It used to be real nice before the cops came and started tearing everything up. They said the toilet and water pump weren't good enough and tore them out. They came after some drug addicts who were hiding in the ceiling and made that hole."

"The cops are a drag," said another. "They can come and raid any time. They could come right now. If they found you here they'd take your baby away from you."

This to Ceres who clutched her child to her bosom and looked wide-eyed.

"They hauled Pam and Larry out of their tree house one night. They grabbed their two-year-old son Siddhartha. Lou ran after their car and said at least leave Siddhartha here with me, but they wouldn't. There was another girl here who lived up in a tent with her three sons. She had the whole tent full of food but the cops said she wasn't feeding the kids properly and took them away . . . Yeah, I've been in jail. You know what's the worst thing about it? They have the TV and radio on constantly from six A.M. to ten P.M. . . . I'm not supposed to come back to Morning Star but I do. It's the spirit of the place."

There did not seem to be much spirit left in Morning Star. It was obviously dying. As an alternative life-style it simply was not valid. And the kids, the flower children who had seemed so promising, now were revealed as bewildered derelicts, lost in dreams, out of touch with reality. They were tramps, not Warriors. They rejected straight society but took its handouts, broke all its rules but expected it to care for them. As for soul glue, they clearly knew nothing about it. They could not learn to live with their neighbors. They could not really agree among themselves. Basically they were anarchists; and anarchy, though appealing in theory, does not work in practice. We live under certain inescapable laws. They are imposed by nature. They cannot be broken.

Actually I had looked in the wrong place for information about soul glue. There had been, in San Francisco during the flower children epoch, a remarkable Warrior whose activity I had overlooked. His name was Steve Gaskin.

Steve was an original, home-brewed, American bodhisattva, thin as a rake and tough as boot leather. I had heard about him and his Monday Night Class but dismissed him as one more long-haired guru who had assembled a teaching out of various odds and ends. I assumed he was like the rest of the flower children, lacking in practicality, lacking in willingness to work, dependent on drugs, on welfare, on free handouts—in short a social parasite.

How wrong I was!

Steve Gaskin had personal power. I don't know where he got it. He was very much influenced by Susuki Roshi, San Francisco's own private Zen saint. But Steve bowed before no teacher, was totally free of the starry-eyed syndrome. He was practical, a real Warrior. He lived strategically, took responsibility for his actions, and managed to teach his associates to take responsibility for theirs. Which was quite a feat, all things considered.

With a following of "kilo dealers and English majors" Steve set off across the country with a fleet of school buses. "Out to save the world," said the leading bus. The trip could have been as directionless as the crazy excursion of Ken Kesey's Merry Pranksters, but Steve had something Ken Kesey lacked: the secret of soul glue and a valid aim. So his group, about six hundred strong, settled in Lewis County, Tennessee, and bought a farm. One thousand and fourteen acres for seventy dollars an acre.

"You can't get a kilo for seventy dollars, can you?" wrote Steve Gaskin. "You can still get an acre of dirt for that. And you can live on an acre of dirt" (*Hey Beatnik! This is the Farm Book*, The Book Publishing Co; The Farm, Summertown, Tennessee, 38483).

So you can, if it's good dirt and you're willing to shed some sweat. This is what the Gaskinites were willing to do. They sweated. They planted beans and beans and beans.

> It's so grossly uneconomical and energy-expensive to run soybeans through a cow and then eat the cow instead of just eating the soybeans that it's virtually criminal.
> We're absolute vegetarians for several reasons—one of them being that I'm as telepathic with animals as I am with people and it's weird to eat them.

So plant beans, eat beans, make soybean milk and soybean cheese. But be sensible about it. None of this macrobiotic nonsense that leaves pregnant women and growing children without enough protein. If you're growing or making a baby, you've got to have those amino acid building blocks, and you've got to have the right ones in the right amounts. Steve's farmers had it all worked out. They had a biochemist on the farm, and he put together a balance sheet: so much for males, so much for females, so much for the pregnant, for the kids. You don't have to suffer from malnutrition just because you're a vegetarian.

Steve Gaskin's farmers were the valuable fruits of the flower children epoch. But for them, the whole episode would have left behind it nothing but wreckage. For though the episode began with flowers it ended with thorns. There was murder, rape, a lot of disease, and much bad tripping. Steve, however, managed to generate the necessary soul glue to hold his people together, to make friends with instead of antagonizing the neighbors, to be truly self-sufficient instead of living on handouts. He offered an example to those who needed it of just how much can be accomplished by a group of young people if they can straighten out their inner chemistry, stop indulging in negative emotions, stop ripping each other off, and stop asking for handouts.

35

SARMOUN
AND PSYCHOTRON

Early in 1967 a rumor began to circulate. It concerned a new Master, a *Sarkar* or leader of the Work, who had supposedly arrived in the Western world from some secret community in the Far East, and whose task it was to initiate a new octave of development. The *Sarkar* had been sent, so went the rumor, by that secret society known as the *sarmoun* or *sarman,* also called the Community of the Bees. It was said to be a very, very ancient society that had existed since before the Flood. As bees gathered nectar and transformed it into honey, so the *sarmouni* gathered knowledge and transformed it into wisdom.

Knowledge and wisdom were not the same thing. Today, so went the story, humanity was in a dangerously unbalanced condition, having a huge excess of knowledge and a grave deficiency of wisdom. Earth's human biomass resembled a vessel heavily loaded on the decks but without enough ballast to keep it on an even keel. In a storm the whole top-heavy craft would capsize and sink. And a storm was on the way. We certainly needed the *sarmouni.*

I needed them personally as badly as anyone. My Missionary was struggling to play the role of teacher without really knowing what he was trying to teach. It was easy enough to replay the old tapes, to repeat, in my own words, the teaching I had received from Ouspensky, to outline what he had called *the* System, as if it were the only system of knowledge worth considering. But my Cynic, my old

Diogenes—a cantankerous character who lived in a barrel somewhere in the lower levels of my brain—kept making rude remarks about my Missionary's efforts. How do you know that? What makes you think that is true? You are only repeating what you've heard from someone else. You're no better than the other True Believers who worked with Gurdjieff and Ouspensky and now replay the old tapes and imagine they are teachers. All they do by this teaching is bolster their own egos as you are bolstering yours. You're a fool and a fraud. Why not admit it?

With all this mockery coming from old Diogenes, my Missionary was having a hard time. He was starting to yell, "Help! I need somebody." Somebody, moreover, who did not belong to the old club, mouldering among its memories and building a mausoleum over the corpses of dead teachers, but who spoke from personal realization and did not merely echo the words of the dead.

So naturally these rumors about the *Sarkar* deeply impressed my Missionary, struggling as he was to play a role that was really beyond his power. The Missionary had always favored the idea that there existed somewhere an Inner Circle of Humanity. He had picked it up from Ouspensky, for whom it had been an article of faith. Ouspensky had always maintained that the *illuminati* could be contacted if one knew where to look, but that they would not be easy to find. They were the guardians of the mysteries, obligated to prevent the sacred knowledge from falling into the hands of those who would degrade it.

So I did not think that the hunt for the *Sarkar* would be easy. I fully expected to be led on several wild goose chases, as indeed I was. The first wild goose chase was hilarious and quite instructive. Somehow the impression was created that a certain bearded Jew of rather formidable presence who had recently arrived in San Francisco was either the forerunner of the Master or the Master himself. I strongly suspected that this "Master" was one of the most outrageous con artists who had ever separated fools from their money. As do all con artists, he demanded large sums for his services and lived very well at his followers' expense. But I could not be certain that my evaluation was correct, so I deliberately exposed all the people who were or had been associated with me to this "Master" to see what would happen. It is a law among players of the Master Game that the level of development of the disciple is shown by the teacher he chooses. This law is expressed in the aphorism: *A fool gets a fool for a teacher, a fraud gets a fraud.*

Even I, who am not an admirer of the species *Homo sapiens*, was astonished at the result of this experiment. Here were cultured, educated Americans, most of them with college degrees, concealing under a mask of sophistication a level of suggestibility and credulity that would have disgraced a savage. The "Master" was really a ringmaster, and the circus he organized around him was quite unbelievable. He had his followers mooing like cows, braying like donkeys, barking like dogs, and mewing like cats. He had them walking around bare-assed and dangling enormous phalluses between their legs. He had them wearing labels that read Special Asshole. He had them rolling around naked in sexual orgies. He had them fighting, dancing, drinking, fucking. He had them accepting teachings concerning man and the universe that were such unadulterated nonsense that even a child could hardly have believed them.

So outrageous was the performance that for a while he had me confused. Had he perhaps really been sent by the *Sarkar* to follow "the way of *malamat*," the way of blame? For the *malamati*, outrageous forms of behavior are part of their practice. They are masters of Outer Theater and can act as they choose. They have gone "beyond praise and blame"; they no longer seek for or care about the good opinion of others.

The way of *malamat* can easily become a trap for fools. People lacking discrimination imagine that merely by being offensive they become liberated. So they strut around insulting others and behaving outrageously, giving themselves airs and imagining themselves to be Masters. In this role they perfectly exemplify the phenomenon called "crow in peacock's feathers." They are showing off in borrowed plumage.

The real *malamati* always know where to draw the line. They may insult, offend, exasperate, and confuse, but they do not deliberately lead people astray. Nor do they make a living by separating fools from their money. You can always tell the genuine *malamati*. They can dish it out, but they can also take it. You cannot flatter them, nor can you insult them, for they are beyond praise and blame.

So I arranged a test. Our "Master" was invited to attend a meeting in my "ashram" and was subjected to the test called "undressing of the false ego." Every follower of the Way must sooner or later face this test, in the course of which all his favorite corns are trodden on, all his pet pretensions exposed, his masks torn away. Under these conditions the true *malamati* remain quite unruffled. They have shed their egos and so have nothing to protect. The phony Master, however, either gets angry or collapses or runs away. We show our level of being by our reactions to insults.

"What makes you think you can teach others?"

"Where did you learn what you think you know?"

"Why do you take large sums of money for your services?"

"Why do you strut around like a crow in peacock's feathers?"

"Look at yourself. Who do you think you are?"

Our "Master" did not do well under these conditions. He ran, not walked, to the nearest exit. After this encounter he could not insult me enough. His favorite term of abuse was motherfucker. I became for him the motherfucker supreme.

No—decidedly not a Master. Just another player of the world's oldest con game. In the end even his followers realized it, though not before he had liberated them from a considerable sum of money. He belonged to the species

Diablerus minor, the Lesser Shaman. He was a little Rasputin. I labeled him, as a taxonomist should, and set him aside.

A new clue now appeared. A book that purported to be written by a certain Rafael Lefort had been published by Gollancz in England. It was called *The Teachers of Gurdjieff*. With some difficulty I obtained a copy.

The book made an odd impression. Here was this Rafael Lefort, who claimed to have met several of the teachers of Gurdjieff, trotting around the Middle East and asking naive questions and being given long lectures by various Sufis on the stupidity of Western man in general and on his own stupidity in particular. All the Sufis spoke in the same way. All adopted the same tone of arrogance: "I am wiser than you are." It read like the work of an amateur novelist whose characters are all derived from the same model.

Who was this Lefort? I really needed to know. *The Master Game* was in the hands of the publishers but had not yet gone to the printer. *The Master Game* drew heavily on Gurdjieff's teachings, and I needed to know as much as possible about the origins of those teachings. I had a scientist's habit of quoting my sources and of trying to distinguish truth from falsehood.

Was *The Teachers of Gurdjieff* fiction or nonfiction? Publishers are supposed to know this. After all, it does make a difference. Gollancz was my English publisher, had published both *Drugs and the Mind* and *Man against Aging*. So I wrote for information and received a statement to the effect that *The Teachers of Gurdjieff* had been certified genuine by a certain scholar who preferred to remain anonymous.

So I wrote to Lefort care of Gollancz.

The correspondence that followed convinced me (a) that Rafael Lefort did not exist, (b) that the teachers of Gurdjieff did not exist, and (c) that somebody who knew a great deal about Sufis and Sufism was staging a rather elaborate masquerade.

What lay behind the masquerade? Obviously the teachers

of Gurdjieff could not still be alive. The book was either a put-on or a rather clever allegory, a teaching story designed to test the intelligence of the reader. It was the sort of test that one might expect from a genuine teacher, designed to weed out the Starry-eyed Believers with their fixed patterns of thought from those who still retained flexibility and adaptability. Despite its obvious absurdities and its tiresome air of superiority, it did convey one message: The times are changing and the methods of presenting the teachings must change with them. One does not mix yesterday's potato peelings with today's soup.

Who had really written the book? What lay behind it? Where could I look for clues? As I thought about it, an idea flashed through my mind. The words formed so clearly that I had the impression I was receiving a message telepathically.

Ask Bennett.

Bennett . . . Of course. If anyone knew what was really going on, it would be John Godolphin Bennett. Had he not, from the beginning, been a collector of information, sent to Turkey while still in his early twenties, to gather military intelligence? He spoke Turkish and several other languages, had traveled all over the Middle East, was a Warrior of the first order, courageous, persistent, intelligent. Moreover he had one feature that separated him from the other True Believers who had gathered about Gurdjieff. He had always retained the capacity to ask questions, to think for himself, to experiment and seek. The shell of concrete in which the True Believer envelops his mind and which renders it incapable of accepting any new ideas had not encased Bennett. He was not stuck in a groove. If anything he tended to explore too many different grooves and to scatter his energies by rushing here and there always seeking new teachers and new teachings. But this, from my point of view, was hardly a drawback. It made him a mine of information, and information was what I wanted.

We who had followed Ouspensky had been forbidden to

have anything to do with Bennett, but that was far away and long ago. There was no need to respect, at that late date, the special brand of paranoia which had befuddled Ouspensky toward the end of his life. I wrote to Bennett and received, to my great surprise, the information that he had indeed tried to contact me telepathically. He planned to visit the United States quite shortly and would be in California in May. He was setting up a new institute in one of the stately homes of England and would be looking for students.

When Bennett arrived in California, I was impressed by his resemblance to Ernest O. Lawrence, the inventor of the cyclotron. They were both big men, both thought in a big way, both were expert politicians, and both were the victims of a consuming ambition. I say victims because, in the end, it was their ambitions that killed both of them. They could not learn to slow down.

I happened to know a lot about E. O. Lawrence because I had just finished writing a book, *The New Prometheans*, that contained a chapter on the atom smashers. Lawrence's cyclotron smashed atoms by accelerating ions to great velocities and hurling them against targets. From the targets so treated, elements could be obtained that had not been in the target. Lawrence had realized the alchemist's dream of transmuting one element into another.

Bennett was an alchemist of a different sort. He was concerned with spiritual transmutations. It was from Bennett that I had learned the phrase "way of accelerated completion." Accelerated completion seemed to be much on his mind. He had always been a man in a hurry.

It occurred to me as I thought about Bennett's new institute that it was really a spiritual particle accelerator comparable in many ways to Lawrence's cyclotron. In the cyclotron ions were accelerated by being kicked across a succession of voltage gradients. Each kick added to the velocity of the ions, which spiraled outward gaining mass all the time until they finally collided with the target. In Bennett's psychotron (Bennettron for short) I envisaged a similar process. It would impart energy to the psyche by means of a series of shocks or stimulations. Shocks could be negative or positive. One can drive a donkey by beating its rear or dangling a carrot before its nose. In the old days under Ouspensky we had learned to expect more stick than carrot. With Bennett, I gathered, there would be more carrot than stick. Emphasize the positive. Don't dwell on the horrors of sleep but think about the pleasures of awakening. The power of positive thinking . . .

Anyway, a good but strenuous time would be had by all. The spiritual particles, accelerated to near relativistic velocities, would be enabled to make the great jump from the Stream of Descent to the Stream of Ascent. The Ascending Stream was essentially the Warrior's Way. It led up to the Mount of Liberation, to reunion with the Sun Absolute. Not many particles could be expected to get that far, but at least they might be saved from the fate of perishing like dogs. It was worth a try.

The young people lapped it up. They adored Bennett. He had just the right touch, the right combination of schoolmaster and scoutmaster, the right blend of knowledge and being. He was an ardent Roman Catholic. If he had only joined the hierarchy of the Church instead of playing around with the ideas of G. Gurdjieff, he would certainly have ended up a cardinal.

And of course he knew all the answers I was seeking. Who wrote *The Teachers of Gurdjieff*? Ah, yes. That was so and so. An allegory of course. Gurdjieff's teachers were all dead. Who was the *Sarkar*? Ah, yes. That's quite a young man. I know him well. A remarkable chap. Did Bennett's new institute mark a different phase of the Work? Yes and no. Gurdjieff gave us the general line but we must develop it ourselves. Rigid adherence to earlier patterns will prove a hindrance to progress. Did he know our celebrated ringmaster and circus manager? Ah, yes. He was a student of mine. Had to throw him out. Always chasing the girls.

So that was where our comedian got his ideas! The plot
thickened.

And how about the famous "Inner Circle of Humanity"?
Was there really such a circle, or was it just an invention
like Madame Blavatsky's *mahatmas* who sent letters through
the ceiling? Bennett really perked up at this question. He
grew eloquent. Yes, there was indeed an Inner Circle of Humanity. He was writing a book about it and would send me
a copy. The circle consisted of adepts who were called the
Kwajagan, a word of Persian origin which he had translated
as the "Masters of Wisdom." Historically the Masters of
Wisdom had all been Moslems and had labored mainly in
Turkey, Persia, and Afghanistan. It was due to the influence
of the Masters of Wisdom that civilization was restored after
the terrible destruction wrought by the Mongol invasions in
the thirteenth century.

Were the *sarmouni* associated with the Masters of Wisdom? It was hard to tell. The *sarman* society was perhaps as
old as the Sumerian civilization. Many schools of wisdom
had existed in the past, among them the Essenes, from
whom both John the Baptist and Jesus had received their
training. It was difficult to trace the various schools, because adepts did not reveal what they knew and did not
write books. The wisdom of the *sarmouni* was preserved by
the Naqshbandi, an order of dervishes founded by Baha ad-
din Naqshband. It was also preserved by the Ahl-i-Haqq,
the People of the Truth. The Ahl-i-Haqq still existed in Persia.

"So the Inner Circle of Humanity still exists?"

Bennett was sure of it. He was also sure that we must do
our best, without necessarily contacting the adepts, to
create something like the *sarman* society in America. The
huge populations of the industrial societies were living in a
fool's paradise, refusing to face facts though the facts were
obvious to anyone. A crash was inevitable. We were running out of everything: fossil fuels, metals, forests, arable
land. He drew a vivid picture of the kind of chaos we might

expect. Our huge extravagant American agriculture was
nothing but a factory for turning oil into food. Stop the oil
and you stop the tractors. Stop the tractors and you stop the
food production. Stop the food production and people
starve. They will not starve quietly. The chaos could be as
bad as that created by the Mongol invasions. We were facing a period of destruction and grave danger. It made sense
to prepare.

"I visualize a series of self-sufficient communities," said
Bennett. "They will consist of candidates who will be training to follow the Way, specialists who teach various skills,
and an initiate who will oversee the whole operation."

Where would he get the initiates? They seemed to be in
really short supply. Bennett thought he had enough of
them. Genuine Masters of Wisdom? Well, perhaps not Masters, but far enough along on the Way to know what was
what. Small self-sufficient communities were the wave of
the future. Bennett was friendly with E. F. Schumacher.
Small is Beautiful—that was the slogan for the coming age of
scarcity.

Right on. Couldn't agree with you more. But there is this
matter of soul glue. How do you hold these very volatile
young people together long enough to create anything? I
had found them almost impossible to work with. They
ripped each other off, stole each other's mates. They re-
sented even the slightest criticism and left the group if you
trod on their toes. They were impossible.

Not so, said Bennett. They were very promising. But one
had to handle them just right. He had it all worked out. If I
wanted to know how it was done, I would have to go and
study at his institute.

No way. I have things to do here. But I shall watch the experiment with great interest. None of the people in my own
group felt like trusting their psyches to Bennett's particle accelerator. But members of a second group led by my friend
the Designer were made of sterner stuff. They scraped the
money together for a passage to England and a ten-month

residence in the stately home. I got letters from them. One contained a reproduction of one of Blake's illustrations from the *Visions of the Daughters of Albion*. "Bound back to back in Bromion's cave terror and meekness dwell." Written on the back of the postcard: "Life in the Bennettron."

Ah yes, terror and meekness, I could imagine it. No bed of roses. The courageous candidates for accelerated development were doubtless being whirled and swirled through every emotion in the spectrum. Love, hate, fear, exhaustion, self-pity, anxiety, ecstasy, discouragement, despair. It was the Warrior's Way and no mistake. Not for cowards and not for weaklings. Meanwhile in California things were happening. The Designer had in his group a young man into whose lap fortune had dumped a quite ridiculously large sum of money. Everyone else in our group was as poor as a church mouse. I had the idea, like Bennett, of creating a self-sufficient rural community, the Church of the Earth. It would be supported on three pillars: the garden, the temple, and the university. The garden would feed the physical body, the temple would feed the spirit, the university would feed the mind. It would be an ark that would hopefully stay afloat during the coming deluge, aboard which we might be able to stay alive, retain our sanity, and perhaps even awaken a little.

This was all very fine in theory, but would it work in practice? Only if our rich young man would provide the wherewithal to make it happen. But was it right that he should do so? The gospel story warned me to be on my guard. The very rich had a way of getting tangled up in their own wealth. It was difficult karma to have a huge sum of money dumped in one's lap, to find oneself surrounded by outstretched hands all eager to help themselves from one's hoard. Very difficult karma. *How hard it is for them that trust in riches to enter into the kingdom of God. It is easier for a camel to go through the eye of a needle. . . .*

On the other hand it was a principle in the Work that the rich must pay for the poor. All Ouspensky's work, both in

England and in America, had been financed by contribu-
tions from a few wealthy people. If you put your money
first and the Work second, you would never make much
progress. Jesus had confronted the rich young man with a
formidable task: *Sell whatsoever thou hast and give to
the poor . . . and take up the cross and follow me.*

Well, we could hardly ask our poor fellow to sell all he
had. That would be going too far. But a modest base for the
work, a meeting place, a few acres of garden . . . We asked
and he gave it. Fifteen acres and a building that we would
put up ourselves.

I had doubts from the start. The doubts came to the surface after the foundations had been dug. We dug them by
hand very carefully, two feet deep as called for by the building code. But my doubts were very strong. This was heavy
karma, a lot of money was involved. Let us give our young
benefactor one last chance to get off the hook. The group
had assembled in my chicken-house ashram. I gave the
message.

"Tell them to fill it in. Why do you let them wreck a perfectly good piece of pasture with a lot of trenches. Tell them
to fill it in."

Clear enough. The proper duty of a disciple is obedience.
Fill it in. I thought of the bomb shelter we had dug at Lyne
Place during the lion-into-rabbit crisis in 1938. Ouspensky
rode by on his horse. "Fill it in." We filled it in.

But times had changed. Evidently our benefactor thought
I was joking. The group did not fill in the foundations. Instead it went ahead and put up the building. There were
two neat three-bedroom houses for the resident students
and a large room for exercises and meditation. We called the
large room the *tekkia*, which was Turkish for a meeting
place for dervishes. Real *tekkias* are very beautiful structures
built with exquisite love and care, every stone washed and
laid in place with devotion, every timber hand-hewn from
selected trees. Things weren't being done that way here. It
was as much as I could do to persuade the carpenters to use

hand tools instead of power tools. Then our benefactor, who was studying *aikido*, wanted to turn the *tekkia* into a *dojo*. Go ahead. Don't mind me. It's your money. So truck-loads of scrap rubber were brought in, over which was spread a huge turquoise-blue carpet. The effect was hideous in the extreme. The *tikkia/dojo* was beginning to look like a rustic branch of the Bank of America.

Heavy karma. Once the building was finished, a sort of lassitude settled over everyone. Perhaps Bennett's accelerated particles would liven things up a bit when they returned. They were certainly taking their time, wandering around Europe and Asia. We had a garden to lay out, vineyards and orchards to plant. We needed help.

When they finally did return, Bennett's spiritually accelerated particles gave me a shock. I had expected well-trained, obedient, ready-for-service disciples. I received rebellious, starry-eyed, self-opinionated "adepts." Yes, adepts. They had been through a ten-month crash course. They had labored and suffered. The course at the Bennettron had certainly not been comfortable. Every one of the students in that first year had come up against obstacles that must have seemed almost insuperable. The struggle with those obstacles had, of course, generated energy in those members of the group who had really made efforts. They had learned the truth of the aphorism: *Strength exerted equals more strength. Weakness indulged equals greater weakness.* Encouraged by Bennett they had exerted themselves. They felt strong. It was a good feeling.

Not only did they have strength, they also had knowledge. They had worked intensively on all manner of exercises, dug the garden, tended the chickens, practiced the sacred dances, studied Turkish, heard lectures by Bennett, studied the works of Gurdjieff, practised *zikr*, fasted, staged theatricals, served the community. There was really no aspect of the Warrior's Way that they had not experienced. Bennett was not one to do things by halves. He understood and practiced the Gurdjieffian maxim: *If you're going on a spree go the whole hog.*

So Bennett's spiritually accelerated particles were whizzing around at velocities approaching that of light, and had as a result of their high velocity gained considerable mass. They were eager to share their newly gained energies with others. They were, as they put it, Messengers of the Higher Powers. Bennett had always been much preoccupied with Higher Powers and had passed on this preoccupation to his disciples. Messengers of the Higher Powers. It sounded great.

I found myself impaled on the horns of a dilemma. How should one handle these Messengers? They had obviously no intention of working under my direction, made it pretty clear that they thought they knew more than I did. Well, perhaps they did. And then again, perhaps they didn't.

I had been nearly forty years "in the Work." Which of course meant nothing except that I had entered it early and was now growing old. *But many that are first shall be last; and the last shall be first.* Was I just an old fuddy-duddy wedded to outmoded methods, a mere leftover from the past? Did these kids really know better than I did just what sort of action was called for by the Spirit of the Age? Or were they merely a bunch of deluded brats, full of self-importance, vibrating with borrowed energy that they would lose in a few months?

And what was Bennett? Was he, in the parlance of the great game, my honorable opponent? The great game is like a multidimensional form of chess. One needs an opponent, and it is best to choose one who is more skillful than one is oneself. One plays not to win but to improve one's skill. So one studies the strengths and weaknesses of one's honorable opponent with a view to understanding one's own strengths and weaknesses.

I thought about Bennett. The man was a Warrior of the first order, but ambitious. That was his problem. There were two men in Bennett. The first was a very sincere Seeker after Truth, who would spare no expense, no trouble, to learn more about the great game. That aspect of Bennett I admired. But there was a second aspect. I called it the Arch-Vainglorious Greek. It was a Gurdjieffian term and referred to Alexander of Macedon, the strutting hero who had spread havoc all the way from Greece to India and then expressed regret that there were no more worlds to conquer.

J. G. Bennett had, from the very beginning, been a battlefield in which the Seeker after Truth struggled with the Arch-Vainglorious Greek. The Seeker after Truth was basically humble and sincere, content with little, modest and retiring. But the Greek was ambitious, full of great schemes, always liable to overextend himself, to attempt too much. That overambitious character would kill Bennett unless he could be restrained. He involved Bennett in more and more large scale undertakings. In addition to the Bennettron in England he planned to open a branch of his institute in America. He was no longer young. He really was not strong. He thought he was, but that was self-deception.

It was not useful to try to persuade Bennett to abandon these big schemes. He would certainly kill himself by overwork, carried forward by a burning spirit that ignored the warning signals from his failing body. It was evidently his fate. Even his nearest and dearest could not persuade him to slow down. My problem was how to cope with those former members of my flock who had returned from England with a serious case of inflated ego. What would Gurdjieff do? Apply the sensitive corn test?

"I resolved whomever I should meet, for business, commerce or any other purpose, I had immediately to discover his 'most sensitive corn' and 'press' it rather hard."

How to make friends and influence people . . .

But of course the rules of the Way are not the same as the rules of life. Shall I submit these crows in peacock's feathers to the sensitive corn test? Better take the aspect of an Arabian storyteller and tell them a genuinely Gurdjieffian parable.

"Gather round, gather round, O ye beloved of Allah, and listen while I relate to you the story of the magician and the sheep.

"Once, long ago, on the plains of Central Asia there lived a magician. That magician was very rich but he was also very stingy. He had great flocks of sheep which kept running away because they knew the magician wanted their meat and their skins. They were pretty smart sheep.

"The magician was too cheap to hire shepherds or to build fences to confine the sheep. One day he had a brilliant idea. He hypnotized the sheep. He told them that he loved them dearly—that as for his taking their meat and skins, that was just a sign of his love and it wouldn't hurt at all; on the contrary it would be very pleasant. As for the more difficult sheep, the sort that might not swallow that suggestion, he persuaded them they were not sheep at all. He hypnotized some to think that they were eagles and some to think they were lions and some to think they were magicians. After that he had no trouble at all. The sheep came willingly to be slaughtered.

"He that has ears to hear let him hear."

A good story, really. Sums up the human dilemma. But it didn't go down well with the accelerated particles. Indeed they began to direct toward me vibrations that were apt to spoil a man's digestion and even give him ulcers if continued long enough. Hell! Have I lived sixty years on this earth only to have my digestion impaired by negative vibrations from a bunch of conceited brats? How did I get mixed up in this crazy scenario? My Missionary's fault. A meddlesome fool if ever there was one. Besides, who can tell, perhaps these young people aren't so dumb after all. They are the players of the future, the candidates for the higher life, the transmitters of the sacred lore. . . .

Had I been too harsh with them?

Never castigate. Babies learn to walk by falling down. If you beat a baby every time he falls down, he'll never care much for walking.

A crest jewel of wisdom from Robert Townsend (*Up the Organization*, New York: Fawcett Publications, 1970). Babies learn to walk by falling down. You can do your best to make it easy for the little darlings, take the furniture out of the way so they won't bruise their noses, or you can leave things alone and let them take their chances. But anyway, never castigate. Those who embark on the Warrior's Way will fall down heavily and frequently. It's inevitable. The Way is full of traps, icy in spots, muddy in others, steep in places, full of enticing detours and dead ends. Even the old and experienced travelers make mistakes. So how can one expect mere kids, barely out of college, not to fall flat on their faces again and again?

Never castigate.

Slowly I was getting the message. I had played the whole movie quite wrongly. I had been far too much influenced by the infallible teacher tradition, by the old authoritarian rigmarole. I had picked it up from Ouspensky and Madame Ouspensky. Always we had been put down, made to feel small, discouraged from taking the initiative. But for these young people of the seventies this would not do at all. They were not going to accept this authoritarian stuff. They were teachers in their own right. Or so they thought.

Okay. So they're hypnotized sheep and they dream they are magicians. Had I not fallen into exactly the same trap myself and with far less excuse? I had been nearly forty years "in the Work" and should have known better. If they wanted to float aloft on a hot-air balloon of self-importance and see themselves as Messengers of Higher Powers, then let them float. Why puncture their balloons? They would come down soon enough when the icy wind of reality cooled the hot air. And as for those who didn't come down, let them float away on the currents of their own ambitions.

Ambition . . . My mind flashed back over the years. The very first book I had read about the Way, the Theosophical work called *Light on the Path and Karma*, started with the words *Kill out ambition*. Ambition, it explained, was the first curse, the great obstacle in the path of those who aimed at self-transcendence. The itch to teach others was a manifestation of ego. Let me show you the way. Let me guide your steps. Let me steer you to heaven. Let me run your life for you. Such was the stock-in-trade of priests and politicians and head shrinkers, the swamp from which bubbled a million sermons and lectures. And underlying it all was a sense of superiority. I am not just anybody but the Reverend So-and-so, or His Holiness, Whose Word Must Not Be Doubted, or the Infallible Leader in whom you must have total faith, or the High Priest of psychobabble with a degree in clinical psychology. Ambition. Ambition.

The only true teacher is one who teaches by example. The true teacher is like Leo in *The Journey to the East.* Who was Leo? He seemed, to the junior Members of the League, to be simply a servant. Leo never lectured anyone, never preached, never gave himself airs. Simply a servant.

He who would be greatest let him be as a servant among you.

But the Journey to the East depended on Leo, and when he disappeared in the Morbio Inferiore the whole enterprise seemed to grind to a halt.

> Without Leo, his handsome face, his good humor and his songs, without his enthusiasm for our great undertaking, the undertaking itself seemed in some mysterious way to lose meaning.

Leo, the perfect teacher of the Way, so well disguised that his fellows did not even know he was their teacher! Teach only by example, never preach, never lecture, never castigate. But in order to teach by example one must have *Being.* And Being cannot be faked. One can fake knowledge. One can lay down a smoke screen of words and confuse all but the discerning few. But one can never fake Being. We show our level of being by our reactions, especially our reactions to insults, disappointments, disasters. You can't fake a reaction.

Did I possess the necessary level of being to play the role of Leo in the great journey? Obviously not. I was not even the right type. One had to be a sanguinic-phlegmatic type to play that role well, not a melancholic-choleric. One had to be a truly mellow dude. I was not a mellow dude. Anything but. In an emergency I tended to blow my cool. Confronted with opposition I tended to lose my temper. Worst of all I was at heart a recluse, a misanthrope. I did not love my neighbor as myself. I did not even love myself. An unpleasant type, objectively speaking.

Well, one must do what one can with the cards one has been dealt. In the great genetic poker game no one can ask for a new deal. My honorable opponent had put me in a bind. Checkmate? So it appeared. In any case that particular game was over. Obviously you cannot teach those who have no desire whatever to learn, who are in fact quite convinced that they are teachers themselves.

So what next? Turn the whole mess over to the Designer? The Designer had created his own group in San Francisco, had managed to persuade his "tail of donkey" that he was a teacher of a sort. Nearly all the returned Messengers from the Bennettron had originally been in the Designer's group. The Designer had helped to construct our *tekkia/dojo*. As far as I was concerned, he could now have it. The Designer, I strongly suspected, saw himself as a Man with a Message. Wanted to be a spiritual big shot. Let us offer him the bait and see if he swallows it.

He did. He swallowed it, hook, line, and sinker. Took over the whole show, didn't even ask for advice from his old teacher. I was glad to let him have it. After all, he had a Ph.D. in clinical psychology. Perhaps he could influence these "Messengers of Higher Powers" that Bennett had produced with his spiritual particle accelerator.

Poor Designer! He tried to play the authoritarian teacher, imitating me who was in turn imitating Ouspensky. So the whole gang turned on him like a pack of wolves and dragged him down. I watched from the sidelines. Messengers of Higher Powers! Heaven protect us from powers that send such messengers. The scrimmage got so rough toward the end that our benefactor, who still owned the property and had problems of his own, threw out the whole squabbling crowd. The *tekkia/dojo* with its pneumatic carpet and miscellaneous bad vibes stood empty. Six years later I walked over to look at it. It was still empty. Seen through the mist of a damp December afternoon, the building had a dreary, unloved appearance. It was a fitting memorial to the maleficent organ Kundabuffer, the consequences of whose properties continue to bedevil us.

So that was the end of the Church of the Earth.

The three pillars of wisdom—garden, temple, university—all collapsed. What went wrong? Seated alone in the chicken coop that I had once called my ashram, I meditated on the problem. A picture from the past appeared before me, the image of Sister Archangel, now dead, glaring at me on that Easter day when I had suddenly appeared, a disgraced and despised deserter, at the ostentatious mansion that was then the center of the Work. "What do *you* want?" The tone a butler uses to a beggar. Yes, that was it! As a group we had always lacked compassion. We lacked the soul glue that can hold a group together. So the whole group flew apart, torn to bits by petty rivalries, jealousies, spiritual ambitions and games of one-upmanship.

Seated there in the empty ashram, already disintegrating and being reclaimed by the rats, I continued to ponder. The "Messengers of Higher Powers" had certainly destroyed everything I had tried to create, and had been unable themselves to construct anything in its place. The unused *tekkia/dojo*, put up at considerable cost by members of my group, all of whom had contributed their labor for free, mocked our fine pretensions, made us all look like hypocrites or fools. Yes, it had been quite a lesson. I understood clearly that the gifts of the very rich tend to be poisoned and to carry within them destructive elements. I understood two principles that Michael Phillips, one of the New Realists, had formulated: *You can never really receive money as a gift* and *You can never really give money away* (*The Seven Laws of Money*, Menlo Park, California: Word Wheel, 1974).

A group that buys its own land and develops its own property is bound together by a very strong link. They *own* the place and it is in their interest to develop it. A group that has been given a piece of property has no such concern. The gift encourages freeloaders, tramps and layabouts. I thought of Lou Gottlieb's Morning Star, that short-lived utopia, "land access to which was denied none." My own Church of the Earth had been even more shortlived than Lou's hippie heaven, destroyed by those very "Messengers of Higher Powers" whose chief task should have been to build and strengthen it.

I had learned a great truth, however. One tries to teach others at one's peril. It is better to leave one's fellow men to sleep in peace than to disturb their slumbers.

Let not those who know unsettle the minds of the ignorant who know nothing.

How could I, a careful student of the Bhagavad Gita, have missed the significance of that verse?

Don Juan offered a similar message: *A warrior does not squeeze his world out of shape. He taps it lightly and passes on leaving hardly a trace.*

That was it. By playing the guru, I had squeezed out of shape the people with whom I had come in contact. I had also squeezed myself out of shape by trying to play a role not in accord with my essence. The Missionary, that babbling fool, had betrayed me.

Well, I had learned a lesson and would not forget it. In the future, no more talk. Live by the rule of the dervish: *Don't volunteer information about the Way, but be willing to answer honest questions.* What are honest questions? Honest questions contain the seeds of their own answers and show that the questioners have tried to solve the problems themselves. Dishonest questions show that the questioners are trying to get something for nothing, making conversation, indulging in idle curiosity, or showing off. Those liable to ask questions about the Way generally want someone else to do their thinking for them. The rest just don't care. So the dervish can continue on his way in solitude, unimpeded by either companions or possessions.

> Down to Gehenna or up to the Throne
> He travels fastest who travels alone.
> (Kipling)

36

SEEKER
AFTER TRUTH

My honorable opponent killed himself by overexertion in December 1974. A serious loss, from my point of view. John Godolphin Bennett was a skilled player of the game, one who kept his mind open and was always ready to experiment. He had charisma. He had personal power. He had a way with people, especially young people. I had debated at length with myself and others whether his influence on his students had been beneficial or disastrous.

No answer came.

It was perhaps too early to tell.

In any case, he was dead. One more link in the old chain was destroyed. Soon that particular chain would vanish entirely. The links were already eroded by the age of its members, their limited understandings, their petty rivalries, their personal ambitions. In accordance with an inexorable law the various groups that wore the label "Gurdjieffian" grew weaker as they grew more numerous. The movement tended, as do all such movements, to turn into a cult of personality.

What could be done to prevent this dreary transformation?

The remedy lay in reassembling the Seekers after Truth. Such seekers would have to consist of hard-headed realists, able and willing to study quite objectively any method of psychotransformism that appeared to be promising. They would have to be able to overcome in themselves those two

obstacles to objective mentation, credulity and suggestibility. They would have to get rid of the tendency to indulge in starry-eyed belief in some teacher or leader, the
tendency to evade responsibility for their actions or decisions and to take refuge in ready-made systems of belief.

The Seekers after Truth.

It is by far the most select club on earth. It is open to everyone; no distinctions are made on grounds of sex, color,
or creed. The cost of admission is our illusions, *all* our illusions. For it stands to reason that if we want the truth we
cannot at the same time take refuge in lies. But this is what
we like to do. We love lies. And our fondest lies are those
that relate to ourselves, lies about our own importance,
about our dignity, our "human rights," our place in nature.

Was Bennett a member of the club? The question drifted
through my mind as I meditated on his life. It had been a
strenuous, stormy life which he had described in some detail
in his autobiography (*Witness*, Tuscon, Arizona: Omen
Press, 1974). He had certainly lived dangerously, experimented fearlessly, traveled widely, and thought deeply. He
had never spared himself, preferring the hard path to the
easy way. He had met and responded to challenges that
would have destroyed a weaker man. He had died an honorable death.

This did not automatically make him a member of the
club, for those subtle defects, suggestibility and credulity,
can operate in people whose life-style is heroic and strenuous. The most destructive form of religious fanatic is one
who fearlessly and strenuously follows his own closed system of fixed beliefs. The Seekers after Truth can never
admit to their company fanatics of any kind. Fanaticism
always involves the closing of the mind, the substitution of
a fixed belief system for the open approach.

My question, Did Bennett belong to the club? was of
course a futile one. We cannot judge the being of another.
The only benefit to be derived from the study of another
person's life is an understanding of laws. Two kinds of laws

govern our lives, laws escapable and laws inescapable. Freedom consists in living under as few laws as possible, substituting intentional, self-made laws for laws imposed by outer circumstances. Richard Burton, translator of the *Thousand and One Nights*, expressed this idea in *The Kasidah of Haji Abdu El-Yezdi*.

> Do what thy manhood bids thee do.
> From none but self expect applause:
> He noblest lives and noblest dies
> Who makes and keeps his self-made laws.

Richard Burton, who was almost certainly a full member of the club, had much in common with Bennett. Both belonged to that category of handsome mesomorphs who, besides being endowed with great physical strength, possess first-class minds and a consuming curiosity about the mysteries of life. Members of the group always live dangerously, and come close to death several times before they actually die.

Bennett was no exception. Scarcely had he come of age before he was swept into the carnage of World War I. On March 21, 1918, he lay on a battlefield with a serious head wound and a body full of shrapnel. The injury had the effect of separating some part of him from his physical body. He was able to observe, with a certain detached curiosity, the efforts a surgeon was making to patch up his wounds. This early experience of almost dying, of entering a realm where all perceptions were changed and physical bodies were not required, impressed Bennett so deeply that it affected the whole course of his life. He became, at the age of twenty, one of "the dead who have returned." He knew that it was possible to leave the physical body and enter a different dimension. He knew also that it was possible to return from that dimension and take up one's body again. This sort of knowledge is not given to everyone.

The knowledge began almost immediately to influence

his line of fate. During that state of semideath he had entered what Hesse called "the Archives of the League" and received a hint of the enormous treasures they contained. No one who has entered the Archives, however briefly, can be satisfied with the ordinary life games. To such a person Hog in the Trough and the Fame Game seem ridiculous. Even the Art Game and the Science Game seem insufficient. They are useful only as stepping stones. The greatest game of all lies beyond science and art, though it can incorporate them both. It involves the *Journey to the East*, a return to the true place of our arising.

Bennett's Journey to the East took him quite literally in an easterly direction. He had learned Turkish and became head of the British Intelligence Office in what was then Constantinople. He was only twenty-three but was placed in a position of such importance that men old enough to be his grandfather came humbly to consult him. Eunuchs and chamberlains from the Sultan's palace, spies, informers, intriguers, assassins, and gossips flocked to his office. Young, tall, handsome in his polished boots and perfectly tailored officer's uniform, aloof, cool, mature and at the same time boyish, he represented the sort of young man who had given to Britain her greatness and whose senseless butchery in World War I was largely responsible for her later decline.

In Constantinople in 1920–21 there was real fear on the part of the Allies of a religious war, a general rising by the Moslems led by the dervishes aimed at the restoration of the glory of Islam and the liberation of all Moslems from the foreign yoke. There were 150 million Moslems who were subjects of the British raj, in India, Malaya, and Africa. The dervishes were well-known as fanatical fighters. Such a revolt of Islam might prove to be a serious matter indeed.

So young Bennett was instructed to move discreetly into certain circles in Turkish society and to find out what the dervishes were doing. Accordingly he attended the meetings of the Mevlevi dervishes and watched the turning exercise that these dervishes use as a means of "pointing the soul toward God." He also visited the *tekke* of the Rufa'i on the Asiatic coast of the Bosphorus. There he saw an elderly dervish draw a sharp scimitar across his bare belly as he lay on the floor. Two other dervishes stood on the sword, which appeared to be cutting the old man in two. The old man remained perfectly calm, lifted the sword, drew a line over his body with his right thumb where the sword had been. His body, which had been practically cut in half, was now completely unmarked. Bennett, who examined the sword, pronounced it sharp as a razor. He later saw many demonstrations of a similar kind and was left in no doubt that, by means of special exercises, it is possible to acquire extraordinary powers over the physical body.

Both Ouspensky and Gurdjieff were in Constantinople at the time, and Bennett met them both. From Ouspensky he learned, at their very first meeting, the idea of the transformation of man, which formed the basis of all Ouspensky's teaching.

"You suppose all men are on the same level," said Ouspensky. "In reality one man can be more different from another than a sheep from a cabbage. There are seven different categories of man."

On a piece of paper Ouspensky drew a diagram having seven compartments. In the lower compartments were instinctive, feeling, and thinking man, in the next was transitional man, in the upper three were integrated man, conscious man, and perfected man. All people we ordinarily meet belong to the first three categories; they are dominated either by instinct, feeling, or thought. All the beings in the higher categories are transformed men; they have brought about in themselves certain changes by intentional work on themselves.

"If man aspires to transformation," said Ouspensky, "he must first acquire balance and harmony of his instincts, his emotions, and his thoughts. This is the first condition for right transformation. The transformed man acquires powers that are incomprehensible to ordinary people. Even man number five (integrated man) is for us a superman."

Ouspensky abruptly terminated his explanation and did not return to the subject. What he did not say, but what Bennett and all Ouspensky's other pupils later learned, was that the work of harmonizing instinct, feeling, and thought is so difficult that few undertake it and even fewer succeed.

Several years later this fact was brought home to Bennett in a very direct way. He had met Gurdjieff in Constantinople; and later, when the Institute for the Harmonious Development of Man was opened in France, he went to work there. The work was intensive and exhausting. It was made more so for Bennett by the fact that he was suffering from dysentery, which he had contracted in Smyrna four years earlier. He was so weak that he could hardly get out of bed, yet he forced himself to carry on, even to perform a certain exercise for a far longer time than did most of the other students. He lost all sense of past and future, was aware only of the present agony of forcing his weakened body to continue to move. Gurdjieff stood watching intently. Bennett became aware of an unspoken demand that was at the same time an encouragement and a promise. He must not give up even if the effort killed him.

Suddenly he found himself filled with an influx of immense power. His whole body seemed to have turned into light, and he could not feel its presence in the usual way. His weak, rebellious body had become strong and obedient. He no longer felt the gnawing abdominal pains that had tormented him for days. So great was this new influx of energy that he could not rest even when the exercise was over. He went off into the kitchen garden and spent some time digging vigorously, then went for a walk in the forest of Fontainebleau. On one of the forest paths he met Gurdjieff. Without any preliminaries Gurdjieff began to talk in Turkish about the energies that work in man.

A certain energy was necessary for work on oneself. No one could make efforts unless he had a supply of this energy. It could be called Higher Emotional Energy. Everyone, by a natural process, made a small amount of it every day. Rightly used, it enabled one to achieve much for one's own

self-perfecting. But one could only get to a certain point in
that way. The transformation of Being that was indispens-
ible for one who wished to fulfill the purpose of his existence required a much greater concentration of Higher Emotional Energy than that which came to one by nature.

There were some rare people in the world who were connected to a Great Reservoir or Accumulator of this energy.
Those who could draw on it could be a means of helping
others. Suppose we need a hundred units of this energy for
our transformation, but we only have ten units and cannot
make more. We are helpless. But with the help of someone
who can draw upon the great Accumulator, we can borrow
ninety more. Then our work can be effective.

Those able to draw on the Great Reservoir belonged to a
special part of the highest caste of humanity. Bennett,
Gurdjieff said, might become such a one, but he would
have to wait for many years. What he had received that day
was a taste of what was possible for him. Until that time he
had known about those things only theoretically, but now
he had experience. When a person had had experience of
Reality, he became responsible for what he did with his
life.

Bennett was not able to stay for long at the Prieuré. He
had to make money and attend to other obligations. Before
he left he had one more talk with Gurdjieff.

"So far you have come here as a trial," said Gurdjieff.
"You have been given something. But if you come here to
work, you must understand that nothing is given. If you
wish to acquire something of your own you must steal.
What I have to give cannot be paid for; it is priceless.
Therefore, if you need it, you must steal it."

Gurdjieff spoke of the enormous obstacles that had to be
overcome if the process of inner transformation was to be
completed. Most people encountered barriers that they
could not pass. Everyone had these barriers; they were in
human nature. Bennett had seen that it was possible to be
connected to the Great Accumulator of Energy. If he could

be permanently connected to this source, he could pass all barriers. But he did not know how it could be done, and he was not ready to be shown. Everything was still in front of him to be done, but he now had proof that it was possible. It might take twenty, thirty, or even forty years before he would be able to enter into possession of the power that had been lent to him for a day.

"Ever since I was a young boy," said Gurdjieff, "I have known of the existence of this power and of the barriers that separate man from it. I searched until I found the way of breaking through them. This is the greatest secret that man can discover about human nature. Many people are convinced that they wish to be free and to know reality, but they do not know the barrier that prevents them from knowing reality. They come to me for help but they are unwilling or unable to pay the price. It is not my fault if I cannot help them."

Gurdjieff spoke about Being and Knowledge. Bennett, he declared, was in danger of losing everything if he relied on knowledge alone. Too much knowledge could make the inner barrier insurmountable. Bennett inquired how long he would need to work with Gurdjieff. He expected him to say that the work of breaking through the barriers would take twenty years at least. To his surprise Gurdjieff gave quite a different estimate. If he would devote all his energies to the task, it might take two years before he could work alone. Until then he would need help, for he could not create the needed conditions for himself. Afterward he would not need help any more. But for those two years he would have to be ready for anything.

Bennett did not continue to work with Gurdjieff. He left the Prieuré and worked with Ouspensky in London. In 1924 Ouspensky called a special meeting of ten of his closest associates, of whom Bennett was one. Ouspensky told them that he had decided to break off all relations with Gurdjieff. All those present would have to decide whether they wanted to work with Gurdjieff or with Ouspensky. If they chose to work with Ouspensky, they would have to promise not to communicate in any way with Gurdjieff or his pupils.

Gurdjieff, Ouspensky explained, was an extraordinary man whose possibilities were quite exceptional. But even Gurdjieff could go wrong. He was, Ouspensky thought, passing through a crisis the outcome of which no one could foresee. Most people had many I's. If those I's were at war, it did not produce much harm, because they were all equally weak. But in Gurdjieff there were only two I's: one very good and one very bad. Ouspensky believed that in the end the good I would conquer. But while the struggle was in progress it was dangerous to be near Gurdjieff. They could not help him, and in his present condition he could not help them. So Ouspensky had decided to break off relations. Which did not mean that he was against Gurdjieff or thought what he was doing was bad.

Bennett decided to work with Ouspensky. At the time I first met him in 1936, he occupied an important position in the hierarchy. Often he presided over those interminable meetings at Warwick Gardens, collecting questions for the teacher when Ouspensky was absent. But Bennett, even in those days, had his own group and taught in his own way. He was by far the most independent of Ouspensky's older pupils. This independence was not appreciated by Ouspensky, who in 1943 issued another ultimatum. If we wished to continue to work with him, we must sever all contacts with Bennett and with members of Bennett's group. Looking back on it I find this ukase highly absurd. It meant that all sorts of old friends who had worked together for years had studiously to avoid each other. But avoid each other we did. How seriously we took our teacher in those days!

In 1945 Bennett found himself confronting a problem. He was cut off from Ouspensky and had lost touch with Gurdjieff. He had quite a large group working with him who regarded him as their teacher. Was he really a teacher? Ouspensky had convinced him that the test of man's Being was his ability to remember himself. Could he do this? No, he could not. Ought he therefore to stop teaching? He could not do this either. The group he had gathered at Coombe Springs had a life of its own and continued to grow and was demanding more of his time. Whether he liked it or not, he was compelled to go ahead. He had to give the work he was doing a form and a name. He chose one that would mean little and convey less, and be so awkward to pronounce that no one would use it—*The Institute for the Comparative Study of History, Philosophy and the Sciences Limited.*

Despite the fact that he was now the head of an institute that attracted as many as two hundred students to its courses, he was not at ease. The signs of the times were not encouraging. It seemed fairly certain that all the sacrifices of World War II had been in vain and that a third world war was inevitable. Why, thought Bennett, should he and his group remain in the danger zone? The unrestrained use of atomic weapons might change the whole of the Northern Hemisphere into a radioactive desert. Ouspensky was dead, Gurdjieff had vanished. There was nothing to hold them in Europe. They should move to the Southern Hemisphere and there build a Noah's ark.

This thought sent Bennett flying off to Africa early in 1948. The Northern Hemisphere was probably doomed, but a new and more interesting civilization might arise in the South. He was deeply interested in black Africa, convinced that the native people had retained many spiritual powers that the rest of the world had lost. In 1948 Africa did indeed seem safe. The Mau Mau troubles had not started in Kenya, and the rest of the continent seemed to be locked in a sort of slumber, unaware of its power. In Nairobi, however, Bennett felt acutely uncomfortable. He was surrounded by people who had run away, who thought themselves clever because they had got out of England before trouble came. Was he not also running away? Why should he suppose that a community hidden in the depths of South Africa or Rhode-

sia would necessarily survive any better than one on the
outskirts of London?

The uncertainties in Bennett's mind were resolved by a
conversation he had in Cape Town with Field Marshal Jan
Smuts. Bennett had met Smuts when, as a young man, he
had been recovering from his war wounds in Cambridge.
Now he had been invited to meet him again. Smuts was a
truly remarkable man: Prime Minister of the Union of South
Africa, a soldier and a philosopher. I myself had been much
influenced as a student by his theory of Holism, especially
as applied to the process of evolution. Now Smuts listened
while Bennett spoke of his plans for an African utopia.

"I believe there is a great danger that European civilization will collapse," said Bennett. "With a group of about
two hundred, I have been wondering whether we ought to
emigrate and found a colony in some remote valley in
Africa, where we could preserve what we have found and
bring it back after the storm."

Smuts rejected the idea. He explained his reason. It was
wrong, he said, to imagine that if European civilization was
destroyed, something could be preserved in Africa. Europe,
for at least another century, would continue to be the bearer
of the hope of the human race. A very ancient and stable
culture had been established in Europe. There was nothing
like it in the rest of the world.

Smuts had been to San Francisco for the signing of the
Charter of the United Nations. It had made a fine start, but
it could not save the world from disaster. Only Europe
could save the world. What good would it do for Bennett
and his group to settle in South Africa? It was a newborn
country. It had not even begun to grow up. All its troubles
lay ahead. There would be no real culture in South Africa
for a hundred years.

Moreover, said Smuts, the same was true of the United
States. The most profound and distressing impression he
had received during his visit to America was of the imma-
turity of that country. It had become the most powerful
country in the world and was being forced into world lead-

ership. But it was not yet fit to play this role, and this was a grave danger.

The crisis in human affairs, explained Smuts, was due to premature acquisition of powers by the human race that it was too immature to use wisely. But the crisis could not be solved by running away from it. If Bennett had understood the situation a little better than others, then his place was at home.

"Go back," said Smuts, "and preach the supreme importance of your European heritage."

Bennett took the old philosopher's advice. He returned to England and shortly afterward made a business trip to America. He wrote to Madame Ouspensky asking if he could see her and was promptly invited to Franklin Farms. There were shocks all round. Bennett the outcast, Bennett the anathematized, suddenly invited to reside among the faithful! Loud squawks resounded, as from a chicken coop into which the farmer himself had introduced a fox. Nor was Bennett the only fox. Madame Ouspensky was talking of inviting Gurdjieff himself to America. Gurdjieff the Terrible, whom we had been forbidden to contact under any circumstances, was alive and active. Bennett had tried to find him in France without success. He had concluded that Gurdjieff had either died or gone mad.

"He is not mad," said Madame Ouspensky. "He has never been mad. He is living in Paris now. Why you not go to him?"

Bennett went immediately to Paris. There in a shabby little flat on the Rue des Colonels Renard was the same man who had told him so much in the old days at the Prieuré in 1923. Gurdjieff was wearing a red fez in the style of the Ottoman Turks, an open shirt, and sloppy trousers. The face, which one of his old students from the Prieuré days described to me as "positively piratical," had aged. The dark sweeping moustaches had turned white. He was old and sad, but he still carried himself erect. And the power was still there.

"You know what is first commandment of God to man?"

While Bennett fumbled for an answer, Gurdjieff supplied it himself.

"Hand wash hand! You need help and I need help. If I help you, you have to help me."

Then he asked: "What do you wish from me?"

"Will you show me how to work for my Being?"

"It is right. Now you have much Knowledge but in Being you are a nullity. If you will do as I say, I will show you how to change. Only you must stop thinking. You think too much. You must begin to sense. Do you understand the distinction between sensing and feeling?"

Bennett said that one was physical and the other emotional.

"More or less. But you only know this with your mind. You do not understand with your whole being. This you must learn."

It was extraordinary. Twenty-seven years had passed since Bennett had first met Gurdjieff at the house of Prince Sabaheddin in Istanbul. On that occasion Gurdjieff had spoken of Knowledge and Being and the futility of developing one without the other. Now here they were on the same subject. Had nothing changed in the interval? Of course it had. Both men were older. Time was running out.

From that point until the day of Gurdjieff's death Bennett stayed close to his old teacher. He was determined to learn all he could and to make use of that knowledge. Bennett seriously believed he was the inheritor of the mantle of the prophet and quoted some words of Gurdjieff that seemed to support this conclusion. Toward the end of Gurdjieff's life, when he had only a few weeks more to live, the following exchange took place between him and Bennett:

"I cannot thank you for what you have done for me," said Bennett. "That I can never repay."

Gurdjieff continued to drink his tea as if he had heard nothing. Later he commented on Bennett's statement.

"What you say about never repay—this is stupidity. *Only* you can repay. Only you can repay for all my labors. . . .

But what you do? Before trip I give you task. Do you fulfill? No, you do just opposite. Never once I see you struggle with *yourself*. All the time you are occupied with your cheap animal."

Later, while sitting with Gurdjieff by the open window of a café looking onto the Avenue des Ternes, Bennett asked about the meaning of the phrase "real unchangeable I." Gurdjieff waved his hand toward the street.

"Those people all look for taxi. Everyone can get on your taxi. But you are beginning to have own motor car. You must not let people get on your taxi. This is real unchangeable I—to keep one's own motorcar. Now you have only taste, but one day you will have such I, and when you know it has come, you will have such happiness as you cannot imagine."

There it was, the key to the whole game, handed out casually in a Paris café. *Have your own motorcar.* Stop being a taxi that anyone can hire. If you are really a Master, you must take responsibility for your own actions. Stop relying on others. Stop expecting others to give you directions. The master builder does not ask others how to build a house. The master artist does not ask others how to paint a picture. The master navigator does not ask others how to plot a course. And if you are going to play the Master Game and have spent years and years learning the game, the time must come when you yourself know how to play. And if you know how to play you do not need to depend on others. Your apprenticeship is over. You are a member of the Guild, a Master.

Bennett, however, continued to search long after most people would have concluded they knew all the answers. In Aleppo he met Farhad Dede, a very holy dervish of the Mevlevi Order. Farhad Dede was not optimistic about the future of the dervishes. He had been a dervish for nearly sixty years and had been trained by a great sheikh formed when the discipline of the parent *tekke* in Konyia had lost none of its traditional rigor. He had, since then, known many sheikhs. He had been in *tekkes* in Istanbul, Cairo, Cyprus, Jerusalem, Afyun Kara Hissar, Aleppo. The sheikhs did not take, as did members of the Dedeghian, vows of poverty and chastity. They had to be worldly men, and everything depended on their training. Farhad Dede was sure of one thing. No one was fit to teach who had not worked under a teacher. Only a true spiritual guide, a *murshid*, could form another *murshid*. True sheikhs had always been rare, and now none were left. Soon the Mevlevi order would die out. All was finished.

As for him, he was content. His soul was delivered to God. Whatever God willed was acceptable.

"If I could come to England and you would accept me, I would take you for my sheikh, for I see that your will is surrendered to God. For me it is enough that I have my ragged cloak and food to eat. I want nothing else in this life."

He made Bennett a cup of tea, "with the slow exquisite care that the Mevlevi dervishes bring to each act, large or small."

In northern Persia Bennett spoke with another dervish, Ahmad Tabrizi, who lived in a hut by the tomb of a forgotten saint. The dervish had wandered far and wide throughout Turkistan and Afghanistan. He had made pilgrimages to Mecca and Kerbela, but had never attached himself to any order.

"All my life I have walked alone," the dervish said. "When I could learn something useful about religion, I stopped. When I had learned all I could, I went on. Now I am satisfied that I have found all that I need on earth and, if it is God's will, I shall remain in this place until the end of my life."

In reply to Bennett's question Ahmad Tabrizi made a distinction between the *tarikat* and the *marifat*. The *tarikat* are the Ways. The Ways are traveled by those who need a guide, a *murshid*. But there were many dangers in the relationship between teacher and pupil. He himself had preferred to rely on *marifat*, illumination that comes directly from God. The beginning and end of religion was surrender to the will of God, and that surrender alone made the true dervish.

A short while later Bennett set off on the track of another teacher, an Indonesian called Pak Subuh, whose method, Subud, involved a practice called *latihan*. For awhile Subud was all the rage, and Bennett, who never did anything by halves, spent all his energy explaining the new method. The *latihan*, declared Bennett, had worked wonders for him and his wife. They had become freer, more open, and above all more hopeful. They could see clearly the harm done "by the unnecessary pessimism and restrictiveness of the Gurdjieff groups." (Gurdjieff by that time had been dead for eleven years. The "Gurdjieff groups" were organized by his pupils.) But the *latihan* did not offer the final solution to this ever restless seeker. He now set off for the Shivapuri Hills below the Himalayas in Nepal to meet a great sage, said to be more than one hundred and thirty years old, called Shivapuri Baba.

His rather brief contact with this sage convinced Bennett that he, Bennett, might be destined to reach—here in this very life—that condition which Gurdjieff had described to him in 1949. *Do not be satisfied with Paradise, but seek only to come to the Sun Absolute.* "For the first time," wrote Bennett, "this audacious quest appeared to be something more than a distant vision."

In June of 1962 Bennett was hot on the trail of yet another teacher. This time the teacher was Idries Shah, who had (so Bennett's informants assured him) been sent to the West from that very brotherhood in Afghanistan where Gurdjieff and Professor Skridlov had talked with Father Giovanni about knowledge and understanding. In a surprisingly short time Bennett convinced himself that Shah was indeed a messenger from the Guardians of the Tradition. He placed himself at Shah's disposal. He handed over to Shah his estate, Coombe Springs, which had been the center of his activities since 1941, and moved to a house in Kingston.

Having given Shah Coombe Springs (which Shah promptly sold) Bennett bought Sherborne House, an enormous building that had been a school for one hundred and forty boys. It was at this point that I met Bennett again, with results already described. He had parted company with Idries Shah and was devoting his attention to a Turkish Sufi called Hasan Shushud. This Sufi was an authority on the *Khwajagan*, the Masters of Wisdom, whose doings Bennett described in the opening chapters of his book on Gurdjieff (*Gurdjieff: Making of a New World*, New York: Harper and Row, 1973). He was also an exponent of the way of Absolute Liberation. He taught Bennett the perpetual prayer of the heart, the *zikr-i-daim*, which has no words and spans all religions. He also taught him the method of breath control that transfers the action of the *zikr* from the physical body to the body Kesdjan, or Astral body, which becomes stronger as a result.

Hasan Shushud did not seem to be impressed by Bennett's students. He saw no reason why this gifted man should spend his declining years playing "nanny to eighty brats" as one of Bennett's own students put it to me in a moment of frankness. "You have been chosen to be one of the rare ones," said the Sufi, "who are destined to go all the way to the final liberation from the conditions of existence. Your only home is the Absolute Void."

If Bennett's home was the Absolute Void, he certainly showed no great eagerness to return there. Though his health was obviously failing and he already had more students than he could handle, he was busily planning to put yet another millstone round his neck. A large and costly estate, Claymont Court in West Virginia, had become available. Bennett was all in favor of buying it and creating a self-sufficient rural community. He was convinced that the top-heavy technological society of the West would crash sometime in the 1980s. He was also convinced that the ideas of E. F. Schumacher offered a blueprint for the alternative society that would grow out of the ruins of the old. So this indefatigable Warrior began once again to plan and to build, joyously announcing that as far as he was concerned life began at seventy.

How much time did he think he still had? At the end of his book *Witness* he declared that there was no obvious reason why a healthy man or woman should not live to a hundred or more. He mentioned Shivapuri Baba, who had been in full possession of his faculties at the age of one hundred and thirty-six. He mentioned also a Turkish Hamil he had met in 1919 with authenticated papers showing that he was born in 1776, twelve years before the French Revolution. Could a self-realized man live as long as he chose?

Who knows? According to the legend, on the night of mid-Shaaban the Tree of Extremity in Paradise is shaken by the archangel and the falling leaves bear the names of all who will die in the coming year. In 1974 one of the falling leaves bore the name of John Godolphin Bennett.

37

THE TRICKSTER'S WAY

Early in 1972 I wrote a letter to Carlos Castaneda. I had discovered, rather late in the day, *The Teachings of Don Juan* and had just finished reading Castaneda's second book, *A Separate Reality*. A series of thoughts passed through my brain. First, this man is either a madman or a genius. Second, as he seems to be living a normal life in Los Angeles he can't be completely mad. Third, if he doesn't watch out he will be. Fourth, we can't afford to lose him.

This last thought of mine was prompted by my acute awareness of the tragedy of Friedrich Nietzsche. I had always been an admirer of Nietzsche. In spite of the dreadful archaic language in which it is written, *Thus Spake Zarathustra* remains one of the finest portrayals of the Warrior's Way. Nietzsche's insanity may have been, probably was, the result of tertiary syphilis, but there were other contributing factors. Utterly alone, without wife, without children, without recognition, this "philosopher with a hammer" always seemed to me a truly tragic figure. He was, as Jung put it, like "a blank page whirling about in the winds of the spirit." A torrent of tremendous ideas surged through his brain, which, like an electric device that receives too much current, was burnt out completely by their power.

In many ways Castaneda resembled Nietzsche. He did not, thank God, use a pseudoarchaic style or resort to poetic devices to convey his ideas. Indeed, one of the most refreshing features of his two main spokesmen, don Juan and don Genaro, was that they were completely down to earth, laughed, spat, shat, cracked jokes like anyone else. But the scope of the ideas, the insistence on impeccability and unbending intent, on the need for courage, on the importance of awareness, the emphasis on the dangers of the way and on the utter aloneness of a Warrior who embarks upon it—all these were strongly reminiscent of Nietzsche's Zarathustra. And the same danger that threatened the creator of Zarathustra also threatened the creator of don Juan. Or so it seemed.

My letter therefore was prompted by a certain concern. I knew enough about schizophrenia to realize that the schizophrenic is a victim of a split in reality. But this split in reality can also be induced intentionally, by people who are not schizophrenic but have a special ability to enter what Aldous Huxley called "the Antipodes of the Mind." Such people are natural mystics and seers. William Blake, Jacob Boehme, Emmanuel Swedenborg, and, of course, Friedrich Nietzsche all belonged to this group. Blake was particularly well endowed. He saw not two but four separate realities.

> Now I a fourfold vision see,
> And a fourfold vision is given to me;
> 'Tis fourfold in my supreme delight
> And threefold in soft Beulah's night
> And twofold Always. May God us keep
> From Single vision and Newton's sleep!
> ("Letter to Thomas Butts")

Castaneda, I thought, had placed himself in a rather more dangerous situation than such natural seers as William Blake. First, he had made extensive use of such drastic psychedelic drugs as the devil's weed (*Datura inoxia*). Second, when not wandering around in the Sonoran desert, he spent his time in Los Angeles. Los Angeles and the practice of shamanism do not mix. It is one thing to pop in and out of separate realities among the cacti and shrubs of the desert, quite another to do it while driving a Volkswagen bus on a Los Angeles freeway. Disassociation under such conditions could be very dangerous. My letter, therefore, carried a warning. It also carried the message that I greatly admired his work and would like to meet him.

Back came a telephone message. Castaneda would be in Sonoma sometime between the twentieth and twenty-fifth of February. More details later.

The promised details, of course, never arrived. I gave up trying to arrange a meeting. Light was beginning to dawn. Castaneda, I realized, was following a Way that involved becoming invisible. It was not a new idea. Gurdjieff had often said that those in the Work should know how to become invisible. The secret lay in not engaging the attention of those around one. One should be able to move through a crowd without being noticed, without making any impression on anyone. Castaneda, for reasons of his own, was cultivating this ability. It was a legitimate method and one which I could appreciate.

So Castaneda became for me a living example of the Invisible Man. He also became an example of the Trickster. Trickster plays a role in the mythology of several tribes of American Indians. Trickster is man in all his complexity. He is crude, primitive, unaware of his powers, a chaos awaiting the creator. But this is only one aspect of Trickster. Seen from another point of view, Trickster is *maya*, the play of nature, the unceasing change that goes on around us and within us, the flow of phenomena, the images real and unreal that chase each other incessantly through the chambers of our awareness. Trickster is also a magician holding us spellbound by his displays, extracting rabbits from hats, turning wands into serpents, sawing ladies in half, causing solid objects to vanish and reappear.

Trickster, in short, is a master at creating illusions, but his tricks are more than ordinary conjuring tricks. Warriors who follow the Trickster's Way learn certain things about both themselves and others. They learn mainly about the power of credulity and suggestibility over the workings of the psyche of people in the state of waking sleep. They learn about the power of hypnotic suggestion. By using the power he develops, a Warrior who follows this Way can make those around him react as he wishes them to react, see what he wishes them to see. This sort of power is used particularly by the shaman and the sorcerer. It is part of their stock-in-trade. The sorcerer is a not very advanced kind of Warrior, being usually trapped on the Mountain of Power. But even Warriors who have gone far beyond the sorcerer's level of development can benefit from learning the sorcerer's tricks. In the course of such learning the Warrior gains insight into his own credulity and suggestibility and thus learns to be on his guard.

All this helped me to understand Castaneda's presentation of the Trickster's Way. Castaneda played the Trickster role with extraordinary skill. Though I had had quite a lot of contact with magic and magicians, I could not help but gasp with amazement at the power of this illusionist. His technique involved blending very vivid descriptions of the laws that govern the Warrior's Way with all sorts of circus stunts and magical tricks, related in such detail and with such verbal skill that I almost believed in them myself. Had he described only magical tricks I would not have read his books. I had, at that stage in my career, not much use for "tales of mystery and imagination." But the circus tricks and special effects (iridescent coyotes, sorceresses who turned into blackbirds, terrifying presences that crawled on the back of one's neck) were blended with so much useful knowledge that I read the books several times.

The Way of the Trickster . . . Yes, it is a valid Way, and it reveals to those clever enough to follow it an enormous amount about themselves and their fellow men. Consider the reactions to Castaneda's books. In Richard de Mille's carefully researched and brilliantly written study, *Castaneda's Journey*, the author addresses a question to the general public. *What do you think of Carlos Casteneda and the teachings of don Juan?* He offers nine answers, four of which will be quoted here.

> A: Don Juan is the most important model for man since Jesus. If he is imaginary, then Carlos Castaneda is the principle psychological, spiritual and literary genius of recent generations.
>
> A: Don Juan is a combination of various spiritual teachers Castaneda has met or read about. Many of the details in the books are factual, though disguised to protect people's privacy.
>
> A: Castaneda is a vulgar hoaxer and cheapjack con man, who writes blatant occultist trash and philosophic piffle, which is gobbled up by the ignorant and gullible but ignored by the informed and discriminating. I have nothing to say about what happened at UCLA.
>
> A: Castaneda's only sorcery consisted of turning the University of California into an ass.
>
> (*Castaneda's Journey*, Santa Barbara: Capra Press, 1976.)

Anyone who can evoke such a varied response is clearly a Trickster of the first order. The unflattering comment on the University of California relates to the fact that Castaneda was awarded a Ph.D. for what appears to be a work of pure fiction (*Journey to Ixtlan*). In his role of Trickster Castaneda would probably consider this his master stroke. Even cynics like myself who are inclined to dismiss anthropology as a pseudoscience and anthropologists as meddlesome pests ("dogs have fleas, Indians have anthropologists") expect an anthropological study to contain some objectively verifiable data. *Journey to Ixtlan* had none—no tape recordings, no photographs, no artifacts, nothing. To have foisted what is evidently a novel on a group of supposedly scientifically trained professors was a trick indeed. Castaneda richly deserved the Ph.D. he was awarded. Only he received it from the wrong department. It should have been offered by the Department of Theoretical and Applied Deception.

What a triumph to be able—not once but five times—to hoist works onto the best-seller list that are clearly fiction but solemnly labeled nonfiction by librarians, critics, and book reviewers! How our Trickster must chuckle now, in 1978, to see at the top of the fiction list Tolkien's *Silmarillion* and creeping up on the nonfiction list Castaneda's *The Second Ring of Power*, though it is obvious that the sorceresses of *The Second Ring of Power* are just as insubstantial as the airy nothings that inhabit Tolkien's fantasies.

Tricks, all tricks. One is reminded of Ken Kesey and his Merry Pranksters. What is the difference between a Prankster and a Trickster? A Prankster invites you to sit down and pulls the chair from under you. A Trickster invites you to sit down on a chair that was not there in the first place. In either case you bruise your arse and feel humiliated. Never trust a Prankster or a Trickster.

Which is all very well—as far as it goes. If it helps to keep us alert and aware, let the Trickster perform his tricks. If we fall for his tricks it shows where we are. Not attending. Not alert. You can't sneak up on a *brujo*. But is all this tricking and pranking really a lawful part of the Warrior's Way? And is Castaneda following the Way himself or simply indulging in a series of literary put-ons and making large sums of money in the process?

I asked myself this question after reading Castaneda's fifth book, *The Second Ring of Power*. I was so disgusted with Castaneda for publishing such nonsense that I summarily banished the four don Juan books from my shelf of sacred books, where they had reposed between William James's *Varieties of Religious Experience* and Carl Gustav Jung's *Memories, Dreams and Reflections*. Now they were placed on a shelf labeled "Spiritually Inspired Fiction." They shared it with Heinlein's *Stranger in a Strange Land*, Talbot Mundy's *Om*, Rafael Lefort's *The Teachers of Gurdjieff*, and Kurt Vonnegut's *Cat's Cradle*.

Having put don Carlos and his sorcerers in their proper place, I asked myself if Castaneda's exposition of the Trick-

ster's Way had taught me anything of real value. The answer was yes. It had taught me that the Trickster's Way was
tricky. One had to be extremely intelligent and superbly detached to avoid becoming the victim of one's own tricks.
The temptation to indulge in mockery and spiritual pride
was very great. I could imagine don Carlos chuckling over
the success of his books. "Well, they've swallowed don
Juan and don Genaro and Catalina and the lizards and
coyotes and ghosts and goblins. I will now write something
completely preposterous and see if these idiots swallow
that." Hence *The Second Ring of Power*. And the idiots did
swallow it. Proving once again that suggestibility and credulity play a major role in the working of the psyche of
Homo sapiens.

As if further proof is needed!

All the same, if one sifted out the supernatural garbage,
there remained in the don Juan books a core of truth. The
chief characteristics of the Warrior's Way were formulated
clearly and vividly, and illustrated in stories which were
often gripping and always good reading. Castaneda had
performed a real service. The fact that he had blended those
challenges into a series of fairy stories could not really be
held against him. The fairy stories were the sugar coating of
the pill. Those who wanted the sugar coating could get it
without swallowing the pill. Those who wanted the pill
would ignore the sugar coating. The don Juan books were
teaching stories, and the teaching story or parable was one
of the oldest ways of passing on certain kinds of knowledge.

Castaneda's basic teachings concerning the Warrior's
Way could be summarized as follows:

A Warrior accepts everything as a challenge. He cannot indulge in self-pity, curse his fate, his god, his mate, his
boss, his luck. He accepts responsibility for everything. If
he puts the blame for his predicament on others, he is not a
Warrior.

A Warrior lives strategically. He knows which life game he is playing and why he plays it. His battles are for power and for knowledge. His enemies are weakness and ignorance. He struggles to live by his own self-made rules and to avoid being pushed about by outside forces.

A Warrior uses death as his adviser. He is aware of the fact that his time is limited, so he cannot afford to waste time on useless fantasies or meaningless activities.

A Warrior has unbending intent. His trained will is his only weapon against the random and chaotic forces that distract, weaken, and can finally destroy him.

A Warrior knows he must confront and overcome four enemies. These enemies were listed by don Juan as fear, clarity, power, and old age. A Warrior must be able to overcome them all.

In addition to these ideas, all of which are simple and have been formulated by many teachers, Castaneda's don Juan introduced others not so simple. Among them was the idea of the ally. The ally was defined as a power a man could bring into his life to help him, to give him the strength necessary to perform certain actions. Don Juan was most emphatic on the subject of allies. He repeated his definition four times in succession.

"An ally will make you see and understand things about which no human being could possibly enlighten you."

Does such a power really exist? Is it equivalent to the Higher Emotional Energy that Gurdjieff described as being available only to a few members of the highest caste of humanity? Castaneda, being tricky, does nothing to enlighten us on the subject but starts playing stunts with the ally, turning it into a ghostly karate instructor, liable, if encountered unexpectedly, to lay one out or even kill one. This ally makes a noise like a jet plane, glows in a certain way, can assume a human form. In this guise it becomes only one more item in don Carlos's celebrated bag of tricks.

The same is true of the concept of the *tonal* and *nagual*. These terms were introduced by don Juan in *Tales of Power* and illustrated with the help of tablecloths, salt and pepper shakers, chili sauce, and mustard. The *tonal* appears to include all manifestations of the phenomenal world, whereas the *nagual* is the world outside of time-space, the noumenal world. In the language of the Vedanta the *tonal* would correspond to the personal self in all its manifestations, the *jiva*, whereas the *nagual* would correspond to the Great Self, the *atman*. But once again Trickster plays his tricks, and by the time he has finished even the devil himself could hardly see through the fog that surrounds the *nagual*. The entity is transformed from a shadowy nonbeing outside time-space into a sinister presence that pops up now here, now there, adopting various weird forms, a furry brown long-legged crocodile that clambers about in the eucalyptus trees or a basket that jumps off the hook on which it was hanging and shakes and squeaks and swells and crawls around.

More circus tricks. The *nagual*, like the ally, finally becomes a concept so obscure as to be virtually meaningless. Meanwhile a lot of hair-raising fun is had by sorcerers and apprentices alike, who end up jumping into some sort of abyss, apparently the "door to the unknown." As Richard de Mille puts it, one wonders what the Sonora Spoofers will come up with next. One wonders also why Castaneda has this queer need to obscure and twist out of shape the concepts he describes, cheapening and vulgarizing the Warrior's Way, turning his characters into clowns and the Way itself into a circus.

For my part, though I felt fully justified in banishing don Juan from the shelf of sacred books, I derived quite definite benefits from his instructions. This was particularly true when my Missionary started becoming active again. The total collapse of the Church of the Earth had put my Missionary in disgrace. It was still aboard my ship of fools but sulked somewhere in the hold, out of sight. From time to time, however, the Missionary would appear on deck and start trying once again to play the Man with the Message, planning to give lectures, organize groups, and engage once more in the old spiritual con game. Whenever this happened I could hear an Indian cackle from somewhere within me and the ghostly voice of don Juan reminding me of certain important aspects of the Warrior's Way:

The Warrior is not available. Never is he standing on the street waiting to be clobbered.

The Warrior is inaccessible. He does not squeeze other people or his world out of shape. He taps it lightly and passes on leaving hardly a trace.

38

LEAVING
THE LAB

Goodbye, gadgets, lovely expensive gadgets. Goodbye, scintillation counter, gas chromatograph, thin layer chromatograph, spectrofluorometer, spectrophotometer, and all the other toys that are the scientist's delight.

Today I leave you, pretty playthings.

I am closing the door of my laboratory for the last time.

I sought out my car in the lower levels of the University of San Francisco parking lot. Strange, so strange. On that twenty-second day of May of the year 1973 my scientific career ended. I closed the lab, climbed into my old grey Chevy, and headed for the hills, the tawny rolling hills of Sonoma County. I felt no regrets. No regrets at all. Only a sense of relief.

Truly the Science Game had deteriorated since I had started to play in the 1930s. The players now were, for the most part, politician-scientists. They had friends in government circles. They knew the right people. They were adept at getting their projects funded. When they weren't rushing around seeing influential people, these pseudoscientists sat in their offices and talked. They rarely even took the trouble to keep up with the literature.

So who did the actual research? Graduate students in some cases. Or technicians, who might if they were lucky get their names on the papers that described the work they had done. Quite often the politician-scientists did not even write the papers, which was not surprising, since they had not done the work and often did not even understand the problem. But they put their names on the papers anyway.

If this was science I wanted out. Oh, for the simple days of Louis Pasteur, of Emil Fischer and Rutherford and Madame Curie and Claude Bernard! They walked like giants on the earth. They worked in the laboratory, they knew exactly what went on. Their equipment might be put together with sealing wax and string, but they got results. They had no need to run around kissing the arses of various bureaucrats to get thousands of dollars for costly equipment. They did not take the credit for the work of underpaid technicians or sit in offices instead of working in the lab.

It was impossible to stay in the rat race of official science without losing one's self-respect. The only way to do honest research was to equip one's own laboratory, choosing a line of work that did not require expensive equipment. Were there such lines? Of course there were. In the field of plant cell culture it was perfectly possible to equip a lab quite cheaply and do worthwhile research. Animal cell culture was a bit more demanding, but even that could be managed.

I could afford to set up a simple lab of my own. But I felt no wish to do so. My Scientist was dead.

Or was he?

The question echoed through my mind as the old car headed across the Golden Gate Bridge. The ocean was calm. Next day, if I felt so inclined, I could go out fishing. I would rather go fishing than play with scientific gadgets, counting the amount of C^{14}-labeled tetrahydrocannabinol in the brains of mice that had been exposed to smoke of marijuana spiked with radioactive THC. Sure enough, there was THC in the brains of those mice. So what? If you smoked marijuana you could expect to find THC in your brain. You didn't need mice to tell you that the drug entered the brain and produced various effects. You could observe those effects first hand. Why bother with mice?

For the last three years I had studied the various effects

the smoke of marijuana exerted on mice that were exposed to it regularly. As controls we used mice exposed to smoke from marijuana from which the active principle had been removed with solvents. The only thing the smoke of marijuana seemed to do was to reduce the breeding activities of the mice. They had fewer and smaller families. We could not detect an increase in the incidence of cancer or any reduction in the length of life of the animals. They just didn't breed as frequently. Which didn't mean much. You cannot safely extrapolate from mice to men, and it was presumably the effect of marijuana smoke on humans that really interested the National Institutes of Health, which had funded the project.

Well, there were plenty of humans around. Experiment with them. Why do we always impose on poor wretched mice to solve our dirty little problems? Or on dogs, cats, monkeys, apes, guinea pigs, rats, horses, and even dolphins? How arrogant and presumptuous we are, we who impose our will on the so-called "lower animals," as if we have some sacred right to poison, mutilate, and kill our fellow creatures so that we ourselves may benefit. How many rats, mice, guinea pigs have I infected, poisoned, or killed in the course of my career? Shall I be held accountable on the Day of Judgment?

But was my Scientist dead? This was the question. Driving on past the fringe of Sausalito I pondered the problem. The Magician and the Scientist, those powerful components of my psyche, had danced their *pas de deux* through my life, related to each other yet separate, friends and yet rivals. I looked back, and back. There in the garden of my grandmother's house was a grubby little boy making mud pies in the round, flat tins in which boot polish was then sold. Those were magical mud pies. Turned out on a flat piece of slate ornamented with violets, daisies, small pansies, they satisfied some special need in the child's soul, the quest not for objects of beauty but for objects of power.

I looked back again. There I was, preadolescent, thirteen years old, deep in the Lithuanian forest, at a place consid-

ered to be endowed with power. Pale orchids bloomed
there and scented meadowsweet and tremulous balsam
with yellow flowers. There I cooked over the sacred fire a
brew of herbs and fungi. Again, as in the case of the mud
pies, I was seeking power, magical power.

Again I looked back. I was standing in a constant temperature room at Lederle. It was dark. Before me, like a phallic
symbol, a tall glass column rose above a fraction collector
filled with test tubes. The air was fragrant with butanol. In
my hand I held a portable UV lamp and directed its deep
purple rays on the column. It was a partition column, white
"Celite" impregnated with water/butanol through which a
steady stream of butanol was forced under pressure. Slowly
the material I was purifying separated into bands on the
column, bands not visible in ordinary light but visible in
the ultraviolet. Again there was the sense of magic, the
sense of power.

Yes, I could see it now. All those scientific manipulations,
whether they involved the culture of cells, the separation of
pharmacologically active substances, or the estimation of
the activity of brain enzymes, had in them an element of
magic.

And what had happened now?

The magic had gone.

I derived no more thrills from those manipulations. They
were as meaningless for my aging psyche as my earlier efforts at making magical mud pies. The fun had gone out of
the game.

What does one do when the fun goes out of a game?

One stops playing it, naturally.

But did that mean my Scientist was dead?

No, it did not. My Scientist had matured. He did not get
pleasure any longer from playing with gadgets. The Scientist had come closer to the Magician and both had grown
wiser. They now had a common aim. Their aim was to enter
the mind of the Old One, to discover the Universal Arcanum, the sign of All and Everything.

One could not do this by playing with gadgets in a laboratory. Gadget science, manipulative science, can take us just so far, can tell us just so much. Let no one belittle its tremendous gifts. It has remade our world. It has given us health, abundance, ease such as no generation before ours has ever known. It has expanded our horizons in space and in time, shown us our place in nature, revealed the forces that shape our fate, the molecular code that fashions our life. It has liberated at least a few of us from the bonds of superstition and compelled us to seek the answers to our questions directly from nature instead of quoting some authority. Believe nothing. Question everything. Where is the evidence?

Never will I abandon the scientific spirit to take refuge in some smelly little rabbit warren of fixed belief or behind some flimsy facade of dogma and ritual. My contempt for faith is as great now as it ever was. How sickly is the human appetite for a fixed belief, for a God, a savior, a redeemer, a heavenly father. I thank the force that created me for installing in the depths of my psyche the old Diogenes, the mocking Cynic, who laughs at all fixed beliefs and refuses to take refuge from ugly realities in any system of comforting illusions.

If I were young again and starting instead of ending a scientific career, what branch of science would I choose? I would choose one in which all the aspects of my being could participate. After equipping myself with a thorough training in medicine, I would knock on the door of the Menninger Foundation and ask to work with the new guides on the Journey to the East, Elmer Green and Alyce Green.

No scientist in my youth could have expected to get official support for research into the psychophysiology of yoga. One would have been considered odd or slightly mad back in the thirties even to have mentioned such research. But now here were these Greens with the resources of a large institute at their disposal, boldly plunging into the unknown region that lies beyond our usual state of con-

sciousness and using all the gadgetry of modern science to
study that area.

Yes, the Greens were actually doing those experiments I
had imagined Carrel and Lindbergh performing in the secrecy of their island. They were reaching out toward the
edge, into the shadowy realm that is usually explored only
by mystics, yogis, or sorcerers. They had brought Swami
Rama to Topeka, the inimitable swami of the Himalayan Institute of Yoga Science and Philosophy, former *sankacharya*
of southern India, master of the heart (he could stop it at
will), master of *siddhis* (he could break a ruler by contact
with the tip of his finger). Not content with bringing the
swami to Topeka, they also brought Topeka, in the form of
a vast array of electronic gadgets, to the swami, and to any
other swamis in India who wished to cooperate in their
research.

They were much more than gadgeteers. They were followers of the Warrior's Way, reaching out in new directions. While the Greens explored the psychophysiology of
yoga, Doug Boyd, Alyce Green's son by a former marriage,
explored the world of an American Indian medicine man.
He worked with Rolling Thunder to transmit to the White
Brother some of the knowledge of the Indian Brother—
knowledge the White Brother badly needed but showed
little sign of acquiring.

Here, if anywhere, was the wave of the future. In this
rich mingling of different streams of culture a more balanced life-style was being born. The new life-style was
manifesting as a philosophy of holism, of which holistic
medicine was only one aspect. Certainly we needed holistic
medicine, a medicine that would treat not isolated symptoms but the whole human being. But even more we
needed holistic consciousness, awareness of our total dependence on the biosphere, of our oneness with the cosmic
process, of our capacity to function as the eyes and ears of
God, of our capacity for inner transformation.

The earth was a living being, said Rolling Thunder to

Doug Boyd. Water was the blood of the earth; it flowed in
streams as blood flowed in our veins. When we pollute the
streams we poison the earth.

> "The Indians have a saying," said Rolling Thunder. "*Never
> trust the water downstream from a white man!* This land was all
> pure at one time. The whole country was pure—the air, the
> water, everything. Now there's hardly any pure water left.
> From the major rivers to even the little streams in secluded
> areas, if the white man's gotten to it, it's no longer pure. And
> it hasn't taken him long, it hasn't taken the white man long at
> all."

> (Doug Boyd, *Rolling Thunder*,
> New York: Random House, 1974.)

The earth was sick, he explained. Pollution in one place
spread to other places. It was like cancer. Some of the natural disasters that were likely to happen in the near future
would happen because the earth was being mistreated.
Various things on the land did not belong there, and the
upheavals that were going to happen in the future would
really be the earth's attempt to get rid of those sicknesses. It
would be like fever or vomiting, a convulsion in the earth.

The earth, he went on, was a living organism. It was the
body of a higher individual who had will and wanted to be
well. As people should treat their own bodies with respect, so they should treat the earth with respect. Too many
people failed to realize that when they harmed the earth
they harmed themselves and that when they harmed themselves they harmed the earth. Even people interested in
ecology who wanted to protect the earth would cram anything into their mouths just for tripping or freaking out.
They would even use the sacred plants of the Indians. Rolling Thunder called those plants helpers and said they were
good if they were taken very seriously. Otherwise they
were useless or even harmful.

Rolling Thunder had been describing the Path of Beauty,
the Warrior's Way. But how could knowledge of the Way be

brought to a spoiled, careless, pampered, town-bred man-swarm, a people who scattered empty beer cans along country roads, who imagined they owned the earth, and had no respect for anyone or anything? How could one ever inform an enormous educational machine that, for young people, training in how to develop *Being* was even more important than acquiring Knowledge? How could one transmit the message that Knowledge without Being had an unbalancing effect and could cause our whole elaborate culture to capsize? Above all, how could one persuade a sloppy, self-indulgent people that only by confronting challenges can one develop strength, that the only way worth following was the Warrior's Way?

These questions buzzed in my mind as I thought about the science of the future. I thought back to the days after my return from Jamaica when I had searched for the secret of the Sly Man's pill and investigated the potentials of the cyborg. I was looking for methods of controlling certain physiological processes normally attainable only through the practice of *hatha* yoga. I wanted a shortcut. Now it appeared that the shortcut had become available. It was called biofeedback.

Biofeedback consisted of making visible or audible certain body processes of which we are normally unaware. The simplest example is the heartbeat. Normally we are quite unaware of the rhythmic contractions of this muscular pump on which our health and our life depends. Under conditions of stress we may become uncomfortably aware that the pump is working too hard for its own good. This is particularly true of emotional stress. In an emotionally stressful situation we may find our hearts pounding away as if we had run a hundred yards uphill. Such overreaction of the heart is useless and dangerous, but we cannot of our own free will slow it down.

There are ways of learning to control the beating of the heart. Swami Rama, an adept in *hatha* yoga, could slow his heartbeat and induce a state of atrial flutter, which in an

untrained person would have indicated the beginning of a
fatal "heart attack" but which the Swami could correct at
will. So the heart is not really beyond reach of conscious
control, but we do not ordinarily perceive what it is doing.
If, by the use of suitable gadgetry, we render the heartbeat
either visible or audible, we can see (or hear) whether our
efforts to control the heartbeat are having any effects. We
are getting the necessary feedback and can thus reinforce
any procedure that proves effective.

So biofeedback is a shortcut to control. It is a legitimate
shortcut. It does no harm and can do a great deal of good. It
gives voluntary control of internal states and can be enormously valuable in treating certain illnesses. Sufferers from
migraine, Raynaud's disease, hypertension, gastrointestinal
disorders, asthma, neuromuscular disorders, tension head-
ache, anxiety tension, epilepsy, and cerebral palsy can all be
helped by biofeedback training. The Greens even described
a case of cancer of the bladder that was much improved
when the patient learned to *voluntarily* cut off the blood
flow to the cancer. It was a technique with great therapeutic
possibilities.

But the important part of the Greens' work, from my
point of view, was that they saw beyond biofeedback. This
was, in fact, the title of their book (*Beyond Biofeedback*, New York: Delacorte Press, 1977)—a book so rich in
facts and ideas that it illuminated for me some quite new
aspects of the Warrior's Way. Consider the question of
growth of Being. All of us who had worked with Gurdjieff
or Ouspensky considered growth of Being to represent the
very essence of the Work. But although I used the term very
glibly I had never troubled really to define what it meant.
After reading *Beyond Biofeedback* the meaning of the term
growth of Being became a lot clearer. People's level of Being
depended on two things, their level of awareness and their
degree of self-control. Self-control in turn depended on a
certain kind of inner awareness. Someone who could relax
at will, slow the heart, control various other autonomic

functions, certainly had more self-control than one who
could not.

Biofeedback could enhance one's inner awareness. It was
for this reason very valuable quite apart from its therapeutic
effect. But a full development of Being depended on en-
hancing one's outer as well as one's inner awareness. Such
expanded awareness was essential if a narrow preoccupation with self was to be avoided. It was, as Rolling Thunder
told Doug Boyd, essential to develop respect for the Great
Spirit, for the living mantle of the earth, the biosphere, of
which we are part and on which we depend for the food we
eat, the air we breathe, and almost all of our impressions.

So what lay beyond biofeedback?

The techniques of biofeedback could be used as a basis
for training a new spiritual elite who could function as
guides and teachers during the very difficult transition
period shortly to begin. Obviously the transition from an
Age of Abundance to an Age of Scarcity could not occur
without a lot of storm and stress. A nation of hogs would
have to learn to be less hoggish and to place more emphasis
on growth of Being than on the accumulation of possessions. It would be a very, very difficult test and one which
would place great strains on the whole fabric of society.

In the period of storm and stress that would accompany
that enforced change in life-style I foresaw that there would
once again develop the "struggle of the Magicians" that had
raged so violently during the Dirty Thirties and the Frightful Forties. There would be once again a battle between the
Light Force and the Dark Force to control the destiny of
man. There would emerge once again a Black Order and a
White Order. There would almost certainly be widespread
death and destruction, possibly accompanied by a series
of natural convulsions—earthquakes, floods, famines,
droughts, possibly a volcanic explosion on the order of mag-
nitude of that which destroyed the island of Thera and
brought to an end the Minoan civilization. Such convulsions were foretold by the holy men of the Hopis. They

called them the Great Purification—the end of one culture, the beginning of another.

During this period of upheaval the White Order would have to play the same role as did the Masters of Wisdom after the Mongol invasions had left civilization in ruins in the thirteenth century. It was realistic to begin training such guides and teachers as soon as possible, using, if possible, the "way of accelerated completion" to bring them to the necessary level of Being. The Masters of Wisdom had operated in a war-ravaged society without taking sides or getting personally involved in the struggle. They had operated so effectively that by the year 1250 (only twenty-seven years after the death of Genghis Khan) a new and splendid civilization was rising on the ruins of the old.

The training of the Masters of Wisdom was designed to produce beings who were "in the world but not of it." They were competent practical men able always to earn a living by some sort of honest work. The practice of living on handouts, which is characteristic of Buddhist and Hindu holy men, was never encouraged by the Masters. Above all they practiced objective love and impartial beneficence.

> The Masters never, in four hundred years, compromised their position as completely independent of all factions and person-alities. The secret of their success was their consistent avoid-ance of positions of wealth and power and the practice of hu-miliation. All accounts agree that their influence was based on the love which they inspired in all who met them.
>
> (J. G. Bennett, *The Masters of Wisdom*, London: Turnstone Books, 1977.)

The Greens in *Beyond Biofeedback* outlined the steps that could be taken to train teachers and guides. They were particularly concerned with protecting unsuspecting people from commercial mind-training programs run by ex car salesmen and other spiritual con artists, whose ignorance of the human psyche is only matched by their greed for gain. The Greens' training method included the following items:

(1) Make it possible for each person to discover "himself" at a proper rate; that is, penetrate into the unconscious at a rate consistent with his ability to keep his feet on the ground, keep his reality-testing powers intact.

(2) Shield the student from the imperfections of the teacher that might otherwise become part of the student's "psychic atmosphere" and hinder his progress.

(3) Evaluate teachers according to their level of insight and awareness, so that as each student progresses existentially he has a properly qualified human advisor with whom to talk.

(4) Pass the student from teacher to teacher as rapidly as his experiences require more advanced advice or suggestions.

(5) Locate training centers for self-awareness within reach of anyone interested in participating in the program and establish the centers on a *nonprofit* basis.

So my meditations brought me to some very clear conclusions. Scientific research in the future would concern itself increasingly with the attainment of control over the inner forces that shape human behavior. A new holistic medicine would replace the excessively expensive, overspecialized medicine of the present. More emphasis would be placed on training people how to stay well than on treating them when they fall ill. Science would become more humanistic and less obsessed with gadgets. Scientists would become more aware of their social responsibility and less liable to wash their hands of all concern with the uses to which their inventions might be put. Methods derived from widely different cultures, from yogis, from Indian medicine men, from neurochemistry and neurophysiology, from biofeedback and behavioristic studies, would be combined to develop a new science of man's totality. On that science the human race would depend to make the dangerous and difficult transition from an Age of Abundance to an Age of Scarcity.

39

THE
WATERCOURSE WAY

In November 1973 I was startled to hear of the death of
Alan Watts. I could not accept the idea of his death. It
seemed inappropriate, a violation of a natural law. By all
the rules of the game he should at about that time have
begun to attain real maturity. Born in 1915, he was two
years younger than I was, a mere boy of fifty-eight. He
should have had as least twenty more years of life. What
did he mean by dying at such a ridiculously early age?
What had gone wrong?

The question was not academic. It concerned me personally. Alan Watts had had an influence on my line of fate.
I had met him in one of the "mystical" bookstores in New
York, and his enthusiastic account of the beauties of Big Sur
had strengthened the forces already drawing me to California.

After my own migration to California I lunched with him
on his ferryboat in Sausalito. The cavernous old S.S. *Vallejo*
reclined on the mud, sluggishly rising and falling with the
tides. It creaked and groaned, as if complaining of rheumatism. Around it clustered colorful houseboats inhabited by
various dropouts from the Great Society who had found a
haven by the shores of Richardson Bay. They lived like
water rats on an assortment of old barges, on which they
had built wooden structures of various designs.

In the midst of this floating community Alan Watts
played the role of an all-purpose guru. He offered a spiritual

smorgasbord, a bit of everything: Vedanta, Zen, Tao, a taste of Sufism, a dash of Christian mysticism. His seminars aboard the old ferryboat were small gatherings, the size of the audience being limited by the size of the boat. At the time I met him he was experimenting with LSD and had just finished writing *The Joyous Cosmology*. He was full of enthusiasm for design in nature. LSD had marvelously sharpened his awareness of those designs, those swirls and whirls, spirals and arabesques that occur throughout the plant and animal kingdoms. He was groping, as I was myself, toward a better understanding of the mind of the Old One, of whose dreams these ever-changing symmetries are an expression.

Alan never plunged madly down the great psychedelic freakway as did Tim Leary and Ken Kesey. He understood that after one has gotten the message one hangs up the phone. He seemed to get the message rather quickly and soon gave up experimenting with LSD.

And what, for him, was the message?

The way of noneffort. The watercourse way. Go with the flow. Flow with the wind, with the water. Just be what you are. Sit back and relax.

Sit back and relax . . . It was a puzzling interpretation of the Warrior's Way which at first made no sense to me. I had always supposed that enlightenment came as a result not of ordinary effort but of supereffort. All my former teachers had told me this. Effort, effort, effort. Only by friction between Yes and No can the heat be generated that fuses the many little I's into one big I, the many little wills into one big will. If you want muscular strength you must exercise your muscles. If you want real will you must exercise your will. You must concentrate and refine it as a metallurgist concentrates and refines a metal. This is the very root of the alchemical process.

Strength exerted equals greater strength; weakness indulged equals greater weakness.

I thought of Gurdjieff. Alan Watts had rejected Gurdjieff.

The way Gurdjieff taught, said Watts, was no longer valid. Too much yang. Too much struggle. Not a balanced way. It was certainly true that Gurdjieff had made a big deal about effort, especially his own. "Forever merciless to my natural weaknesses . . . almost unceasing day and night work . . ." He really had been merciless to his natural weaknesses and to the natural weaknesses of those who worked with him. And what had been the result of that merciless driving? A "charge and a crash" in a car traveling ninety kilometers an hour, a crash that destroyed the Institute for the Harmonious Development of Man.

Too much yang? So it would seem.

Gurdjieff had taught that the human machine is a carriage built to travel rough roads and that we "civilized" fat cats make things far too easy for ourselves. This is certainly true. But it is also possible to drive the carriage too hard, too far, and too fast, over roads so rough that they practically shake it to pieces. Is such overdriving an essential feature of all those daring spirits who follow the Warrior's Way? I could not accept the idea. Consider the fakir who develops physical will by holding up his arms until they become fixed at the joints. What agonies he must suffer, what struggles he must endure! But then, when he has attained physical will, he does not know what to do with it. He has spoiled his body for nothing. Is the fakir a Warrior or a fool?

These thoughts trickled through my head on a foggy winter morning as I lay in bed listening to the *bonsho*. The group of Zen Buddhists who had bought the ranch next to my property used it to announce the time for morning *zazen*. It was not a real *bonsho*. Those big brass bells cost a lot and can only be obtained from Japan. The Zens were hard up, so they had removed the bottom of an old propane gas tank and used the tank as a *bonsho*. Every morning at five fifteen they belted this contraption, to the great annoyance of their neighbors, for the clanging racket was more like the sound one might hear in a boiler factory than a harmonious voice calling on all and sundry to take refuge in the *dharma*.

So . . . awakened by the "old propane sound" I continued to ponder. Who was this Alan Watts, this all-purpose guru? Was he merely an entertainer, a spiritual stunt man? He had written and left unfinished at the time of his death a very beautiful study, *Tao: the Watercourse Way*, which his Chinese collaborator, Al Chung-liang Huang, had completed (New York: Pantheon Books, 1975). It contained some advice that I found challenging.

> There is no point in trying to suppress the babble of words and ideas that goes on in most adult brains, so if it won't stop, let it go on as it will, and listen to it as if it were the sound of traffic or the clucking of hens.
>
> Let your ears hear whatever they want to hear; let your eyes see whatever they want to see; let your mind think whatever it wants to think, let your lungs breathe in their own rhythm. Do not expect any special results, for in this wordless and idea-less state, where can there be past and future, and where any notion of purpose?

Furthermore, in his very readable autobiography (*In My Own Way*, New York: Pantheon Books, 1972) he had written as follows: "I should have known by then that self-improvement is a dangerous form of vanity."

These ideas stuck like bones in my throat. I could neither swallow them nor spit them out. The statement about self-improvement was particularly offensive to my earnest Seeker for Perfection. This was sheer nonsense! It undermined the whole idea of the Work. If I am a wastrel, a weakling, a drug addict or alcoholic, am I simply to accept this fact and let myself sink lower and lower? No effort, no struggle, let it slide? A fool's philosophy!

My Cynic was not so sure. The urge toward self-improvement was a two-edged sword. A tricky instrument, one apt to inflict injury on the user. My Cynic was very fond of the word *bovarism*. It had been coined by Aldous Huxley. Flaubert's Madame Bovary, always trying to pretend to be something she was not, was the archetypal bovarist. Bovarism, essentially, consisted in trying to imitate someone else. There was high bovarism and low bovarism. Even such an exalted work as Thomas à Kempis's *Imitation of Christ* was an invitation to bovarism.

So my Cynic was able to accept Alan Watts's statement. The urge to self-improvement really could be a form of vanity. It was a part of the personal salvation syndrome, a form of anxiety that distracted one from living in the here and now and set one to fussing over heaven and hell. It was a form of neurosis encouraged by the Judeo-Christian guilt cult, a neurosis that at times attained the status of a full-blown psychosis. Obsessed by fears of the devil and the threat of eternal damnation, one ruined one's enjoyment of this world by worrying over one's fate in the world to come. So one squeezed one's whole being out of shape by struggling to become something one was not, an imitation of Jesus, of a saint or a holy man.

Bovarism, all bovarism. Just be what you are. There is nothing to attain, no enlightenment, no *samadhi*, no *satori*. There is no heaven, no hell, no reward, no punishment. Your strivings are in vain. Enjoy what comes. Live in the now. Sit back and relax.

This seemed to be the essence of the message. Alan Watts had received it from Krishnamurti, who had spent the best part of a long life offering his nonteaching to a large group of nondisciples. Stop putting labels round your necks, Krishnamurti would say. Stop taking refuge in dogmas and rituals. Stop letting others do your thinking for you. Stop following gurus, guides, teachers, leaders. Be guides to yourselves. Be lamps to your selves.

Which, after all, was only what Gautama Buddha had said two thousand five hundred years earlier.

Krishnamurti echoed Gautama. Alan Watts echoed Krishnamurti. And my Cynic, who by that time was heartily sick of teachers of all kinds, accepted the message as being the best available. Which did not alter the fact that Alan had somehow or other become confused toward the end of his life. He really seemed to lose his way. He ate too much, smoked too much, drank far too much alcohol, never took any exercise. In a word he indulged, and a Warrior cannot indulge. It tarnishes his spirit.

"I don't like myself sober," confided Alan to a friend of mine, "so I spend much of my time drunk."

The statement aroused my wonder. How could it be that Alan Watts, so thoroughly familiar with the principles of Buddhism and Taoism, had missed the central truth? *There is no self, either to like or to dislike.* There is merely an agglomeration, a ship of fools committed to voyage from birth to death. But those who have understood the secret of the Way know better than to identify with the fools. Fools come and go. Now one predominates, now another. But the whole meaning of liberation or enlightenment lies in this, that we have the power to separate from the fools, to stop calling them "I," to regard them objectively as mechanical dolls, wound up by outside circumstances, programmed to go through certain motions. So, if I am quite objective toward my dolls, why should I have to drug myself with alcohol in order to be able to endure their antics? They come and go. Nothing is permanent. None of them is important. As one grows older the antics of the dolls become less and less interesting. Their performances seem shadowy, unreal. One becomes increasingly convinced that old Omar had the right idea.

> We are no other than a moving row
> Of visionary Shapes that come and go
> Round with this Sun-illumined lantern held
> In Midnight by the Master of the Show;
>
> Impotent Pieces of the game he plays
> Upon this Chequer-board of Nights and Days;
> Hither and thither moves, and checks, and slays,
> And one by one back in the Closet lays.

This realization may, in the uninitiated, awaken feelings of despondency or even despair. But those who have passed through the shadow and emerged into the light find nothing to worry about in Omar's verses. For we are both the pieces and the player. We are part of the Master of the Show, who is the Old One, who is God. Not "old Nobodaddy aloft," that ridiculous creation of the Judeo-Christian guilt cult, but the mind or soul of the biosphere of which our own minds are a part. When we have contacted that higher mind, why should we bother about the personal self? It comes, it goes, is doomed in any case. So let it do what it will.

In spite of this realization I could not help feeling a certain sadness as I meditated on the line of fate of Alan Watts. We were very similar, born only two years apart, products of the same atrocious English educational system, endowed with the same wide-ranging curiosity. When I was a follower of Ouspensky he had been a follower of Dmitrije Mitrinovic, "a high initiate into the mysteries of the universe" who had much in common with Gurdjieff. Being restless and rebellious, never one to accept the dominance of a teacher, he did not stay as long with Mitrinovic as I did with Ouspensky. He went to America along with the rest of the intellectuals who quit what seemed to be a sinking ship in the mid-thirties. Later he had migrated to California, and I shared with him his passion for its brown hills, redwood groves, and rocky shores. Both of us recognized northern California as our spiritual homes.

Watts had a restless vigorous intellect that made it impossible for him to fit into any accepted pigeonhole in American society. His short stint as a priest in the Episcopal Church only served to prove that there was no place in the Christian establishment into which he could fit. Possessed of a vigorous, lusty nature he plunged into the carnival of life, eagerly sampling its joys and entangling himself in vast amounts of karma. He left behind him two broken marriages, numerous children and grandchildren, a huge pile of cigarette butts and empty bottles, some Chinese calligraphy, and a vast collection of words both in books and on tapes.

His repertoire, unfortunately for him, did not include any really down-to-earth elements that might have prevented him from being "whirled about in the winds of the spirit." He was neither a gardener nor a carpenter nor a boat builder nor a fisherman. Nor had he discovered, as I had done at a fairly age, those vitally important *hatha* yoga exercises that can keep the physical body harmonized and in good shape. He knew about them, of course, but did not practice them. So there was nothing to offset the flood of words that poured day and night through his brain. He could not turn off the jabber by spading the garden or taking a kayak out through the surf and listening to the voice of the ocean. Moreover, owing to his status as all-purpose guru, he was exposed to an endless stream of "Seekers after Truth," those spiritual leeches that suck the lifeblood out of any weak enough to let them.

Like all of us, he reaped exactly what he sowed, so my feeling of regret when I thought about him was merely a form of indulging. But surely such a bright spirit should have known better than to take a wrong turn on the Way during the last stage of his life. He had any number of good friends who could have told him the truth. I could even have given him a few tips myself, but he had labeled me a Gurdjieffian and did not trust me.

So he continued to play a role that had become increasingly distasteful, the role of spiritual entertainer, a sort of aging clown laughing through tears. "On with the motley, the paint and the powder . . ." It was a bore, a real drag. He had said everything there was to say, written everything there was to write. But still he ran around, whirled here and there—trips to Japan, trips to Europe—deafened by the roar of jet planes, his biorhythms disrupted by constant travel across different time zones. He had become increasingly dependent on alcohol. His once vigorous and quite athletic body was rapidly deteriorating. He had run out of games worth playing, was sick of lectures, seminars, talking, writing. He had seen it all, said it all, known it all. There was nothing left to do but die. And so he died.

Meditating on his death, I had the feeling that he had really missed the best part of the show. But perhaps I was wrong. How can one judge the being of another? He left me a piece of Californian jade and two Zen poems, which I like to murmur at intervals whenever I wish to redefine for myself the subtle essence of the watercourse way:

> The wild geese do not intend to cast a reflection,
> The water has no mind to retain the image.

> The bamboo shadows
> Sweep the steps
> But raise no dust.

40

ON
THE BEACH

Waves.

They followed each other endlessly, swelled, broke, swept up the beach, vanished. I sat with my back against the rock wall, looking out to sea. The rock was a conglomerate. It told me its history. It had once been part of a beach, had then sunk deep into the earth, where the pebbles had been fused by heat and pressure. Then it was heaved aloft by enormous pressures and towered above me as a cliff. Now the ocean nibbled away at it, and it became a beach again.

Rocks, ocean, sky. The endless cycles. The sky was perfectly cloudless and the sea was calm. I would spend the night in my tent by the beach and go out in my kayak in the dawn light. Meanwhile the planet rolled and the evening sun was swallowed by the sea. A flush of crimson filled the sky. A line of brown pelicans made their way to the rock on which they roosted. Above the place where the sun had vanished the planet Venus emerged.

Waves, waves. As the darkness came there was only the voice of the sea, and a whispering wind from inland as air drained from the slopes and flowed gently along the canyon. It was a very warm wind. I could hardly believe that this was December. Not a drop of rain had fallen all that month. The creeks that should have been flowing were all dry. Another dry winter. Some new weather cycle was starting. A thought crossed my mind. If the climate really went bad on us, it could shake us out of the country like fleas out of a blanket. We might have to flee as the Okies fled from the dust bowl. The Okies fled to California. But where could the Californians go?

Perhaps, like lemmings, they would migrate in swarms to the coast and plunge into the sea. I could imagine the land breathing a sigh of relief.

Cycles, huge cycles.

All round me monstrous movements were taking place. The very land beneath my body was shifting. The continents drifted like barges on the plastic mantle, carried by enormous plates that plunged above or beneath each other. There, in the direction of the sunset, under that calm ocean, the Pacific plate plunged under the North American plate, heaving up the Coastal Ranges in the process. Horrendous stresses were generated, stresses that must be released in the form of earthquakes. We lived on top of a system of coiled springs. They could go off at any time, shaking cities to pieces. This grinding crushing motion of plate against plate would tear off Baja California along with the city of Los Angeles and transport it northwards until the site of L.A. would be level with that of San Francisco and located on an island in the Pacific.

When?

In about ten million years.

In ten million years what will be left of Los Angeles? Or of San Francisco? Or of *Homo sapiens*?

Could a species so volatile, disharmonious, and paranoid possibly endure for ten million years? Or one million? Or ten thousand? Or one thousand?

Alone on the beach at night I find a new time-scale. My little life becomes as brief as the flash of a meteor across the sky. And yet, if I like to think so, this scene is all for me. Only I, with my man-brain, can take in its significance, can realize that the planet Venus hanging above the ocean is a world as big as the earth, is shrouded in carbon dioxide, and has a surface as hot as molten lead. Only I can know, as the big moon rises, that not so long ago men stood on its surface and left footprints in its dust. Only I can tell that this massive continent was once part of Pangea, the supercontinent that broke up 200 million years ago. All this I know because I am part of a superbrain, the collective brain of humanity. No other creature has such a collective brain. The birds roosting on the rocks, the fish in the ocean, the plants and insects, the sheep on the hills—they do not even know their own histories, let alone the history of the planet.

The moon, low in the sky, appeared to be enormous. It illuminated the beach, the sparse willows along the creek, the lapping waves, the huge expanse of ocean. A night bird called. Some bleating sounds came from the sheep in the hills. From the direction of Route 1 came the sound of a logging truck changing gear.

I walked back from the beach to my tent and crawled inside. From there I could go where I wished, leaving my body, traveling in spirit. My teacher in the spirit realm was called Fong. He was a Taoist hermit, or had been when alive. Fong had told me the secret of Tao, of balancing the yin and the yang. That was the essence of the balanced way, which avoided extremes. Too much yin and one became slothful and self-indulgent. Too much yang and one became tense and ambitious. A Taoist hermit goes with the flow. He is like the fog that rolls in from the ocean. The fog enshrouds and envelops the redwood trees, but it does not distort them. It touches everything, but leaves everything unchanged.

Ah, yes. Before I contacted Fong I was prone to think in terms of supereffort. Now I go with the flow. It was possible, if one was quiet enough and relaxed enough, to project one's awareness clear out of the body. It was said of the Taoist hermits that they could fly like dragons. Fong, who really existed (he was described by Rowena Farre in *The Beckoning Land*), was a master of flying. One flew in the subtle body by perfectly balancing on the back of the bird of time. The bird of time has two wings called past and future. But between the two wings is a spot on which the sage can balance. He flies in the subtle body on the back of the bird of time.

Balance, balance. Ascending out of the body I rose on the bird of time above the Californian shore. Reflected light, bouncing off the moon, illuminated the earth. On such trips I became aware of my body lying there by the beach, a speck no bigger than a grain of sand. Sometimes the bird of time journeyed so far that I wondered if I would be able to return. What would happen to my speck of a body without the "I am"? But there was a thread like the string of a kite between me and the body, and always it wound me back. My body slept. The planet rolled. In the east the sky began to lighten.

I ate breakfast in a blend of dawn and moonlight, dismantled my tent, and took it back to the car. Lifting my kayak over my shoulder I carried it to the ocean. It was a new kayak, shorter and lighter than my old one, quite a different design, more like a decked canoe. It had a watertight compartment for my gear and a keel to help it track. The old kayak was flat-bottomed as a scow and waddled like a duck. I had made the new kayak myself and named it *Small Porgy*.

I arranged my gear in the forward compartment and bolted the bulkhead in place. Dragging *Small Porgy* down the beach I lined it up to face the surf. The surf was always high at Russian Gulch. It was a lot easier to go out from Fort Ross, but a new breed of bureaucrats had taken charge of the park and made it practically impossible for a fisherman to get down to the beach. I had grown tired of pleading and arguing with them. Better face the surf than the bureaucrats.

So. One lined up one's boat and waited for the right moment. A tricky business. The moment of truth. Experience had taught me one thing. Once you launched you had to go on. No hesitating, no turning back. That was disastrous. You would be rolled by the breakers and lose equipment.

So I launched, plunged on and was hit by a breaker. Poor timing. *Small Porgy* took on gallons of water. But my new design allowed for that; fore and aft *Small Porgy* was filled with urethane foam. A floating soufflé. She stayed afloat even when full of water.

Now she was half full. I paddled clear of the breakers and baled out the water. I was wet, but the sun was rising. It would be a beautiful day, clear sky, calm sea. I would dry out.

A sudden blast behind me and a small cloud of vapor caused me to look back. It was Little Orphan Alfie (or was it Annie?) the lonely grey whale. It had been in the cove all summer, left behind in the great migration. A student of whales informed me that Alfie (or Annie) would starve. There was not enough food in that cove to keep it alive. It had lost touch with the great cycle that governed whale behavior. Too bad. Alfie was friendly. He seemed to enjoy coming up close to the kayak and giving me a start.

"Now, Alfie, I love whales in general and you in particular, but don't you think you could play just a wee bit further off?"

After all, the beast was at least fifteen feet long and encrusted with barnacles. Suppose it took it into its head to scratch its back on *Small Porgy*'s keel?

Fortunately Alfie had other things in mind and rolled off, blowing at regular intervals. I let down my jig and started fishing. On the floor of the ocean were hordes of white sea anemones. I could feel their tentacles grabbing at the bait.

A hang-up.

I could tell by the feel of the line that I was held by a sea anemone. There is a rubbery feel about sea anemones. I jiggled the line. The sea anemone failed to release the hook. I pulled more forcibly. Extraordinary that those rubbery creatures could hold on so strongly that the fifty-pound-test line would break before they would loosen their hold on the rock! But this time the line was stronger than the anemone. I hauled it up, cautiously cut the creature loose, and dropped it back in the water. It would settle back on the rock. A soft machine capable of repairing itself.

Those soft machines! Once again I marveled at the inventive power of the Old One. To create that enormous variety of soft machines out of carbon compounds and a few mineral salts—to make them self-repairing, self-reproducing, and even, in the case of man, self-aware—what a feat that was! All the basic mechanisms had been invented quite early, at the time when the ancestors of my sea anemone appeared on the scene, some time in the Cambrian, five to six hundred million years ago. Already the Old One had dreamed up muscular contraction, nervous conduction, sexual reproduction, stinging cells that would paralyze the prey. What a device! The nerve fibers of the sea anemone were not very different from my own: extremely thin tubes filled with a dilute solution of sodium and potassium salts. Imagine trying to build a complex computer with only thin tubes of salt solution to transmit the signals! Out of this early device developed the human brain, which could generate the theory of relativity, write the sonnets of Shakespeare, the symphonies of Beethoven, design the Gothic cathedrals, originate the Gospels, the Sutras, the Upanishads. Not to mention invent and explode an atomic bomb.

All done with minute tubes filled with dilute salt solutions!

The ingenuity of the Old One is truly unbelievable. I had long ago given up trying to explain the mechanisms of evolution. The old neo-Darwinian clichés about natural selection acting on random mutations were so puerile that I could not take them seriously. I was satisfied to be aware that the Old One existed, that it could not be represented in any way, that it was forever beyond my power to understand. One could call it the soul or mind of the biosphere, but this explained nothing.

My kayak rocked and rolled on the Pacific swells. In some deeper level of my mind vaguely erotic images followed one another, like a flock of nymphs chased by satyrs.

Symbols of the Old One.

Had I the wealth and resources of the Gupta kings, I would build on one of those smooth slopes by the Pacific a temple dedicated to the Old One. It would be even more complex than the great temples at Khajuraho and even richer in ornaments. The temple would celebrate the entire dream of the Old One, three billion years of organic evolution. All forms of life would there be represented. Fungi would sprout from the cornices, fantastic orchids from the eaves. There would be beetles and butterflies. There would be trilobites, graphtolites, coelocanthes, and crocodiles. In forests of cycads and tree ferns would be brontosaurs, allosaurs, tyrannosaurs, and mososaurs. Pterodactyls would grimace like gargoyles. Sea anemones would link arms with giant squids. Snakes, worms, crinoids, starfish, eels would coil and writhe in undulating heaps. There would be carnivores and herbivores, the hunters and the hunted, horses, mammoths, antelopes, giraffes, anteaters. In the midst of all this teeming life a few naked apes at various stages of evolution would scuttle around—not the lords of creation at all, but simply one more product of the Old One's dream.

Ah, yes, that would be quite a temple, the whole squirming mass held together by endless strands of DNA, the code of life. And to that temple I would invite the young, fresh folks, he and she, to celebrate their nuptials, using the energies liberated during sexual union to enhance their awareness of the force that gave them life. Indeed it is true that through sexual union one can come to awareness of the Old One. This was well known in ancient India, where the *devadasi*, temple girls trained in the arts of love, helped the worshiper attain the proper state through the practice of the sacred *maithuna*. This greatly shocked the proper British, who imagined that God was as uptight about sex as they were.

Once again I was hung up. This time the sea anemone got the better of the struggle. Another jig lost on the bottom. I paddled south to Pinnacle Rock. There were some big fish in its vicinity and fewer sea anemones. On every ridge of the rock stood brown pelicans, prehistoric in appearance, like pterodactyls or gargoyles. They took off awkwardly as my kayak approached. A large fish grabbed the jig, bending my rod, making me suddenly alert. It was an orange rockfish. I could tell that even before I reeled it in. They never put up a fight but came in passive as lumps of lead. Lingcod, on the other hand, fought like tigers. In a kayak one had to land them in one's lap. A large, struggling lingcod heavily armed with dorsal spines could be quite a lapful. But I caught no lingcod, only orange, black, blue, and vermilion rockfish—and a nice-looking flounder. What was a flounder doing on a rocky reef? One normally catches them on a sandy bottom.

A hang-up again. My mind had been wandering. Philosophical speculations. I swore and jerked the line. It came up with a starfish attached. I removed the starfish, put on fresh bait, gave my full attention to fishing. Alone on the ocean in a small kayak, one indulged in daydreams at one's peril.

Stop!

Stop thinking, commenting, interpreting, asking questions.

But the chatter of my accursed talk machine continued to interfere with my simple awareness. The idiot wanted to know the *meaning* of things.

What is the sense of significance of life on the earth in general and of human life in particular?

Gurdjieff's great question.

A calypso from the Books of Bokonon drifted through my head.

> Tiger got to hunt
> Bird got to fly
> Man got to sit and wonder, "Why, why, why?"
> Tiger got to sleep
> Bird got to land
> Man got to tell himself he understand.

The itch to interpret. The mania for meaning. They concealed the real world as clothes conceal the body of a woman. If you're a lover you want the woman, not the clothes. You want her warm, naked, as she really is.

The naked truth.

Sense and significance?

What is the sense and significance of these white sea anemones who steal my jigs? What is the sense of these pelicans that look like pterodactyls, of Little Orphan Alfie, the lost grey whale, of the rocks, of the ocean, of the earth, of the galaxy, of this elderly hominid paddling around in a kayak of fiberglass and resin, trying to catch himself a few fish dinners?

They have no sense. They have no significance. They simply are. The itch to interpret is a sickness of the mind. It merely obscures the here and now with a fog of speculation.

Energy, matter, life, mind. The pyramid of Being. At the level of mind the cosmic process becomes conscious of itself. It becomes a witness. I am a witness, here on this ocean. I can see some way into the past, a little into the future. I can see a great deal of the present if I don't ask questions about sense and significance.

Those who insist on asking such questions must invent their own answers. They can believe anything they wish to believe.

Another Bokonon calypso trickled through my head:

> I wanted all things
> To seem to make some sense,
> So we could all be happy, yes,
> Instead of tense.
> And I made up lies
> So that they all fit nice,
> And I made this sad world
> A par-a-dise.

Kurt Vonnegut, who had invented both Bokonon and Bokononism, should really have taken the religion seriously.

He could have come to California, where the appetite for
new religions is insatiable, and founded the First Bokonon-
ist Church. Bokononism made far more sense than a lot of
the far-out religions that bloomed under the Californian
sun.

Really you can believe whatever you like. Whatever answer you give to questions about the sense and significance
of life will be guesses. You can never prove anything. So
why bother to guess?

I was ready to go in. My legs were stiff. The fish had
stopped biting. From the look of the beach the surf was rising. It was best to go in at slack tide, but I had forgotten to
check the tide tables. I packed away my sack of fish, my
tackle box, bang stick, gaff, and the lower part of my fishing
pole, closed the door of my watertight bulkhead, and
started for the beach.

When coming in always be ready for a wipeout. Have no
loose gear in the boat. Put your watch in a waterproof
pocket, take off your sunglasses, and pick up the rhythm of
the waves. I shifted into a kneeling position and waited just
behind the surf line. It was important to keep one's cool
and to time things properly. There were two schools of
thought about landing a boat through surf. One, the heroic
school, said pick the biggest wave and ride it all the way up
the beach. This was fine if you balanced just behind the
crest of the wave, but if you got too far ahead you'd get
pitch poled, and if you were too far behind you would be
swept back by the undertow and the next wave would roll
you. I preferred the cautious school, which said wait out the
big ones and come in during a quiet spell.

I waited. A series of big ones lifted me high in the air and
crashed on the beach in a welter of creamy foam. The quiet
spell was a long time coming. The surf had really risen since
the early morning. Some far-off storm, presumably. One
had to be patient. Wait.

Finally things calmed down a bit and I glanced over my
shoulder. Never start in without checking what's coming up
behind you. No big ones in sight. I picked up the crest of

the next wave and swooshed toward the beach. A little too far forward, but the keel did its work and the boat was not sideswiped. I jumped out fast. *Small Porgy* was swept back by the undertow and took a breaker over the stern, but I had her safely by the bowline attached to my paddle, hauled her up the beach, bailed out the water.

I carried my gear up the beach, placed *Small Porgy* well out of reach of the ocean, sat down and ate lunch. The ocean was beautiful, a dreamy blue, but the surf was heavy and becoming heavier. I had come in not a moment too soon.

I gazed gratefully at the ocean. It was so enormous and my boat was so very small. It could crush me as easily as I could swat a fly. But it hadn't. It had let me sneak out, get my fish, and return with nothing worse than a wetting. What a teacher it was! How much better than the human teachers with their endless talk about higher consciousness and the sense and significance of life and of man. The ocean did not talk of higher consciousness. But woe betide those who did not watch what they were doing, who came in or went out carelessly through the surf, who failed to watch out for the rising of the wind.

I looked at Pinnacle Rock. The rising surf smashed against it, smothering it in spray. Pinnacle Rock had a strange quality. In its shadow I felt aware of the presence of death, as if death was perched among the seagulls and pelicans and watched me. Don Juan informs us that a Warrior dances before his death, that that dance is performed in a special place of power. Death must watch the Warrior's last dance, in which he recounts all the battles he has won and lost.

One needs a myth for living and a myth for dying. This myth of the Warrior's last dance pleases me. My spirit will dance there in the shadow of that rock, among seagulls and pelicans, sea lions and starfish. I would like to give my flesh back to the ocean to feed the fish whose bodies have so often fed me.

I know that death will scatter all the elements of my personal self, as a necklace of beads is scattered when the string breaks. But I know that the archetypes recur again and again, endlessly playing their roles in the cosmic drama, each with its own memory deeply rooted in the collective unconscious. It is this, the memory of the archetypes, that gives us the sensation that we have been here before. The personal ego perishes at death. But the archetypes are long-lived, because they are projections of the mind of the Old One. So though my personal ego perishes, my archetypes will appear again and again and dance together on the stage of life.

The show must go on. It must go on forever, eternally recurring. My spirit, in its dance of death, will turn and whirl like the Mevlevi dervishes. What is the theme underlying this sacred dance? The turning, whirling bodies symbolize change, death and rebirth, the days and nights of the cosmos. The outstretched arms—one hand facing up, the other down—symbolize the great cosmic interchange, "one hand gives, the other takes." But the spirit of the dancers is beyond being and nonbeing, focused on the One.

La Ilah Illa Allah.

No God but God.

The whirling of the dervishes, the endless rolling of the wheel of rebirth, proclaim the message of Zarathustra's animals—the eagle, knower of the heavens, the serpent, knower of the earth.

> "O Zarathustra," said his animals, "to those who think like us, all things dance: they come and hold out the hand and laugh and flee—and return.
>
> Everything goes, everything returns; eternally rolls the wheel of being.
>
> Everything dies, everything blooms again; eternally runs the year of being.
>
> Everything breaks, everything is united anew; eternally builds itself the house of being.
>
> Everything parts, everything meets again; the ring of being remains eternally true to itself.

Being begins in every 'Now,' around every 'Here' rolls the sphere of 'There.'

The middle is everywhere.

CROOKED IS THE PATH OF
ETERNITY."

(*Thus Spake Zarathustra*)

INDEX

à Kempis, Thomas, *Imitation of Christ*, 380

Aging, 1–2

Aikido, 326

Albedo, 299

Alchemy, 18, 93, 237, 299, 301

All and Everything (Gurdjieff), 207, 212

Alpert, Dick, 284

America, 157–158, 163

Anarchy, 311–312

Antic Hay (Aldous Huxley), 88–89

Archangels, 171–172, 182, 186–187, 200–201

Archives of the League (Hermann Hesse), 217, 339

Arch-Vainglorious Greek, 328

Ashokhs, 206, 207, 216

Australia, 33–38

Bacteriologist, 141, 143–148, 149

Baraka, 173

Baron, The, 123–128

Beelzebub's Tales (Gurdjieff), 192–193

Beethoven, Ludwig von, 229–230

Benda, Julian, *The Treason of the Intellectuals*, 67

Bennett, John Godolphin, 336–353; on barriers, 341–342; early life of, 338; on energy, 341–342; and Gurd-
jieff, 200, 341–343, 347–349; *Gurdjieff: A Very Great Enigma*, 215; *Gurdieff: Making of a New World*, 352; and the Institute, 345; *The Masters of Wisdom*, 374; and Ouspensky, 101, 170, 171, 340–341, 343–344; and search for teachers, 349–352; as Seeker of Truth, 337–338; and *The Teachers of Gurdjieff*, 319–323; *Witness*, 353

Bennetron, 324, 326, 328

Bernard, Theos, 246

Beyond Biofeedback (Elmer and Alyce Green), 372, 374–375

Bhagavad-Gita, 85

Bhakti yoga, 91, 188

Biofeedback, 242, 371–373

B.J., 65–66

Black Order vs. White Order, 248–249, 373

"Blackening, The," 299

Blake, William, on Jehovah, 60; "Jerusalem," 54; on realities, 355; *Visions of the Daughters of Albion*, 324

Blavatsky, 84, 94, 322

Bloomsbury Set, 88, 90

Boehme, Jacob, 355

Bokononism, 393–394

Bomb shelters, 120–121

Bonsho, 378

Books of Bokonon, 392, 393

Bovarism, 379–380

Boyd, Doug, *Rolling Thunder*, 369–370

Brand, Steward, 289, 290

Brave New World (Aldous Huxley), 89, 279

Breckenridge, Colonel Henry, 264

Brucella abortus, 141, 144–147, 148

Buddha, 59–60, 76, 380

Burns, Robert, 162–163

Burroughs, William, 283–284

Burton, Richard, *The Kasidah of Haji Addu El-Yezdi*, 338

Cancer research, 175–177, 232–233

Carrel, Alexis, 242–254; and Charles Lindbergh, 245, 264, 268; *Man the Unknown*, 242, 243, 246–247; *Reflections on Life*, 251–252

Cassady, Neal, 287–288

Castaneda, Carlos, 354–363; *Journey to Ixtlan*, 358; *The Second Ring of Power*, 359–360; *A Separate Reality*, 354; *Tales of Power*, 361–362; *The Teachings of Don Juan*, 354; as Trickster, 356–362

Castaneda's Journey (Richard de Mille), 357–358, 362

Cathedral, 9–12

Chamberlain, Neville, 127, 263

Cheam School, 13, 15

Children, with E., 130–132, 141; with Tessa, 219–220, 225–227, 234

Church of the Earth, 324, 333

Churchill, Winston, 135, 139

Cleaver, Eldridge, 285

"Climb Mount Everest" fallacy, 169

Clynes, Manfred, 240

College, 56–61

Communist movement, 62–67, 77

Compost heaps, 134–135

Creative Psychology, 294–297

"Crossing the Bar," (Alfred Lord Tennyson), 13–14

Curtis, John Hughes, 260

Cyborg, 240–242, 371

Daladier, Edouard, 263

Darwin, Charles, 58

Daudzegir, 19, 20–21

Death, 395–396

Dede, Farhad, 349–350

de Mille, Richard, *Castaneda's Journey*, 357–358, 362

de Ropp family, 3, 19–20

Designer, 324, 332

Dock life, 39–43

"Domestic Oaf," 194, 196, 218, 225, 228

don Juan, *see* Juan, don

Doors of Perception, The (Aldous Huxley), 279

Dostoevsky, 77

Drugs, 233–239

Drugs and the Mind, 241

Dunkin, Major G.W., 147

Dust storms, 33–38

E., breakdown, 149, 152–155, 158–159, 232; children with, 130–132, 141; diary, 172, 173; and Madame Ouspensky, 150–151; meeting, 116–117

Easter, in Ouspensky's group, 184–185

Education, 9–11, 15, 16, 26–32, 56–61

Electric Kool-Aid Acid Test (Tom Wolfe), 288–289

Energy, 341–342

Eroica (Beethoven), 229, 230

Eyeless in Gaza (Aldous Huxley), 89

Farming, 34–38, 108–112, 168–169

Farre, Rowena, *The Beckoning Land*, 387

Fascism, 62–63, 77
Fate, 2, 42, 105
Faust, 60–61
Fisher, Cordelia (Cork), 45–48
Flower children, 303–313
Fourth way, 107, 108, 182–183, 297
Fragments of an Unknown Teaching (Gurdjieff), 169, 191
Franklin Farms, 168, 178, 186, 192
Freud, Sigmund, 52

Galileo, 66
Gandhi, 90, 91
Gaskin, Steve, 312–313
Gift from the Sea, A (Anne Morrow Lindbergh), 265
Gilbert, J.M., 149
Gilgamesh, 206, 216
Ginsberg, Allen, 283–284
God, concept of, 73, 77–78
Goddard, Robert, 269
Goering, General, 262, 263, 264
Goethe, 60–61
Gottlieb, Lou, 304–305, 309, 310
Greens, Elmer and Alyce, 242, 368–369; *Beyond Biofeedback*, 372, 374–375
Gregg, Richard, 86
Gregory, F.G., 68–78
Gulliver's Travels (Jonathan Swift), 89
Gurdjieff, 186–187, 210, 212, 292, 318–319; *All and Everything*, 207, 212; *Beelzebub's Tales*, 192–193; criticisms of, 217; doubts about, 196, 201–203; *Fragments of an Unknown Teaching*, 169, 191; great question, 392; impressions of, 197–205; knowledge from, 214, 295; *Life Is Real Only Then, When "I am*," 212; life of, 205–217; *Meetings with Remarkable Men*, 193, 198–199, 206, 211, 286–287; and

Ouspensky, 102–104, 191–192, 200, 343–344; "sly man's pill," 237–238; teachings of, 107, 238, 296, 356, 378; "third series," 212, 213
Gurdjieff: A Very Great Enigma (J.G. Bennett), 215
"Gurdjieff groups," 351
Gurdjieff: Making of a New World (J.G. Bennett), 352
Gurjef, Lydia, 3

Haldane, J.B.S., 66, 69
"Hanbledzoin," 214
Hatha yoga, 239, 240, 245, 371
Hauptman, Bruno Richard, 260
Hayling Island, 82, 83
Heard, Gerald, 90, 91, 98, 113–114, 115, 139, 185, 188
Henley, W.E., 159; "Invictus," 42–43
Herald of the Coming Good, The, 215
Hesse, Hermann, *Archives of the League*, 217, 339; *Bead Game*, 284; *The Journey to the East*, 331, 339; "Morbio Inferiore," 174–175
Hibernation, 239–240
Hippocrates, 300
Hitler, 124–126, 141, 264
Hoffer, Abram, 279
Hoffman, Albert, 233
Hopis, 373–374
House building, 194, 223
Huxley, Aldous, 87–91, 98–99, 139; *Antic Hay*, 88–89; "The Antipodes of the Mind," 355; *bovarism*, 379–380; *Brave New World*, 89, 279; *The Doors of Perception*, 279; *Eyeless in Gaza*, 89; *Island*, 279–280; and Ouspensky, 113, 115; *The Perennial Philosopher*, 115; on Tim Leary, 284–285
Hvareno, 215, 255
Hymns Ancient and Modern, 13–14

IFIF (International Federation of Internal Freedom), 280
I Speak for the Silent (V.V. Tchernavin), 66
If the Invader Comes, 135
Île de France, 163, 165
Illumination, 186, 189
"in the Work," 93, 327
Inner Circle of Humanity, 322
Institute of Creative Psychology, 297–298
Institute of Man, 251, 252, 253
Intelligentsia, 113–114
"Invictus" (W.E. Henley), 42–43
Island (Aldous Huxley), 279–280

James, William, *Varieties of Religious Experience*, 155
"Jerusalem" (William Blake), 54
Jesus, 17–18, 76, 325
Journey to Ixtlan (Carlos Castaneda), 358
Journey to the East, The (Hermann Hesse), 331, 339
Joyous Cosmology, The (Alan Watts), 377
Juan, don, 267, 334, 395; *see also* Castaneda, Carlos
Julius Caesar (William Shakespeare), 119
Jung, Carl, 25, 354

Kennedy, Joseph, P., 262
Kesey, Ken, 284, 287–289
Kew Gardens, 160–162
Kinemadrama (Ouspensky), 105
Kipling, Rudyard, 16, 126, 335
Kline, Nathan, 240–241
Krishnamurti, 76, 84, 380
Kwajagan, 322, 352

Lao-Tze, 76, 293
Latvians, 21–25
Lawes, J.B., 149
Lawrence, Ernest O., 320
Leary, Timothy, 280–286, 287, 288, 309
Lederle Laboratories, 222, 232–233, 273
Lefort, Rafael, 318
Levi, Eliphas, 151
Liberté, 231, 232
Life, definition of, 69–70
Life games, 2, 42
Life Is Real Only Then, When "I am," (Gurdjieff), 212
Light on the Path and Karma, 84, 330
Lilly, John, 239
Lindbergh, Anne Spencer Morrow, 256, 260–262, 264, 267, 270; *A Gift from the Sea*, 265
Lindbergh, Charles, and Alexis Carrel, 243–246, 264, 268; life of, 257–270; *Of Flight and Life*, 266; and "Ring of Power," 255–256; *The Spirit of St. Louis*, 257, 259
Lipsky, 148–149
London, Jack, 275, 276
Low, David, 116
LSD, 233, 281, 282
Luftwaffe, 262–264
Lyne Place, 109, 118, 129, 133, 138
Lysergic acid diethylamide, 233, 281, 282

McCoy, Don, 309
Madness, 155–156
"Magician," 8–9, 23–25, 47–48, 366
Magnum Opus, 93
Malamat, 215, 283, 316, 317
Man the Killer, 75–76
Man the Unknown (Alexis Carrel), 242, 243, 246–247
Marriage, 131, 194

Master Game: Beyond the Drug Experience, The, 294, 318
Masters of Wisdom, The (J.G. Bennett), 374
Meditation, 87, 90, 91
Meetings with Remarkable Men (Gurdjieff), 193, 198–199, 206, 211, 286–287
Merry Wives of Windsor, The (William Shakespeare), 53–54
Metzger, Ralph, 284
Miller, James, 89–90
"Missionary," 181, 182
Mitrinovic, Dmitrije, 382
"Morbio Inferiore," 174–175, 182, 189, 224
Morning Star Ranch, 303–305, 308–311
Moseley, Oswald, 62–64
Mosley, Leonard, 257–258
Muggeridge, Malcolm, 65
Murshid, 350

Nature, 47–48, 73–74
Nazis, 77, 90, 92, 118, 120, 135, 262, 263
New Model of the Universe, A (Ouspensky), 93–94, 104
New Prometheans, The, 320
Nietzsche, Friedrich, 2, 104, 261, 287; *Thus Spake Zarathustra*, 12, 242, 354–355, 396–397
Nigredo, 299
Nirvana, 115, 291
Nyland, Ilonka, 192, 198
Nyland, Wym, 190, 191, 192, 198

Obeahs, 234, 235–236
Of Flight and Life (Charles Lindbergh), 266
"Old One," 216, 390–391
Orage, A.R., 191, 198

Original sin, 74–75, 76
Origins of man, 75–76
Osokin, Ivan, 228–229
Ouspensky, 93–106, 138–140, 157, 271; characteristics of, 99–100, 170, 172–173; 178–181; *Fragments of an Unknown Teaching*, 91, 108–109; group, 185–186, 304, 324–325; and Gurdjieff, 103–104, 107–109, 191–192, 343–344; ideas, 104–105, 130, 132, 340–341; and J.G. Bennett, 340, 343–344, 347; knowledge from, 105, 295; *A New Model of the Universe*, 93–94, 104; "Notes on the Decision to Work," 100; *The Strange Life of Ivan Osokin*, 105, 180; teachings, 97, 100–101, 120, 127–128, 133
Ouspensky, Madame, 101, 108–110, 112–115, 139, 150–151, 170, 171, 172, 181–183, 188–189
Outer Theater, 298–300

Paderewski, 131–132
Pasteur, Louis, 174
Peace Pledge Union, 86, 87, 168, 279
Peasants, living with, 21–32
Perennial Philosophy, The (Aldous Huxley), 115
Pétain, Marshal, 250, 253
Philips, Michael, 290, 333
Political unrest, 62–67
Port Adelaide, 39–42
Prayers and Meditations, 90
Psychedelic freakway, 270–291; and Aldous Huxley, 279–280; and Ken Keasy and Merry Pranksters, 287–289; and LSD, 281–282; and Tim Leary, 280–285; and Tom Wolfe's *Electric Kool-Aid Acid Test*, 288–289
Psychomimetic, 233
Pythagoras, 302

Quack, Quack (Leonard Woolf), 90

Rama, Swami, 369, 371
Raymond, Dick, 290
Reflections on Life (Alexis Carrel), 251–252
Religion, 16–18, 73–74
Research, with abnormal plant growth, 177; with bacteria, 141–148; cancer, 175–177, 232–233; with drugs and the mind, 233; industrial, 221–222
Revolt in the Tree House, 310
"Ring of Power," 255–256
Rockefeller Institute, 175–176, 243
Rolling Thunder, 369–371
Roosevelt, Franklin D., 264
Roshi, Susuki, 312
Rossetti, Dante Gabriel, *Sudden Light*, 271
Royal College of Science, 56, 68

Sally, 219–220, 225–227
Sarkar, 314–317
Sarmoun, 314, 322
Satyagraha, 90–91
Saviors, 76–77
Schizophrenia, 183, 232, 355; E.'s 152–153, 158–159; Tessa's, 225
Schumacher, E.F., 323, 352
"Scientist, The," 47–48, 57–58, 366
"Season in hell," 39–43, 50
Second Ring of Power, The (Carlos Castaneda), 359–360
Secret Doctrine, The, 84
Seekers after Truth, 336–337
Separate Reality, A (Carlos Castaneda), 354
Shah, Idries, 351–352
Shakespeare, William, 53, 300; *Julius Caesar*, 119; *The Merry Wives of Windsor*, 54

Shaw, George Bernard, 65
Sheppard, Dick (Peace Pledge Union), 86, 87, 168, 279
Shushud, Hasan, 352
Sir John in Love (Ralph Vaughan Williams), 54
Sita, 306–310
Skridlov, Professor, 209, 210
Slack, Charles W., *Timothy Leary, the Madness of the Sixties and Me*, 286
Slaves, 2, 42
Sly Man, and the Devil, 107–108
"Sly Man's pill," 237–238, 371
"Small Porgy," 388–389, 395
Smerdiakovs, 77–78, 132
Smith, Major Truman, 262
Smith, Rodney Colin, 166, 168, 169, 179–180, 181
Smuts, Jan, 346–347
Song of the Redwood Tree (Walt Whitman), 164
"Soul force," 98, 113
"Soul glue," 304, 312, 323
Spirit of St. Louis, The, 257, 259
Stalin, 129, 130, 132, 141, 265
Stevenson, Robert Louis, *The Silverado Squatters*, 276
Stonehenge, 9, 25
Strange Life of Ivan Osokin, The (Ouspensky), 105, 180
Subuh, Pak, 351
Sudden Light (Dante Gabriel Rossetti), 271
Suicidal feelings, 227–230
Swedenborg, Emmanuel, 355
Swift, Jonathan, *Gulliver's Travels*, 89
System, The, 181, 314

Tabrizi, Ahmad, 350
Tales of Power (Carlos Castaneda), 361–362
Tchernavin, V.V., *I Speak for the Silent*, 66

Teacher of the Way, 173–174
Teachers of Gurdjieff, The, 318, 321
Teachings of Don Juan, The (Carlos Castaneda), 354
Teagle, 81–83
Tekkia/dojo, 325–326, 332
Tennyson, Alfred Lord, "Crossing the Bar," 13–14
Tessa, breakdown, 225, 231–232; children with, 218–219, 234; desire for, 160–163, 172, 190, 194
Textbook of Bacteriology (Gopley & Wilson), 145
Thaelmann, 62, 63
Theosophy, 84, 98
Thoreau, Henry David, 303
Thus Spake Zarathustra (Friedrich Nietzsche), 12, 242, 354–355, 396–397
Todd, John, 290
Tolstoy, Leo, 31
Townsend, Robert, 329
Treasure of the Intellectuals, The, (Julian Bender), 67
Trickster's Way, 356–357; *see also* Castaneda, Carlos

Undine, 8

Vansittart, 126
Varieties of Religious Experiences (William James), 155
Voltaire, 301
von der Ropp family, 3, 19–20
Vonnegut, Kurt, 393–394

Warrior, definition of, 2
Watts, Alan, 283–284, 376–384; *In My Own Way*, 379; *The Joyous Cosmol-* ogy, 377; and LSD, 377; on self-improvement, 379–380; *Tao: the Watercourse Way*, 379
Way, The, 292
Way of the Good Man, 54–55
Way of Objective Morality, 54–55
Webb, Sidney and Beatrice, 65
Wheeler, Bill, 309
White Gates, The, 48, 49, 51, 52
White Order vs. Black Order, 248–249, 373
White, Philip R., 175
"Whitening, the," 299
Whitman, Walt, *Song of the Redwood Tree*, 164
Whole Earth Catalog, 290
Williams, Adeline Vaughan, 48–55, 81, 82
Williams, Ralph Vaughan, 48–55
Wilson, Dr. G.S., 145, 146
Wolfe, Tom, *Electric Kool-Aid Acid Test*, 288–289
Woolf, Leonard, *Quack, Quack*, 90
Woolf, Virginia, 52
Work, The, 93, 156, 157, 168, 170–171, 178, 183, 186, 327
World War I, 4–5, 86–87, 88
World War II, 129, 134–139, 163–164
Wormwood, 80, 92
Wyatt, James, 10, 12

Yoga, 83–85, 91; bhakti, 91, 188; hatha, 239, 240, 245, 371
Yogis, 83–85, 91

Zen Buddhists, 378
Zepplin, 5, 6
Zikr, 195, 326

THE AUTHOR

Robert S. de Ropp, a biochemist and formerly a visiting investigator at Rockefeller Institute, has carried out research in the fields of cancer, mental illness, and drugs that affect behavior. He has published forty-five scientific papers and eleven books, including *The Master Game*, *Drugs and the Mind*, *Sex Energy*, *Eco-Tech*, and *The New Prometheans*. He lives in California where he grows his own vegetables and fishes from his kayak in the Pacific.